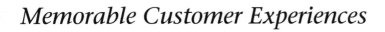

Memorable Customer Experiences

To faster and Orla, in loving memory – AL

To Elizabeth, with all my love – JV

To Emma, lots of love – MBB

Memorable Customer Experiences

A Research Anthology

Edited by
ADAM LINDGREEN,
JOËLLE VANHAMME and
MICHAEL B. BEVERLAND

GOWER

Published by
Gower Publishing Limited
Wey Court East
Union Road
Farnham
Surrey
GU9 7PT
England

Gower Publishing Company
Suite 420
101 Cherry Street
Burlington
VT 05401-4405
USA

www.gowerpublishing.com

Adam Lindgreen, Joëlle Vanhamme and Michael B. Beverland have asserted their moral right under the Copyright, Designs and Patents Act, 1988, to be identified as the editors of this work.

British Library Cataloguing in Publication Data
Memorable customer experiences : a research anthology.
  1. Relationship marketing. 2. Consumer satisfaction--
Evaluation. 3. Marketing research.
  I. Lindgreen, Adam. II. Vanhamme, J. III. Beverland, M.
  658.8'343-dc22

ISBN: 978-0-566-08868-1 (hbk)
       978-0-566-09207-7 (ebk)

Library of Congress Control Number: 2009934928

Mixed Sources
Product group from well-managed forests and other controlled sources
www.fsc.org Cert no. SGS-COC-2482
© 1996 Forest Stewardship Council
FSC

Printed and bound in Great Britain by
TJ International Ltd, Padstow, Cornwall.

Contents

List of Figures

List of Tables

About the Editors

Adam Lindgreen

After graduating with degrees in chemistry, engineering, and physics, Dr Adam Lindgreen completed an M.Sc. in food science and technology at the Technical University of Denmark. He also finished an MBA at the University of Leicester, as well as a One-Year Postgraduate Program at the Hebrew University of Jerusalem. Dr Lindgreen received his Ph.D. in marketing from Cranfield University. Since May 2007, he has served as a Professor of Strategic Marketing at Hull University Business School. Dr Lindgreen has been a Visiting Professor with various institutions, including Georgia State University, Groupe HEC in France, and Melbourne University; in 2006, he was made an honorary Visiting Professor at Harper Adams University College. His publications include more than 70 scientific journal articles, seven books, more than 30 book chapters, and more than 80 conference papers. His recent publications have appeared in *Business Horizons*, *Industrial Marketing Management*, *Journal of Advertising*, *Journal of Business Ethics*, *Journal of the Academy of Marketing Science*, *Journal of Product Innovation Management*, *Psychology & Marketing*, and *Supply Chain Management*; his most recent books are *Managing Market Relationships*, *The New Cultures of Foods*, *The Crisis of Food Brands*, and *Market Orientation*. The recipient of the "Outstanding Article 2005" award from *Industrial Marketing Management* and the Christer Karlsson Award at the 2007 *International Product Development Management* conference, Professor Lindgreen also serves on the board of several scientific journals; he is the editor of *Journal of Business Ethics* for the section on corporate responsibility and sustainability. His research interests include business and industrial marketing management, consumer behaviour, experiential marketing, and corporate social responsibility.

Adam Lindgreen has discovered and excavated settlements from the Stone Age in Denmark, including the only major kitchen midden – Sparregård – in the south-east of Denmark; because of its importance, the kitchen midden was later excavated by the National Museum and then protected as a historical monument for future generations. He is also an avid genealogist, having traced his family back to 1390 and published widely in scientific journals related to methodological issues in genealogy, accounts of population development, and particular family lineages.

Joëlle Vanhamme

Joëlle Vanhamme is Associate Professor at the IESEG School of Management at the Catholic University of Lille and Assistant Professor at the Rotterdam School of Management at Erasmus University. Dr Vanhamme has a degree in business administration and two master degrees (psychology and business administration), all from the Catholic University of Louvain. She also has been awarded the CEMS master degree from the Community of European Management Schools. Subsequently, Dr Vanhamme received her Ph.D. from the Catholic University of Louvain. Her Ph.D. thesis examined the emotion of surprise and its influence on consumer satisfaction. She has been a Visiting Scholar with Delft University of Technology, Eindhoven University of Technology, and the University of Auckland; she is currently a Visiting Professor with Hull University Business School. Dr Vanhamme's research has appeared in journals including *Business Horizons, Industrial Marketing Management, Journal of Business Ethics, Journal of Consumer Satisfaction, Dissatisfaction and Complaining Behavior, Journal of Customer Behaviour, Journal of Economic Psychology, Journal of Marketing Management, Journal of Retailing, Psychology & Marketing,* and *Recherche et Applications en Marketing.*

Michael B. Beverland

Dr Michael Beverland is Professor of Marketing at Royal Melbourne Institute of Technology. Professor Beverland received his Ph.D. from the University of South Australia. He is currently a Visiting Professor with Hull University Business School. He has published in *Business Horizons, European Journal of Marketing, Industrial Marketing Management, Journal of Advertising, Journal of Business & Industrial Marketing, Journal of Business Research, Journal of Consumer Research, Journal of Management Studies, Journal of Personal Selling and Sales Management, Journal of Product Innovation Management,* and *Journal of the Academy of Marketing Science,* among others. His research interests include the design–brand marketing interface, consumer interaction with design, the marketing of authenticity, consumer responses to design aesthetics, creative processes associated with new product design, and brand management. His forthcoming book is entitled *Building Brand Authenticity* (Palgrave). He serves on the boards of *Industrial Marketing Management, Journal of Business Ethics, Journal of Business & Industrial Marketing,* and *Journal of Business Research.*

About the Contributors

Barry J. Babin

Dr Barry J. Babin is the Max P. Watson Professor of Business and Department Head of the Department of Marketing and Analysis, Louisiana Tech University, USA. The research for his chapter in this book was conducted while visiting Reims Management School, France. Dr Babin has published articles in many outlets, including *Journal of Consumer Research, Journal of Marketing, Journal of Retailing, Journal of the Academy of Marketing Science,* and many others. His research interests focus on the concept of value as a result of human activity. He serves as associate editor for marketing for *Journal of Business Research* and is on the editorial board of many academic journals. He is co-author of several books, including *CB: A Value-Based Approach, Exploring Marketing Research* (4LTR Press, 2009), and *Multivariate Data Analysis* (Prentice Hall, 2006).

Michael Basil

Dr Michael Basil received his Ph.D. from Stanford University in 1992. He is a Professor of Marketing at the University of Lethbridge in Canada. His Italian and Hungarian heritage predisposed him to a love of fine food, and some of his research has investigated food selection. Recently, he has developed a taste for ultra-fine restaurant dining. He would like to dedicate this chapter to those dedicated chefs who work long hours to bring their artistry to bear on their culinary creations.

Debra Z. Basil

Dr Debra Basil received her Ph.D. from the University of Colorado. She is an associate professor in marketing at the University of Lethbridge in Canada. Her primary interest is in non-profit marketing and volunteerism. However, she developed an interest in fine dining after a visit to the French Laundry.

Michael B. Beverland

Dr Michael Beverland is Professor of Marketing at Royal Melbourne Institute of Technology. Dr Beverland received his Ph.D. from the University of South Australia. He has published in *Business Horizons, European Journal of Marketing, Industrial Marketing Management, Journal of Advertising, Journal of Business & Industrial Marketing, Journal of Business Research, Journal of Consumer Research, Journal of Management Studies, Journal of Personal Selling and Sales Management, Journal of Product Innovation Management,* and

Journal of the Academy of Marketing Science, among others. His research interests include the design–brand marketing interface, consumer interaction with design, the marketing of authenticity, consumer responses to design aesthetics, creative processes associated with new product design, and brand management. He serves on the board of *Industrial Marketing Management* and *Journal of Business & Industrial Marketing*.

Adilson Borges

Dr Adilson Borges is the IRC Professor of Marketing and the Auchan Chair of Retailing at Reims Management School, France. Dr Borges has published articles in various journals, including *International Journal of Retailing and Distribution Management*, *Décision Marketing*, and *Revista de Administração de Empresas da FGV*, among others. His research interests include consumer behaviour in retailing, memory and price perceptions, price image, and social marketing. He serves on the editorial review boards of the *Journal of Business Research* and *Journal of Marketing Theory and Practice*.

Stephen Brown

Dr Stephen Brown is Professor of Marketing Research at the University of Ulster, Northern Ireland. Best known for *Postmodern Marketing*, he has written numerous books, including *Free Gift Inside*, *The Marketing Code*, *Agents & Dealers*, and *Wizard: Harry Potter's Brand Magic*. He is currently working on *The Customer Key*, the final volume in his "management thriller" trilogy.

Roy F. Cammarano

Roy F. Cammarano is a principal with Customer Performance Group, LLC, a management and marketing strategy consulting firm. He has served as president of several service organisations, including Voicecomm, Premiere Conferencing, and Enhanced Calling Services (all part of Premiere Global Services [NYSE: PGI]), and as an executive officer and consultant in the publishing, leisure, retail, and consumer product industries. Mr Cammarano is the author of two books and a dynamic leader with a track record of success and accomplishments in all phases of business growth and development. As a senior executive, he specialises in leading high-growth, dynamic environments. Mr Cammarano received his MBA from the University of Phoenix.

Lewis P. Carbone

Lewis P. Carbone is founder and chief experience officer of the Minneapolis-based consulting firm Experience Engineering, Inc. He is a pioneer in experience management methods and tools, and author of *Clued In: How to Keep Customers Coming Back Again and Again* (Prentice Hall, 2004, 8th printing).

Adam Finn

Dr Adam Finn is the RK Banister Professor of Marketing at the University of Alberta School of Business. He received his Ph.D. from the University of Illinois at Urbana-Champaign. Dr Finn has published research in *International Journal of Research in Marketing, Journal of Cultural Economics, Journal of Marketing Research, Journal of Public Policy & Marketing, Journal of Retailing, Journal of Service Research*, and *Marketing Science*, among others. His current research interests include marketing measurement, assessment of service, store and mall patronage, new product development, and consumer trade-offs for setting public policy. He is a co-author of *Global Television and Film: An Introduction to the Economics of the Business* (Clarendon Press, 1997) and of *Media Economics: Applying Economics to New and Traditional Media* (Sage, 2004).

Alexandra Ganglmair-Wooliscroft

Dr Alexandra Ganglmair-Wooliscroft is a Lecturer in the Department of Marketing at the University of Otago, where she received her Ph.D. with a dissertation on "Measuring Affective Consumption using Rasch Modelling". She has published in several journals, including *Der Markt Zeitschrift für Absatzwirtschaft und Marketing, Journal of Satisfaction, Dissatisfaction and Complaint Behaviour*, and *Kotuitui: New Zealand Journal of Social Sciences*. Dr Ganglmair-Wooliscroft's research interests include consumer behaviour and marketing research with a special interest in post-consumption emotions, quality of life research, and Rasch modelling.

Frank M. Go

Dr Frank M. Go is Professor and Director of the Centre for Tourism Management at the Rotterdam School of Management, Erasmus University. Prior to his present post, he served on business faculties at universities in Canada and Hong Kong. His research focus is on marketing strategy, destination images and brand identity, ICT and innovation, and sustainable business development. He is a Visiting Professor at Rikkyo University in Tokyo, Japan, and the Open University Business School, UK. Currently, he cooperates with the United Nations Conference on Trade and Development, Geneva, on the development of e-tourism in emerging economies. He has carried out projects funded by Accor, IATA, Carlson Wagon Lit, Maclean Hunter, Marriott, Microsoft, and the Economist Intelligence Unit, and he has co-authored more than 125 articles, official reports, and book chapters. Most of his writing has focused on the need to integrate technological, market, and organisational change in travel, destination, and hospitality contexts to improve the effectiveness of organisations. He is an editorial board member of *Journal of Tourism and Hospitality Planning & Development, Journal of Information Technology & Tourism New York: Cognizant, Journal of Tourism Analysis, Journal of Travel & Tourism Marketing, Journal of Hospitality & Leisure Marketing*, and *International Journal of Sports Marketing & Sponsorship and Tourism Review*. He is a member of the Academy of Marketing, the International Association of Scientific Experts in Tourism, the International Federation of Information Technology and Tourism, and the Media Tenor Network.

Suzie Goan

Suzie Goan is Director of Development and Marketing at Experience Engineering, Inc. She has been instrumental in writing about and conducting experience management research, design, and implementation for the firm since 1999.

Robert Govers

Robert Govers is currently serving as Assistant Professor of Marketing and Strategy in the Master in Tourism programme of the Consortium University of Leuven, Belgium, where he was also Project Manager at the Flemish Center for Tourism Policy Studies. He is a freelance lecturer and consultant and works with The Hotel School, The Hague, Rotterdam School of Management, IULM University in Milan, and several institutes in Dubai. Together with Professor Frank Go, he is the author of *Place Branding: Glocal, Virtual and Physical Identities, Constructed, Imagined and Experienced* (Palgrave Macmillan, 2009). He has also co-authored several journal articles and conference papers in the fields of place branding, tourism, hospitality and quality management, e-commerce in tourism, and tourism research and marketing. As a project manager, Robert has been involved in many consultancy projects for reputable organisations such as IATA, the European Commission, the Flemish Government, and various Dutch ministries and tourism promotion boards.

Ronald D. Hampton

Dr Ronald D. Hampton is an associate professor and Chair of the Marketing Department at the University of Nebraska-Lincoln. His research interests include experiential marketing, consumer imagination, spirituality and marketing, retail management, and international marketing. He has recently received grants to study the global impact of human trafficking. He has taught managerial marketing, with an emphasis on experiential marketing, to executives of many *Fortune* 500 companies around the world. He has published articles in *Journal of Business Research, Journal of Marketing Research, Journal of Retailing,* and *Journal of the Academy of Marketing Science.*

Michael J. Healy

Michael J. Healy is a Ph.D. candidate with the University of Melbourne and is currently completing his thesis, entitled "Experiential Retail Strategies: Understanding their Impact on Consumer In-Store Assessments and Brand Identity – An Ethnographic Approach". Mr. Healy specialises in retail marketing using qualitative research techniques, including ethnography, participant observation, and in-depth interviews. He recently published in *International Journal of Market Research*'s special issue on ethnography.

Morris B. Holbrook

Dr Morris B. Holbrook is the W.T. Dillard Professor of Marketing in the Graduate School of Business at Columbia University. Professor Holbrook graduated from Harvard College with a BA degree in English (1965) and received his MBA (1967) and Ph.D. (1975) degrees in marketing from Columbia University. Since 1975, he has taught courses at the Columbia Business School in such areas as marketing strategy, sales management, research methods, consumer behaviour, and commercial communication in the culture of consumption. His research has covered a wide variety of topics in marketing, consumer behaviour, and related fields – with a special focus on issues related to communication in general and to aesthetics, semiotics, hermeneutics, art, entertainment, music, jazz, motion pictures, nostalgia, and stereography in particular. Recent books include *Daytime Television Game Shows and the Celebration of Merchandise: The Price Is Right* (Bowling Green University Popular Press, 1993); *The Semiotics of Consumption: Interpreting Symbolic Consumer Behavior in Popular Culture and Works of Art* (with Elizabeth C. Hirschman, Mouton de Gruyter, 1993); *Consumer Research: Introspective Essays on the Study of Consumption* (Sage, 1995); and *Consumer Value: A Framework for Analysis and Research* (edited, Routledge, 1999). Professor Holbrook pursues such hobbies as playing the piano and vibraphone, attending jazz and classical concerts, going to movies and the theatre, collecting musical recordings, taking stereographic photos, and being kind to animals, especially cats.

Peter C. Honebein

Dr Peter C. Honebein is a principal with Customer Performance Group, LLC, a management and marketing strategy consulting firm. He is also an adjunct professor at the University of Nevada, Reno and Indiana University, where he teaches marketing, customer experience design, human performance technology, and instructional systems courses. In addition to authoring two books, Dr Honebein designed the system that tracked the clean-up of the Exxon Valdez oil spill and has consulted on the design, strategy, and launch of numerous innovations and products, including the system that sequenced the human genome and smart meter systems and services. Dr Honebein received his Ph.D. from Indiana University.

Karsten Kilian

Karsten Kilian is currently completing his Ph.D. at the Institute of Marketing and Retailing at the University of St Gallen in Switzerland. Karsten studied in the MBA programme at the University of Florida and received his graduate degree of a Diplom-Kaufmann (equivalent to an MBA) at the University of Mannheim in Germany. He worked for several years as a consultant for Simon-Kucher & Partners (Prof. Dr Hermann Simon). In line with his research interests, Mr Kilian has contributed to a wide range of anthologies and texts on experiential marketing, brand management, audio branding, multi-sensory branding, and relationship marketing. He recently published his first book on cult brands. In the last five years, he has built Markenlexikon.com, the most-respected website on brand management in the German-speaking world.

Clinton D. Lanier, Jr.

Dr Clinton D. Lanier, Jr. is an assistant professor of marketing at the University of St Thomas. He recently received his Ph.D. in marketing from the University of Nebraska-Lincoln and also holds two degrees in philosophy. His dissertation, "Experiential Marketing: Understanding the Dimensions, Characteristics, and Logic of Firm-Driven Experiences", explores the nature of experiential marketing and what constitutes an experience as a market offering. His broader research focuses on experiential marketing and experiential consumption, symbolic consumption, consumer imagination, consumer participation, and consumer privacy. He has published in *Academy of Marketing Science Review* and *Research in Consumer Behavior: Consumer Culture Theory*.

Kathryn A. LaTour

Dr Kathryn A. LaTour is an associate professor of hospitality marketing at the William F. Harrah College of Hotel Administration at the University of Nevada, Las Vegas. Kathryn received her Ph.D. from the University of Iowa in 1997. Her research has focused on the malleability of memory and the development and application of research tools to "dig deeper" into customers' minds. Dr LaTour's research has been published in marketing journals such as *Journal of Consumer Research, Journal of Marketing, Psychology & Marketing, Journal of Business Research, Journal of Advertising*, and *Journal of Advertising Research*, as well as hospitality journals such as *Cornell Hospitality Quarterly, Annals of Tourism Research*, and *Journal of Travel Research*.

Adam Lindgreen

Dr Adam Lindgreen is Professor of Strategic Marketing at Hull University Business School. Dr Lindgreen received his Ph.D. from Cranfield University. He has published in *Business Horizons, Industrial Marketing Management, Journal of Advertising, Journal of Business Ethics, Journal of Business and Industrial Marketing, Journal of Marketing Management, Journal of Product and Innovation Management, Journal of the Academy of Marketing Science*, and *Psychology & Marketing*, among others. His books included *Managing Market Relationships* (Gower, 2008). His research interests include business and industrial marketing, consumer behaviour, experiential marketing, relationship and value management, and corporate social responsibility. He serves on the boards of many journals.

Harmen Oppewal

Dr Harmen Oppewal is Professor of Marketing with Monash University. Professor Oppewal specialises in research on store and consumer choice and reactions to in-store environmental variables. He has published in *International Journal of Research in Marketing, Journal of Marketing Research, Journal of Retailing*, and *Journal of Retailing and Consumer Services*.

Joëlle Vanhamme

Dr Joëlle Vanhamme is Associate Professor at the IESEG School of Management at the Catholic University of Lille and Assistant Professor at the Rotterdam School of Management at Erasmus University. Dr Vanhamme has a degree in business administration and two master's degrees (psychology and business administration), all from the Catholic University of Louvain. She also has been awarded the CEMS master degree from the Community of European Management Schools. Subsequently, Dr Vanhamme received her Ph.D. from the Catholic University of Louvain. Her Ph.D. thesis examined the emotion of surprise and its influence on consumer satisfaction. She has been a Visiting Scholar with Delft University of Technology, Eindhoven University of Technology, and the University of Auckland; she is currently a Visiting Professor with Hull University Business School. Dr Vanhamme's research has appeared in journals including *Business Horizons, Industrial Marketing Management, Journal of Business Ethics, Journal of Consumer Satisfaction, Dissatisfaction and Complaining Behavior, Journal of Customer Behaviour, Journal of Economic Psychology, Journal of Marketing Management, Journal of Retailing, Psychology & Marketing*, and *Recherche et Applications en Marketing*.

Fabian von Loewenfeld

Dr Fabian von Loewenfeld is Senior Manager Corporate Intelligence & Strategy at Dubailand Parks & Resorts. He received his Ph.D. from Johannes Gutenberg University Mainz, Germany. Before joining Dubailand, he worked for four years as a consultant at The Boston Consulting Group and for almost four years as a consultant in the European Marketing & Sales Practice at McKinsey & Co. His key areas of expertise include branding, customer insights, customer relationship management, and digital marketing. Besides his Ph.D. thesis about success factors and economic relevance of brand communities, he has published several articles in management journals.

Luming Wang

Luming Wang is a marketing Ph.D. student at the University of Alberta School of Business. Luming completed her MA in Economics at the University of Alberta in 2005. She has presented research papers at INFORMS Marketing Science conferences in Singapore and Vancouver. Her research interests include branding, brand equity and brand management, research methodology, market structure, Bayesian modelling, consumer choice modelling, and international marketing.

Ben Wooliscroft

Dr Ben Wooliscroft is a Senior Lecturer in the Marketing Department of the School of Business at the University of Otago, where he received his Ph.D. after writing his dissertation on "The Loss of Wroe Alderson's Theories of Marketing". He has published in several journals including *European Business Review, Journal of the Academy of Marketing*

Science, *Marketing Theory*, and *Tourism Analysis*. He has edited, with Robert Tamilia and Stanley J. Shapiro, *A Twenty-first Century Guide to Aldersonian Marketing Thought* (Springer, 2006). His research interests include the history of marketing theory, consumer behaviour, experiential marketing, and the impacts of complexity, chaos, and self-organised criticality on marketing systems. He serves on the editorial boards of *European Business Review*, *Journal of Historical Research in Marketing*, and *Journal of Macromarketing*.

Introduction

In today's high-velocity environment, and with hypercompetition all around, it takes more than incremental changes to keep up. But, lo and behold, companies are surrounded by a plethora of snappy marketing approaches that promise to be universal panaceas for the challenges they face.

Experiential marketing – or memorable customer experiences – is one such marketing approach. The scramble to achieve a presence among experience providers, combined with a lack of knowledge of what experiential marketing is all about and how it can be used for commercial advantage, however, has led many companies to rush to design and implement experiential marketing. Sadly, with little idea as to what they want to achieve by means of experiential marketing as part of their overall marketing strategy, these companies often have ended up dissatisfying their customers rather than delighting them.

The objective of this research anthology is to investigate different angles of experiential marketing. Together, the chapters fill holes and explore new fields. The book's 16 chapters are organised in six sections: Conceptual foundations, Brands and brand communities, Design of customer experiences, Management of customer experiences, Methodological issues, and Critique of experiential marketing. The sections and the chapters are briefly outlined below.

Conceptual Foundations

An important question pertains to whether memorable customer experiences result from the use of traditional marketing practices, perhaps implemented more effectively than previously, or require entirely new practices with new foundations that turn companies into experience providers. The first section of this book therefore expressly considers experiential marketing and its conceptual foundations.

Chapter 1, by Clinton Lanier and Ronald Hampton, relates the strategic marketing logics behind experiential marketing to other proposed strategic marketing logics (i.e., goods-dominant and service-dominant). The authors propose that the strategic logic of experiential marketing depends on assumptions of symbolic resources, engaging transactions, and internalised value. Their critical relativism implies multiple marketing logics, each with its own specific assumptions, available to firms. In their extended research study of 10 experiential contexts, the authors confirm their three assumptions. In particular, this chapter provides important lessons about how to translate these assumptions into memorable customer experiences.

In Chapter 2, Karsten Kilian suggests an experiential marketing and brand experience framework that may enable companies to become experience providers that establish and manage real or virtual experience products and worlds. The framework details components and success factors for brand experience worlds, based on a review of prior experiential marketing research and a comparison of the content and coverage of experience markets. In an attempt to designate experience product categories, the author suggests a value triad: experience, prestige, and function. Finally, this chapter illustrates (real and brand) experience worlds with real-life companies to identify the key factors for creating such worlds.

Brands and Brand Communities

How does the experiential marketing concept translate into practice? How can experiential marketing help companies build their brands and make them distinctive in the marketplace? This section of the book details ways providers, including manufacturers and retailers, seek to build brands through experiential marketing.

Chapter 3, by Michael Beverland, sets the scene by proposing that brand experiences allow customers to achieve self-authentication and authoritative performances. With the historical accounts of the Morgan Motor Company, his own experiences, interviews with the chair and marketing manager of the company, and interactions with Morgan owners as input, the author provides examples of self-authentication (i.e., individual brand experiences) and authoritative performances (i.e., collective brand experiences). He draws key conclusions about how marketers can enhance a brand's authenticity and provide consumers with an experiential platform.

In Chapter 4, Adam Lindgreen and Michael Beverland also consider the challenges of authenticity and how to market authentic product clues. In this case, the context involves Trappist breweries that hope to reinforce their brand identity, command price premiums, and differentiate themselves. Objective (i.e., real attributes) and subjective (i.e., rhetorical attributes) sources can both create impressions of authenticity; the Trappist breweries in particular must downplay scientific and business expertise in favour of religious imagery and time-honoured traditions. This chapter's detailed examination of breweries' six types of authenticity should inspire marketers in other industries.

With their focus on different types of brand communities, in Chapter 5 Fabian von Loewenfeld and Karsten Kilian explain ideal management approaches and circumstances in which official brand communities can provide memorable customer experiences. Nine different brand community experiences emerge in a classification of usage types, media usage, and status or orientation. Thus, there are three brand community management options that entail unique success factors. Equally important, these authors list the criteria for establishing a successful brand-centred community. This chapter's brand community management framework provides solid managerial input to marketers.

The last chapter in this section, Chapter 6 by Michael Healy, Michael Beverland, and Harmen Oppewal, considers how some retailers provide larger-than-life spectacles to build brand identity and presence. Whereas prior research cannot explain how to translate the experiential marketing concept into smaller retail spaces, these authors use ethnographic research techniques to show how brand adoption occurs intimately at Mag Nation, a small-scale experience store in Australia. The chapter provides an excellent example of experience deconstruction into areas of the store, its touch points, and various activities. The retailer's product offering is just as much a result of the customer's creation as the retailer's, achieved by scripting dedicated (staff) and impromptu (customer) behaviour to maintain the core values of the brand.

Design of Customer Experiences

So even if we accept that experiential marketing is, at least sometimes, fundamental to a brand and its owner's marketing success, the question of how customer experiences should be designed is much trickier. Is it possible to offer general guidelines, or are various consumption contexts just too different? This third section attempts to understand how marketers might design customer experiences.

To start, in Chapter 7, Peter Honebein and Roy Cammarano integrate nearly 50 fieldwork studies to reveal that to create customer delight, designers must balance emotional and relational customer experiences. The authors' memorable experience model contributes to a better understanding of the possible memories that customers form, depending on the effectiveness and interaction of emotional and rational experiences (delighted, dissatisfied, dysfunctional, and directed). The model also identifies which ingredients an experience needs to attain delight: memorable customer experiences must be rational first and then emotional, the customer should be involved in designing the experience, and the experience should be harmonised and balanced.

Three hundred and fifty-two online reviews of upscale dining experiences at Michelin three-star restaurants in the United States also give Michael Basil and Debra Basil insights into assessments of luxury purchases. In Chapter 8, they identify two evaluative frames: a hedonic one related to the experience as special or "splurge" (which tends to induce positive reviews) and a more rational "value" perspective (more frequently related to negative reviews). With the value frame, the restaurant's ability to meet expectations provides the most important criterion for interpreting the experience, consistent with service quality literature that demonstrates that people interpret experiences relative to expectations. Finally, in contrast with many, many service quality studies, these authors suggest that the aesthetic and hedonic aspects of food may be more important than service quality in an ultra-fine dining context.

Finally, in Chapter 9, Ben Wooliscroft and Alexandra Ganglmair-Wooliscroft provide an empirical investigation of the consumption of hot chocolate drinks in Belgium. Customer involvement in co-producing hot chocolate makes the experience theatrical and magical. The authors identify several elements that likely extend to other memorable consumption experience contexts.

Management of Customer Experiences

The fourth section continues the preceding theme: now that a company has made the strategic decision to provide customer experiences, how will it manage those experiences? Again, can frameworks outline the mechanisms by which customers and experiences interact? This section seeks to examine such management questions.

In Chapter 10, Barry Babin and Adilson Borges investigate how retail memories create shopping value and how value shapes retail memories. Customers' memories result from the totality of interactions that constitute the shopping experience, not just the products that they purchase. Through its theoretical and practical insights, the retail memory framework proposed in this chapter emphasises the need for research into memory in retailing studies, as well as specific mechanisms by which customer memory may link to value. According to these authors, a memorable shopping experience must feature four elements: noticeable, performance, exciting, and valuable.

According to Kathryn LaTour, Lewis Carbone, and Suzie Goan, in Chapter 11, hospitality organisations can systematically manage their customers' experiences and encourage favourable memories by making guests an integral part of the experience, creating intimacy with customers, considering encounters from the customer back, understanding emotional aspect of customers' experiences, using atmospheric elements to create an authentic representation, paying attention to signage, showing customers the best face, attending to entrances and exits, managing the experience before customers arrive and after they leave, and offering customers valuable advice. Using examples from Las Vegas, the authors discuss the implications of the new "science of the mind" for framing customer experiences and recommend techniques for hospitality researchers.

In Chapter 12, Frank Go and Robert Govers explain how one company – TUI Travel plc, the world's largest tour operator – has applied packaged tour innovations to create memorable customer experiences. It bridges three critical gaps: tourist demand specifications, tourism delivery and supply, and tourism development strategy. The authors offer a detailed examination of factors that may help or hinder the creation of memorable travel experiences.

Methodological Issues

Managing customer experiences assumes access to a reliable evaluation method, yet various evaluations have yet to be resolved. Are existing methods, such as behavioural and physiological measures of emotions, useful? This fifth section offers a discussion of the methodological issues relating to experiential marketing.

Chapter 13, by Adam Finn and Luming Wang, investigates self-reported measures of emotions provided by a random sample of consumers about a random sample of online service providers. The minimal variance in self-reported emotions due to service providers, but more significant variance between customers and in the interaction between customers and service providers, suggests that the usefulness of self-reported emotion measures is questionable, which means that so too is the assumption that service providers can measure and manage the emotions that make for memorable service experiences.

The second and final chapter in this section is firmly based in literature on customer delight. Although most people might agree that customer delight offers a marketing advantage, Joëlle Vanhamme recognises that competing conceptualisations, methodologies, and stimuli in existing studies leave the relationship between surprise and delight ambiguous. Chapter 14 therefore assesses these different conceptualisations and overviews existing empirical evidence to reveal that during highly hedonic experiences, surprise indirectly influences satisfaction (through joy) and can increase satisfaction overall. The author also discusses an original experiment that sheds light on the surprise–satisfaction causality.

Critique of Experiential Marketing

"Experiential marketing changes everything!" claim the management gurus, but is it really so significant that to not join this race is dangerous? This last section of the book offers a much needed critique of experiential marketing.

In Chapter 15, Stephen Brown argues that despite the hype, experiential marketing is not new and, more important, that what experiential marketing envisages is not really attainable. Companies may say they are engaged in experiential marketing, but their customers more often have experiences that are anything but pleasant, as the author so eloquently demonstrates throughout his chapter.

Finally, in Chapter 16, Morris Holbrook questions whether the widely touted concept of experiential marketing fits all situations in general and the special case of academia in particular. His anecdotal illustrations and detailed example involving the branding of his own business school suggest some fundamental problems with analogies between the "commercialization of education and the selling of toothpaste or the glorification of the shopping mall".

Closing Remarks

We extend a special thanks to Gower and its staff, who have been most helpful throughout the entire process. Equally, we warmly thank all the authors who submitted their manuscripts for consideration for this book. They have exhibited the desire to share their knowledge and experience with the book's readers – and a willingness to put forward their views for possible challenge by their peers. Finally, we thank Elisabeth Nevins Caswell for her editorial assistance.

There are companies that have built themselves entirely around experiential marketing and have been remarkably successful, yet one clear message from the chapters of this book is that not all companies can or should proceed down the experiences lane. There is still a lot we do not know about experiential marketing. We are hopeful that the chapters in this book will fill knowledge gaps for readers but also that they will stimulate further thought and action pertaining to experiential marketing issues.

Adam Lindgreen, Hull
Joëlle Vanhamme, Lille
Michael B. Beverland, Melbourne

Part I
Conceptual
Foundations

1

Experiential Marketing: Understanding the Logic of Memorable Customer Experiences

CLINTON D. LANIER, JR.* AND RONALD D. HAMPTON†

Keywords

experiential marketing, symbolic consumption, symbolic resources, engaging transactions, internalized value, marketing logic

Abstract

To address the question of what memorable customer experiences are, exactly, this chapter attempts to understand the nature of experiential marketing. Are memorable customer experiences simply the result of traditional marketing practices implemented more effectively, or are they the outcome of a completely different marketing strategy? Although it is indeed possible for firms to enhance customers' experiences using traditional marketing practices, this chapter argues that the specific strategy of producing memorable customer experiences is part of a distinct marketing logic that is separate from the goods-dominant and service-dominant logics.[1] For marketers to produce memorable customer experiences, they need to understand this experiential marketing logic and its implications. The purpose of this chapter is to outline this strategic logic and thus explore the underlying factors that contribute to memorable customer experiences.

Before we begin, it is necessary to define the domain of experiential marketing. Experiential consumption literature has pointed out that people have consumption experiences in almost every aspect of their lives.[2] More important, these consumption experiences can be both market-based and non–market-based.[3] Even within market-based

* Clinton D. Lanier, Jr., University of St. Thomas, Opus College of Business, MCH 316, 2115 Summit Avenue, St. Paul, MN 55105-1096, USA. Telephone: (651) 962-5887. E-mail: lani1820@stthomas.edu.

† Ronald D. Hampton, University of Nebraska-Lincoln, Department of Marketing, 310B CBA, P.O. Box 880492, Lincoln, NE 68588-0492, USA. Telephone: (402) 472-5321. E-mail: rhampton1@unl.edu.

exchanges, experiences can be either intentional or unintentional and driven by the firm, the customer, or both.[4] This chapter specifically focuses on firm-driven, market-based experiences. Experiential marketing refers to the strategy of creating and staging offerings for the purpose of facilitating memorable customer experiences.[5] This definition is not meant to imply that the firm is in total control of these experiences or their specific effects. Rather, it simply means that these experiences are the result of a market-based transaction that involves some type of interaction between a firm and its customers.

Strategic Marketing Logics

To understand what constitutes experiential marketing and memorable customer experiences, it is helpful to examine the underlying logic of this particular form of marketing in relation to the other proposed strategic marketing logics. One way to distinguish between marketing logics is to examine their assumptions regarding resources, transactions, and value.[6] Generally, resources refer to anything utilized by producers and consumers to generate an effect.[7] Transactions refer to the process by which producers and consumers engage in exchanges.[8] Value refers to the relative worth, utility, or importance of something to someone.[9] Some scholars have suggested though that these concepts only apply to traditional, economic-based conceptualizations of marketing and do not really capture the essence of alternative forms of marketing that are socially and culturally based such as experiential marketing.[10] Using the schema of one form of logic to explain another form inevitably restricts the explanation to the domain of the schema; however, this chapter uses the concepts of resources, transactions, and value to provide a consistent framework for comparing the different logics. At the same time, we acknowledge that other concepts may help explain this new form of logic better.

The strategic marketing logic of goods is based on tangible (operand) resources, discrete transactions, and exchange value.[11] The goods marketing logic focuses primarily on the use of material resources in the production and distribution of physical offerings.[12] During the production process, goods are embedded with value by being imbued with qualities that are sought by the market.[13] According to this logic, goods constitute the fundamental unit of exchange.[14] As a result, the main foci of the goods marketing logic are managing costs, optimizing time and place utility, and providing reliable and dependable products.[15] For example, firms using this logic to manufacture home appliances (e.g., toasters, microwaves, washing machines) focus primarily on the cost of raw materials, the efficiency of the manufacturing process, and the effectiveness of their channels of distribution. The main assumption underlying this logic is that if the firm meets customers' needs at a low cost, customers will continue to purchase the products. The inherent focus on the firm underlying this perspective is captured by the marketing mix (i.e., product, price, place, and promotion).[16]

In contrast with the goods marketing logic, the strategic marketing logic of service is based on intangible (operant) resources, relational transactions, and use value.[17] Although not confined to what is traditionally considered services marketing, the service marketing logic focuses primarily on the use of specialized knowledge and skills to produce value propositions that are useful to customers.[18] As Vargo and Lusch explain, service is defined as "the application of specialized competences (operant resources – knowledge and skills), through deeds, processes, and performances for the benefit of another entity or the entity itself".[19] The main focus of the service marketing logic is to understand customers in order to provide them with the proper instrumental resources needed to help them accomplish their goals.[20] The use of knowledge and skills, rather than their exchange, constitutes the source of value for the customer. For example, automobile repair businesses provide specialized mechanical knowledge and skills as instrumental resources to help customers resolve problems with their vehicles. These operant resources are customized to the specific problem of the automobile and the customers' desired level of repair. To institute this logic, firms can develop relationships with customers and involve them in the production process,[21] an option especially prevalent with automobile repairs, in which customers rely on the relationship with their mechanics to mitigate their fear of being taken advantage of due to their lack of mechanical knowledge. These types of transactions are important because they ultimately lead to value creation for the consumer.

In keeping with the structure of the other logics, this chapter proposes that the strategic marketing logic of experiences is based on the assumptions of symbolic resources, engaging transactions, and internalized value.[22] Unlike the goods marketing logic, which is focused on satisfying customers' needs through material products, or the service marketing logic, which is focused on helping customers reach their goals through instrumental knowledge and skills, the experiential marketing logic focuses on fulfilling customers' desires through symbolic practices. The experiential marketing logic is based on utilizing, integrating, and instantiating a wide range of symbols in creative and imaginative ways to create stimulating offerings and generate positive customer memories.[23] Thus, it is not the type of resource that is important (i.e., operand or operant); rather, it is the perspectives and meanings that the resources present to the consumer that lie at the heart of the experiential marketing. Likewise, it is not simply the duration of the transaction or the level of involvement of the parties that is important but rather the degree to which the offering stimulates the customer and leaves a lasting impression. For example, the value of a visit to Disney World is not reducible to the tangible souvenirs and food that the "guests" purchase or their interactions with the "cast members". Rather, it lies in the perspective and meanings that these resources stimulate in the guests. As Pine and Gilmore write, "However, while the *work* of the experience stager perishes upon its performance, the *value* of the experience lingers in the memory of any individual who was engaged by the event."[24] In addition, we argue that customers do not have to be directly involved in the material production of the offering (e.g., co-production) for it to have this effect. Instead, customers simply need to be involved in the symbolic appropriation and interpretation of the offering in order for it to become a memorable customer experience.[25]

It is important to note that we are not arguing that the goods or service logics are inherently incorrect or that they cannot be used to great effect. If anything, this chapter challenges the idea that the goods marketing logic has evolved into the service marketing logic and that the service logic is, or should be, the dominant paradigm in marketing.[26] Moreover, we do not argue, as do some experiential marketing researchers,[27] that the experiential marketing logic is the next step in the marketing evolutionary ladder. Instead, this chapter takes a more postmodernism stance against grand marketing narratives and argues from a critical relativism position that there are multiple logics in marketing, each with its own specific assumptions, that firms may utilize.[28] For firms to be successful, they need to understand these different logics and their assumptions and decide which one fits their objectives and goals. In fact, it may be the creative incorporation of multiple logics into a single venue (e.g., Disney World) that can lead to a sustainable competitive advantage.[29]

If producing memorable customer experiences is the primary goal of a firm's strategy, we argue that the firm needs to utilize a strategic marketing logic that is directly focused on achieving this goal. That is, the goods and service marketing logics are based on assumptions that are not focused on the specific dimensions and characteristics of experiences. If the firm wants to produce memorable customer experiences, it needs to utilize a logic that addresses the creation of a symbolic experiential offering, the management of an engaging interface between the offering and the customer, and the facilitation of personal meaning and enjoyment. From a managerial perspective, the proper strategic mix depends on the creative resources and capabilities of the firm, the type of experience it wants to create, and the degree to which the experience is related to the goals of the firm.[30]

Experiential Marketing Logic

To understand the experiential marketing logic and how it affects the creation of memorable customer experiences, we conducted an extended research study of 10 experiential contexts (e.g., amusement/theme parks, concerts, cruises, festivals, museums, national parks, performances, resorts, sporting events, zoos) in which we collected qualitative data from both producers and consumers (see Appendix, pp. 19–20). The participants in the study were recruited using theoretical sampling, and the data were collected through observation, interviews, and open-ended questionnaires. Data analysis followed the accepted methods proposed for qualitative data analysis.[31] Due to space limitations, we present the results from our study as aggregate findings.

SYMBOLIC RESOURCES

The first foundational premise is that experiential marketing is based on symbolic resources. A symbolic resource is defined as anything used by producers and consumers as a sign to convey a particular perspective and meaning.[32] Although experiential offerings often consist of both tangible and intangible stimuli, as well as tangible and intangible effects, we find that what makes these resources experiential is not what they are but rather what they represent. For goods, resources represent functions; for services, resources represent solutions; for experiences, resources represent perspectives and meanings. It is the instantiation‡ of these perspectives and meanings through various stimuli that consumers seek from these offerings.[33] These perspectives and meanings can be transmitted and received in many different ways and depend partly on the offering and partly on the consumer. Although consumers seek offerings that use these resources, they are not necessarily confined to the perspectives and meanings proposed by the firm. Rather, it is the active participation (physically, mentally, and/or emotionally) in these resources that consumers really seek.

---

‡   Instantiate means to the represent an abstraction (e.g., concept, idea, meaning, theory) in a concrete or tangible form.

While much of the experiential literature focuses on the specific type of stimuli associated with an experiential offering (e.g., sensorial, emotional, intellectual, fanciful, social, emotional, physical, and spiritual),[34] we find that the type of stimuli is less important than the effect it produces. Although an experiential strategy might simply involve incorporating as many different stimuli as possible into an offering in the hopes of producing some type of experiential effect,[35] we find that most successful experiential offerings start with an intended dramatic effect.[36] That is, experiential marketing strategy is not driven by the motivation to satisfy a consumer's need, but rather by the intentionality of the producers to create some type of dramatic effect. As a result, the effect determines which stimuli are instantiated in an experiential offering. More important, the stimuli are carriers of perspectives and meanings that underlie the intended dramatic effect. Ultimately, it is the symbolic relationship, rather than a causal connection, between the stimuli and the effect that lies at the heart of these types of offerings. For example, a Holocaust museum might provide a lot of informational stimuli, but the actual effect can be extremely emotional.

The experiential effect is the result not simply of some type of conditioning process but of consumers' interaction with and interpretation of the symbolic resources. The interaction between the intentions of the producers and the intentions of the consumers underlies the perspectives and meanings of the symbolic resources. At the same time, we find that the level and degree of interaction and interpretation can vary greatly among consumers. A critical factor in encouraging consumers' interaction and interpretation is the liminal characteristics of an experiential offering.[37] Because experiential offerings often provide consumers with a different sense of time and space,[38] the consumers must actively interpret the perspective and meanings of the various stimuli to participate in the intended effect. For example, most consumers of Renaissance festivals engage their imaginations to transport themselves back in time and participate in the offering. The stimuli of the festivals help facilitate this process, yet most consumers also filter and/or interact with specific aspects of the experience to incorporate the offering into their personal perspectives and meanings.

This focus on the symbolic nature of experiential marketing does not negate the importance of the material elements;[39] it simply means that the visceral aspects of an experiential offering have to be interpreted by consumers to become an experience.[40] In general, the visual appearance of an experiential offering and the physical sensations that it produces can have powerful symbolic effects on consumers. We find that the material aspects of experiential offerings can affect consumers' level of anticipation, enjoyment, and evaluation. In addition, the symbolic nature of an experiential offering can affect its material enjoyment. For example, the thrill of a roller coaster is not simply the physical sensations associated with the ride but also the combination of perspectives and meanings (e.g., highest, fastest, longest) surrounding the ride. As a result, the symbolic and the material aspects of an experiential offering are often intimately intertwined. In fact, it is the tangible dimensions of an experiential offering that actual separate experiential marketing from branding. For example, Disneyland and the Disney brand, though very similar and consistent, are not the same: Disneyland instantiates the Disney brand in a very particular and material way.

How can producers use symbolic resources to produce memorable customer experiences? One of the difficulties with an experiential offering is that the producers are not fully in control of its perspective and meaning. We suggest that the producers only provide the symbols; it is up to the consumer to interpret and embrace them. Although this gap may seem like a weakness of this form of marketing, it is really one of its strengths. Because consumers have to interact and interpret experiential offerings, the offerings have a very strong effect.

Ceding a certain lack of control inherent in experiential marketing, marketers can do several things to instantiate the symbolic aspects of their offerings and produce a dramatic effect. First, marketers need to decide on both the general and specific perspectives and meanings that they want to transmit through the offering. While it is true that there is a symbolic dimension to every offering,[41] a marketing experience is unique in that it focuses on and promotes a particular sign system.[42] This sign system usually revolves around a set of themes,[43] which establish the perceptual and conceptual context in which the material aspects of the offering are situated. Although themes can integrate the symbolic perspective and meanings of the experiential offering, this process cannot occur arbitrarily or cavalierly. Just placing labels on aspects of the offering that are consistent with the theme does not necessarily incorporate them into the symbolic nature of the experience. The marketers must ensure that both the symbolic and material aspects of the offering fully instantiate the perspectives and meanings of the particular experience. For example, many Renaissance fair consumers complain that simply labeling French fries as the King's fries and cheese sticks as fairy wands does not incorporate them into the ethos of the festival. In fact, many consumers attribute this lack of symbolic connection to manipulative marketing.

Second, marketers must confirm that the symbolic resources associated with an experiential offering fit with the perspective and meanings. It is not simply the instantiation of various stimuli into the offering that leads to the experiential effect; rather, it is the interaction among all of the symbolic resources that contributes to a particular perspective and meaning. For example, many museum curators state that creating a successful exhibit is a multidisciplinary effort, in which everyone offers their particular expertise to add layers and depth to the perspective and meanings of the exhibit. The symbolic connections among all of the elements facilitate the intended dramatic effect. In turn, we find that when consumers participate in the relationships among these symbolic resources, rather than the resources themselves, they exercise their desires and intentions and convert the intended effect into a memorable customer experience.

Third, overt commercialism can interfere with and detract from the symbolic nature of an experiential offering. On the one hand, most consumers realize and accept the commercial nature of such offerings. On the other hand, the commercial aspects of an experiential offering can draw consumers out of symbolic participation and cause them to focus on the business motives surrounding the offering. Drawing on the previous example, most consumers of Renaissance festivals accept the commercial nature of the venues and willingly participate in them; but when they perceive that the commercial elements do not fit with the symbolic elements (e.g., the King's fries), this dissonance interferes with their enjoyment. The integration of all elements, including the commercial, into the overall symbolic perspective and meaning of the offering usually causes consumers to participate in the sign system surrounding these offerings. As a result, the producers should minimize the commercial in favour of the symbolic. It is the symbolic nature of the resources, rather than their commercial potential, that attracts consumers and produces the overall effect.

ENGAGING TRANSACTIONS

The second foundational premise is that experiential marketing logic is based on engaging transactions.[44] An engaging transaction is defined as an exchange process that sustains a person's interest and attention. Whereas the marketing literature addresses consumer interest in transactions in terms of motivation and involvement, our study finds that these concepts may not be adequate to explain engagement in an experiential offering. Most consumers in our study suggest that involvement and engagement in an experiential offering differ and that the level of involvement does not necessarily correlate with the level of engagement. In fact, many consumers relate situations of low involvement but high engagement. In general, involvement refers to the activities that a person initiates to satisfy a goal based on needs and wants,[45] whereas engagement refers to the process by which a person's desire gets intentionally projected onto an object.[46] Our study finds that most consumers do not associate the consumption of experiential offerings with drives, motives, preferences, or purpose. Instead, consumers focus on engagement with aspects of the offering that they find fascinating, engrossing, attractive, or even tempting (i.e., which actually indicates something contrary to goal-striving behaviour).[47] For example, consumers of performances (e.g., plays, musicals, concerts) deny being involved in the production of the offering but claim they were completely engaged and engrossed in the experience.

These findings raise an important question: What constitutes an engaging transaction? The answer to this question is quite complex. First, what is engaging for one consumer may be disengaging for another. For example, some consumers of Renaissance festivals are engaged by their interactions with the various characters at the fairs, whereas others are turned off by this interaction and attend strictly to observe. Second, a consumer may be engaged and disengaged by different aspects of the offering. For example, most consumers of zoos note animals that they found very engaging and others that were not. Third, engagement can be elicited anywhere along the consumer participation continuum.[48] For example, a consumer of a performance may be a passive participant but still very engaged in the story. Fourth, the type and level of engagement can differ among experiential venues. For example, what is engaging at a sporting event may be disengaging at an art museum.

With all of this variance, it seems almost impossible to determine what constitutes an engaging transaction, yet a deeper analysis of the data suggests some commonalities among experiential offerings that underlie consumer engagement. First, to create an engaging transaction, marketers need to produce a holistic offering. One of the definitions of engagement is to hold attention, which firms can do by ensuring that all of the elements of the marketing experience fit together holistically. For example, among the consumers who attribute the most satisfaction with an experiential offering, almost all had difficulty pinning down specifically what they liked about the offering. Most fans of sporting events stated that it was everything about the event (e.g., the stadium, the other fans, the game) that contributed to their enjoyment and that the removal of any element would have diminished the experience. Holistically, the sum is greater than the parts. Because all aspects of an experiential offering are important, it is their combined effect that influences consumers. We even find that if one element does not fit with the others, it can distract consumers and potentially cause them to disengage from the offering or prompt a negative reaction. As with symbolic resources, marketers can employ themes and stories to create an engaging holistic experience. A theme can be used to organize the elements of an offering, and the story can establish the relationships among the elements. To create and maintain an engaging transaction, all of these elements must come together and produce a holistic experience.

Second, marketers need to manage the temporal aspects of an experiential offering to create an engaging transaction. The data suggest that how the offering unfolds over time directly influences consumer engagement. Not only should all of the elements "fit" together to produce a holistic object, but they should also "flow" together to produce a holistic process. This process is important because it keeps customers engaged throughout their consumption of the offering. If there are gaps or breakdowns in the temporal process, consumers will often disengage from the offering. For example, many consumers of musical concerts in our study comment on how much they enjoyed a particular performance because it flowed seamlessly from one song to the next without any substantial breaks. The degree of temporal continuity also influenced the perceived quality of the concert. The holistic nature of the process is also important because it encourages consumers to participate in the offering by projecting what will come next. Many sports fans talked about how they would try to anticipate what plays and/or strategies would be undertaken, based on all of the other aspects of the game. As a result, engagement often grows over the course of an experiential offering as all of the elements come together to produce the intended dramatic effect.

Third, to produce an engaging transaction, marketers need to manage not only the connection between the producers' intention and the actual performance of the offering,[49] but also the connection between the producers' intentions and the consumers' intentions. Unlike experiential consumption that focuses exclusively on the intentions of consumers,[50] experiential marketing also involves the intentions of producers. One of the things that makes an experiential offering unique is its position as the interface between these two sets of intentions. The intentionality of the producers is captured in those aspects of the offering that direct the consumers' attention. In a sense, it is the perspective being advocated.[51] The intentionality of the consumers refers to how consumers direct their attention to interpret and ascribe meaning to the offering.[52] For example, though most museum curators acknowledge that their exhibits provide a particular perspective, they still try to provide enough resources for consumers to explore their own interests and create their own experiences. Many of the museum curators we interviewed indicate that they struggle with how much information, especially in terms of labels and signs, to provide with a particular exhibit. Although marketers cannot directly manage consumers' intentionality, by providing a symbolically rich offering in which the perspectives of both the producers and the consumers can be explored, they can encourage consumers to remain engaged throughout the transaction, ascribe their own meanings and perspectives to the offering, and create enduring memories.

INTERNALIZED VALUE

The third foundational premise is that experiential marketing logic is based on internalized value, or the degree to which an offering facilitates a subjective, hedonic response by an individual or group.[53] Unlike use and exchange value, which are primarily utilitarian and extrinsically focused on achieving some goal, internalized value is primarily auto-telic and intrinsically focused on the experience for its own sake.[54] While the experiential literature suggests that internalized value relates directly to the memories of an experience,[55] we find that what makes an experience memorable is often idiosyncratic and sometimes only tangentially associated with the offering. This section explores three factors that underlie the internalized value of experiential marketing.

First, internalized value is strongly affected by consumers' personal connectivity with an experiential offering, which can range from a broad association with the general nature of the offering to a deeper personal connection with specific aspects of the experience. For example, many consumers state that they like to go to zoos and aquariums because of their personal interest in animals, nature, and conservation. Part of the value of these offerings lies in the fact that they provide consumers with an object on which to project their broader personal desires and in which they can directly participate. At the other end of the continuum, consumers may value an experiential offering because it relates to some important aspect of their lives. For example, many consumers in our study state that they choose to go to concerts because the band is one of their favourites and they feel more connected to the artists at a live performance. In contrast with existing literature, part of the value of these offerings is that it allows consumers to participate in the "real", or at least what they perceive as real, and thus experience unmediated desire.

Second, internalized value is strongly affected by the extraordinary characteristics of an experiential offering. Consumers value an unusual experience because it exposes them to things that they may have never encountered before and stimulates them in many unexpected ways. For example, by going to the zoo, consumers can see and learn about many exotic animals that they would never experience in everyday life. Whereas experiential literature often focuses primarily on escape as a primary characteristic of an experiential offering,[56] we find that it is only part of the equation. Getting away from the real world is often simply the condition that allows consumers to experience new things and take on different perspectives.[57] That is, the value of an experiential offering is not merely that it provides an escape, but also that it allows for a sense of discovery. The subjective excitement brought on by this sense of adventure increases the value for the consumer. Although the excitement and value can diminish when the "real world" (i.e., the ordinary and usual) intrudes on the adventure, this feeling is often restored through the sense of exploration.

Third, internalized value depends strongly on the social connectivity of the experience. Most consumers, whether attending a theatrical performance, a sporting event, or a zoo, consume an experiential offering with others. The importance of this social engagement is not simply the proximal characteristics of being with others with similar interests (i.e., not spoiling the experience), though such benefits can definitely add to the enjoyment, but rather is a function of sharing and creating the experience. The internalized value of an experiential offering seems to increase when consumers can talk about it with others before, during, and after the engagement.[58] Our data suggest that this social engagement may be more valuable than the offering itself. Several consumers in our study state that the particular venue is less important than experiencing it with others. For example, one informant states that a particular roller coaster ride would not have been the same had he not been sitting with his best friend in the first car screaming their heads off and laughing about it afterwards. An experiential offering, given its symbolic nature, often facilitates conversations, which enables consumers to play with the perspective and meanings of the experience. Providing opportunities for consumers to share the experience (e.g., snapping photos of them on the roller coaster) enhances the internalized value of the offering and can lead to more memorable customer experiences.

Conclusions

While the ultimate goal of a firm may be to provide a memorable customer experience, what constitutes a memorable customer experience and how to achieve this goal remains relatively unknown. To compound this problem, current marketing strategies do not address this issue. That is, simply providing higher quality goods or more instrumental services is not necessarily going to translate into memorable customer experiences. Instead, firms need to employ a strategic marketing logic that directly focuses on experiences and proposes specific elements to facilitate consumer memories. We argue that by understanding the strategic logic of experiential marketing, we can understand what constitutes memorable customer experiences and how to facilitate them.

On the basis of our study, we find that the experiential marketing logic is a complex form of marketing that differs significantly from the strategic logic of goods and services and which is based on the assumptions of symbolic resources, engaging transactions, and internalized value. The real trick for marketers is to translate these assumptions into offerings that produce memorable customer experiences. First, marketers must manage the symbolic nature of their offering by deciding on the intended dramatic effect(s), as well as the particular perspective and meanings underlying those effect(s). This effort will help them determine exactly which stimuli they need to incorporate in the offering to facilitate the desired effect. Because it is the overall sign system in which the stimuli are embedded that provides them with a particular perspective and meaning, it is vitally important that marketers manage all of the stimuli and their relationships. When consumers intentionally project their desires into this sign system, they convert the intended effect into a memorable experience.

Second, marketers need to provide an engaging transaction. While much of the experiential literature has focused on customer involvement in the production of an offering as a means to facilitate the experience, this study finds that "co-production" does not necessarily translate into an engaging experience. Instead, marketers should focus on producing a holistic experiential offering in which all of the stimuli that constitute the offering influence the intended dramatic effect. Every element should have some connection to the intended effect or it should be removed. In addition, it is not enough to manage the "fit" among all of the elements; marketers must also manage the "flow" of elements. Anything that interrupts the flow may detract from the intended effect. To manage fit and flow, marketers should facilitate the connection between the producers' and consumers' intentionality. Each comes to the offering with a particular perspective. The exploration of these perspectives, rather than their imposition, underlies an engaging transaction. That is, by engaging consumers in the connections among the physical, temporal, and intentional aspects of the offering, marketers are more likely to convert the transaction into a memorable customer experience.

Third, marketers must enhance the internalized value derived from the offering, with an understanding that consumers are not merely passive recipients of these offerings but come to the offering with their own desires. It is not really possible to manage these desires, but it is possible to provide an offering that accommodates, and even encourages, them. As a result, it is important to understand both the general and the specific personal connections that consumers have with an experiential offering. This is not simply the standard practice of trying to determine consumers' needs and wants; rather, it is the process of understanding what the offering means to consumers. Most people do not consume an experiential offering to fulfil a particular goal, but to engage something on which they can project their interests and desires. Therefore, marketers should promote the experiential offering not as a means to an end, but as a means unto itself. Furthermore, consumers value an experiential offering because it allows them to experience something different and out of the ordinary. In a sense, their desires and interests are not to be fulfilled, but explored and enhanced. One way that consumers explore these types of offerings is by sharing the experience with others. This communal discourse helps consumers access their particular perspective, assign their own meanings, and create lasting memories.

Although creating memorable customer experiences may be the primary goal of firms that decide to engage in experiential marketing, the main way to reach this goal is to actively manage the symbolic resources associated with the offering, create an engaging transaction, and enhance customers' internalized value. The specific memories that a customer has of an experiential offering are almost impossible to create and manage, but it is possible for firms to facilitate the memory process and create a lasting impression in the minds of consumers. The logic of experiential marketing underlying this goal can shed some light on this process and the steps that need to be taken to create a truly memorable customer experience.

Appendix

To study the logic of memorable customer experiences, this study uses an interpretive qualitative research design.[59] The existence of empirical research on various aspects of experiential marketing and consumption prompted us not to use a grounded theory approach. Instead, we use a descriptive-theoretic framework and build on prior research by utilizing a priori themes,[60] though we still employ an inductive method to facilitate discovery. The purpose of the study is to discover, interpret, and describe the various assumptions of experiential marketing and their relationships.

Unlike most qualitative studies that focus on a single context, and because the phenomenon of interest is the logic of experiential marketing, we look across different experiential contexts. No consensus currently exists about what constitutes an experiential offering; as such, we use Pine and Gilmore's "four realms of experience" framework[61] to identify experiential contexts: (1) entertainment experiences (e.g., sporting events, performances, concerts), (2) escapist experiences (e.g., amusement/theme parks, cruises, resorts, festivals), (3) aesthetic experiences (e.g., fine arts museums, national parks), and (4) educational experiences (e.g., natural science and history museums, zoos, aquariums).

In terms of participants, we theoretically sampled both consumers and producers from the various contexts who could contribute to our understanding of the logic of experiential marketing.[62] Using purposive sampling, we chose participants on a continuous basis to develop and test our theoretical interpretations.[63] In total, we interviewed 188 consumers and 18 producers across 10 different contexts.

In terms of data analysis, we followed a four-stage process based on the procedures advocated by McCracken and Spiggle.[64] In the first categorization stage, we read and coded all of the qualitative data. We also wrote memos based on our initial insights and issues that arose during the coding process. The second stage involved abstraction and dimensionalization, during which we grouped the codes into descriptive themes and identified the properties and elements of each theme. In the third integration stage, we identified the relationships among the descriptive themes. Rather than looking for causal connections, we sought holistic relationships. Finally, in the fourth stage of interrogation and refutation, we evaluated the findings in relation to the raw data and the original a priori themes to determine if our findings hold across contexts and to understand the boundary conditions of the findings. We also conducted member checks with both consumers and producers during this stage. The whole process was iterative as we moved back and forth between the data and the interpretations.

Notes

1.   Vargo, Steven L. and Lusch, Robert F. (2004), "Evolving to a new dominant logic for marketing", *Journal of Marketing*, Vol. 68, No. 1, pp. 1–17.
2.   Carù, Antonella and Cova, Bernard (2007), "Consuming experiences: an introduction", in A. Carù and B. Cova (eds), *Consuming Experience*, Routledge, New York, pp. 3–16; Fuat Firat, A. and Venkatesh, Alladi (1995), "Liberatory postmodernism and the reenchantment of consumption", *Journal of Consumer Research*, Vol. 22 (December), pp. 239–67; Holbrook, Morris B. and Hirschman, Elizabeth C. (1982), "The experiential aspects of consumption: consumer fantasies, feelings, and fun", *Journal of Consumer Research*, Vol. 9 (September), pp. 132–40.
3.   Edgell, Stephen, Hetherington, Kevin, and Warde, Alan (eds.) (1997), *Consumption Matters: The Production and Experience of Consumption*, Blackwell, Oxford.
4.   Kozinets, Robert V., Sherry, John F. Jr., Storm, Diana, Duhachek, Adam, Nuttavuthisit, Krittinee, and Deberry-Spence, Benet (2004), "Ludic agency and retail spectacle", *Journal of Consumer Research*, Vol. 31 (December), pp. 658–72.
5.   Pine, B. Joseph and Gilmore, James H. (1999), *The Experience Economy: Work is Theater and Every Business is a Stage*, Harvard Business School Press, Boston.
6.   Vargo and Lusch, "Evolving to a new dominant logic for marketing".
7.   Barney, Jay B. (1991), "Firm resources and sustained competitive advantage", *Journal of Management*, Vol. 17, No. 1, pp. 99–120; Constantin, James A. and Lusch, Robert F. (1994), *Understanding Resource Management*, The Planning Forum, Oxford, OH; Hunt, Shelby D. (2000), *A General Theory of Competition: Resources, Competencies, Productivity, Economic Growth*, Sage, Thousand Oaks, CA.
8.   Bagozzi, Richard P. (1975), "Marketing as exchange", *Journal of Marketing*, Vol. 39, No. 4, pp. 32–9; Dwyer, F. Robert, Schurr, Paul H., and Oh, Sejo (1987), "Developing buyer–seller relationships", *Journal of Marketing*, Vol. 51, No. 2, pp. 11–27; Rindfleisch, Aric and Heide, Jan B. (1997), "Transaction cost analysis: past, present, and future", *Journal of Marketing*, Vol. 61, No. 4, pp. 30–54.
9.   Holbrook, Morris B. (1999), "Introduction to consumer value", in M.B. Holbrook (ed.), *Consumer Value: A Framework for Analysis and Research*, Routledge, London, pp. 1–28; Narver, John C. and Slater, Stanley F. (1990), "The effect of a market orientation on business profitability", *Journal of Marketing*, Vol. 54, No. 4, pp. 20–35; Woodruff, Robert B. (1997), "Customer value: the next

source for competitive advantage", *Journal of the Academy of Marketing Science*, Vol. 25 (Spring), pp. 139–53.

10. Brown, Stephen (1999), "Devaluing value: the apophatic ethic and the spirit of postmodern consumption", in M.B. Holbrook (ed.), *Consumer Value: A Framework for Analysis and Research*, Routledge, London, pp. 159–82; Fuat Firat, A. and Dholakia, Nikhilesh (1998), *Consuming People: From Political Economy to Theaters of Consumption*, Routledge, New York; Venkatesh, Alladi, Peñaloza, Lisa, and Fuat Firat, A. (2006), "The market as a sign system and the logic of marketing", in R.L. Lusch and S.L. Vargo (eds), *The Service-Dominant Logic: Dialog, Debate, and Directions*, M.E. Sharpe, Armonk, NY, pp. 251–65.

11. Constantin and Lusch, *Understanding Resource Management*; Vargo and Lusch, "Evolving to a new dominant logic for marketing".

12. Cherrington, Paul T. (1920), *The Elements of Marketing*, Macmillan, New York; Nystrom, Paul (1915), *The Economics of Retailing*, Ronald Press, New York.

13. Beckman, Theodore N. (1954), "The value added concept as applied to marketing and its implications", in S.H. Rewoldt (ed.), *Frontiers in Marketing Thought*, Bureau of Business Research, Indiana University, Bloomington, pp. 83–145; Shaw, A. (1912), "Some problems in market distribution", *Quarterly Journal of Economics*, Vol. 12 (August), pp. 703–65; Venkatesh et al., "The market as a sign system and the logic of marketing".

14. Weld, Louis D.H. (1917), "Marketing function and mercantile organizations", *American Economic Review*, Vol. 7 (June), pp. 306–18.

15. Converse, Paul D. (1921), *Marketing Methods and Politics*, Prentice Hall, New York; Cowan, Alan (1964), *Quality Control for the Manager*, Pergamon, Oxford; Garvin, David A. (1983), "Quality on the line", *Harvard Business Review*, Vol. 61 (September–October), pp. 65–73.

16. McCarthy, E. Jerome (1960), *Basic Marketing: A Managerial Approach*, Richard D. Irwin, Homewood, IL.

17. Vargo and Lusch, "Evolving to a new dominant logic for marketing".

18. Day, George (1994), "The capabilities of market-driven organizations", *Journal of Marketing*, Vol. 58 (October), pp. 37–52; Evans, Philip B. and Wurster, Thomas S. (1997), "Strategy and the new economics of information", *Harvard Business Review*, Vol. 75 (September–October), pp. 71–82.

19. Vargo, Stephen L. and Lusch, Robert F. (2006), "Service-dominant logic: what it is, what it is not, what it might be", in R.F. Lusch, and S.L. Vargo (eds.), *The Service-Dominant Logic: Dialog, Debate, and Directions*, M.E. Sharpe, Armonk, NY, pp. 43–56, at p. 43.

20. Kohli, Ajay K. and Jaworski, Bernard J. (1990), "Market orientation: the construct, research propositions, and managerial implications", *Journal of Marketing*, Vol. 54, No. 2, pp. 1–18.

21. Dwyer et al., "Developing buyer–seller relationships"; Norman, Richard and Ramirez, Rafael (1993), "From value chain to value constellations: designing interactive strategy", *Harvard Business Review*, Vol. 71, (July–August), pp. 65–77; Prahalad, C.K. and Ramaswamy, Venkat (2004), *The Future of Competition: Co-Creating Unique Value with Customers*, Harvard Business School Press, Boston, MA.

22. Holbrook and Hirschman, "The experiential aspects of consumption"; Pine and Gilmore, *The Experience Economy*; Venkatesh et al., "The market as a sign system and the logic of marketing".

23. Kozinets et al., "Ludic agency and retail spectacle"; Santoro, Chiara and Troilo, Gabriele (2007), "The drivers of hedonic consumption experience: a semiotic analysis of rock concerts", in A. Carù and B. Cova (eds.), *Consuming Experience*, Routledge, New York, pp. 109–25; Venkatesh et al., "The market as a sign system and the logic of marketing".

24.   Pine and Gilmore, *The Experience Economy*.

25.   Lanier, Clinton D., Jr. and Schau, Hope Jensen (2007), "Culture and co-creation: exploring consumers' inspirations and aspirations for writing and posting on-line fan fiction", in R.W. Belk and J.F. Sherry, Jr. (eds.), *Research in Consumer Behavior: Consumer Culture Theory*, Vol. 11, Elsevier, Oxford, pp. 321–42.

26.   Vargo and Lusch, "Service-dominant logic".

27.   Pine and Gilmore, *The Experience Economy*; Venkatesh et al., "The market as a sign system and the logic of marketing".

28.   Anderson, Paul F. (1986), "On method in consumer research: a critical relativist position", *Journal of Consumer Research*, Vol. 13 (September), pp. 155–73; Brown, Stephen (1995), *Postmodern Marketing*, Routledge, London; Lyotard, Jean-François (1984), *The Postmodern Condition: A Report on Knowledge*, trans. Geoff Bennington and Brian Massumi, University of Minnesota Press, Minneapolis.

29.   Bryman, Alan (2004), *The Disneyization of Society*, Sage, London.

30.   Badot, Olivier and Filser, Marc (2007), "Re-enchantment of retailing: toward utopian islands", in A. Carù and B. Cova (eds.), *Consuming Experience*, Routledge, New York, pp. 166–82; Podestà, Stefano and Addis, Michela (2007), "Converging industries through experience: lessons from edutainment", in A. Carù and B. Cova (eds), *Consuming Experience*, Routledge, New York, pp. 139–53; Schmitt, Bernd H. (1999), *Experiential Marketing: How to Get Customers to Sense, Feel, Think, Act, and Relate to Your Company and Brands*, Free Press, New York.

31.   McCracken, Grant (1988), *The Long Interview*, Sage, Newbury Park, CA; Spiggle, Susan (1994), "Analysis and interpretation of qualitative data in consumer research", *Journal of Consumer Research*, Vol. 21 (December), pp. 491–503.

32.   Levy, Sidney J. (1959), "Symbols for sale", *Harvard Business Review*, Vol. 37 (July–August), pp. 117–24; Mick, David Glen (1986), "Consumer research and semiotics: exploring the morphology of signs, symbols, and significance", *Journal of Consumer Research*, Vol. 13, No. 2, pp. 196–213; Venkatesh et al., "The market as a sign system and the logic of marketing".

33.   Lanier and Schau, "Culture and co-creation".

34.   Hirschman, Elizabeth C. and Holbrook, Morris B. (1982), "Hedonic consumption: emerging concepts, methods and propositions", *Journal of Marketing*, Vol. 46 (Summer), pp. 92–101; LaSalle, Diana and Britton, Terry A. (2003), *Priceless: Turning Ordinary Products into Extraordinary Experiences*, Harvard Business School Press, Boston, MA; Schmitt, *Experiential Marketing*.

35.   Schmitt, *Experiential Marketing*.

36.   Baron, Steve, Harris, Kim, and Harris, Richard (2001), "Retail theatre", *Journal of Service Research*, Vol. 4, No. 2, pp. 102–17.

37.   Belk, Russell W. and Costa, Janeen Arnold (1998), "The mountain man myth: a contemporary consuming fantasy", *Journal of Consumer Research*, Vol. 25 (December), pp. 218–40; O'Guinn, Thomas C. and Belk, Russell W. (1989), "Heaven on Earth: consumption at Heritage Village, USA", *Journal of Consumer Research*, Vol. 16, (September), pp. 227–38.

38.   Arnould, Eric J. and Price, Linda L. (1993), "River magic: extraordinary experience and the extended service encounter", *Journal of Consumer Research*, Vol. 20 (June), pp. 24–45; Celsi, Richard L., Rose, Randall L., and Leigh, Thomas W. (1993), "An exploration of high-risk leisure consumption through skydiving", *Journal of Consumer Research*, Vol. 20 (June), pp. 1–23; MacLaran, Pauline and Brown, Stephen (2005), "The center cannot hold: consuming the utopian marketplace", *Journal of Consumer Research*, Vol. 32 (September), pp. 311–23.

39.   Heilbrunn, Benoît (2007), "The blandness and delights of a daily object", in A. Carù and B. Cova (eds.), *Consuming Experience*, Routledge, New York, pp. 79–91.

40. Hoch, Stephen J. (2002), "Product experience is seductive", *Journal of Consumer Research*, Vol. 29 (December), pp. 448–54.

41. Levy, "Symbols for sale".

42. Venkatesh et al., "The market as a sign system and the logic of marketing".

43. Bryman, *The Disneyization of Society*; Gottdiener, Mark (1998), "The semiotics of consumer spaces: the growing importance of themed environments", in J.F. Sherry, Jr. (ed.), *Servicescapes: The Concept of Place in Contemporary Markets*, NTC, Chicago, pp. 29–54; Pine and Gilmore, *The Experience Economy*.

44. Pine and Gilmore, *The Experience Economy*.

45. Arnould, Eric J., Price, Linda L., and Zinkhan, George M. (2004), *Consumers*, McGraw-Hill/Irwin, New York.

46. Belk, Russell W., Ger, Guliz, and Askegaard, Soren (2003), "The fire of desire: a multisited inquiry into consumer passion", *Journal of Consumer Research*, Vol. 30 (December), pp. 326–51; Cova, Véronique and Rémy, Eric (2007), "Consuming experiences: an introduction", in A. Carù and B. Cova (eds.), *Consuming Experience*, Routledge, New York, pp. 51–64.

47. Hoch, "Product experience is seductive".

48. Lanier, Clinton D. and Hampton, Ronald D. (2008), "Consumer participation and experiential marketing: understanding the relationship between co-creation and the fantasy life cycle", *Advances in Consumer Research*, Vol. 35, pp. 44–8.

49. Deighton, John (1992), "The consumption of performance", *Journal of Consumer Research*, Vol. 19 (December), pp. 362–72.

50. Cova and Rémy, "Consuming experiences: an introduction".

51. Lanier and Schau, "Culture and co-creation".

52. Cova and Rémy, "Consuming experiences: an introduction".

53. Hirschman and Holbrook, "Hedonic consumption".

54. Holbrook, "Introduction to consumer value".

55. Pine and Gilmore, *The Experience Economy*.

56. Firat and Dholakia, *Consuming People*.

57. Belk and Costa, "The mountain man myth".

58. Ibid.; Arnould and Price, "River magic"; Ladwein, Richard (2007), "Consumption experience, self-narrative, and self-identity: the example of trekking", in A. Carù and B. Cova (eds), *Consuming Experience*, Routledge, New York, pp. 95–108.

59. Holbrook, Morris B. and O'Shaughnessy, John (1988), "On the scientific status of consumer research and the need for an interpretive approach to studying consumption behaviour", *Journal of Consumer Research*, Vol. 15 (December), pp. 398–402; Hudson, Laurel Anderson and Ozanne, Julie L. (1988), "Alternative ways of seeking knowledge in consumer research", *Journal of Consumer Research*, Vol. 14 (March), pp. 508–21.

60. Philipsen, Gerry (1977), "Linearity of research design in ethnographic studies of speaking", *Communication Quarterly*, Vol. 25, No. 3, pp. 42–50.

61. Pine and Gilmore, *The Experience Economy*.

62. Spiggle, "Analysis and interpretation of qualitative data in consumer research".

63. Belk, Russell W., Sherry, John F., Jr., and Wallendorf, Melanie (1988), "A naturalistic inquiry into buyer and seller behavior at a swap meet", *Journal of Consumer Research*, Vol. 14 (March), pp. 449–70.

64. McCracken, *The Long Interview*; Spiggle, "Analysis and interpretation of qualitative data in consumer research".

2 Experiential Marketing and Brand Experiences: A Conceptual Framework

KARSTEN KILIAN*

Keywords

experiential marketing, experience products, brand experiences, brand experience worlds

Abstract

In this chapter, I propose a conceptual framework for experiential marketing and brand experiences. The framework is linked to three types of values. It enables companies to become experience providers, establishing and managing real or virtual experience products and worlds. In particular, I provide the components and success factors for brand experience worlds and memorable brand experiences.

I will name the dynamics behind experience societies and markets; present relevant experience market ranges and realms; propose a systematization for real and virtual experience products and worlds; and introduce the value triad with value dimensions of products and services. Also, I will denote the characteristic components and success factors of real experience worlds, as well as provide an overview of brand experience worlds and their characteristics.

Experience Societies on the Rise

In former times, when people wanted to experience something, they went on journeys, strolled around a public park, or visited the local zoo. Today, more and more industries have become "experience-oriented". For example, the largest aquarium in Berlin, the German capital, is not

* Karsten Kilian, University of St. Gallen, Switzerland. E-mail: kilian@markenlexikon.com. Telephone: + 49 9343 509 031.

the public zoo's aquarium but rather appears in the lobby of the five-star Radisson SAS hotel. The hotel-owned AquaDom, a 25-meter-tall saltwater aquarium, was conceived consciously as a salient landmark for the hotel and functions like a magnet, attracting and astonishing hotel guests, inviting them to stay, and encouraging them to come back.[1]

On the basis of social changes, experiences become crucial differentiation and success factors for many industries, especially as highly developed countries increasingly transform themselves into "experience societies". The term "Erlebnisgesellschaft" (experience society) was first coined by the German sociologist Gerhard Schulze in 1992. Until the 1980s, people's view of life primarily depended on external factors, but with the proclaimed rise of the experience society, this orientation has shifted toward the individual and his or her inner orientation.[2] In the search for infinite experience worlds, "experience and existence flow more indiscriminately into one another than ever before".[3] Affluent Western societies tend to "comprehend the entire life as [an] experience project",[4] such that "a person's life is quite literally the sum of his or her experiences".[5] Four aspects are responsible for this increasing experience orientation:[6]

- Social expansion, by which broader portions of the population have access to experiences.
- Relative portion, in that greater shares of people's time budgets are dedicated to experiences.
- Penetration, such that increasing areas of everyday life are affected by experiences.
- Central role, as experiences move from the periphery of personal values toward the center and increasingly define the purpose of life.

Among the causes of this intensified experience orientation is the significant increase in life expectancy, combined with longer training periods, earlier exits from working life, and temporary breaks in between, such as sabbaticals. For example, in Europe, an academic spends roughly 40–45 percent of his or her life working. As a result, humans have more free time, which they must fill with experiences. Time-saving inventions also have contributed to an experience orientation, because "the time saved has to be disported once again".[7]

Even during a person's working life, the portion of working time has decreased. Whereas in the 1950s and 1960s, 50–60 hours per week over six working days was standard, today, the five-day week with 35–45 working hours prevails, and paid vacation averages 25–30 days annually. Moreover, consumers spend relatively less time and money on their basic needs, such as food. Consequently, an ever greater portion of their income becomes available for upscale consumer goods (e.g., books), consumer durables (e.g., cars), and services such as restaurant visits and holidays.[8] Accordingly, the principal purpose of experience consumption is the facilitation of a pleasant life: "We devote a considerable portion of our resources to the pursuit of 'the good life' – one of contentment, pleasure, and happiness."[9] The quest for a beautiful, successful life moves more people in Western cultures than ever before.[10]

Experiential Marketing as Key

The alteration of the social environment has led to changes in consumer needs. Beyond necessity and usefulness, indulgence and amusement become cornerstones of consumption. Experiences in this context can best be described as individualized events that develop in the consumer's world of feelings and experiences, which have beneficial effects on the consumer and therefore cannot be called up completely or in a well-planned manner.[11] Experiences do not contribute to consumers' quality of life until the moment they are demanded, which increases subjective consumer risk. At this point, branding comes into play, because brands can offer subjective security and association-rich recall,[12] which help ensure that the experiences will work well for the consumer.

In general, experiences provide customers with "short-term access to simulated worlds and altered states of consciousness".[13] They are triggered stimulations to the senses, the heart, and the mind, and they evolve as a "result of encountering, undergoing, or living through situations. Experiences connect the company and the brand to the customer's lifestyle and place individual customer actions and the purchase occasion in a broader social context."[14]

Pine and Gilmore move even beyond this assertion.[15] They understand experiences as an independent economical value, which contrasts with raw materials, products, and services so much that it might be considered a fourth economic factor. Whereas products as material (mass) offerings serve anonymous customers, services represent immaterial activities conducted expressly for them.[16] Experiences then go beyond pure services. By nature, they are memorable and personally affect the recipient over time. A consumer "pays to spend time enjoying a series of memorable events that a company stages – as in a theatrical play – to engage him in a personal way".[17] Thus, experiences can be interpreted as stage-managed events that serve to provide a fulfilled pastime by personally involving consumers. A salesperson stages the experience, and the consumer is the guest whose perceptions define the happening and who is therefore willing to pay a significantly higher price for this experience compared with experience-poor products or services.

Although this experience approach by Pine and Gilmore is well thought-out and logical, their view of experiences as independent economic goods may go too far. Furthermore, their definition greatly restricts the spectrum of possible experiences to staged services. They almost entirely neglect products, which prevents them from embracing the total observable experience spectrum.

It therefore appears appropriate to apply a value- or benefit-based demarcation of experiences to differentiate the utilitarian, socially expressive, and experience-oriented contributions of an offer. Whereas utilitarian benefits are functionally coined and their achievement is objectively examinable, socially expressive and experience-oriented benefits of products and services only subjectively emerge in the understanding of the consumer, who must interpret and reconstruct a symbolic, association-rich achievement. The two symbolic benefit categories also can be differentiated with respect to their orientation: socially expressive benefits emerge extrinsically from their effect on other persons, whereas experience-oriented benefits unfold intrinsically within the mind and body of the consumer. Aesthetic sensory impressions and associated feelings and dispositions are beneficial for experiences, whereas socially expressive benefits arise from interrelations with others and the role a person plays within a family, a circle of friends, or another social group. Figure 2.1 summarizes the typical characteristics and attributes of the three value-based achievement classes.

As the quintessence of these definitions, experiences represent individually perceived incidents that develop in the emotional and knowledge-based sphere of a person. They unfold subjectively felt beneficial effects in the interior perspective at the situational

Value	utilitarian	socially expressive	experience-oriented
Orientation	external (extrinsic)		internal (intrinsic)
Assessment	objective (functional)	subjective (symbolic)	
Tangibility	tangible, verifiable	interpretable, associative	
Focus of Offering	offering itself	mind of user	
Imagery Attributes	brand attributes	brand personality	
Self-Concept	functional	actual	ideal
Emotionality	low	distinct	intense
Aim	"functioning well" (inform: be qualified)	"appear more" (differentiate: be distinctive)	"live more richly" (enjoy: be enthusiastic)
Characteristic	function, usefulness	prestige/uniqueness, affiliation	self-expression, hedonism, sensation
Manipulation (Impact)	oneself (personally)	others (interpersonal)	oneself (personally)
Motivation (Value System)	Perfectionist (qualitatively)	Veblen (visible, conspicuous), Snob (unique), Bandwagon	Hedonist, Aesthete (emotional)
Objective	control problem-solving	self, role family, group	emotions mood/disposition
	⇨ Function	⇨ Prestige	⇨ Experience

Figure 2.1 Value-based classification of offerings[18]

moment of usage. Thus, experiences go beyond the definition of products and service, but at the same time, they cannot claim to be a separate kind of economic offering. Rather, they can be interpreted as a contingent type of value that stands side-by-side with utilitarian and socially expressive benefits, and they can be drawn on to differentiate offerings. Therefore, experiential benefits supplement the functional benefit contribution of an offering and possibly even substitute for it.

Experiential marketing in turn refers to companies that provide and market experiences to consumers. As experience providers, experiential marketers offer an adequate environment or setting for the desired customer experience to emerge, because experiences are not self-generated but induced. The basic assumption of experiential marketing is that the best opportunity to influence brand perception is during the post-purchase or consumption phase: customers want to be stimulated, entertained, and educated, as well as emotionally affected and creatively challenged. The enriched consumption experience then strongly influences customer satisfaction and brand loyalty.[19]

In turn, experiential marketers must arrange experiences to be convincing, fascinating, unforgettable, and applicable in the long run.[20] The emotional added value through experiential marketing entails an image-shaping factor with a short-term impact at the point of the event, as well as in the long run in the minds of consumers. Innumerable practical examples reveal that experiences increase consumers' attention to messages from the provider, extend the time spent at the point of sale (POS), and directly promote sales.[21] Thus, experiential concepts represent gratifications that provide consumers with a pause from everyday life and contribute to the overall benefit of an offering through strong, personal emotions. Experiential concepts get offered in experience markets that can be described best as environments in which experience products are being exchanged and/or experience worlds are being staged.

Experience Market Dynamics

The growing importance of experience markets can be attributed to five forces that account for a significant portion of their growth in the past decade:[22]

- experience-oriented change of the product structure;
- expansion of the exchange volume through intensification;
- spatial expansion of the areas of distribution;
- corporatization and concentration;
- missing collective saturation.

The experience-oriented change of the product structure can be characterized by three experience-oriented trends: innovation, diversification, and reinterpretation. First, many new product types have emerged, such as cinema, radio, television, the Internet, and mobile television. New film and music storage devices, new kinds of sports activities, mass tourism, and computer games also have formed new product categories. The increasing diversification of the offer spectrum has thus led to increased homogeneity and greater needs for differentiation. Finally, a reinterpretation of products can take place. Former consumer durables like food, sporting clothing, and kitchen furniture might be reconsidered as experience goods.

Second, new product types strengthen the experience-oriented exchange volume, such that the value and number of consumption activities per time unit become crucial measures of the constant intensification of experience consumption. In a first step, experiences follow in ever greater density; consumers go on vacation more frequently, dine out more regularly, or page through more magazines. At a certain point, further compression is no longer possible, so an increasing shortening of the average experience duration follows. Consumers zap through television programs, book short trips, or replace their clothes more often (fashion chains like H&M and Zara change their collections up to 15 times per year). When the shortened duration is no longer sufficient, experience episodes start getting overlaid. While watching television, a consumer leafs through a magazine while also talking to a friend on the phone and eating a sandwich. Finally, as a last possibility, intensification through refinement, enrichment, and extravagance remains.

Third, the spatial expansion of the areas of distribution lends additional thrust to experience markets. The omission of most trade barriers and the rapid development of modern communication and transportation technologies have strongly increased the spatial mobility of consumers while dissolving the traditional relationship of spatial proximity and confidence. Regional particularities have degenerated. The accompanying globalization experience can, among other outcomes, lead to the worldwide marketing of experience products such as perfumes, cars, and watches.

Due to its greater efficiency, the corporatization, privatization, and concentration of experience providers has become generally accepted. The professional solidification of experience providers penetrates cultural areas and commercializes once-private experiences. Birthday parties, for example, are offered professionally by fast-food chains. Public cultural policy increasingly suffers financial pressures and therefore opens to private suppliers.

A collective saturation point is missing though. A general reorientation toward asceticism might be expected, though few current publications support the idea.[23] Only wars, epidemics, environmental changes, and their results temporarily slow down the experience urge, as did the terrorist attacks of 9/11, the bird flu epidemic, and the 2004 tsunami. Overall, "the processing of the world for experience purposes" continues to progress.[24] In particular, weariness and the increasing difficulty of producing experiences by one's own efforts ensure that experiential demand remains insatiable. This trend grows stronger in response to consumers' fear they will miss something: "The fear of escaped joy of life is an inexhaustible source of the experience market."[25]

Experience Market Systematization

A comparison of different experience ranges plainly shows that, to date, experiences have not been clearly systematized. Schulze only lists various experience examples without systematically categorizing them;[26] Weinberg differentiates between product formation, communication, and shop organization;[27] Schmitt and Simonson distinguish between retail spaces, environments (e.g., transport systems such as airports, bus stops, busses, and trains), and the Internet;[28] and Pine and Gilmore differentiate among four experience realms: entertainment, education, escapist, and aesthetic.

Typical examples of passively absorbing entertainment include viewing a performance, listening to a piece of music, or reading a book for pleasure. The education realm can be best described as the absorption of an event through active participation. A person is truly informed (and increases his or her knowledge or skills) by actively engaging the mind (e.g., in a business seminar) and/or body (e.g., fitness course). For experience realms that combine education with entertainment, the term "edutainment" applies. Typical examples include interactive exhibits in museums or, on a larger scale, science centers, such as the ten currently existing in Germany, with eight more scheduled to open soon.[29] Similar trends emerge in almost all industrial countries. The third realm, escapist experience, involves the complete immersion of consumers, such that they become actively involved participants, such as when visiting theme parks and casinos or playing a game of paintball or using virtual reality headsets. Online computer games also belong to this experience realm. Finally, aesthetic experiences include experiences in which people immerse themselves but have little or no effect on the event. The environment remains untouched; they do not. Examples include visits to museums and art galleries, trips to lookout points like the Grand Canyon, or attendance at sports events.[30]

In contrast to this classification of four experience realms, Steinecke considers trade services and cultural and leisure offers as experience markets that he summarizes as mixed-use centers. Typical characteristics of mixed-used centers are their multi-functionality, leisure and experience character, and convenience aspects; for example, they offer an easygoing opportunity to satisfy different accommodation and leisure interests in a single location.[31]

Mikunda divides experience markets into five categories. First, Brand Lands, fairs, and expositions cluster as "visits to brand and plant". Second, a category encompasses city events, urban entertainment, and hip bars and taverns, which Mikunda classifies as possible arrangement forms of "going out and celebrating a festival". Third, flagship and concept stores, as well as design malls, belong to the category referred to as "purchase places as entertainment". Fourth, the "convenience entertainment" category consists of "optimized places" and "bricks and clicks". In tourism, optimized places depict the smooth organization of check-in, luggage transport, and dinner seating at a resort, because these adjacent experiences have significant impacts on the evaluation of the entire vacation experience. In retail trade, an optimized place might include a system of hidden mini-elevators that transport goods from underground storage to different sales levels, as in some Niketown stores. "Shops in traffic", most frequently found at train stations and airports, also belong to this category, as do unusual places for sports, such as indoor ski-resorts. Bricks and clicks are also part of "convenience entertainment", because they describe the affiliation of real and virtual places, such as telepresence in virtual rooms or teleportation. Fifth, the last category encompasses "mood management", which consists of "lobbies and lounges" and "new hiking". Lobbies and lounges describe temporary places of arrival (e.g., hotel lobbies) or waiting (e.g., theater lounges) that turn into main places and contribute to customers feeling relaxed or lively or considering a place exciting. "New hiking" describes fascinating experiences with nature, such as theme trails and historic locations like museums and memorial places.[32] Figure 2.2 summarizes the experience ranges mentioned by these different authors.

A comparison of experiential dimensionalities shows that some authors focus primarily on trade and services, whereas others embrace products and their composition.

Schulze	Weinberg	Schmitt/Simonson	Pine/Gilmore	Steinecke	Mikunda
"Experience Society"	"Experience Value"	"Marketing Aesthetics"	"Experience Purchase" "Experience World"	"Consumption World"	"Experience World"
Purchases ■ Cosmetics ■ New Hairstyles ■ Clothing ■ Trendy Accessories ■ Furniture ■ Domestic Appliances ■ Food/Drink ■ Magazines ■ Fiction ■ TV/Radio Programs ■ Music CDs ■ Car Components ■ Automobiles ■ To Go Out/ ■ To Stroll ■ Concerts ■ Theater ■ Exhibitions ■ Museums ■ Sports ■ Vacation Trips	**Product Composition** ■ Quality ■ Brand ■ Design ■ Packaging ■ Fringe Benefits **Communications** ■ Mass Communications ■ Pitch/Sales ■ Conversation ■ Nonverbal **Store Composition** ■ Showcase ■ Merchandise Presentation ■ Showrooms	**Retail Floor Spaces** ■ Department Stores ■ Regional Malls ■ Strip Malls ■ Supermarkets ■ Boutiques ■ Superstores ■ Factory Outlets ■ Theme Stores ■ Restaurants **Environmental Spaces** ■ Transportation Systems ■ Recreational Spaces ■ Cultural Spaces ■ Political Complexes **Internet** ■ Cyberspace	**Escapist ("do")** ■ Casinos ■ Theme Parks **Esthetic ("be there")** ■ Museums ■ Viewpoints **Entertainment ("sense")** ■ Read Books ■ Listen to Music **Educational ("learn")** ■ Intellectual Education ■ Physical Training	**Mixed-Use-Centre** Retail Markets, Services, Culture and Leisure: ■ Urban Entertainment Centre ■ Leisure Parks ■ Holiday Parks ■ Brand Lands ■ Theme Hotels/ Restaurants ■ Musical Centre ■ Infotainment-Centre ■ Museums ■ Zoological Garden ■ Parks/ Allotments	**Visits with Brand & Plant** ■ Brandlands ■ Fairs/Expos **Going Out & Celebrating a Festival** ■ City Events ■ Urban Entertainment Centre ■ Hip Taverns **Purchase Places as Entertainment** ■ Flagship Stores ■ Concept Stores ■ Design Malls **Convenience Entertainment** ■ Optimized Places ■ Bricks & Clicks **Mood Management** ■ Lobbies/ Lounges ■ Hiking

Figure 2.2   Content and coverage of experience markets[33]

Both restrictions seem unjustified. Therefore, I define experiences to encompass both products and services and their pertinent worlds.

According to this literature review, experience markets can be differentiated on the basis of reality or virtuality, and with respect to their composition as experience products or experience worlds. Real experience worlds, which are extended or delimited by real experiential products and/or virtual experience worlds, form the core of most experience markets.

One example of virtual experience worlds are "fantasy worlds", the experiences that can occur when a consumer watches movies, listens to audio books, or reads a novel that creates a fantasy world in his or her mind. "Cyberspace", defined as a virtual room, similarly opens new experience opportunities. Digitally created virtual experience worlds can range from simple visits to an online store to computer games that bring three-dimensional themed areas into virtual existence to chat forums that allow for the anonymous exchange of ideas. Figure 2.3 summarizes the most important experience markets.

Typical examples of real experience products include mountain bikes and motocross motorcycles, mainly used for fun trips on gravel roads. Real experience worlds consist of six categories, each of which encompasses larger, potentially experience-oriented material environments or worlds. Consumer centers, for example, feature restaurants and shopping malls, whereas brand centers take the form of Brand Lands or brand events. Transport systems include gas and train stations, as well as airports and seaports. Hotels and amusement parks belong to recreational areas. In contrast, cultural places comprise opera houses, museums, and folk festivals, whereas institutional complexes include political, social, and religious worlds and spaces. Finally, virtual experience worlds might come alive in fantasies or in cyberspace.

With respect to branding, story-based communication can enhance the experience-oriented intermediation of brands, because storytelling creates lively context. Ideally, stories should be simple, concrete, credible, and emotional, and contain unexpected elements.[34] According to Brown, strong brands tell stories, awaken curiosity, and provide

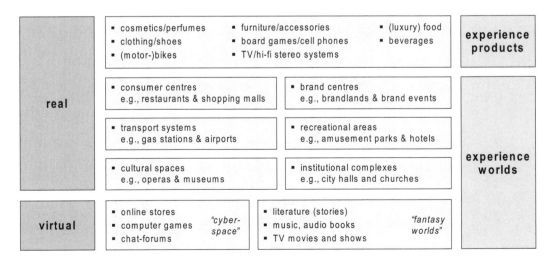

Figure 2.3   Real and virtual experience products and worlds

for wondrous astonishment. Thus, brands "create imaginary fantasy places that consumers want to visit and project themselves into. Gucciworld, Nokialand, Virginville, Auditown, Blackberry Way are mystical, magical, wonderful settings that we desperately want access to. Products are the price of entry. We get telling tales in return."[35]

Before taking a closer look at experience worlds and the sub-category of brand experience worlds (brand centers) in particular, in the following section I examine experience products in greater detail. Experience products cover products and services delivered both at home or away from home, whereas experience worlds are characterized by consumers entering them virtually or in reality.

Experience Products

The basic problem when categorizing experience products is its imprecision. Nearly all industries provide experience-oriented products while at the same time offering primarily functional and prestige-oriented offers. Thus, it is meaningful to make an intra-industry differentiation. Accordingly, I apply the value-based classification from the introductory part of this chapter to differentiate utilitarian, socially expressive, and experience-oriented offerings. Products and services can be classified according to the functional, prestige, or experience value they provide; in most cases, two or all three value dimensions exist with varying degrees of impact. Figure 2.4 provides an overview of the three value dimensions.

The fundamental prerequisite for any product or service is to be found within its functional elements. To achieve prestigious offerings, branding plays a crucial role, whereas multi-sensory enrichment of products or services is key for experience-oriented offerings. Experiential or prestigious components can add value to a functional offering;

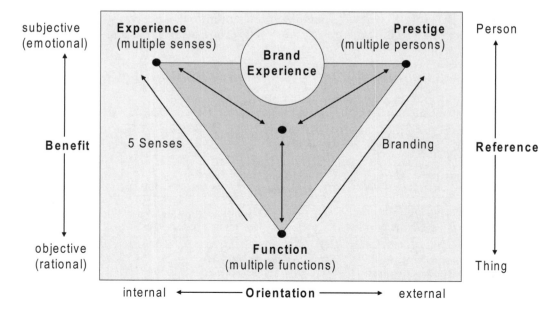

Figure 2.4   Value triad

these elements may also become the main value providers. This value deferral relates closely to a shift from objective, rationally comprehensible benefits toward subjective benefits that can be felt only emotionally and evaluated only by the individual consumer. The point of reference for functional offerings is the "thing" itself; for experience and prestige products, the person is crucial.

Within the value triad, brand experiences take an intermediate position between inner- and outer-directed orientation. They combine prestige and experience. The brand helps ensure a positively felt experience by minimizing the negative experience risk. A prestigious brand also ensures the desired external effect – an evening gown from Chanel, a sound system by Bang and Olufsen, or a BMW Cabriolet. In this context, two possible brand experience paths are conceivable: either the brand turns into a brand experience, or the experience turns into an experience brand. In both cases, the result is a branded experience, inseparably connecting experiences to one or more brands. The same product might lead to varying positions within the value triad for different consumers. For the primary allocation of an offering, the consumer's own intention is crucial, because "experiential purchases are those made with the primary intention of acquiring a life experience: an event or a series of events that one lives through".[36]

Thus, a Jeep might primarily be an experience vehicle for an adventure holiday-maker, but a manager living in the city might drive the same off-road vehicle predominantly for prestige reasons. Someone currently building a house might use the all-terrain vehicle for functional considerations, focusing on the loading capacities and traction power (see left side of Figure 2.5). For a hunter, a Jeep represents a combination of function (e.g., loading materials), prestige (e.g., among hunter colleagues), and experience (e.g., driving on gravel roads). The weights of the three value dimensions might vary depending on the situation. Cruising along a highway in a Cabriolet might be motivated mainly by the experience derived from it, whereas a convertible parked in the yard might be prestigious, and a picnic trip with friends might be a combination of both.

In a similar way, a company offering no-name crystal glass provides functionality from a glass, whereas a Swarovski crystal glass is not purchased solely for functional reasons but rather for the prestige linked to it. The Swarovski Crystal Worlds in Wattens, Tyrol, the second-largest tourist destination in Austria, have been visited since their opening in 1995 by more than 8 million people. The brand center predominantly serves as a stimulus for brand experiences. In the shop, referred to by Swarovski as a "crystal stage" and "glittering shopping world" that provides "a special shopping experience",[37] consumers can satisfy both prestige and experience desires (see right side of Figure 2.5).

Real Experience Worlds

Real experience worlds consist of consumer centers, brand centers, transport systems, recreational areas, cultural spaces, and institutional complexes. Figure 2.6 lists typical examples of these six categories. Note that some experience worlds can overlap, such as flagship, theme, and brand stores, cruises, or kindergartens. Other experience worlds, depending on their configuration, might be assigned to different categories or represent a combination of several categories.

The "Europa Park" in Rust, Germany, represents a recreation area, whereas Disneyland Paris clearly belongs to brand centers, because its innumerable characters are marketed

Industry Example: Automotive   Product Example: Swarovski

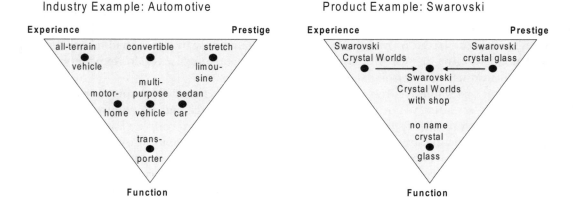

Figure 2.5   Two value triad examples

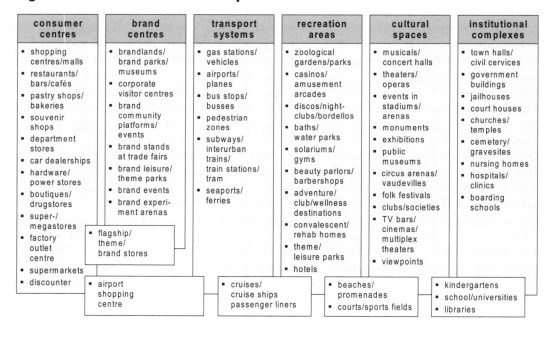

consumer centres	brand centres	transport systems	recreation areas	cultural spaces	institutional complexes
• shopping centres/malls • restaurants/bars/cafés • pastry shops/bakeries • souvenir shops • department stores • car dealerships • hardware/power stores • boutiques/drugstores • super-/megastores • factory outlet centre • supermarkets • discounter	• brandlands/brand parks/museums • corporate visitor centres • brand community platforms/events • brand stands at trade fairs • brand leisure/theme parks • brand events • brand experiment arenas	• gas stations/vehicles • airports/planes • bus stops/busses • pedestrian zones • subways/interurban trains/train stations/tram • seaports/ferries	• zoological gardens/parks • casinos/amusement arcades • discos/night-clubs/bordellos • baths/water parks • solariums/gyms • beauty parlors/barbershops • adventure/club/wellness destinations • convalescent/rehab homes • theme/leisure parks • hotels	• musicals/concert halls • theaters/operas • events in stadiums/arenas • monuments • exhibitions • public museums • circus arenas/vaudevilles • folk festivals • clubs/societies • TV bars/cinemas/multiplex theaters • viewpoints	• town halls/civil cervices • government buildings • jailhouses • court houses • churches/temples • cemetery/gravesites • nursing homes • hospitals/clinics • boarding schools

• flagship/theme/brand stores

• airport shopping centre

• cruises/cruise ships passenger liners

• beaches/promenades
• courts/sports fields

• kindergartens
• school/universities
• libraries

Figure 2.6   Overview of real experience worlds

separately as soft toys, animated films, computer games, and comics under the Disney brand. The park-owned hotels can be assigned to recreational areas as well, whereas the souvenir shops are part of the consumer center category. Similarly, the Deutsche Museum in Munich is an example of a cultural area, whereas the Mercedes-Benz Museum in Stuttgart is a typical brand center.

Discounters are listed within the range of consumer centers, which might initially come as a surprise. However, consider the purchase experience a bargain hunter has when striving for the latest special offer; even discounters like Aldi, Lidl, and Netto provide – at least temporarily – purchase experiences. By artificially initiating temporal scarcity, these retailers induce customers to make impulse purchases, usually by triggering an emotional response that warns, "I could miss a unique offer." The trend toward experiential purchases similarly emerges in the boom of extensive shopping centers. Consumers in the United States spend 51 percent of their total expenditures at shopping centers; Europeans, on average, spend only 12.6 percent, and German consumers, at only 8 percent, spend even less.[38] Current developments imply that these differences will be lessened. While there were only 93 shopping centers (more than 10,000 square meters each) in Germany in 1990, there were already 279 in 2000 and 372 at the end of 2006. From 1990 to 2006, the total shopping area grew from 2.8 million to 11.7 million square meters.[39] At the end of 2008, 414 shopping centers existed in Germany, and that number is expected to increase to 456 by 2010.[40] According to Gobé, buying as a sterile activity will be outdated in the stores of tomorrow, "and in its place will stand 'the art of shopping' which is less about purchasing and more about experiencing the brand".[41]

Before closely examining brand experience worlds, I highlight similar structural changes in the category of transport systems, using airports as an example. All over the world, airports are moving away from pure aviation, turning their locations into shopping centers with runway connections. Rainer Beeck, the head of real estate management at Munich Airport, describes this change as follows: "Airports today are also places of events, conferences and presentations, gastronomic experience worlds and purchase miles."[42] With a brewery, a hospital, and a furniture house of its own, which operate almost 24 hours a day, Munich Airport has removed itself from a classical airport. Similarly, Frankfurt Airport plans to extend its retail trade surfaces from its current 14,000 square meters of sales area to 27,000 square meters by 2011. With the development of a third terminal, it projects that it will have 42,000 square meters eventually.[43] Thus, Frankfurt Airport does business with parking lots, shops, and other services – such as conference areas, kindergartens, gambling casinos, and beauty salons – which are becoming its main source of income. On average, 44 percent of the turnover of European airports comes from non-aviation business. By 2010, this share should be 55 percent.[44] Consequently the design of experiential worlds created by people for people becomes ever more important.

According to Mikunda, four components of experiential worlds are characteristic: landmark, malling, concept line, and core attraction (see Table 2.1). In summary, experience worlds contain points of reference that take the form of highly visible emblems and an

Table 2.1   Four characteristic components of experience worlds[45]

Component	Description	Elements	Examples
Landmark	Emblems with signalling effect ("built headline")	Header Replica	Gigantic climbing wall Celebrity statue/figure
Malling	Promenade as a result of cognitive maps (mental representations of a place)	Axles/centers Cross-ways Mark spots Districts	Promenade, parkway Giant flat-screen Monument Style, light, aroma
Concept line	Framework, holistic entity ("leitmotif")	Image contrasts Central theme	Old and new combined Genuineness, design
Core attraction	Ensuring curiosity and appeal	Wow effects Show effects	Wine cellar as tower Illuminated advertising

entertaining core attraction that invites customers to promenade within the conceptual framework. Thus, unforgettable consumption experiences are triggered.

Brand Experience Worlds

Brand centers represent one of the six experience markets, but they can also be referred to as brand experience worlds, which consist of four main types: corporate visitor centers and Brand Lands; flagship, theme, and brand stores; brand leisure and theme parks; and brand experimentation arenas and brand events. Figure 2.7 provides selected examples of the brand experience world types and two intermediate worlds, namely brand appearances at exhibitions and brand community platforms and events.

One of the most well-recognized examples of a Brand Land is the "Autostadt" (automotive city) of Volkswagen in Wolfsburg, Germany. At the Autostadt, six brands of the Volkswagen Group are presented in an experience-oriented fashion. Similarly, BMW opened its "BMW Welt" in October 2007, mainly to create a direct connection with customers whom the carmaker has been promising "Freude am Fahren" (the "joy of driving") since 1965. BMW uses a somewhat different claim in the English-speaking world, focused more on engine performance and thus the source of the driving pleasure, namely, "the ultimate driving machine".[46] The motivation for the BMW Welt, according to former CEO Helmut Panke, is as follows: "The range offered in the premium segment becomes ever larger. We therefore did not only plan the BMW Welt as a delivery center

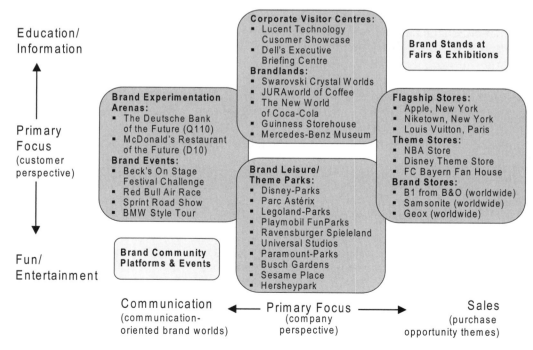

Figure 2.7   Types of brand experience worlds

but as a kind of brand world, a brand showcase in which one can become acquainted with the brand and the products more profoundly. This goes beyond the rational."[47]

As Beiersdorf CEO Thomas-Bernd Quaas points out, brand worlds try to strengthen brand value, perhaps "by boosting the brand emotionally, by making it possible for consumers to experience the brand".[48] The company-owned "Nivea Haus" in Hamburg, for example, provides not only the full range of Nivea products but also applications, massages, and cosmetic treatments, such as a spa typically offers, as well as an event area for experiences centered on the Nivea brand. Furthermore, it enables the brand to establish, through its representatives, direct contacts with customers. Essential associations linked to the brand can be embodied effectively in the (potential) customer's mind through direct, emotionally enriched interactions.[49]

Flagship, theme, and brand stores form the second class of brand experience worlds. Flagships are typically the largest stores, found at prominent locations, such as the Apple flagship store on Fifth Avenue in New York, whose landmark, a glass cube, is probably as well known as the glass pyramid of the Louvre in Paris. Apple currently owns 207 brand stores in representative locations worldwide, which are visited by 34 million customers annually.[50]

A third category of brand experience worlds consists of brand leisure and theme parks. Most prominent are the 11 Disney theme parks in five locations on three continents, which attract 100 million visitors worldwide each year.

Finally, brand events and brand experimentation arenas form the fourth category of brand experience worlds. Brand events are temporary, by definition, offering a transient opportunity to experience a brand "live". One example took place in December 2005 in Berlin, when ING bank temporarily built an ice house in the German capital to express the transparency of the banking house.[51] Brand experimentation arenas have a more permanent character. They typically involve pilot projects that enable brand managers to test new ways to present, compose, and enrich the brand in the future.

Another example in the banking industry illustrates this concept. Deutsche Bank established "Die Deutsche Bank der Zukunft" (The Deutsche Bank of the Future) in Berlin.[52] The futuristic spot showcases and tests new service offers and innovative future retail banking concepts. Instead of waiting at counters, customers arrange themselves around stand-up bistro tables to discuss banking issues with bank representatives. Storage shelves for the forms and brochures have been replaced with flat touch-screens operated by customers. Information boxes appear on shelves like packaged goods in a supermarket. After consumers scan the barcode on the back of the box, the appropriate infomercial comes onto the screen. Movable walls with water-colour paintings by local artists, which is common to banks in Germany, have disappeared in favour of a "gallery of desires", with jam from Harrods, Ritz-Carlton wellness packages, Nike golf bags, and a Porsche Cayman. In the integrated lounge and bar, coffee and small snacks are served, with a shelf of books available to customers, along with a short shoulder-and-neck massage. Die Deutsche Bank der Zukunft is bank, coffeehouse, and shop all in one. In the futuristic store, money appears not only as an emotionally enriched product but also in the form of its possible uses.[53]

All the types of brand experience worlds have four characteristics in common: they are multi-functional per se, are run by the brand owner, provide a platform for brand communications, and employ brand-adequate multi-sensory staging techniques. From a customer perspective, brand experience worlds might be differentiated with respect to the type of experience provided, whether education and information or fun and entertainment. From a company perspective, differences arise with respect to the main goal, whether mere brand communication purposes or activities that directly and effectually push sales.[54]

Brand experience worlds can also be characterized by a profound "urge forward". Brand providers desperately search for direct relationships with their customers. Only through forward integration can they provide multi-sensory experiences at the point of personal encounters. In addition to the interaction quality, they try to increase the quantity of these touch-points, effectively establishing and/or maintaining product differences and brand preferences. Brand experience worlds not only attune the design of the place and environment with the brand but are also able to link appropriate acoustic impressions, tactile stimuli, and olfactory and gustatory appeals to the brand.[55] An exchangeable point of sale (POS) thus turns into a brand-specific world that provides distinctive, memorable brand experiences. The POS becomes a point of experience (POE) and thus an agitation field that shapes images of a brand. If the everyday use of the branded product corresponds to a brief brand experience locally, such as at a brand event, high brand loyalty is almost guaranteed. In both experience situations, the brand product demonstrates what it can do for the consumer, and if the experience is as promised, the brand earns profile and profits.[56]

Five factors are crucial in arranging brand experience worlds.[57] First, it is necessary to ensure brand recognition through a continuous and consistent corporate design that pinpoints the core values of the brand. Second, the personal commitment of the target group should be increased through positive product and/or service experiences. In this way, the brand and desired positive associations and feelings inseparably become interconnected. Third, to enhance this connection, brand experience worlds should initiate enthusiasm among consumers. Employees play a key role here; if they display brand-adequate behaviour, they become brand ambassadors. Thus, brand behaviour and internal branding strategies are crucial, because every positively experienced customer contact increases brand value.[58] Fourth, successful brand experience worlds typically provide some kind of a surprise, often through technical effects or visionary aspects. Fifth, it is advisable to treat customers as guests, perhaps by offering gastronomy, hotel-like business approaches, and entertainment, as well as a customer-friendly infrastructure, proper information, and promotional follow-ups, such as mailings or customer magazines.

When all five factors are in action, experience worlds in general and brand experience worlds in particular turn into "third places".[59] These homes away from home transform the semi-public habitat into places of personal habitat. Their functional core has been enriched and supplemented with emotional extras. Although the core function still prompts the visit, the auxiliary function makes the customer stay for a long time and possibly come back again.[60]

The Ultimate Experience

Experiences strengthen customer retention because they make people happier than material goods. Simply put, experiences are more likely to provide happiness, one of the strongest modes of satisfaction. Van Boven and Gilovich examined which resource allocation helps people pursue happiness: material purchases (e.g., clothing, jewellery) or experiential purchases (e.g., fees, admissions). Material purchases mainly aim at "having" tangible goods in one's possession, whereas people's intentions for experiential purchases are geared toward "doing" things, such as living through an event.[61]

In this context, material possessions can be physically retained over time, but experiences can be enjoyed further only in an indirect manner as pleasant memories, favourable self-perceptions, or enjoyable stories to tell. In return, material possessions may be afflicted with prejudices or regarded unfavourably, whereas people with an experience-rich life are perceived favourably. From four studies, the researchers discovered that "experiential purchases – those made with the primary intention of acquiring a life experience – made [people] happier than material purchases".[62]

The effect can be specified further. These differences are more likely among younger, more affluent, and better educated people, as well as women and people living in urban or suburban communities. Furthermore, experiential purchases are more frequently "mentally revisited" and open to increasingly favourable interpretations over time. Three causes may exist for this "experience effect" that makes consumers happier. First, experiences are open to positive reinterpretations over time. Incidental annoyances and distractions get forgotten, but mental representations can be sharpened, levelled, embellished, or otherwise reconfigured to appear much better in retrospect. Second, experiences are more central to a person's identity because they – and the positive stereotypes associated with them – contribute more to the construction of the self. Experiences are more self-defining and self-actualizing, satisfying intrinsic goals and enabling personal growth. Third, experiences have greater social value. They provide more pleasure when discussed with others and more effectively foster social relationships, because they tend to be viewed positively and contain a typical narrative structure. Most experiences also are inherently social, such as dining, dancing, and dating.[63]

Experience demands, contrary to basic needs, are thus unlimited: "Experience needs are not to be compared with hunger and thirst. Eventually, one has eaten and drunk enough. Experiences, however, do not satiate, but stimulate the appetite for further experiences. They collapse in themselves and only leave behind a memory and the desire for a new psycho-physic activation: 'What's next?'"[64]

We must keep in mind, however, that experiences, as subjectively felt emotions, cannot be "guaranteed" by providers. Evoking favorable inner feelings and thus converting an experiential offer into an actually felt experience depends on the reception and processing by the individual customer: "One can in all cases only purchase the experience offer, not the experience itself – everyone has to produce this under his or her own direction."[65]

Rosy times thus appear on the rise for brand companies as experience providers that understand how to inspire consumers with appropriate ingredients for experiences, which will turn them into insatiable, loyal experience customers who are ready, again and again, to invest time and money into unforgettable brand experiences.

Notes

1.   Klesse, H.-J. (2006), "Paradies Deutschland", *WirtschaftsWoche*, No. 5, pp. 58–66, at p. 59.
2.   Schulze, G. (2000), *Die Erlebnisgesellschaft, Kultursoziologie der Gegenwart*, 8th ed., Campus, Frankfurt/New York. First published in 1992.

3. Gross, P. (1994), *Die Multioptionsgesellschaft*, Suhrkamp, Frankfurt, at p. 63.
4. Kemper, P. (2001), "Vorwort", in P. Kemper (ed.), *Der Trend zum Event*, Suhrkamp, Frankfurt, pp. 7–9, at p. 7.
5. Van Boven, L. and Gilovich, T. (2003), "To Do or To Have? That is the Question", *Journal of Personality and Social Psychology*, Vol. 85, No. 6, pp. 1193–202, at p. 1200.
6. Schulze, *Die Erlebnisgesellschaft, Kultursoziologie der Gegenwart*, p. 59.
7. Gross, *Die Multioptionsgesellschaft*, p. 155.
8. Opaschowski, H.W. (2004), *Deutschland 2020, Wie wir morgen leben – Prognosen der Wissenschaft*, VS Verlag, Wiesbaden, p. 139.
9. Van Boven and Gilovich, "To Do or To Have?", p. 1193.
10. Schulze, *Die Erlebnisgesellschaft, Kultursoziologie der Gegenwart*, p. 314.
11. Opaschowski, *Deutschland 2020*, pp. 138f.
12. Engeser, M. (2006), "Kick im Kopf", *WirtschaftsWoche*, No. 7, pp. 81–3, at p. 83.
13. Rifkin, J. (2000). *The Age of Access: The New Culture of Hypercapitalism, Where All of Life Is a Paid-for Experience*, Tarcher/Putman, New York, p. 43.
14. Schmitt, B. (1999), *Experiential Marketing: How to Get Customers to Sense, Feel, Think, Act, and Relate to Your Company and Brand*, Free Press, New York, pp. 25f.
15. Pine, J. and Gilmore, J.H. (1999), *The Experience Economy: Work is Theatre and Every Business a Stage*, Harvard Business School Press, Boston, MA, pp. 2ff. and 11ff.
16. Ibid., pp. 2 and 6f.
17. Ibid., p. 2.
18. Vershofen, W. (1959), *Die Marktentnahme als Kernstück der Wirtschaftforschung*, Heymanns, Cologne et al., p. 89; Park, C.W., Jaworski, B.J., and MacInnis, D.J. (1986), "Strategic Brand Concept-Image Management", *Journal of Marketing*, Vol. 5, October, pp. 135–45, at p. 136; Fournier, S. (1991), "A Meaning-Based Framework for the Study of Consumer-Object Relations", *Advances in Consumer Research*, Vol. 18, pp. 736–42, at pp. 737ff; Strebinger, A., Otter, T., and Schweiger, G. (1998), "Wie die Markenpersönlichkeit Nutzen schafft: Der Mechanismus der Selbstkongruenz", Working Paper, University of Vienna, pp. 16f; Vigneron, F. and Johnson, L.W. (1999), "A Review and a Conceptual Framework of Prestige-Seeking Consumer Behavior", *Academy of Marketing Science Review*, Vol. 1, pp. 1–15, at pp. 7f; Schulze, *Die Erlebnisgesellschaft, Kultursoziologie der Gegenwart*, p. 35; Kressmann, F., Herrmann, A., and Magin, S. (2003), "Dimensionen der Markeneinstellung und ihre Wirkung auf die Kaufabsicht", *Die Betriebswirtschaft*, Vol. 63, No. 4, pp. 401–18, at pp. 402f; Van Boven and Gilovich, "To Do or To Have?", p. 1194.
19. Schmitt, *Experiential Marketing*, pp. 29, 32 and 60f.
20. Bekmeier-Feuerhahn, S. (2004), "Erlebnisorientierte Markenstrategien", in Bruhn, M. (ed.), *Handbuch Markenführung*, 2nd ed., Vol. 1, Gabler, Wiesbaden, pp. 879–902, at p. 884.
21. Mikunda, C. (2007), *Marketing spüren: Willkommen am Dritten Ort*, 2nd ed., Redline Wirtschaft, Frankfurt/Vienna, p. 19.
22. Schulze, *Die Erlebnisgesellschaft, Kultursoziologie der Gegenwart*, pp. 444ff.
23. For example, Boorman, N. (2007), *Bonfire of the Brands: How I Learned to Live Without Labels*, Canongate Books, Edinburgh.
24. Schulze, *Die Erlebnisgesellschaft, Kultursoziologie der Gegenwart*, p. 449.
25. Ibid.
26. Ibid., pp. 420ff.
27. Weinberg, P. (1992), *Erlebnismarketing*, Vahlen, Munich, pp. viiff.

28. Schmitt, B. and Simonson, A. (1997), *Marketing Aesthetics: The Strategic Management of Brands, Identity, and Image*, Free Press, London, pp. 279ff and 302ff.

29. Greiner, T. (2007), "Land der Leuchttürme", *Der Spiegel*, No. 49, pp. 26–9, at p. 27.

30. Pine and Gilmore, *The Experience Economy*, pp. 31ff.

31. Steinecke, A. (2004), "Zur Phänomenologie von Marken-Erlebniswelten", in A. Brittner Widmann, H.-D. Quack, and H. Wachowiak (eds.), *Von Erholungsräumen zu Tourismusdestinationen*, Facetten der Fremdenverkehrsgeographie, Trierer Geographische Studien, No. 27, pp. 201–19, at pp. 19ff.

32. Mikunda, *Marketing spüren*, pp. 7ff and 52ff.

33. Schulze, *Die Erlebnisgesellschaft, Kultursoziologie der Gegenwart*, pp. 420, 422, and 427; Weinberg, *Erlebnismarketing*, pp. viiff; Schmitt and Simonson, *Marketing Aesthetics*, pp. 343ff; Pine and Gilmore, *The Experience Economy*, pp. 52ff; Steinecke, "Zur Phänomenologie von Marken-Erlebniswelten", p. 19ff; Mikunda, *Marketing spüren*, pp. 8f.

34. Heath, C. and Heath, D. (2007), *Made to Stick*: *Why Some Ideas Survive and Others Die*, Random House, New York.

35. Brown, S. (2005), *Wizard!: Harry Potter's Brand Magic*, Cyan Books, London, p. 177.

36. Van Boven and Gilovich, "To Do or To Have?, p. 1194.

37. Swarovski Kristallwelten (2008) available at <http://kristallwelten.swarovski.com/Content. Node/besucher infos/shopping_experience.php> (accessed 24 August 2008).

38. Opaschowski, H.W. (2000), *Kathedralen des 21. Jahrhunderts: Erlebniswelten im Zeitalter der Erlebniskultur*, Germa Press, Hamburg, p. 51.

39. *Der Spiegel* (2006), "Boom bei Einkaufszentren", No. 3, p. 57.

40. Gobé, M. (2001), *Emotional Branding*: *The New Paradigm for Connecting Brands to People*, Allworth Press, New York, p. xxv.

41. Becker, T. (2008), "Rosa Risenferkelei", *KulturSpiegel*, No. 10, pp. 30–35, at p. 32.

42. Beeck, R., quoted in R. Kiani-Kress (2006), "Nur die Hälfte", *Der Spiegel*, No. 4, pp. 46–50, at p. 48.

43. Kiani-Kress, R. (2006), "Dampf im Kessel", *Der Spiegel*, No. 3, pp. 50–51, at p. 51.

44. Kowalski, M. and Schwab, F. (2006), "Einkaufszentren mit Startbahn", *Focus*, No. 2, pp. 146–9, at p. 146.

45. Mikunda, C. (2005), *Der verbotene Ort oder die inszenierte Verführung*: *Unwiderstehliches Marketing durch strategische Dramaturgie*, Redline Wirtschaft, Frankfurt/Vienna, pp. 50ff and 217ff; Mikunda, *Marketing spüren*, pp. 27ff.

46. Kilian, K. (2009), "From Brand Identity to Audio Branding", in K. Bronner and R. Hirt (eds.), *Audio Branding: Brands, Sound and Communication*, Nomos/Edition Reinhard Fischer, Baden-Baden, p. 36.

47. Biskamp, S. and Katzensteiner, T. (2005), "Verlierer sind die Massenhersteller", *WirtschaftsWoche*, No. 52, pp. 92–104, at p. 96.

48. Klesse, H.-J. (2006), "Mühsam, aber erfolgreich", *WirtschaftsWoche*, No. 8, pp. 60–64, at p. 64.

49. Kilian, K. (2008), "Hersteller handeln, Marken suchen den direkten Kundenkontakt", *Promotion Business*, No. 3, pp. 44–7, at pp. 44 and 47.

50. Ibid., pp. 46f.

51. van Leesen, C. (2005), "Eiskalt wohnen im Frosthaus am Potsdamer Platz", *Der Tagesspiegel*, Vol. 12 (December), p. 12.

52. Die Deutsche Bank der Zukunft (2008), available at <http://www.q110.com> (accessed 23 August 2008).

53. Schnaas, D. (2005), "Bank mit Botschaft", *WirtschaftsWoche*, No. 52, pp. 112–15, at pp. 112ff.

54. Steinecke, "Zur Phänomenologie von Marken-Erlebniswelten", pp. 205ff.

55. Kilian, K. (2008), "Vertikalisierung von Markenherstellern", in Meyer, H. (ed.), *Marken-Management 2008/2009*, dfv, Frankfurt, pp. 181–205, at p. 201.

56. Kilian, "Hersteller handeln, Marken suchen den direkten Kundenkontakt", p. 47.

57. Pflaum, D. (2008), "Markenbildung durch Markenparks", in N.O. Herbrand (ed.), *Schauplätze dreidimensionaler Markeninszenierung*, Edition Neues Fachwissen, Stuttgart, pp. 167–76, at pp. 171ff.

58. Tomczak, T., Esch, F.-R., Kernstock, J., and Herrmann, A. (eds.) (2008), *Behavioral Branding: Wie Mitarbeiterverhalten die Marke stärkt*, Gabler, Wiesbaden; Schmidt, H.J. (ed.) (2007), *Internal Branding: Wie Sie Ihre Mitarbeiter zu Markenbotschaftern machen*, Gabler, Wiesbaden.

59. Oldenburg, R. (1999), *The Great Good Place: Cafés, Coffee Shops, Bookstores, Bars, Hair Salons, and other Hangouts at the Heart of a Community*, Marlowe and Company, New York, p. xvii. First published in 1989. Oldenburg used this term in a sociological sense to describe the unification of local neighborhoods (pp. xvii and xxiii), whereas marketing research extends it to signify public places with a sense of feeling at home. Starbucks, for example, considers itself a "third place".

60. Mikunda, *Marketing spüren*, pp. 15 and 44.

61. Van Boven and Gilovich, "To Do or To Have?", pp. 1194f.

62. Ibid., p. 1193.

63. Ibid., pp. 1196ff and 1200f.

64. Schulze, *Die Erlebnisgesellschaft, Kultursoziologie der Gegenwart*, p. 450.

65. Ibid., p. 548.

Part II
Brands and Brand Communities

3 Tally Ho, Chocs Away! The Morgan Motoring Experiences

MICHAEL B. BEVERLAND*

Keywords

authenticity, self-authentication, authoritative performance, brand experience, motoring

Abstract

In this chapter, I propose that brand experiences allow consumers to achieve self-authentication and authoritative performances. Using the case of the Morgan Motor Company, I identify how consumers use this brand to achieve an authentic self. Building on insights from Morgan owners, I identify seven ways in which marketers can enhance their brand's authenticity and provide consumers with an experiential platform. I will provide background on the Morgan Motor Company, provide consumer examples of self-authentication and authoritative performances, and identify seven ways in which marketers can enhance the authenticity of their brand.

Introduction

Mike (Interviewer): What about the criticism that the car has a "hard ride"?

Charles: You can take it both ways. Don't forget a hard ride also gives you an incredible feel, so the handling of the Morgan right up to 1980s was better than any other car in terms of

---

* Professor Michael B. Beverland, School of Economics, Finance and Marketing, Royal Melbourne Institute of Technology, GPO Box 2476V, Melbourne, Vic 3001, Australia. E-mail: michael.beverland@rmit.edu.au. Telephone: + 61 3 9925 1475.

responsiveness. The classic line about Morgans is that you can tell whether a coin is heads or tails just by running over it. What that says is that the steering wheel is giving you every bit of information, which as a driver is exactly what you want – the last thing you want to do is feel out of control. On the other hand, of course your passenger didn't like the hard ride.

Charles Morgan, Chairman, Morgan Motor Company

Mike (Interviewer): Why do the cars have that leather strap on their bonnet?

Matthew: Oh to make you feel like Biggles and that's all, does absolutely nothing. Cars in the 20s did have a strap on and it's just carried across. Some people like them.

Matthew Parkin, Marketing Manager, Morgan Motor Company

Every Morgan fan can remember the first time they encountered the brand. Mine is more unusual than most, though this formative experience is perhaps why I've sought redemption through writing about brands that confound mainstream marketing theory. I first heard of the Morgan Motor Company (MMC) in 1993 while studying organizational change at university. A group of colleagues had used the famous (or infamous) *Troubleshooter* TV series featuring the (sadly) late Sir John Harvey Jones (former ICI Chairman), seeking to fix well-known British firms that found themselves in trouble. Sir John's advice seemed perfectly rational – break up the business into profitable units, increase quality and production, and all would be well. Morgan mythology is clear on the result – Peter and Charles Morgan had the temerity to ignore the guru's advice and be one of the few firms in the series to survive and prosper. As a naive student, my reaction was simple – here were these old school English toffs refusing to face reality, when everyone knew that embracing the market and modern marketing was the order of the day. In my view, the brand's days were numbered (my lecturer dutifully rewarded me with an 'A' for the course and all was well with the world).

Well, like Sir John, I had to eat humble pie. Not only did Morgan survive and prosper by ignoring modern marketing principles, worse still, I became a member of the brand cult (though sadly yet without my very own car or "Moggie"), started reading Biggles, began collecting toy soldiers, and spent a good part of my academic career writing about brands that reject marketing principles to achieve success. A few years ago, while wondering how it was Chateau Margaux and other so-called "old world" brands were successful for so long, my mind wandered back to that strange car brand I saw in 1993. I wondered what happened to it (and let's face it, I was after another good case study). To my surprise, I found Morgan alive and well. Since then, it has been a downhill slide. In 2006 I visited the factory and met the owner; in 2007 I got to ride in a Morgan (thanks Doug) and later on drive one (thanks Paul). I have the jacket, the t-shirt, the club membership, and the pen made out of an old ash frame. The car is no more than a few consulting jobs away.

But enough of me. After all, as one informant (John) says, "The car is the star. You'll die, the car will live on." How has this British car brand survived for 100 years (Morgan celebrates its centenary in 2009) without investing heavily in marketing, seemingly ignoring its customers, making just four models in 100 years, and keeping customers waiting for up to four years or more for delivery? And don't forget that the car is expensive. Both Charles Morgan and the owners interviewed here admit car owners can get better performance for the price. Clearly, "Mogs" are not brought for their functional benefits. For example:

But having said that with the weather, over here on hot days in summer you can't drive it either because you just fry, and I'd imagine in Australia it'd be ever worse. If you leave it out in the sun you're going to destroy the leatherwork, and I mean that's one of the things, when you go places you end up having to find an overhanging tree to park it under. And I've parked on the pavement under the shade rather than leave it out in the sun. And again that's sort of the trip; if you're rushed for time it's not the car to take.

(Peter, 4-seater 4/4)

Interviewer: I mean, why not get a practical car?

Paul: I've never been practical. Yeah, with a Morgan you need a daily driver.

(Paul, 1991 4/4)

As the opening passage states, the ride is hard, the technology on the car is ancient (the suspension was developed in 1909 and based on old horse-drawn carts), the design dates to the 1930s, the frame is made of wood, and things that would be standard on most cars are extras on the Morgan. And when you drive in it, it shakes, rattles, is deafening, and exposes riders to the elements. This is clearly no boring Lexus. And yet, people love them. Clearly, this brand has built a cult following on the basis of an experience, and it is this experience and its lessons for today's marketers that this chapter explores. First, though, I will provide a brief history of the Morgan Motor Company.

100 Years of Motoring: The Morgan Motor Company Story

The Morgan story begins in 1909 when H.F.S. Morgan founded a motoring firm in the Malvern Hills in the United Kingdom (the current factory is located in Pickersleigh Road, Malvern Link). H.F.S. began making a three-wheel car that quickly became known for its speed, road holding, and performance. The firm continued with a three-wheeled version until the 1930s, when tax changes in favour of four-wheeled cars started to hurt the brand's competitiveness. In the 1930s, the firm launched its first four-wheeled version, the +4. This car evolved slowly over the next few decades, the biggest change being the movement from a flat radiator to the familiar rounded grill of today. In 1968, a new model was released – the +8, which was simply a larger, more powerful version of the +4 and which remains for many the gold standard Morgan experience. In each case, the car's design evolved little – the 1930s sports lines and running boards stayed, as did the horse-and-cart suspension and the wooden (ash) frame.[†] Production techniques also remained firmly craft-based, resulting in lengthy delays between ordering and receipt of the car. Marketing relied largely on word of mouth, the odd advertisement, and surprise racing successes at Le Mans.

---

† The +4+, made out of fibreglass and featuring a hard top, was the sole exception, though it was quickly phased out due to lack of popularity – 24 were made, and today they are the most elusive and expensive Morgans.

Figure 3.1   Morgans through the ages (3-wheeler and Flat Rad)

Figure 3.2   Morgans through the ages (Modern 4/4 and Aero 8)

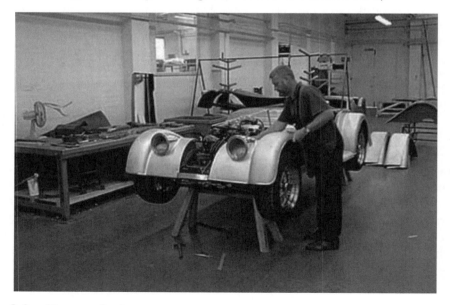

Figure 3.3   Morgan factory

Throughout this time, the firm weathered wars, competition, takeover threats, the death of H.F.S., generational changes in leadership, emissions and safety legislation that locked many UK sports car manufacturers out of international markets, ridicule following the *Troubleshooter* series, the 1980s boom and bust, and the decline of the UK motoring industry (at one time, Morgan, with a maximum annual production of 400 cars, was the largest surviving British car maker). In 2001 the firm also released a new model – the Aero, which threatened to divide enthusiasts (though many still believe that a true Morgan only has three wheels) with its BMW engine, modern technology, and radically new take on the original design. This car eventually won over a new legion of fans and converts from old Mogs. Again, despite investments in Japanese quality methods and better production planning, which resulted in increased production and decreased waiting lists, the firm appears to be much the same as it was 50 years ago.

Consumers have not changed much either (except for getting older). Legions of fans form clubs across the United Kingdom and the world to celebrate the car, people continue to put up with the hard ride and ancient technology, and they happily put down money in advance (now months rather than years) for a new car made exactly to their specifications. And they continue to pay high prices for what remains a vintage-styled car (the Aero and limited-edition Aeromax are exceptions, though even their functional performance does not justify the pricing). So how do consumers experience the Morgan brand?

The Morgan Experience

In discussions with owners, the Morgan brand is experienced in two ways, both of which reinforce brand loyalty: individually and collectively. These experiences allow owners to achieve two important goals – what Eric Arnould and Linda Price call authenticating acts and authoritative performances.[1] An authenticating act allows a person to reinforce a desired identity and thus focuses on the self. In contrast, an authoritative performance allows the person to express the desired self socially, achieved with others. Because both of these goals allow consumers to experience authenticity in an era when so much is fake and contrived, brands that provide consumers this experience are particularly loved. The following sections provide an overview of the two forms of Morgan experience according to the voices of car owners interviewed for this chapter.

SELF-AUTHENTICATION: INDIVIDUAL BRAND EXPERIENCES

Consumers build an emotional bond with the brand through their experiences with the car. These experiences go beyond performance features and include self-relevant motives, such as feelings of flow, competence and mastery, and mystique. The informants identified three ways in which they experience the car – prior to purchase, in use, and caring for the car.

The first time consumers experience *their* car is when they place an order with Morgan. As mentioned, Morgan has a waiting list that forms part of the brand's mystique. Although the length of the list is often overstated, each new Morgan is hand built to customer specifications. Once an applicant has chosen a car and selected the add-ons (nearly everything is), he or she must pay a non-refundable deposit to receive a list number and an estimate of when the car will go into production. When the car is scheduled for production, the applicant must settle the account in full. The owners that informed this study reported that this initial experience of the car was one of anticipation, concern, and shock. In many ways, this initial experiential period reflects the boundary-less nature of the relationship between the owner and the brand, because the experience is so uncertain. For example:

> When you order you don't hear much from Morgan initially. You pay your deposit and name your specs and they send you a build slot, then nothing. All of a sudden you get a letter that says "if you don't settle the account by such a date you will lose your build slot." This is quite a shock, especially when we're always told the customer is king. You get quite apprehensive, but then you realise this is all part of the brand story, but initially you wonder what you've got yourself into when you get a letter demanding money without the niceties.
>
> (Paul, 1991 4/4)

> I brought the first Aero 8 in NZ. I'd always wanted a sports car and loved BMW, so a Morgan with a BMW engine was the perfect union. However, as someone who buys a lot of cars, I'm used to testing the product before purchase, especially when the car is very expensive, as the Aero was. I was visiting the UK when I paid my deposit, and thought I could rock up to the factory and test drive one, well they would have none of that, in fact Morgan were pretty abrasive about it. At this stage the Aero was a new car with no real track record of performance and I suddenly realised the enormous risk of buying a $200,000 sports car, sight unseen so to speak. The first time I'd get to drive it and see how good it was, was when it was shipped to New Zealand, and if I didn't like it, it was too bad.
>
> (Grant, 2002 Aero 8)

These two passages reflect the mixed emotions consumers have when purchasing a Morgan. They are obviously excited about closing in on the prize of a Morgan but also apprehensive about the uncertainty of the process, which is not helped by the lack of customer centricity. As a brand, Morgan undertakes little by way of marketing and more closely resembles an old-world artisan focused solely on getting on with the task. Such an approach gives the brand a strong sense of authenticity precisely because of its focus on substance over style.[2] Similar to extreme sport encounters,[3] the experience of the Morgan brand is characterised by a heightened sense of uncertainty and apprehension, which paradoxically increases the excitement customers feel towards the brand. In these cases, relationships with the brand are "boundary open" in that the customer has little knowledge of what to expect from the brand encounter, yet nevertheless enters into a partnership with the provider.

Although the receipt of the car results in initial excitement, driven by the emotional reaction to the iconic design and the sense of receiving a car built personally for you – customers can choose the model, colour, fixtures, style, and materials, and Morgan provides a full build portfolio for an extra charge – apprehension continues, because unlike modern cars (derisively referred to as "tin tops" by the informants), Morgans need "running in" (just like cars of old). Throughout this period, the owner is getting used to the car, resisting the urge to use it to its full capacity, and identifying any problems. With regard to post-production problems, the informants were effectively on their own, as Morgan takes the view that its responsibility for the car ends with delivery. Usually prospective owners place an order through a licensed dealer that then deals with them regarding any complaints. However, for international owners, this relationship is more difficult, because orders are often placed directly with the factory or through agents that place orders for parts with the factory and then wait for them to be shipped. After this initial blooding period, the new owner can truly experience the intense emotional experience of the brand.

The most powerful experience of Morgan relates to driving the car. My own experience bares this out. Despite having acquainted myself with the brand through DVDs, books, magazines, and a factory visit, nothing beats the first time one experiences a Mog in full flight. At the end of an interview in 2007, my informant, Doug, offered me a ride in his +8 – (until the Aero 8) the most ferocious of the Morgans. Doug prided himself on his ability to modify the car and improve its performance. Riding in a Morgan, you are close to the road and seated much lower down than most everyday cars. The +8 is a powerful V8 car. The wooden construction of the Morgan means it is incredibly light. When combined, the effect is terrific. As we drove out of the parking lot, Doug simply floored the car. The noise was overwhelming and the feeling overpowering. The engine roars, and you are propelled like a rocket down the road. The closeness to the road and the ancient suspension means you feel one with the car and its environment. The engine feels like a dog taking its owner for a walk – it feels as though it is alive, wanting to be let loose and do its job. I arrived back at the parking lot euphoric, tingling with excitement, and shaking all over (oblivious to the soreness in my backside).

My second experience was more powerful because it involved me driving the car. Now, my experience with fast cars is non-existent. I have only ever owned two cars (and currently own none): a 1956 VW Beetle and a 1990s Honda automatic. Both were useful but hardly fun or sporty. My experience is therefore with low torque cars (little power) or low effort cars. A Morgan is completely different. First, the engine gives it tremendous torque, meaning high performance at low speeds (as Paul said, "you can be silly and have fun even at the speed limit"), which eliminates the need for downward gear changes (à la the VW). Second, the wooden body literally moves while driving – something Paul pointed out to me, forcing me to feel the car moving with (not against) the road's surface. This experience is uncanny for a first-time driver, and the sensation is virtually indescribable other than to say that you bond with the car almost immediately, feeling at one with the vehicle and the road.

Third, the feeling of power is exhilarating. Sensing that I was timid when driving the 4/4, Paul asked me to pull over and then instructed me about when to change gears using the rev counter as a guide (previously I had learnt to change gears in relation to speed-based rules of thumb). As I took off, aiming to get the car to 5,000 revs in first gear, Paul started shouting "Push it, come on, go for it!" I did, and again the feeling was simply amazing. Here was this vintage-looking car, delivering amazing performance, seemingly well beyond either its looks or its years.

These experiences are akin to what Czikszentmihalyi calls "flow".[4] Flow experiences are crucial for achieving self-authentication and are achieved individually rather than with others.[5] Huang notes that flow experiences represent the intrinsic motivation of enjoyment in an activity.[6] Flow experiences thus are achieved when there is a sense of seamless interaction between the consumer and the event or activity in which that consumer engages. Research indicates that such outcomes represent the peak level of experience that marketers can hope to achieve using experiential strategies.[7] For example:

> *People do drive incredibly fast. I found out later why, but after I had mine about three or four months, this trip to Akaroa and we came back over the top road, which is a really twisty road with big drop offs, and I was really sweating trying to keep up with people. And there's all these people who seem to be quite conservative and quite stately, you put them behind the wheel and they let loose. I scared myself senseless … There's supposed to be a tour of South Island next year, and that'll be quite fun. It'll be good to just have a whole lot of cars like that just driving around South Island. Days like this [interview conducted on a glorious spring day] you crank it out and take it out for a drive. And I think it's a bit like another metaphor if you like as sailing boats as opposed to motorboats; I'm definitely in the sailing boat brigade. Part of the joy of boating is the travelling in a sailing boat, you may or may not ever get to actually where you wanted to go, because where you are going normally is the thing anyway, you say well we'll sail from here around to the next bay or whatever, and some days you'll get there, and other days you just won't. Whereas a motorboat you just put your foot down, and how boring is that.*
>
> (Peter, 4-Seater 4/4)

Peter's description provides a number of examples of flow-like experiences. Central to these experiences is a feeling of "letting go" and attempting to embrace the fear that comes with using a high-performance object in risky conditions and uncertainty about performance limitations (in this case, stopping power and road handling). As well, Peter's passage identifies the transcendent nature of the driving experience when observing that seemingly conservative people go wild when behind the wheel of a Morgan. Flow is also observed in Peter's focus on the journey, a preference for the process over the outcome. Finally, flow is achieved through the enactment of the sailboat metaphor that expresses a key identity motive.[8] These flow experiences enhance the owners' relationship with the brand.

The final way that owners bond with their cars is through efforts at repair, restoration, and customization. In each case, owners were able to express feelings of control, competence, and mastery because the non-computerized technology of all pre-Aero 8 models (excluding the three-wheeled versions, which were truly vintage) meant that repairs could be conducted by amateur mechanics. The lack of computerization also reinforced perceptions that the car had character. For example, Paul has rebuilt old Morgans from scratch, and the basic technology of the car has enabled Andrew to feel competent even though he believes he has limited mechanical skills. For example:

> *And I'm not that mechanically minded, I'm a sort of do-it-yourself type thing, and I've had the car completely in bits because it was a bit of a wreck when I got it, and I had the whole front end off, rings and everything else and repaint motors and stuff, which is a major mission. Unbelievably it's held together with wood screws, I mean that's just incredible; you have a car held together with wood screws. And they use steel wood screws.*
>
> (Andrew, 1972 4/4)

Andrew's passage reflects further aspects of the Morgan experience. First, being able to work on the car allows him to reinforce his self-image as a "do-it-yourself type". Second, there is the sense of satisfaction that comes with stripping down a car and rebuilding it. Third, the ability to work on the car means that Andrew experiences one aspect of the Morgan myth directly, thus reinforcing his relationship with the brand. A common misconception about Morgans is they are made entirely of wood. In fact, only parts of the frame are made with English ash. This construction is unique in cars today and a true throwback to pre-1940 construction methods. Through his efforts at repairing the car, Andrew directly experiences a key part of the brand myth, which brings up images of heritage, authenticity, and craftsmanship and further reinforces his sense that the car gets purchased by eccentrics who want something a little different.

AUTHORITATIVE PERFORMANCES: COLLECTIVE BRAND EXPERIENCES

Experiences that enable self-authentication primarily are experienced individually. In contrast, authoritative performances involve collective experiences.[9] These experiences allow consumers to reaffirm part of their desired self-image socially. In the case of Morgan, the second quote at the beginning of this chapter, by Matthew Parkin, the Marketing Director, provides an example of how informants build a desired identity using the car. Many owners adopt add-ons – such as leather straps across the hood, World War II leather flight jackets, flying goggles, scarves, and old leather flying helmets (from World War I) – to signify their association with an idealized pre-World War II era (summed up with a reference to the famous fictional boyhood hero Biggles), when Britain retained an empire, men were men, and action was the name of the game. Several informants identified that some of their motivation for owning the car was that it represented the eccentricity of the English. For example:

> Being one of the more English people living over here it's nice to sort of take you back to your roots to some extent, it's eccentricity I suppose, it's a way of sort of saying you're a bit different. And I think it's also a bit of a backlash against all cars being the same; you look at a Honda, you look at all sorts of cars, and you've got to look at the badge to see what it is, they all are very similar ... Oh I think it's the whole tweed coat, cane, sort of eccentric, fly in the face of technological change. I mean the Brits do that like nobody else does, it's one thing you've got the Americans with this, that, and the other, but you can't take the establishment out of the UK – you've got the Queen, the States will never have the Queen, and it's got this upper class, because it's seen as an upper class type thing. Yeah it's all the tweed; I mean you see the advertising blurbs for Morgan and that and they've always got the picnic baskets strapped to the back, I mean how many people do that? I went out and bought a picnic basket [laugh]. You buy into the whole thing. And you tend to drive down to the coffee shop these days or whatever. But you try and buy into that whole scene, the green gumboots and the rest of it. [Interviewer: You said you had the flying goggles and stuff like that, the association with the kind of old flying?] I think it's that eccentricity of the whole thing, yeah there's no point in doing it in half measures. If you're going to do it, do it well. I think again its part of it. People who buy Morgans have got a leaning towards that sort of side.

> (Peter, 4-seater 4/4)

Peter's passage identifies several aspects of an authenticating act that is part of the Morgan brand experience. Authenticating acts represent attempts by consumers to reconnect to time and place in postmodern markets in which traditional markers of authenticity, such as state, culture, and authority, have been undermined by globalization and hyperreality. For Peter, the seeming sameness of modern car brands does not provide the necessary vehicle for him to assert his sense of self to the world. In contrast, the Morgan, with its widely known design and brand name, allows him to engage in an authenticating act that connects him back to an idealised lifestyle – that of an English country gentleman. The car provides a platform upon which Peter can build with his "Biggles-like" driving attire and accompaniments such as the picnic basket tied to the back of the car (clearly an act of impression management, because the basket is not acquired for utilitarian purposes but rather to enhance Peter's public self).[10] Furthermore, this image reasserts Peter's English heritage and the "class" and "style" associated with it (living in New Zealand's most English city, Christchurch, such an image would likely reinforce local traditions and class distinctions).

A second means of engaging in an authenticating act via a Morgan is through club membership. Morgan has been kept alive by clubs of enthusiasts who organise touring events, racing days, skill enhancement sessions, celebratory brand days, and general social events. Clubs often keep track of cars within the country and assist members in gaining spare parts or selling their cars. For example, John was recognised as the leading authority on local Morgan history and revelled in his status as a font of knowledge. He recounted many stories of previous owners and events, drawing on a huge assortment of recent and vintage photos of Morgans, owners, and events in New Zealand. Such actions allow him and other owners to connect to a historical movement of like-minded people. As part of this movement, informants believe they are carriers of history and contributors to a unique aspect of New Zealand life. For example:

Interviewer: And what's valuable to you about the club?

What's valuable to me is the original intention of the club, and that was to record the whereabouts and the information and as much detail as possible of every Morgan in New Zealand that could be located. And people say how many Morgans have we got in New Zealand I can tell you, because you don't know how many are tucked away in sheds. There's supposed to be one three-wheeler sitting somewhere. And every now and again one will pop out that's been around for eight years, five years or whatever. So that original intention is to me the most valuable thing about the club, apart from obviously contact with people, is the records are there and we record everything. And at the moment I've been researching all the racing history, getting as much racing information and old photographs and chasing up the actual history of Morgans in New Zealand I suppose you could say.

(John, 1957 4/4)

Club events enable owners to engage in authenticating acts in a variety of ways. First, because membership is contingent on owning a car, owners become part of an exclusive club. Second, club events allow experienced members to demonstrate their expertise – in terms of both driving skill and skill in repairing and restoring cars to their original condition (clubs regularly run judging events that assess the extent to which restored cars are indexically authentic). For example, Doug is known for his mechanical expertise, especially when it comes to increasing a car's performance. He takes a lot of pride in his widely recognised expert status. Third, because club tours involve multiple members and whole fleets of cars, they represent a very public spectacle. For example:

If you go in a Morgan, it becomes an adventure. You come back to your car and its, "Gosh, that's a nice car." You get out, people are looking round. It just becomes an occasion, every time you use it. Instead of just using it as a means from getting to A to B, the actual getting from A to B is the whole reason for having it. I remember shortly after I bought it I was in a doctor's surgery and this rep came round and we were talking about the car and she said, "What, you've actually gone out in a car just for the fun of driving?" "Yeah." "Why?" I said, "Well, come and have a look at the car." "Right," she said. I said, "Do you want a spin?" And she couldn't quite comprehend that anyone would drive for fun because she drives thousands of miles a year for her job. But to go out in one is just – it's different.

(Paul, 4/4)

It is not uncommon for convoys of 10–20 cars to drive together, pass through cities and towns, book into hotels, and stop at cafés. When adding in the staged eccentricity of many owners, tours represent a highly visible authenticating act. For example, Allan's daughter insisted that Morgans be used at her wedding – 14 cars turned up and were featured in the UK club magazine *Miscellany*. Given the importance of such an occasion, such an act is highly symbolic; as others note, when one marries someone with a Morgan, one marries the car as well.

Fourth and finally, club membership and participation are a means by which like-minded people (as Doug notes, Morgan people are warm people – just like the friendly looking car) can connect and celebrate shared values and interests. For example:

So everyone's got everybody's email addresses, and if people were going on a trip somewhere in the Morgan they seem to contact people and say I'm coming through, do you want to meet up or whatever. And that's where I met John, John was in town so we all went, that's what it always is really, it's always an excuse to go and do it.

(Peter, 4-seater 4/4)

Peter's passage identifies how the car enables him to connect with others. This act allows Morgan owners to join groups as they pass through towns, thus connecting dispersed owners with a larger whole. Grant and Allan both mentioned that one of the nicest and unexpected benefits of car ownership was the social contacts they had made – many of whom had become firm friends and, in Grant and Allan's case, business partners as well. Both are also part of a group planning to take their cars back "home" to England in 2009 to participate in the centenary celebrations put on by the Morgan Motor Company and various English-based clubs. Part of their excitement is that they will be part of a worldwide network of owners and will have the special status of travelling the farthest to the event, thus publicly demonstrating their loyalty and commitment.

What can Marketers Learn from Morgan?

The informant passages in the previous section demonstrate that the Morgan brand provides a platform upon which consumers can gain a range of self-relevant experiences.

The brand allows informants to achieve feelings of flow, mastery, and social interaction, as well as reflect their desired self to others. Based on the informant accounts, and my own experiences, I believe that providing a platform by which consumers can achieve both forms of experiences – self-authentication and authoritative performances – can enhance brand loyalty. When combined, both experiences enable consumers to reconnect to a sense of time and place, culture, and others in a postmodern market characterised by fragmentation, globalisation, and the triumph of style over substance. The use of brands like Morgan to achieve these experiences and thereby reconnect to a sense of self, place, and society (important markers of identity) enables consumers to find authenticity in a postmodern world in two ways. First, Morgan allows consumers to achieve personally relevant experiences, including flow, mastery, and enjoyment. Second, Morgan allows consumers to express important values through authoritative performances. Thus, despite claims that postmodern markets render authenticity impossible (because ubiquitous marketing imagery makes it difficult for consumers to tell real from fake), brands such as Morgan can provide the range of consumer experiences necessary to reach a state of self-authentication.[11]

The use of a Morgan to achieve self-authentication has important implications for marketers. I propose that brand authenticity can be built in seven ways. First, brands such as Morgan invest in storytelling rather than traditional, brand-driven marketing communications derived from a very narrow positioning statement. The brand thus seeds the consumption community with stories about the car, workers, owners, and successes and failures. The company is happy for consumer-based stories to emerge, because these stories can perpetuate the Morgan myth. For example, Charles Morgan admits he has given up trying to counter claims that the car is built entirely from wood (a particularly prevalent myth in France) or that the company rejected all of Sir John Harvey Jones's advice (much of his advice on improved production planning was used). Second, despite investing in improved quality systems (borrowed from Japanese total quality management practices) and improved business practices, the firm plays up its image of an artisanal amateur, seemingly out of touch with modern business practices.

Third, Morgan staff immerse themselves in the world of sports car racing and ownership. Rather than investing directly in formal market research, the brand's myth is kept alive by a policy of continuous ethnographic engagement with the community though four methods: (1) the staff are universally passionate about sports cars (not all of them Morgan) and are thus active members in various clubs and communities; (2) the firm actively works with Morgan clubs and provides a regular series of events to celebrate the brand; (3) the firm's senior managers work with a range of universities, racing teams, and like-minded car firms (e.g., BMW) to keep abreast of material developments that will enable performance improvements; and (4) the firm welcomes suggestions from owners about improvements. Because of their stance on rejecting formal market research, the brand's owners are able to present an image of passionate creators, untainted by crass commercial considerations. Moreover, they often can develop innovations or make improvements because of how they absorb information from their markets on a regular basis. Thus, they seem timeless and strangely innovative.

Fourth, the firm stresses the value of a product orientation. For Morgan and its owners, the car (rather than the customer) is king. In contrast to modern marketing dictates that suggest a product orientation is myopic, Morgan recognises that product consistency, repetition of timeless traditions, and craft techniques allow consumers to achieve self-authentication because they provide a direct contrast with the safe, focus group-tested products and services so predominant today. Fifth, Morgan stays true to its roots. Morgan remains committed to producing a good value sports car, based on a standard open top design. Rather than rejecting old methods of production, it revels in them. The company remains a family business committed to the sports car fraternity rather than an overtly profit-driven business.

Sixth, Morgan has become part of the cultural landscape through its use of clubs and events, as well as by aligning its history with that of the British motor industry – in particular the British sports car tradition. By celebrating its history, the car becomes an important cultural artefact, relatively unchanged over time, which thus confirms an important British myth of triumph in the face of adversity (particularly evident when the car performs well in Le Mans against more fancied and wealthier rivals). Seventh, Morgan publicly recognises its staff, agents, and repairers, who are passionate about the car. As a result, consumers perceive that their car has a human face, made by people as passionate about the product as they are (which helps connect them to the community).

Together, these seven strategies create a platform on which consumers can achieve authenticating experiences.

Notes

1. Arnould, E.J. and Price, L.L. (2000), "Authenticating acts and authoritative performances: Questing for self and community", in S. Ratneshwar, D.G. Mick, and C. Huffman (eds), *The Why of Consumption: Contemporary Perspectives on Consumer Motives, Goals, and Desires*, Routledge, London, pp. 140–63.
2. Beverland, M.B. (2005), "Crafting brand authenticity: The case of luxury wines", *Journal of Management Studies*, Vol. 42, No. 5, pp. 1003–30.
3. Arnould, E.J. and Price, L.L. (1993), "River magic: Extraordinary experience and the extended service encounter", *Journal of Consumer Research*, Vol. 20, No. 1, pp. 24–45; Celsi, R.L., Rose, R.L., and Leigh, T.W. (1993), "An exploration of high-risk leisure consumption through skydiving", *Journal of Consumer Research*, Vol. 20, No. 1, pp. 1–23.
4. Czikszentmihalyi, M. (1991), *Flow: The Psychology of Optimal Experience*, Harper, New York.
5. Arnould and Price, "River magic"; Celsi, Rose, and Leigh, "An exploration of high-risk leisure consumption through skydiving".
6. Huang, M.-H. (2006), "Flow, enduring, and situational involvement in the web environment: a tripartite second-order examination", *Psychology & Marketing*, Vol. 23, No. 5, pp. 383–411.
7. Arnould and Price, "River magic".
8. Huang, "Flow, enduring, and situational involvement in the web environment".
9. Arnould and Price, "Authenticating acts and authoritative performances".
10. Goffman, E. (1959), *The Presentation of Self in Everyday Life*, Penguin, Harmondsworth.
11. Arnould and Price, "Authenticating acts and authoritative performances"; Beverland, M.B. (2006), "The 'Real Thing': Branding authenticity in the luxury wine trade", *Journal of Business Research*, Vol. 59, No. 2, pp. 251–8.

4

Hush, It's a Secret: How Trappist Breweries Create and Maintain Images of Authenticity Using Customer Experiences

ADAM LINDGREEN* AND MICHAEL B. BEVERLAND†

Keywords

authenticity, brands, corporate reputation, experiential marketing, impression management, Trappist breweries

Abstract

We examine the practices of Trappist breweries that seek to build value and create competitive advantage by appearing authentic. In doing so, we identify the need for breweries to engage in experiential marketing. For the breweries, appearing authentic is critical to reinforce their brand identity, command price premiums, and differentiate themselves from larger breweries. We examine two sources of authenticity: objective (real attributes) and subjective (rhetorical attributes). The Trappist breweries create impressions of authenticity by stressing both real and rhetorical aspects of their operation/image when building a brand aura that projects authenticity. Projecting authenticity also involves downplaying scientific and business expertise, in favour of religious imagery and time-honoured traditions. In addition, breweries decouple their day-to-day operations from their espoused approach. Our examination of authenticity helps us understand how images of authenticity can be created and maintained through an engagement in experiential marketing.

* Professor Adam Lindgreen, Hull University Business School, Cottingham Road, Hull HU6 7RX, UK. E-mail: a.lindgreen@hull.ac.uk. Telephone: + 44 1482 463 096.

† Professor Michael B. Beverland, School of Economics, Finance and Marketing, Royal Melbourne Insititute of Technology University, GPO Box 2476V, Melbourne, Victoria 3001, Australia. E-mail: michael.beverland@rmit.edu.au. Telephone: + 61 416 102 492.

Introduction

The requirements of today's marketing are not just bringing a product to the market, crafting a superior design, creating a strong brand, *or* delivering good customer service. What companies need to consider holistically is all of these requirements: product, design, brand, and service. In short, companies must deliver memorable customer experiences.[1] Also in consumer behaviour literature, the importance of customer experiences has been the topic of much discussion.[2]

Despite the considerable amount of literature on the topic, there is a general feeling among academics and practitioners that we have only just begun to understand what is meant by "memorable customer experiences". Many different angles of customer experiences have been investigated. However, holes remain to be filled, and new fields need to be explored. Our study addresses this lacuna in the literature. Specifically, we examine the practices of Trappist breweries that seek to build value and create competitive advantage through appearing authentic. In doing so, we identify the need for breweries to deliver customer experiences.

The chapter has the following structure: first, following an introduction to the creation and management of authenticity, we present a brief review of the nature and sources of authenticity. An overview of the Trappist brewing industry follows. Next, we present the qualitative research design employed. Subsequently, the findings section focuses on the strategies used by Trappist brewers to craft images of authenticity and maintain them, as well as how the breweries might engage in experiential marketing to build authentic brands. A discussion and conclusion completes this chapter.

CREATING AND MANAGING AUTHENTICITY

Increasingly, organisations are turning to brand histories and historical associations as sources of market value[3] and "cultural marker[s] of legitimacy and authenticity".[4] Authenticity is a core component of successful brands because it forms part of a unique brand identity.[5] Consumers also seek out authentic brands and experiences.[6] As Brown et al. state, "the search for authenticity is one of the cornerstones of contemporary marketing".[7] Yet little is known about how organisations create and maintain images of authenticity.[8]

Brand management and the projection of ideal images represent a form of impression management.[9] However, to date, impression management research has focused solely on responding to crises or challenges to legitimacy.[10] In contrast, brand management represents a positive and proactive form of impression management that builds market-based equity (and hence legitimacy) for the organisation through building and reinforcing a corporate reputation that ensures future resource flows.[11] However, research is needed to examine how organisations build such reputations through careful impression management.[12] This chapter addresses these gaps by examining the means by which Trappist breweries create and maintain images of authenticity through their brand programmes.

The deliberate creation and management of authenticity presents several difficulties for organisations. Creating authenticity involves a number of paradoxes, because brands must remain true to their core identity while also remaining relevant.[13] Brand managers must constantly manage the paradox at the heart of strong brands by balancing actions that reinterpret (in response to changing tastes) symbolic stories involving moral conflicts and solutions, evoke aspects of an idealised past in brand imagery, and create an aura which Brown et al. describe as pertaining "to the presence of a powerful sense of authenticity that original works of art exude".[14] This aura is a core brand component because it directly reflects the core values for which the brand stands. However, no research reports on how organisations create and maintain such auras.

The findings of Brown and colleagues present some problems for extant brand management literature, which has been overwhelmingly dominated by a top-down view of creating brand image, according to which brand managers, through a planned process of marketing communications, position their products around desired attributes with little consideration of how the interactions between consumers and brands may alter these images.[15] Brand management literature also pays little attention to the importance of institutional and social contexts, though many brands depend on institutions for their sources of authenticity and legitimacy.[16] Brands are important cultural objects and possess significant symbolic value, an important artefact of institutionalisation.[17] This chapter examines whether wider institutional effects and social contexts may occur that affect the perceived credibility of brand-related actions and symbols of authenticity – a theoretical area ignored by marketing researchers.[18]

Although brand managers play a critical role in developing authenticity, the persistence of authenticity also lies in the legitimacy of established institutions, which is partly achieved through the constant use of classifications, routines, scripts, and schemas, many of which are derived from the day-to-day interaction in which society members construct mutually shared impressions.[19] That is, brands must gain cognitive and/or moral legitimacy.[20] To gain legitimacy, brands may "attempt to establish themselves as central to the cultural traditions of their societies in order to receive official protection".[21] Also, brand-related actions may be shaped by the prestige connected with a particular offering and a shared industry culture.[22] This relation suggests that brand development is similar to the production of culture perspective that focuses on the ways symbolic artefacts are shaped by the institutional environments that they inhabit.[23]

Understanding the relationship between management action and institutional constraints is important particularly for understanding the sources of authenticity; authentic images need to be adapted and updated constantly, because they represent interplay between creators, commercial interests, critics, competitors, and consumers.[24] Peterson's examination of country music performance reveals that organisers manage the conflicting pressures of remaining true to perceived views of authenticity (in this case, rustic hillbilly imagery and spontaneous informal amateurism among the players) and the need to craft a viable commercial product.[25] This consideration is similar to the strategy of decoupling, in that the performances are far more tightly programmed and scripted than consumers realise.[26] Studies in self-taught art and jazz music similarly identify the tension between commercial motives and credible claims of authenticity.[27]

The Nature and Management of Authenticity

THE NATURE OF AUTHENTICITY

The term "authenticity" remains problematic because few authors define the term, nor is a generally accepted definition available; what is often seen as authentic is asserted arbitrarily.[28] Also, commentators discussing the sources of authenticity ignore how consumers and marketers view authenticity.[29] These views are limited because consumers with different levels of cultural capital search for different cues to signal authenticity, and connotations of authenticity shift over time.[30]

We have identified two broad types of authenticity – the objective ideal (real attributes) and the subjective ideal (rhetorical attributes). These types provide a framework by which to classify various approaches to authenticity.

The objective ideal of authenticity

At one extreme, authenticity is intrinsic to the object – what Postrel identifies as the "objective ideal of authenticity," which states that authentic objects cannot involve alterations against history, quality, or art.[31] For example, authenticity gains moral authority by being linked to a creator; perpetuating the organisation's history can also be a source of authenticity.[32]

Objective sources of authenticity are non-personal and include "authenticity as purity", which condemns dilution and thereby grants authority to the natural and functional (i.e., form follows function). Postrel also identifies "authenticity as tradition" as an oft-quoted objective source of authenticity; this form can include items that are handmade or seek to rely on traditional methods of production.[33] For example, Alain Ducasse seeks to build a link between his cooking and the past by referring to how "haute cuisine is the perpetuation of tradition that takes its roots in the past".[34] Finally, "authenticity as aura" refers to objects/persons that show signs of history (i.e., someone who ages without plastic surgery is authentic). For example, re-launches of brands such as Stars Wars and the VW Beetle attracted considerable controversy among long-time fans who questioned any departure from the originals.[35]

The subjective ideal of authenticity

Various questions challenge the originality of tradition, with many suggesting it can be fabricated, or at least stylised.[36] History or culture may be evoked by either an exact replica or "simulations that rely to a large extent on pseudo-history or pure invention. The purpose of this 'heritage industry' is not to replicate the past, but to improve it, to remove all contradictions, ambiguities, and inconsistencies from the era."[37] Writing about the commercialisation of Hawaiian culture, Borgerson and Schroeder state, "we learned that most of the popular songs were written by white tunesmiths and were produced by mainlanders, though the liner notes attempt to represent the music as authentically Hawaiian by focusing on the use of Hawaiian instruments, musicians, and song lyrics that invoke the natural qualities of island paradise".[38]

In contrast to the objective ideal of authenticity, consumers and creators also impart authenticity to objects.[39] This type of authenticity is socially constructed or based on consumers' mental frames of how things "ought to look".[40] For example, cultural tourists often desire the trappings of authenticity without the hardships often faced by local inhabitants.[41] Postrel proposes a number of subjective forms of authenticity, including authenticity as formal harmony, balance, and delight; thus, updated styles of old brands such as the new VW Beetle are authentic for some because they work and give pleasure, rather than being true to the original.[42]

Also, authenticity as connection to time and place is important for consumers because it affirms tradition, which may be particularly important for low-cultural capital consumers.[43] For example, chains of "Authentic Irish Pubs" draw on Celtic symbolism or Irish names such as O'Neill's to create an "ersatz setting of the 'real' Irish public house".[44]

Finally, authenticity as self-expression implies a brand is authentic because it is a genuine expression of an inner personal truth; this type of authenticity can also be an expression of identity through community membership, such as the gay community.[45] Also, consumers may adopt a collection of mass-marketed goods to construct a personal identity; for example, the adoption of used clothing by the 1960s' counterculture reflected a desire for identity represented by the adoption of natural fabrics.[46]

We hold that rather than representing competing sources of authenticity, marketers continually craft together these diverse sources to create rich brand meanings.[47] These sources must constantly be renewed if the brand is to remain relevant, though previous decisions also constrain the ability of marketers to adopt just any claim of authenticity.[48] Literature posits that authenticity can be inherent in an object, can come from a relation between an object and a historical period, an organisational form, or nature, or be given to an object by marketers and consumers. Authenticity can also be true and/or contrived. What matters is that consumers perceive the aspects of authenticity as real, regardless of the truth of the claims.

THE MANAGEMENT OF AUTHENTICITY

Authenticity often is more contrived than real.[49] Small, specialist firms bolster claims of authenticity by strategically employing their identity in the marketplace, portraying themselves as small craft producers who use time-honoured ways and natural ingredients as a means of competitive differentiation.[50] Thus mass-market brewers often find their size detrimental when attempting to enter smaller segments.[51]

Meyer and Rowan propose that the more an organisation's identity is derived from institutionalised myths, the more organisations maintain elaborate ceremonies to display confidence to external and internal publics.[52] Creative activities or authentic brands risk devaluing themselves by being perceived as too commercial or too effective at understanding and exploiting their franchise (the market may taint claims of authenticity).[53] Instead they must, to some extent, appear distant from commercial considerations.[54] For example, Brown et al. argue that as part of a "retro-marketing" strategy, many professions "importune us with allusion to epochs untainted by crass commercialism ('faithfully serving the local community since 1954')".[55] Also, "small specialty brewers try various tactics to differentiate and distance themselves from other types of brewing firms, which are presumed to pursue baser goals".[56]

One way of achieving this objective is to decouple formal structures and day-to-day work activities to maintain legitimacy and conform to institutional norms. Rather than lose legitimacy, organisations positioning themselves around authenticity may downplay their actual prowess and conform to the expected rules of craft production, intuitive expertise, historical continuity, conservative attitude to change, and being "above commercial considerations".

For our purposes, authenticity can be defined as a story that balances industrial (production, distribution, and marketing) and rhetorical attributes to project sincerity through the avowal of commitments to traditions (including production methods, product styling, firm values, and/or location), passion for craft and production excellence, *and* the public disavowal of the role of modern industrial attributes and commercial motivations. This definition is based on a review of the literature and guides the subsequent inquiry.

Background: Trappist Breweries

Trappist monks belong to the order of Cistercians of the Strict Observance. The Cistercians monasteries are divided into two great orders, one of which was founded in 1662 by Armand de Rancé in the Normandy town of La Trappe. From this abbey the popular name "Trappist" originates. The monks from this order follow the Rule of Saint Benoit that goes back to the sixth century. To be self-sufficient, the order of the Cistercians allowed the monks to sell production not needed for the abbey. When the abbeys of these monks were raised again after Belgian independence in 1830, they started to brew their own beer, selling it under the label "Trappist beer".[57]

Due to increased standards of living, tourism, and improved distribution following the Second World War, Trappist beer moved beyond the confines of local communities and gained an international reputation. During this time a mass-produced alternative to Trappist beers emerged in the form of "abbey beers", which refer to tradition and religion in their imagery though they are not brewed in an abbey. An example of an abbey beer is Leffe, manufactured by Interbrew. During 1980–2000, the difference between Trappist beers and abbey beers became less visible to consumers for several reasons. Commercial breweries had licensed the names of existing abbeys, used names from abbeys that no longer existed, or simply invented names, such as Grimbergen brewed by Alken-Maes.[58] This practice allowed abbey beer brands to engage in misleading advertising using images of monks to suggest a monastic origin.[59]

To counter this competitive threat, in 1997 the appellation of origin "Trappist" was created by the International Trappist Organization. This logo, which states "Authentic Trappist Product", guarantees that the beer originates from a Trappist abbey, is produced by monks/nuns or secular collaborators controlled by Trappist monks/nuns, and that the majority of income is dedicated to social programmes.[60] In the beginning, only six abbeys could use the Authentic Trappist Product label: Orval, Chimay, Rochefort, Westmalle, and Westvleteren in Belgium and La Trappe in the Netherlands (Table 4.1). Achel (Belgium) was added in 1999, but La Trappe lost the right to the Trappist label because the brewery was sold to a commercial brewer.

Trappist beer production represents 1.9 per cent of total Belgian beer production. Total Trappist production was 302,000 hectolitres (hl) in 2002, up from 278,000 hl in 1998. Belgian consumption was static at around 220,000 hl in the same period. Export markets account for just over 25 per cent of production.[61] Trappist breweries would be classified as specialists and represent a fertile field for the study of creating and renewing sources of authenticity in the face of increased competitive threats. A study of Trappist breweries therefore contributes to emerging research on the production of cultural value within high-status industry fields.[62]

Table 4.1   Production volumes and market shares of Trappist breweries in 2002

Trappist brewery	Production volume (1,000 hl)	Market share of Trappist market (%)	Market share of abbey market (%)	Different beers per abbey (alcohol content in %)
Westmalle	120.0	39.7	7.6	Double (8), Triple (10)
Chimay	115.0	38.1	7.3	Red (7), Triple (8), Blue (9)
Orval	45.0	14.9	2.9	Blond (6)
Rochefort	15.6	5.2	1.0	6 (6), 8 (8), 10 (10)
Westvleteren	4.5	1.5	0.3	Blond (6), 8 (8), 12 (11)
Achel	2.0	0.7	0.1	Blond (5), Double (8)

Method

A case study design was chosen for several reasons. First, there is a lack of research on the development of authentic brands, suggesting that a more exploratory/theory-building approach is appropriate. Second, the long histories of each brand and the use of that history mean that each brand's development is path dependent. To understand and analyse path-dependent processes requires detailed case histories; such approaches can also help marketers gain new insights about market behaviour, forcing them to reconstruct their views of market realities.

Interviews were conducted at all six Trappist breweries, plus La Trappe, which had ceased being a Trappist brewery. La Trappe provided an interesting foil against which to compare the other six cases, because it is now operating on a standard commercial basis and no longer adhering to Trappist traditions. As Table 4.2 details, seven interviews were conducted across these firms with the person responsible for brand marketing in each brewery. Each interviewee was contacted via telephone. Following this first contact, a letter with more in-depth information about the research was sent. Interviews were conducted with case respondents at their place of business and lasted, on average, two hours. The first author conducted the interviews in Dutch or English.

The authors together developed a question guide for the interviews with the breweries, centred on the firm's history (when it was founded, early aims and decisions), guiding philosophy, important events in the life of the brand, marketing practices (knowledge of market, marketing activity, relationship use, promotional activity), positioning, product quality (including a description of how the product was produced), and competitive pressures (future concerns and aims). All interviews were taped and then transcribed resulting in 133 A4 single-spaced pages (10-point font) of transcript.

At each brewery, a tour of the production facilities was taken to carry out observations and ask further technical questions (each tour lasted one hour on average). Next, interview data were integrated with secondary information from the specialist brewing media, news media,

Table 4.2   Interview details

Interviewee type	Organisation	Founding year (year of first brew)	Position of interviewee	Sources of information
Industry organisation	Belgische Brouwers	1951	Director of external relationships	1 interview, 1 company specific newspaper article, 1 brochure, 2 magazines, company Website
Trappist brewery	Achel	1846 (1999)	Sales manager	1 interview, 1 tour of facilities, 2 brochures, 1 company folder, 2 newspaper articles, company Website
	Chimay	1850 (1863)	Marketing and communications manager	1 interview, 1 tour of facilities, 1 industry history, 1 specific report, 1 newspaper article, 1 annual report, company marketing materials, 3 brochures, 1 folder, company Website
	La Trappe	1868 (1884)	Commercial director	1 interview, 1 tour of facilities, 11 newspaper articles, company Website
	Orval	1926 (1934)	Administrative and commercial director	1 interview, 1 tour of facilities, 1 industry history, 1 specific report, 11 newspaper articles, company marketing materials, company Website
	Rochefort	1887 (1907)	Retired manager	1 interview, 2 tours of facilities, 2 newspaper articles
	Westmalle	1804 (1836)	Sales director	2 interviews, 2 tours of facilities, 1 industry history, 2 brochures, 1 company folder, 2 newspaper articles, company marketing materials, company Website
	Westvleteren	1831 (1839)	Manager	1 interview, 2 newspaper articles, company Website

Table 4.2   *Concluded*

Distributor	Brouwketel	1962	Horeca sales manager	2 interviews, 1 tour of facilities, 1 newspaper article, 1 company specific article, company marketing materials, company Web site
	Daems	1982	Manager	1 interview, 1 newspaper article, company Website
Retailer	Delhaize Group	1860	Category (of drinks) manager	1 interview, 1 annual report, 1 brochure, company Website
	Mitra	1978	Assistant product (non-food) group manager Marketing manager	2 interviews, 2 brochures, company marketing materials, company Website
Café	Het Trappistenhuis	N/A	Manager	1 interview, 1 tour of facilities, company marketing materials, company Website

specialist beer books, and information gained from the firms to provide further background and help triangulate the data and identify the nature of the industry. These sources included brochures, company reports, and Internet sites. In all, more than 50 sources were reviewed.

Four sources of primary data were used. In-depth interviews were carried out with five consumers of Trappist beers (two women and three men aged between 20 and 54 years) to triangulate the producer data. To further identify marketing practices for these beers, two specialist distributors, two retailers, and one restaurant buyer were interviewed. The two distributors were specialists in distributing niche products, including Trappist beers. Of the retailers, one was a specialist niche retailer, whereas the other was a generalist liquor retailer who carried Trappist beers. An interview was also arranged with the manager of the Het Trappistenhuis café. This buyer stocks all the Trappist beers and a large assortment of other Belgian specialty beers. Finally, one interview was conducted with the industry organisation (Belgische Brouwers) in Belgium. These multiple sources enabled us to triangulate the case material.

Analysis of each interview was conducted prior to the next, so the results could inform subsequent questioning and help replicate the emerging results across cases. Cases were analysed through within-case and cross-case analysis by all authors independently. Copies of each case were returned to the relevant interviewee. A final report was presented and discussed with two previous interviewees. Throughout the study, a number of methods for improving the quality of the research were adopted. First, data were triangulated from multiple primary and secondary sources, three researchers provided independent interpretations of the findings, an author read widely about the industry, and respondents had the opportunity to provide feedback about initial findings, all of which reinforced reliability and construct validity. The authors together performed the independent coding of the transcripts, but the interviews were conducted by the same interviewer (the first author) to reduce the role of bias.

Findings

The presentation of the findings centres around two key research questions. First, we briefly provide evidence of the use of authenticity by the Trappist breweries, which provides the basis for addressing the first question. Second, we examine the dual pressures of remaining authentic and maintaining market relevance to address the second question.

All of the interviewees (breweries, buyers, consumers, and the industry organisation) identified authenticity as central to the identity of Trappist beer brands. The identification of authenticity emerged without prompting in each interview. For example:

> *The labeling and packaging are very important to communicating the atmosphere, culture, and history. Imagine if you made a trendy product out of it! Where you have an attractive monk on a nice trendy label – it wouldn't be believable. Rather, the authenticity, the monk is brewing the beer and with his quill writing the name of the abbey on the label – that's the idea you need.*
>
> (Buyer, Mitra-Dost)

> *What is more important is the taste, the aura, the authenticity. It's the combination with the religion that makes it special. A beer that has been made by the monks is special. That gives it the mystique. The tradition is very important, very special and the traditional recipes they still use, and the Trappist name is very important and well known.*
>
> (Consumer)

These quotations evince elements of our definition of authenticity, including the perpetuation of traditions and input by the monks, images conveying cultural stories, and the need to manage both objective and subjective elements to reinforce perceptions of authenticity. The literature review identified two categories of authenticity – objective and subjective ideals. Evidence for the use of each type and various examples of each are provided in Table 4.3.

THE OBJECTIVE IDEAL OF AUTHENTICITY

Authenticity as purity

Authenticity as purity was identified in a number of cases. For example:

> *We have room to produce more, but the objective is not to. It is true that with our capacity we can produce more because we are only working four days a week with one team. Our objective is to help them to sell beer to fund the abbey and social programmes, not to have a growth rate of 10 per cent to satisfy a board of directors who want to have money for investments and the investors who want to have money as a return of their investment. It is completely different to a commercial company. Our investors are the monks. I think that it was the father at Westmalle who said: it is not an abbey in a brewery but it is a brewery in an abbey.*
>
> (Chimay)

Table 4.3   Sources of authenticity

Type of authenticity	Sub-types of authenticity	Derived from	Example from the cases	Frequency of use by cases
Objective ideal	Authenticity as purity	Nature; function; values	1. Commitment to use natural ingredients 2. Commitment to religious values rather than commercial opportunity 3. No dilution of style in the face of consumer demand for changes 4. "Hands-on" involvement of monks in brewing process 5. The use of the "Authentic Trappist Product" appellation	7 6 6 5 6
	Authenticity as tradition	Traditional practices and methods	1. Unique expression of historical beer style 2. The projection of simplicity 3. Commitment to traditional recipes	6 6 6
	Authenticity as aura	Shows signs of history	1. Using old buildings rather than replacing them 2. Slow change in labels and bottles 3. Offering formal proof of heritage	7 6 7
Subjective ideal	Authenticity as formal harmony, balance, and delight	Provides pleasure or functional performance	1. Projection of "mystique" 2. An integrated marketing programme	7 7
	Authenticity as connection to time and place	A sense of traditions	1. 'New' technology must complement "old" methods 2. Few changes to product 3. Claim to historical heritage 4. Projection of religious artefacts (e.g., Gothic letters, abbeys, etc.)	7 6 7 7
	Authenticity as self expression	Inner-self, expression of Trappist values	1. Workmanship of the monks 2. Self-expression projected through product, bottle, label 3. Desire to make a product with a personal imprint 4. Appearing above commercial interests	6 6 7 6

This quotation demonstrates the emphasis placed on ongoing commitment to social activities at the expense of commercial activities. Authenticity is provided through purity of motive, whereby the end result of financial success is merely a means to fund the activities of the monks. This commitment set the Trappist breweries apart from the (often larger) breweries using a Trappist style in the production of their beer. In the cases studied, La Trappe was often used as a constant point of comparison by the Trappist breweries. La Trappe was brewed in an abbey but because the company was profit driven, it could not use the Trappist logo. These commitments to Trappist ideals were seen as being central to the meaning of an authentic Trappist product. Consistent with the objective ideal of authenticity, these commitments represented actual tangible commitments to past traditions and practices rather than surface-level links to images of abbeys and religious imagery. For example:

The abbey beer also has a label like the Trappist beers, but what is behind it I don't know. What restrictions are behind it? To be an abbey there always has to be a link to an abbey, that is for sure. Whether these abbeys still exist is not so important. And it is not so important that beer is made in the abbey. We have also an abbey beer for which we use a name from an existing abbey – there are a few nuns in the abbey, so they had nothing to do with beer but we could use the name. So the abbey exists, but the abbey doesn't have to make the beer. This logo will have an effect on the Trappist market, because people don't know the difference between a Trappist beer and an abbey beer. So that is why we repeat this [the participation of the monks in beer production and the social commitments]. So they can see, ok that is what Trappist beers are.

(Delhaize)

This quotation identifies the use of social commitments and the commitment to hand-crafted production by monks as a form of competitive differentiation. This interviewee considers the constant use of such commitments through marketing practices as a means to recognise the subtle difference between abbey beers and Trappist beers. By repeating marketing information, the Trappists hope to build brand salience with their audience and ensure ongoing loyalty. These investments represent proactive forms of impression management that seek to build a source of brand value.

All of the Trappist cases indicate the necessity that monks brew the beer for the beer to be an authentic Trappist product. Buyers and consumers also reinforce this point – part of another form of authenticity as purity. In this case, authenticity as purity also relates to commitments to stylistic consistency. For example:

Of course the taste can differ, as with all the Trappist breweries, but the Trappist identity is in the taste. So the taste is not totally the same but the main tone of the tastes is the same. When I buy hops from Poland or the Czech Republic the taste will be different compared to the hops from Scotland. The intention is to keep the same taste. The tone of the taste will be for 95 per cent the same. So we certainly don't try to change the taste of the beer in response to consumers. The large breweries do that.

(Achel)

For this firm, the beer should retain the consistent "tone" of a Trappist style while allowing for some variation due to naturally occurring differences in raw material inputs. As part of this commitment, the emphasis rests on retaining this tone or style, regardless of marketplace preferences, as a means of competitive differentiation and commitment to past styles.

Authenticity as tradition

Real commitments to maintaining traditions also occur, achieved through commitments to traditional individual beer styles, production practices, and methods. For example:

> It is difficult to be different, but we all try to be different in our taste. Look at Orval, or Westmalle, or Rochefort, these are totally different. The Trappist beers are quite different in terms of taste. We each try to put our history into our beer.
>
> (Chimay)

As this quotation highlights, maintaining individual stylistic consistency allows brands to build up their salience.[63] Maintaining an individual beer style for each case differs from the commitment to a Trappist tone, identified in the previous section on authenticity as purity. In maintaining individual traditional styles, each individual brewery builds a point of difference, beyond the consistent Trappist base style. This distinction helps provide each brewery with an individual identity and differentiates one from the other. Maintaining past styles involves more than just replicating old recipes. For example:

> I think that the credibility of brewing in the Trappist abbey, under the control of the monks, with the goal of providing a living for the community is also very important in the marketing of the Trappist beers. More important than the beer itself. If they were brewing a type of beer that was not made previously by Trappist breweries – a commercial beer – this could totally damage the credibility of the Trappist beers. White beers belong to a certain area. They answer to other criteria, as do fruit beers. If tomorrow a Trappist brewery were to decide to brew a fruit beer this would have a negative effect on the consumers.
>
> (Belgische Brouwers)

This quotation identifies the importance of an integrated, credible approach, as well as the communication of that approach to the marketplace, as essential to images of authenticity and reinforcing the Trappist market position. The production process must be actually controlled by monks (in contrast to many mass market brewers), and the producer must be committed to social goals. The quotation also includes a deliberate refusal to make beer styles that, though popular, are not in keeping with Trappist traditions. As part of this broader commitment to tradition, the beer styles are not suited to changing trends in the marketplace. For example:

> The taste is never suited to the market. We actually brew with the recipe from the past. I remember in the 1990s we had a discussion that we should make the beer sweeter. We said no at that time. We'd rather go without sales, but we'll stick to our traditional recipe. This is not appreciated by younger people, but it is appreciated by the older people and the experts. We could if we want introduce a beer tomorrow for which we could get something like a few 100,000 euros. The taste would be the same, only the alcohol content would be less. But these businesses are not a part of the discussion. Even if we could earn a few 100,000 euros a year, we have asked this of the monks, because we felt obligated to ask it. They were looking at us; what are you asking now? The answer was obvious.
>
> (Westmalle)

This rejection applies to what is commonly identified as a market orientation (or customer responsiveness). In this case, traditions must be maintained at all costs, which adds significant credibility to the brand but also results in an inability to leverage the brand into growth markets.

Authenticity as aura

Authenticity as aura involves showing signs of age rather than trying to defeat decay. In the case studies, this demonstration occurred in two forms: retaining ruins of older buildings rather than clearing them to make room for more modern facilities and verifying an established history of Trappist beer production. For example, the newest Trappist brewery, Achel, struggled in the marketplace until it found historical records showing beer production prior to the First World War. Research on creative industries similarly reveals that artists effectively have to "pay their dues" before their work gains moral legitimacy.[64]

THE SUBJECTIVE IDEAL OF AUTHENTICITY

Authenticity as formal harmony, balance, and delight

Authenticity as formal harmony, balance, and delight provides pleasure or functional performance. For example:

> They are different because they don't communicate – that is strange but that is the most important difference. I cannot say that they have a higher quality than the others because the other's quality is also very high. No actions and no communication – those are the largest difference. For the rest, yeah, ok, the atmosphere that is around it, that is in the authenticity, and the mystique.
>
> (Delhaize)

This quotation identifies that these brands have value because of the atmosphere surrounding the product. Although this atmosphere does not improve the functional performance of the product, the decision by the breweries not to engage in mass marketing adds to the brands' collective mystique and thereby provides pleasure for this buyer.

Authenticity as connection to time and place

Authenticity could be created through building real or perceived links to time and place. The subjective form of this type of authenticity is believed to add value by reaffirming tradition. For example:

> An image of a beer with a cross does not make you happy. No I don't think so – the only thing is the abbey. But you have to think about the general consumer. The Gothic letters make sure that most of the consumers will know that this has something to do with religion but it is not traceable.
>
> (Mitra-Dost)

A sense of authenticity is derived from the use of Gothic lettering in the branding of the beers. Rather than overtly building a connection between religion and the brand, the use of Gothic letters reaffirms tradition because it appears old, and it is related to consumers' views of religion. In this sense, the use of such lettering conforms to consumers' mental frames of what a Trappist beer brand "ought to look like".

Building such links represents part of the core of a Trappist beer brand and thus limits the strategic moves such breweries can undertake. For example:

> *The introduction of the white Trappist is a problem. The image is authenticity, then the customers will think, how is this possible? Where is the beer coming from? Achel is one of the Trappist beers that has not been on the market so long. They have to provide a very serious explanation that before the war they were making a beer over there. They have found papers from which you can conclude that they had a brewery. In the war a lot of copper kettles were stolen so they had to stop their brewing activities. And by finding these original papers they were able to label their beer as Trappist beer.*
>
> (Delhaize)

This quotation identifies how the Trappist brewer Achel built credible links with the past to add authenticity to the brand. Although the link built to the past was objective (that is, it had produced beer prior to the First World War), there was no continued tradition of product, and as a result, the link with a past tradition of brewing provided subjective authenticity. In both cases, the ability to reaffirm tradition was critical to building brand credibility. The Trappist breweries downplay the brand and focus on pictures of abbeys in all of their external communications. For example:

> *The Trappist breweries are not commercial. But the marketing is focused to underscore the authenticity. Hereby the Trappist logo plays an important role. The Internet sites are also important. When you want to search for the brand names you first come to the abbeys and after that you can go to the brand names. For other breweries the priority is the product. After this you can read what is happening in the company. It is the other way around on purpose for the Trappist breweries.*
>
> (Belgische Brouwers)

This quotation identifies how the breweries reinforce perceptions of authenticity as connection to time and place by emphasising the Abbey in the logo, as well as the dominance of the abbey per se in all forms of marketing communication. These projections of historical images all help reaffirm tradition and as a result communicate authenticity, even when the media through which these images are created are very modern, such as the Internet.

Authenticity as self-expression

Authenticity as self-expression involves either projecting or responding to images that reflect deeper personal truths. For both buyers and brewers, the projection of images reflecting personal truths is important. For example:

We thought our labels were too exuberant, too colourful. We want to go back to the simplicity. We think our old labels did not communicate what we wanted to communicate. This also has a lot to do with the soberness of the monks, of course.

(La Trappe)

I liked the statement that a special beer is more enjoyment alone, just sitting on a bank. That I recognise. In contrast with lager beers which are more about social interaction. And the authenticity of the special beers, you imagine you are on a bench just enjoying and go back to the workmanship which is in your hands. You see this also in the commercials.

(Mitra-Dost)

Authenticity as self-expression emerges in the first quotation, because the interviewee from La Trappe identifies the motivation for changing the label to reflect the soberness of the monastic lifestyle, rather than exuberance or gaiety. In the second quotation, a buyer identifies the value derived from appreciating the workmanship that has gone into producing a traditional product. These beers are identified as special because they are associated with self-contemplation and being enjoyed alone in quiet contemplation.

Summary: Building Images of Authenticity

The discussion so far identifies several types of authenticity that conform to our proposed definition. For example, the breweries use both industrial and rhetorical aspects of their operation and image when building a brand aura that projects authenticity. Also, buyers and consumers associate both aspects with images of authenticity. Industrial aspects involve maintaining past traditions, hand-crafted methods, select distribution, stylistic consistency, monks' involvement in the production, the use of natural ingredients, and targeted marketing communications that emphasise these aspects of production and commercial operation. Rhetorical aspects include stylised images of religious life, the deliberate creation of track record (e.g., Achel established a prior history of beer production), the preservation of the old monastery, the communication of these values through public tours, and a commitment to social programmes.

Consistent with our definition, the breweries selectively communicate or downplay certain aspects of their story to project an idealised and consistent image of authenticity and sincerity. This effort involves the use of both real (objective) and stylised (subjective) sources of authenticity to create a positive impression in the marketplace and build a point of competitive differentiation. For example, the breweries are committed to furthering social causes (purity) and retaining traditional methods, as well as to ensuring stylistic consistency (albeit within a range, because exact replication of taste from one batch to the next is impossible). Also, the projection of commitment to religious or social values at the expense of commercial exploitation is real – the breweries forgo commercial opportunities because of these values, rather than motivations related to building brand image. For example:

It is not possible to visit the abbey. In the abbey of Westmalle we miss opportunities. We try to pick all the right press but we don't let TV teams film here. The monks don't have a good feeling about that. We respect the fact that the monks don't want that, ok sometimes we think it is a shame.

(Westmalle)

However, evidence also indicates that the breweries deliberately and selectively downplay aspects of their operation, due to a real commercial understanding of what the market sees as an authentic Trappist beer image. For example:

We are present in the higher category and we actually are not allowed to grow. So we want to make sure that the customers of today are the consumers of tomorrow. This we try to do by creating a high quality level but also by a good image. It is important to keep the image of Orval in the mind of the consumer. We try to achieve this in several ways. We have about 80,000 visitors a year who hear our history and tradition. Also we're filmed for television every year, which makes sure that the history and culture is communicated to the customers.

(Orval)

Tours of the plants focus on the Abbey (to suggest a link with religion and the past) and traditional production practices rather than on the modern production systems in place. Also, their publicly espoused values are centred on aspects of authenticity other than the commercial benefits that come from commitment to these values. That is, these values are a key part of their brand identity, but when communicated, they are not linked to the language of brand marketing.

Finally, downplaying commercial motivations appears critical to aspects of authenticity. However, the quotations presented herein identify the real commercial pressures faced by these breweries. Further analysis reveals that the breweries effectively meet these pressures through investments in production quality and brand marketing strategies. This production and business prowess sits in contrast with the espoused statements of the interviewees and the public pronouncements made by the breweries, as explored further in the next section, which addresses the second question about maintaining images of authenticity.

MAINTAINING IMAGES OF AUTHENTICITY

Tensions between real commercial pressures and appearing above commercial considerations

The actions of the abbey beers place considerable competitive pressure on the Trappist breweries. In particular, marketers of abbey beers have closed the perceptual gap between their beers and Trappist beer. Abbey beers have positioned themselves around images of religious orders to trade on the positive associations created by the Trappist breweries. Abbey beers have also delivered a more consistent product due to their greater investments in industrial production methods which have driven the Trappist breweries to respond with their own investments in marketing and production. For example:

Our volume was going down six years ago. We needed to react otherwise it would be very difficult to keep our place in the market. We try to be active in the market with marketing that informs the customer why we are a Trappist beer, why the abbey is important and why we are different than the others.

(Chimay)

When the Trappist breweries respond on development in the market they only react very slowly. In the time when the Leffe was coming up, the distributors were saying to Westmalle that they had to do something because the image was collapsing. Only very late did the monks do the promotional and distribution tasks. When this happened, more commercial people made sure that the image of Westmalle survived. Now they have a commercial director and I see the difference. They are absolutely more commercial. This was around 1990. Before this situation we did not have a salesman of Westmalle; since this situation we have one.

(Daems)

These quotations identify commercial drivers of changes in the operations of the Trappist breweries, including investments in marketing communications and delegating tasks previously done by monks to professional marketers. Such actions challenge objective ideals of authenticity – in particular, authenticity as purity. No longer are the monks involved in key commercial decisions, and in many breweries, neither are they involved in beer production. For example:

In the past there was a monk responsible for the brewing, selling and for the packaging. And there was a monk who was the director of the brewery. All three would then go back into the abbey again. For the same function there are hired laymen. Our brewer who is brewing now has been brewing for 10 years with the brewer-monk. So he knows the process very well but he is still a layman.

(Westmalle)

Increased professionalization thus marks the commercial side of Trappist production. This actual practice is a far cry from the one portrayed in communications to the public. Nevertheless, such changes are necessary to deal with very real commercial pressures. Other changes include the importance of stylistic consistency in their beers. Because they use natural production processes, each batch of Trappist beer can have some variation in taste. In the past, these variations could be large, resulting in very different styles of beer and varying quality. In response to the threat posed by abbey beers, this variation needed to be reduced, and the Trappist breweries therefore increased quality controls and made significant investments in production (e.g., Westmalle made an 80-million euro investment in computerised production systems). Again, this shift challenges objective claims of authenticity, in particular authenticity as tradition.

Despite these necessary changes, the espoused view of the breweries has not altered. For example, the breweries often emphasise their commitment to stylistic consistency, regardless of market fashions:

It is true that we are not responding to developments in the market. The incorporation of developments in our strategy is not done, we are really doing nothing. The only thing I can think about is that in the past the gift packages had only one colour, now there are more colours, so these packages are refined. But that is the only thing I can think of. And I assume that in the coming 10 years there will also be some small changes, but not many.

(Westmalle)

In contrast, evidence from business buyers suggests that this brewery was particularly active in the marketplace and responding to market-driven changes, on a far greater scale than the peripheral changes mentioned in this quotation. All of the case studies took the approach of downplaying their real commercial prowess and investments in modern production processes, while playing up traditional images as part of a deliberate attempt to reinforce perceptions of authenticity. This strategy is similar to the strategy of decoupling, whereby firms decouple formal structures and day-to-day practices to maintain ongoing legitimacy.[65] This point thereby addresses the second aim of the chapter.

Use of the "Authentic Trappist Product" appellation

To counter the competitive threat from abbey beers, in 1997, the appellation of "Trappist" origin was created by the International Trappist Organization. This logo, which states "Authentic Trappist Product", guarantees that the beer originates from a Trappist abbey, is produced by monks or secular collaborators controlled by Trappist monks, and that the majority of income is dedicated to social programmes (e.g., Chimay is the biggest employer in the most economically depressed area of Belgium). As noted previously, six abbeys initially were allowed to use the "Authentic Trappist Product" label: Orval, Chimay, Rochefort, Westmalle, and Westvleteren in Belgium and La Trappe in the Netherlands. Achel (Belgium) joined this list in 1999, but La Trappe lost the right to the Trappist label because it was sold to a commercial brewer.

To provide a coherent and differentiating account to consumers, each Trappist brewery uses the Trappist logo on its products (on the back label, with the exception of Chimay). This strategy attempts to explain the difference between Trappist and abbey products and thus regain cognitive legitimacy, which is used actively by specialist retail buyers. For consumers, such an overt declaration of authenticity has the opposite effect, however:

Authentic Trappist product – brown sign, says nothing more than that, can associate colour with the beer, the brown, the double ... too explicit I think. You can't be explicit, you have to believe through the signs it's authentic, you can't read it. You can't see it is authentic.

(Consumer: Bram)

The first is a small sign saying authentic Trappist product, when you have to say you are honest it looks like you have something to hide, when you have to claim you are authentic, it's suspicious, so that is why I don't trust such a sign. On the Westmalle and La Trappe bottle there is a back label, it doesn't help to convey an authentic Trappist product, again they shouldn't claim it too explicitly, like this one has factual information [Westmalle double] this one the triple Westmalle says clear golden yellow brewed under the supervision of the monks, natural ingredients, it is already claiming the supervision of the monks in the first line and if they have to claim it too hard too explicitly I don't believe it.

(Consumer: Hans)

Rochefort, it is a big bottle, the logo is a problem, the authentic Trappist product, if they need that logo to make sure I believe it is authentic then it is no good, The logo, I wouldn't associate a logo directly with authenticity, a logo is mainly to recognise a product but there are a lot of steps to make a logo authentic.

(Consumer: Tim)

Far from providing the necessary normalising account (recommended for repairing cognitive legitimacy), such an explanation only reinforces the Trappists' lost taken-for-grantedness, because it is believed to be a façade or a marketing gimmick. All three consumer passages are representative of the reaction of sampled informants to beers displaying the "Authentic Trappist Product" logo. Consumers viewed such overt explanations sceptically, which undermines the intentions of the Trappists. The consumers also all note that the explanation does not provide a comprehensible account (consistent with cognitive legitimacy) and that the use of the logo actually further distances them from preconceived images of authenticity – images now owned by abbey breweries. Only in cases in which consumers had seen behind the scenes of the brewery in question – that is, had experienced the brewery – did such explanations have a positive or neutral effect.

Discussion and Conclusions

This chapter contributes to the concepts of memorable consumer experiences in several ways. First, we have developed a definition of authenticity and supported this definition with data from the Trappist breweries. Authenticity involves creating a sincere story from both industrial and rhetorical attributes relevant to the brand. Selectively emphasising and de-emphasising objective and subjective forms of authenticity creates sincerity. Thus, authenticity is a combination of the real and the stylised, rather than one or the other. We find support for the view that authenticity is real or intrinsic to the object or brand, as well as contrived and/or subjective. What matters is that the impression created is consistent with the expectations of consumers and/or business buyers.

Second, we identify various attributes of authenticity in the commercial arena, such as building links to place, history, and culture; the use of production methods; a projection of non-commercial values; myths surrounding the brand; and reflections of inner truths. Again, rather than choosing one over the other, the interviewees skilfully blended several attributes of authenticity to create powerful positive impressions and differentiate themselves from competitors. By doing so, the breweries gained and retained both cognitive legitimacy (i.e., they fit their institutional context) and moral legitimacy by pursuing pro-social actions. Legitimacy was also achieved by continued relevance through investments in production quality and marketing activities. Thus, moral claims complemented brand relevance and contributed to the development of a positive corporate reputation.[66] By drawing on literature from brand management and organisation studies, we provide an example of how organisations can proactively create positive market impressions.

Third, we identify the importance to claims of authenticity of appearing distant or disinterested in commercial motives,[67] which contrasts with brand management literature that calls for the constant communication of product improvements and performance equivalence with competing brands. That is, brand managers should constantly communicate relevance to the marketplace.[68] Instead, relevance may be shown through product performance, but the investments leading to ongoing relevance should be downplayed as part of a deliberate impression-management strategy that attempts to create the appearance of authenticity. This finding also contributes to our understanding of decoupling, in that rather than appealing to rational rules of production and commercial practice,[69] these organisations must conform to more subjective rules relating to timeless images, hand-crafted production methods, and traditional values, while simultaneously engaging in rational production and business practices behind the scenes.

Fourth, we shed light on brand management practices by noting that brand meaning is not the sole province of marketers but also draws on the institutional environment surrounding the brand. For example, each Trappist brand draws on the shared identity of the shared culture and history of the Trappist order,[70] as well as the mutually shared impressions of consumers and business buyers. Brand managers clearly draw on these attributes to inform brand meaning, which suggests that the development of a brand aura or impression involves a complex interplay between brand managers, the institutional environment, and consumers and business buyers. Examining these three sources of brand meaning in other contexts would add significantly to our understanding of brand development and maintenance.

Despite some limitations, this research advances work on the actions of specialists, emerging research on the production of cultural value in high- and low-status industry fields, and the production of culture perspectives.[71] We also add to emerging literature on authenticity in other fields by identifying the importance of downplaying commercial considerations to make credible claims of authenticity. To date, this point has been identified only in cultural fields such as self-taught art and music.[72]

LIMITATIONS AND FURTHER RESEARCH

These findings have several limitations. For example, further research is needed to replicate these findings and extend them to other industries and thereby identify other sources of authenticity in the commercial arena and allow for a more comprehensive view of authenticity. Research is also needed in contexts that are more overtly commercial than the quasi-religious organisations examined here. This extension would allow for the examination of both generalist (e.g., Coca-Cola) and specialist (e.g., Krispy Kreme) producers who use authenticity as part of their image. Likewise, examinations of how firms respond to challenges to claims of authenticity are also needed. Longitudinal studies of how marketers balance commercial needs and the claims of authenticity are also encouraged.

Further research could identify how organisations reinterpret expressions of authenticity over time as the institutional context surrounding the brand changes. Are certain brands or product categories more prone to draw on certain attributes of authenticity over others? This tendency might suggest a contingency approach to authenticity, whereby brand managers are limited by institutional restraints regarding which attributes of authenticity they can use (e.g., using place makes sense in the wine industry because of rules protecting regional place names). How do organisations manage to exploit their authenticity without being seen as too successful or too mass-marketed? For example, adoption and diffusion models posit that the mass-market adoption of ideas or products may turn innovators or early adopters away from the product.[73] Research reveals that the quick exploitation of the adoption of Dunlop Volley shoes in Australia by innovative teens would destroy the value of this brand with these teens and result in the brand being seen as a short-term fad by the mass market, thereby destroying any potential for longer-term value.[74]

Finally, research is needed to examine the differences between perceptions of authenticity held by consumers, including the differences in construction of authenticity by low- and high-cultural capital consumers. Holt notes that consumers characterised by low levels of cultural capital are less likely to respond to claims of authenticity or to value the cues that would signal authenticity to high-cultural consumers.[75] Research could also compare novice consumers of products such as wine or beer with experts to examine whether the source and importance of authenticity changes with increased product experience and knowledge or over time.[76] Finally, research should examine how consumers respond to information that challenges claims of authenticity made by brand marketers (i.e., does it matter if authenticity is real or contrived?).

MANAGERIAL IMPLICATIONS

Key managerial implications arise from the findings. First, authenticity matters in the brand arena. Firm owners and marketers should seek to exploit aspects of their history, links to place, production approaches, associations with past events or key cultural elements, and important guiding values for commercial benefit. To do so, marketers must skilfully blend these aspects into a sincere story that has meaning for their target market. Although a sincere story is necessary, not all aspects of the story need to be fully true or to represent a complete version of events. The breweries studied create mystique around their brands by deliberately holding back some aspects of their story and placing greater emphasis on aspects that may no longer be completely true. To avoid potential backlash, brand managers must keep tight control over the story communicated to the public.

Second, the findings highlight the importance of brand relevance. Authenticity, though clearly a useful point of differentiation, is not sufficient. Merely repeating past claims and past practices cannot address new competitive threats (i.e., in this case the abbey beers). Authenticity instead should complement commitments to quality control, consistency, and marketing investments.

Third, a key attribute of creating a sincere story (critical to claims of authenticity) involved deliberately downplaying scientific and commercial prowess, which conflicts directly with current business practices that celebrate expertise and effectiveness. To create images of authenticity, we suggest managers should deliberately appear less competent and modern than they really are. Organisations might adopt a strategy of decoupling, whereby the behind-the-scenes investments and activities that ensure relevance get deliberately downplayed in favour of public pronouncements that emphasise attributes of authenticity. Essentially, to be seen as authentic, one needs to say one thing and do another.

In closing then, to be successful, Trappist breweries need to engage in experiential marketing, involving for example, the opportunity for consumers to visit the breweries within the confines of heritage-rich monasteries that date back many centuries. Such visits would allow consumers to verify how the breweries are connected to time and place and how they are imbedded in the local environment and committed to social activities, rather than appearing interested in commercial opportunities. As well, it allows consumers to see how Trappists monks are involved, with their "hands on" the production of old-style, simple, yet unique beers using traditional brewing practices. Such visits give consumers the opportunity to experience the authentic harmony, balance, delight, and mystique of the Trappist monasteries, where the silent monks live and work. When all of these elements come together, the breweries have achieved an integrated, credible approach to authentic Trappist beer production; the monks have paid their dues, and their beer production has gained moral legitimacy. Only then will the Trappist breweries be successful in creating a sincere story that has meaning for their consumers.

Notes

1   Pine, B.J. and Gilmore, J.H. (1999), *Experience Economy*, Harvard Business School Press, Boston, MA; Schmitt, B.H. (2003), *Customer Experience Management*, John Wiley & Sons, Hoboken, NJ; Shaw, C. and Ivens, J. (2005), *Building Great Customer Experiences*, Palgrave Macmillan, Basingstoke; Smith, S. and Wheeler, J. (2002), *Managing the Customer Experience*, Prentice Hall, Harlow.

2   Arnould, E.J. and Price, L.L. (1993), "River magic: extraordinary experience and the extended service encounter", *Journal of Consumer Research*, Vol. 20, June, pp. 24–45; Csikszentmihalyi, M. (1990), *Flow: The Psychology of Optimal Experience*, Harper & Row, New York; Holbrook, M.B. and Hirschman, E. (1982), "The experiential aspects of consumption: consumer fantasies, feelings, and fun", *Journal of Consumer Research*, Vol. 9, September, pp. 132–40.

3   Brown, S., Kozinets, R.V., and Sherry, J.F. Jr. (2003), "Teaching old brands new tricks: retro branding and the revival of brand meaning", *Journal of Marketing*, Vol. 67, No. 3, pp. 19–33; Grayson, K. and Martinec, R. (2004), "Consumer perceptions of iconicity and indexicality and their influence on assessments of authentic market offerings", *Journal of Consumer Research*, Vol. 31, No. 2, pp. 296–312; Peñaloza, L. (2000), "The commodification of the American West: marketers' production of cultural meanings at the trade show", *Journal of Marketing*, Vol. 64, No. 4, pp. 82–109.

4   Brown, Kozinets, and Sherry, "Teaching old brands new tricks", p. 19.

5   Aaker, D.A. (1996), *Building Strong Brands*, Free Press, New York; Keller, K.L. (2003), *Strategic Brand Management: Building, Measuring, and Managing Brand Equity*, 2nd edn, Prentice Hall, Sydney.

6   Fine, G.A. (2003), "Crafting authenticity: the validation of identity in self-taught art", *Theory and Society*, Vol. 32, No. 2, pp. 153–80; Grayson and Martinec, "Consumer perceptions of iconicity and indexicality"; Holt, D.B. (1997), "Poststructuralist lifestyle analysis: conceptualizing the social patterning of consumption on post–modernity", *Journal of Consumer Research*, Vol. 23, No. 4, pp. 326–50; Peñaloza, "The commodification of the American West"; Thompson, C.J. and Tambyah, S.K. (1999), "Trying to be cosmopolitan", *Journal of Consumer Research*, Vol. 26, No. 3, pp. 214-41.

7   Brown, Kozinets, and Sherry, "Teaching old brands new tricks", p. 21.

8   Fine, "Crafting authenticity"; Grayson and Martinec, "Consumer perceptions of iconicity and indexicality"; Peñaloza, "The commodification of the American West".

9   Elsbach, K.D., Sutton, R.I., and Principe, K.E. (1998), "Averting expected challenges through anticipatory impression management: a study of hospital billing", *Organization Science*, Vol. 9, No. 1, pp. 68–86.

10   Ibid.

11   Ibid.; Fombrun, C. and Shanley, M. (1990), "What's in a name? Reputation building and corporate strategy", *Academy of Management Journal*, Vol. 33, No. 2, pp. 233–58.

12   Fombrun and Shanley, "What's in a name?"

13   Aaker, *Building Strong Brands*; Keller, *Strategic Brand Management*.

14   Brown, Kozinets, and Sherry, "Teaching old brands new tricks", p. 21.

15   Kates, S.M. (2004), "The dynamics of brand legitimacy: an interpretive study in the gay men's community", *Journal of Consumer Research*, Vol. 31, No. 2, pp. 455–64.

16   Grayson and Martinec, "Consumer perceptions of iconicity and indexicality"; Kates, "The dynamics of brand legitimacy".

17   Belk, R.W. (1988), "Possessions and the extended self", *Journal of Consumer Research*, Vol. 15, No. 2, pp. 139–68; Holt, "Poststructuralist lifestyle analysis"; Holt, D.B. (2002), "Why do brands cause trouble? A dialectical theory of consumer culture and branding", *Journal of Consumer Research*, Vol. 29, No. 1, pp. 70–90; Scott, W.R. (2001), *Institutions and Organizations*, 2nd edn, Sage, Thousand Oaks, CA.

18   Grayson and Martinec, "Consumer perceptions of iconicity and indexicality"; Handelman, J.M. and Arnold, S.J. (1999), "The role of marketing actions with a social dimension: appeals to the institutional environment", *Journal of Marketing*, Vol. 63, No. 3, pp. 33–48.

19   Douglas, M. (1986), *How Institutions Think*, Syracuse University Press, Syracuse, NY; Phillips, M.E. (1994), "Industry mindsets: exploring the cultures of two macro-organizational settings", *Organization Science*, Vol. 5, No. 3, pp. 384–402; Powell, W.W. and DiMaggio, P.J. (1991), *The New Institutionalism in Organizational Analysis*, University of Chicago Press, Chicago; Scott, *Institutions and Organizations*.

20   Kates, "The dynamics of brand legitimacy".

21   Meyer, J.W. and Rowan, B. (1991), "Institutionalized organizations: formal structure as myth and ceremony", in W.W. Powell and P.J. DiMaggio (eds), *The New Institutionalism in Organizational Analysis*, University of Chicago Press, Chicago, pp. 41–62, at p. 49.

22   Anand, N. and Watson, M.R. (2004), "Tournament rituals in the evolution of fields: the case of the Grammy awards", *Academy of Management Journal*, Vol. 47, No. 1, pp. 59–80; Benjamin, B.A. and Podolny, J.M. (1999), "Status, quality, and social order in the wine industry", *Administration Science Quarterly*, Vol. 44, No. 3, pp. 563–89; Carroll, G.R. and Swaminathan, A. (2000), "Why the microbrewery movement? Organizational dynamics of resource partitioning in the U.S. brewing industry", *American Journal of Sociology*, Vol. 106, No. 3, pp. 715–62; Peterson, R.A. and Anand, N. (2004), "The production of culture perspective", *Annual Review of Sociology*, Vol. 30, pp. 311–34; Phillips, "Industry mindsets"; Uzzi, B. (1997), "Social structure and competition in interfirm networks: the paradox of embeddedness", *Administration Science Quarterly*, Vol. 42, No. 1, pp. 35–67.

23   Anand and Watson, "Tournament rituals in the evolution of fields"; Benjamin and Podolny, "Status, quality, and social order in the wine industry"; Peterson and Anand, "The production of culture perspective".

24   Carroll and Swaminathan, "Why the microbrewery movement?"; Grazian, D. (2003), *Blue Chicago: The Search for Authenticity in Urban Blues Clubs*, University of Chicago Press, Chicago; Kates, "The dynamics of brand legitimacy"; Peterson, R.A. (1997), *Creating Country Music: Fabricating Authenticity*, The University of Chicago Press, Chicago; Phillips, "Industry mindsets".

25   Peterson, *Creating Country Music*.

26   Meyer and Rowan, "Institutionalized organizations"; Peterson, *Creating Country Music*.

27   Fine, G.A. (2004), *Everyday Genius: Self-Taught Art and the Culture of Authenticity*, University of Chicago Press, Chicago; Grazian, *Blue Chicago*.

28   Boyle, D. (2003), *Authenticity: Brands, Fakes, Spin and the Lust for Real Life*, Harper-Collins, London; Grayson and Martinec, "Consumer perceptions of iconicity and indexicality".

29   Holt, "Why do brands cause trouble?"; Postrel, V. (2003), *The Substance of Style: How the Rise of Aesthetic Value is Remaking Commerce, Culture, & Consciousness*, HarperCollins, New York.

30   Holt. D.B. (1998), "Does cultural capital structure American consumption?" *Journal of Consumer Research*, Vol. 25, No. 1, pp. 1–25; Postrel, *The Substance of Style*.

31   Postrel, *The Substance of Style*.

32   Benjamin & Podolny, "Status, quality, and social order in the wine industry"; Fine, "Crafting authenticity".

33   Fine, "Crafting authenticity"; Postrel, *The Substance of Style*.

34   Hetzel, P.L. (2003), "Contemporary haute cuisine in France: when French chefs are paying their tributes to the past", in S. Brown and J.F. Sherry Jr. (eds), *Time Space, and the Market*, M.E. Sharpe, Armonk, NY, pp. 3–18, at p. 14.

35   Brown, Kozinets, and Sherry, "Teaching old brands new tricks".

36   Grayson and Martinec, "Consumer perceptions of iconicity and indexicality"; Peterson and Anand, "The production of culture perspective".

37   Patterson, A. and Brown, S. (2003), "Comeback for the *Craic*: a literary pub crawl", in S. Brown and J.F. Sherry Jr. (eds), *Time Space, and the Market*, M.E. Sharpe, Armonk, NY, pp. 75–93, at p. 76.

38   Borgerson J. and Schroeder, J. (2003), "The lure of paradise: marketing the retro-escape of Hawaii", in S. Brown and J.F. Sherry Jr. (eds), *Time Space, and the Market*, M.E. Sharpe, Armonk, NY, pp. 219–37, at p. 226.

39   Holt, "Does cultural capital structure American consumption?"; Lewis, D. and Bridger, D. (2001), *The Soul of the New Consumer: Authenticity – What We Buy and Why in the New Economy*, Nicholas Brealey, Naperville, IL; Peterson, *Creating Country Music*.

40   Grayson and Martinec, "Consumer perceptions of iconicity and indexicality".

41   Costa, J.A. and Bamossy, G.J. (2003), "Retrospecting retroscapes: form and function, content and context", in S. Brown and J.F. Sherry Jr. (eds), *Time Space, and the Market*, M.E. Sharpe, Armonk, NY, pp. 253–70.

42   Brown, Kozinets, and Sherry, "Teaching old brands new tricks"; Postrel, *The Substance of Style*.

43   Holt, "Does cultural capital structure American consumption?"; Postrel, *The Substance of Style*.

44   Goulding, C. (2003), "Corsets, silk stockings, and evening suits: retro shops and retro junkies", in S. Brown and J.F. Sherry Jr. (eds), *Time Space, and the Market*, M.E. Sharpe, Armonk, NY, pp. 54–74, at p. 55; Patterson and Brown, "Comeback for the *Craic*".

45   Grayson and Martinec, "Consumer perceptions of iconicity and indexicality"; Kates, "The dynamics of brand legitimacy".

46   Goulding, "Corsets, silk stockings, and evening suits"; Kates, "The dynamics of brand legitimacy".

47   Grayson and Martinec, "Consumer perceptions of iconicity and indexicality"; Kates, "The dynamics of brand legitimacy".

48   Carroll and Swaminathan, "Why the microbrewery movement?"

49   Brown, Kozinets, and Sherry, "Teaching old brands new tricks"; Holt, "Why do brands cause trouble?"; Peterson, *Creating Country Music*.

50   Carroll and Swaminathan, "Why the microbrewery movement?"

51   Ibid.

52   Meyer and Rowan, "Institutionalized organizations".

53   Fine, "Crafting authenticity"; Fine, *Everyday Genius*; Grayson and Martinec, "Consumer perceptions of iconicity and indexicality"; Holt, "Why do brands cause trouble?"; Kates, "The dynamics of brand legitimacy".

54   Holt, "Why do brands cause trouble?"

55   Brown, Kozinets, and Sherry, "Teaching old brands new tricks", p. 4.

56   Carroll and Swaminathan, "Why the microbrewery movement?", p. 730.

57   Van den Steen, J. (2003), *Trappist: Het Bier en de Monniken*, Allmedia, Leuven, Belgium.

58   Lodahl, M. (1994), "Belgian Trappist and abbey beers", *Brewing Techniques*, Vol. 2, No. 6, pp. 28–34.

59   Van den Steen, *Trappist*.

60   Van den Einde, J. and Gillard, P. (2002), *België, het bierparadijs: een ronde van België van het bier*, *Speciaal Dossier*, No. 5, Belgische Dienst voor de Buitenlandse Handel (BDBH), Brussels.

61   Cooreman, R. (2003), "Sector overzicht van de Belgische brouwnijverheid", *Het Brouwersblad*, 6 June, p. 32.

62   Benjamin and Podolny, "Status, quality, and social order in the wine industry"; Carroll and Swaminathan, "Why the microbrewery movement?"; Delacroix, J., Swaminathan, A., and Solt, M.E. (1989), "Density dependence versus population dynamics: an ecological study of failings in the California wine industry", *American Sociological Review*, Vol. 54, No. 2, pp. 245–62; Fine, "Crafting authenticity"; Peterson and Anand, "The production of culture perspective"; Uzzi, "Social structure and competition in interfirm networks".

63   Keller, *Strategic Brand Management*.

64   Caves, R.E. (2000), *Creative Industries: Contracts between Art and Commerce*, Harvard University Press, Cambridge, MA; Fine, *Everyday Genius*.

65   Meyer and Rowan, "Institutionalized organizations".

66   Fombrun and Shanley, "What's in a name?"

67   Holt, "Does cultural capital structure American consumption?"

68   Keller, K.L., Sternthal, B., and Tybout, A. (2002), "Three questions you need to ask about your brand", *Harvard Business Review*, Vol. 80, No. 9, pp. 3–8.

69   Meyer and Rowan, "Institutionalized organizations".

70   Anand and Watson, "Tournament rituals in the evolution of fields"; Carroll and Swaminathan, "Why the microbrewery movement?"; Phillips, "Industry mindsets"; Uzzi, "Social structure and competition in interfirm networks".

71   Benjamin and Podolny, "Status, quality, and social order in the wine industry"; Caves, R.E. (2000), *Creative Industries: Contracts between Art and Commerce*, Harvard University Press, Cambridge, MA; Carroll and Swaminathan, "Why the microbrewery movement?"; Delacroix, Swaminathan, and Solt, "Density dependence versus population dynamics"; Fine, "Crafting authenticity"; Grazian, *Blue Chicago*; Peterson, *Creating Country Music*; Peterson and Anand, "The production of culture perspective"; Uzzi, "Social structure and competition in interfirm networks.

72   Fine, *Everyday Genius*; Grazian, *Blue Chicago*; Peterson, *Creating Country Music*.

73   Rogers, R. (1995), *Diffusion of Innovations*, 4th edn, Free Press, New York.

74   Beverland, M.B. and Ewing, M.T. (2005), "Slowing the adoption and diffusion process to enhance brand repositioning: the consumer driven repositioning of Dunlop Volley", *Business Horizons*, Vol. 48, September–October, pp. 385–91.

75   Holt, "Does cultural capital structure American consumption?"

76   Postrel, *The Substance of Style*.

5 *Brand Communities as Experience Drivers: Empirical Research Findings*

FABIAN VON LOEWENFELD* AND KARSTEN KILIAN†

Keywords

brand communities, brand community quality, brand community management, brand community experiences

Abstract

In this chapter, we discuss different types of brand communities, explain how they should be managed, and identify circumstances in which official brand communities are appropriate for providing memorable customer experiences. As our empirical research findings imply, mutual member support and brand–member interactions are the two dominant drivers of unforgettable brand community experiences. Overall, nine drivers can be measured, evaluated, and combined into the brand community quality (BCQ) construct.

Specifically, we will define and classify brand community experiences; propose a management concept for brand community experiences; provide a scheme for brand community suitability evaluations; introduce the construct of brand community quality (BCQ); and name the influential factors for brand community quality.

Brand Experience "Drivers"

On 7 July 2007, a seemingly endless convoy with more than 170 luxury cars was cruising on a German autobahn. Out of respect, other cars exited the fast lane and made way

* Fabian von Loewenfeld, UAE. E-mail: loewenfeld@gmx.de. Telephone: + 971 5065 97811.

† Karsten Kilian, University of St. Gallen, Switzerland. E-mail: kilian@markenlexikon.com. Telephone: + 49 9343 509 031.

for the motorcade. The drivers got a sense of what it must feel like to be a head of state, travelling to an important summit with counterparts from abroad. Once the convoy reached its destination, the proud owners met for lunch and dinner, exchanged anecdotes, and made new friends.[1] The rally was the 2007 highlight of the brand community 7er, a privately initiated brand community of the BMW 7 Series. At the same time, it was a vivid example of a memorable customer experience surrounding a specific brand and its community of fans.

As a starting point, we note that the vast majority of customer experiences take place in two distinct situations: when purchasing and when using a product or service. With respect to the latter, which mostly extends over a longer period of time, brand communities play an essential role in creating exceptional experiences with the brand, such as the BMW 7 Series. In the past decade, brand communities have become increasingly important for the manifestation and development of brand–customer relationships.[2] Whereas previous branding efforts mostly focused on the relationship between the customer and the brand,[3] brand community and tribal marketing research[4] opens a second avenue of relationship building: the interaction among brand-loyal customers and their role in creating memorable customer experiences.

As a key success factor for "sticky" brand experiences, brand communities are the main focus of this chapter. We first define and classify brand communities as means for creating memorable customer experiences. Next, we propose a framework for brand community management and introduce brand community quality (BCQ), a construct that can help managers plan, implement, and control platforms for generating loyalty-enhancing brand community experiences.

Brand Community Experiences

Brand communities bring together brand fans and help them share their thoughts and feelings about the brand, as well as experience the pleasures derived from interpersonal brand activities. By doing so, brand communities address the fundamental human need to belong to a group of individuals – the tribal or animal herd instinct. As Earls frankly puts it, "Man is a social animal."[5] In accordance with this statement, interactions among participants, such as when they watch a commercial or evaluate a drink, increase the enjoyment of the experience when others display similar reactions.[6] When people express similar opinions and display analogous behaviour, they may reflect a brand community. Brand communities as a whole also influence the perceptions and actions of their members persistently and broadly,[7] enhance the rapid dissemination of information,[8] and boost evaluations of new offerings and competitive actions.[9] Finally, brand communities provide a vast range of opportunities to engage and collaborate with loyal brand customers.[10] They provide the nucleus of what Holbrook and Hirschman call the "experiential view" of consumption, because they provide an ideal platform for "a steady flow of fantasies, feelings, and fun".[11] They also offer a hedonic consumption environment that enables the "multisensory, fantasy, and emotive aspects of product usage experience".[12] Altogether, the characteristics of brand communities provide and enhance memorable customer experiences with branded products or services.

The role model for joint customer–brand experiences is H.O.G., the Harley Owners' Group.[13] Since its formation in 1983, H.O.G. has become the largest official brand community in the world, with more than 1 million members, each of whom pays up to US$45 as an annual fee. In exchange, members receive pins, patches, and the H.O.G. magazine. They also become part of "much more than just a motorcycle organization. It's one million people around the world united by a common passion: making the Harley-Davidson dream a way of life."[14] Many companies have attempted to mimic Harley-Davidson, mostly on a smaller scale, and achieved similar success when measured in terms of their brand community targets, such as the PlayStation community of Sony, the beer club of Krombacher, and "the driver's club for transport professionals" of MAN. As Algesheimer, Dholakia, and Herrmann point out, "brand communities offer a fresh, effective, and viral approach to building brands in the present-day, unresponsive marketing environment".[15]

According to Muniz and O'Guinn, a brand community is "a specialized, non-geographically bound community, based on a structured set of social relationships among admirers of the brand".[16] The relationships are based on a shared consciousness, expressed through rituals and traditions, as well as a sense of moral responsibility to members. McAlexander, Schouten, and Koenig also consider a brand community "a fabric of relationships in which the customer is situated".[17] They note four key relationship dimensions for memorable customer experiences: between the customer and the brand, with the firm, with the product in use, and among fellow customers. As we will see, the first and the last relationship dimensions exert especially significant impacts on the quality of the community experience.

Brand Community Types

As a prerequisite for establishing and managing brand communities, it is important to understand the different community types in the marketplace. In general, we can differentiate nine types of brand communities, classified according to the type of their existence or media usage (offline or online) and with respect to their status or orientation (unofficial or official). Unofficial brand initiatives can be traced back to private initiatives, usually through a strong positive or negative connection to a certain brand, whereas official brand communities are initiated and run by the company.

Figure 5.1 provides an example of each brand community type. Starbucks Gossip monitors "America's favourite drug dealer" solely online, but the unofficial fan clubs of the German soccer club Bayern Munich meet regularly in person at soccer matches. Whereas Microsuck is representative of the anti-Microsoft movement, which currently consists of more than 160 websites and two-dozen usenet groups,[18] the Star Wars Union is a private Star Wars brand community that exists alongside the official Star Wars fan club set up by Lucasfilm.

The vast majority of brand communities are unofficial in nature, mostly privately founded by people who are either fans or haters of the brand. With the emergence and growth of user-generated content published on weblogs, forums, and user groups, brand community management has become of even greater importance to companies seeking to connect customer experiences with their brands.

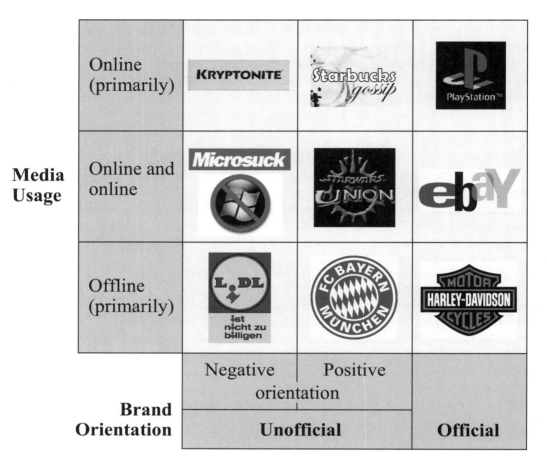

Figure 5.1   Classification of different types of brand communities

Brand Community Management

The challenge for brand managers thus is twofold. On the one hand, companies must specify how existing, unofficial brand communities should be handled, such as whether to monitor them. On the other hand, companies must decide whether to establish an official brand community. Both approaches can be complementary, but whereas the second approach is voluntary, the first one is not – at least when unofficial brand communities exist. In this case, it would be negligent of brand companies not to respond to, or possibly anticipate, negative developments within these communities and beyond, whether in the form of product complaints or harsh criticism of brand behaviour. Figure 5.2 summarises the different complementary options in brand community management.

MONITOR AND/OR COOPERATE WITH BRAND COMMUNITIES

As a starting point, mechanisms to detect brand communities can be established and implemented. Thus, some unofficial communities might be identified and segmented

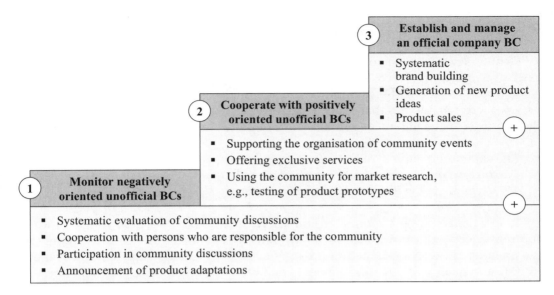

Figure 5.2   **Options in brand community (BC) management**

according to the preceding classification. Alternative courses of action then can be defined on the basis of regular monitoring of the identified communities and the discussions and events taking place there. This step might lead, for example, to initiating contact with the people in charge of the unofficial brand communities, and possibly even to participation in their community activities such as ongoing forum discussions. After contact is established and a relationship developed, the next attempts should establish cooperation agreements with one or several brand communities that are positively attuned toward the brand and the intensification of the relationship over time. To achieve this objective, the company might try to build trust, perhaps with preview announcements of product adjustments and new product releases, which communicate the community's importance to the brand. Another option is to provide support to unofficial brand communities by organising community events. In addition, exclusive product and service offerings for community members should be considered at this stage, while the brand gains access to the product and service knowledge of the community members for market research (e.g., analysing community discussions, providing selected members with prototypes for testing).

The different activities undertaken to build a relationship with unofficial brand communities adds to the customer experience of the members who are part of that community. Although monitoring and cooperating with unofficial brand communities might be sufficient for some companies, it might not be enough for others, for three reasons. First, there might not be an unofficial brand community in existence. Second, existing brand communities might not be accessible, perhaps because they want to stay independent. Third, the company might not be satisfied with community cooperation. It might instead see a potential for brand experience and loyalty and therefore prefer not just to influence but to fully control a community organised around its brand. In these three cases, the company should consider a third option of brand community management: establishing its own official brand community.

RESEARCHING BRAND COMMUNITIES

To identify key success factors for establishing brand communities, we conducted two extensive online surveys, covering both official and unofficial brand communities, which contain roughly 70 brand-community related questions. Of the questions, 46 derive from previous research findings that relate to nine brand community constructs. For example, the construct "need fulfilment within the community" uses the following three items:

- The community entirely matches my expectations.
- The matters of the community exactly meet my interests.
- My needs are being fulfilled by the community.

Respondents answer the questions on a seven-point Likert scale, on which 1 means "do not agree at all" and 7 means "totally agree". To compare the construct findings, the questionnaires also include two broad questions that directly measure the strength (BCQ1) and quality (BCQ2) of the brand community in question, again using a seven-point Likert scale:

- Overall, I would classify the strength of the community around brand XY as high.
- Overall, I regard the quality of the brand community around brand XY as high.

To represent official brand communities, we selected the German Sony PlayStation online community. More than 3,000 respondents completed the online survey, of whom 966 were members of the community and 2,084 were non-members. Almost 90 per cent of the respondents were men, which is not surprising given the type of product. The average age was 20.8 years for members and 21.5 for non-members. After applying several consistency checks, we retained 863 community members and 1,513 non-community members for further analyses. To investigate unofficial brand communities, we selected members of five car communities: three BMW, a Mercedes-Benz, and a Skoda community. Overall, 371 respondents to this survey passed all consistency checks and thus appear in the analysis. The proportion of men, at more than 90 per cent, is similar to that in the official PlayStation brand community sample, but the average age of 31.9 years is significantly higher.

During the analysis, an exploratory factor analysis first revealed that three of the nine constructs loaded on two factors. Therefore, we deleted five items from the two constructs and split the construct "friendship and support" into two constructs. The confirmatory factor analysis led us to delete six additional items for which the indicator reliability was less than 0.50. Finally, non-weighted averages of the 10 identified factors indicated three brand-community quality dimensions: customer–brand relationship, customer–customer relationship, and customer–community relationship. Structural equation modelling (LISREL and partial least squares (PLS)) showed an insignificant regression parameter for customer–customer interaction, so we removed it from further analyses. This finding first came as a surprise, because we considered interaction among members a key element of brand communities. However, this kind of interaction tends to be reflected in other factors, such as friendship and support. Moreover, interaction among customers usually is not an aim in itself; rather, it is a means to accomplish higher-rank goals, such as resolving problems.

As a result of our analysis, we reduced the initial set of 46 German-language items to 30 (see the translations in the Appendix, pp. 97–98). We also removed one factor and split another factor. Figure 5.3 reveals the PLS path coefficients for both official and unofficial brand communities. Overall, the results are consistent across both types of communities. The three brand community dimensions and nine factors provide effective guidance for establishing a company-led brand community.

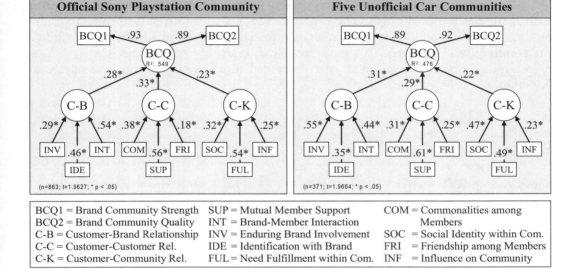

BCQ1 = Brand Community Strength	SUP = Mutual Member Support	COM = Commonalities among
BCQ2 = Brand Community Quality	INT = Brand-Member Interaction	Members
C-B = Customer-Brand Relationship	INV = Enduring Brand Involvement	SOC = Social Identity within Com.
C-C = Customer-Customer Rel.	IDE = Identification with Brand	FRI = Friendship among Members
C-K = Customer-Community Rel.	FUL = Need Fulfillment within Com.	INF = Influence on Community

Figure 5.3   Structural equation models for both brand community types

ESTABLISH AND MANAGE A COMPANY BRAND COMMUNITY

Before establishing a company-run brand community, a firm needs to examine the suitability of the brand for a brand-centred community. Five questions provide guidance:[19]

1. Can the brand arouse enduring interest among customers?
2. Does the brand play an important role in customers' everyday lives?
3. Do customers identify with the brand?
4. Does the brand appeal emotionally to customers?
5. Does the brand provide an appropriate frame or theme for entertainment and further interactive activities?

To establish a successful official brand community, ideally the firm can answer all five questions with a clear "yes", indicating long-lasting customer interest, because the brand plays an important role in everyday life and provides identification, emotional appeal, and a frame or theme for entertainment and joint activities to customers. The PlayStation community, for example, fulfils all these requirements. Computer game players tend to be highly involved, spending hours playing their preferred games over long periods of time, as our PlayStation online survey reveals. Furthermore, they strongly identify with "their" console and thus their brand (e.g., not Microsoft's Xbox or Nintendo's Wii). The PlayStation console per se is an entertainment device that allows customers to play games together off- and online. Thus, PlayStation enables players to engage in memorable joint experiences and provides an ideal platform for a brand community.

However, most cases cannot meet all these requirements, at least initially, as an evaluation of five brands by a group of community experts reveals. As a minimum, several questions provoke a "weak" yes, as the overall evaluation for Ryanair in Figure 5.4 indicates. In the case of Eon, the German utility giant, on four of the five questions, the scoring implies minimal or no suitability. Nevertheless, Eon moved forth with its "Ich-bin-on" community ("I am on"). Despite vast media coverage and advertising spending, the community closed two years later because of declining access rates. Only when a minimum level of all five questions can be reached should a more thorough analysis be undertaken.

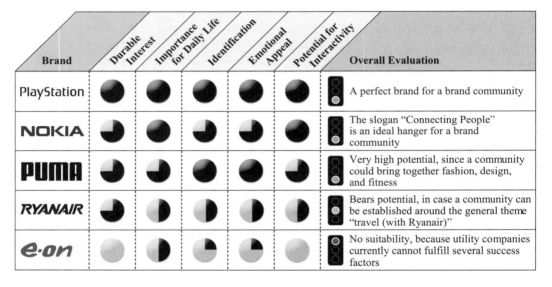

Figure 5.4   Brand community suitability evaluation

The next step includes defining targets for the brand community and developing a business model. One option is to focus on transactions with third parties, such as partners advertising on the website, selling merchandise, or appearing as sponsors. In most cases, however, creating additional customer revenue will be attempted through increased brand loyalty, customer acquisition based on word of mouth, or cross- and up-selling.

The third step consists of clarifying brand community success factors. From our two online surveys, we identified nine factors as relevant from the 1,234 participating community members and which we aggregated within the construct "brand community quality". Two factors are of high relevance, five rank at medium levels, and only two are of minor importance. The nine factors and their impact on brand community quality are summarised in Figure 5.5.

The two predominant factors of brand relationship quality, according to our analysis of six brand communities, are mutual support among brand community members and interaction between the brand (i.e., company behind the brand) and the member. Within

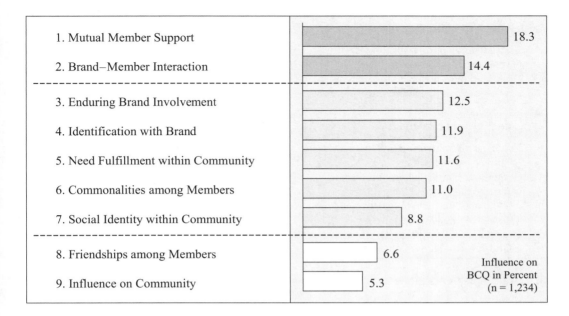

1. Mutual Member Support — 18.3

2. Brand–Member Interaction — 14.4

3. Enduring Brand Involvement — 12.5

4. Identification with Brand — 11.9

5. Need Fulfillment within Community — 11.6

6. Commonalities among Members — 11.0

7. Social Identity within Community — 8.8

8. Friendships among Members — 6.6

9. Influence on Community — 5.3

Influence on BCQ in Percent (n = 1,234)

Figure 5.5   Influencing factors of brand community quality (BCQ)

the Sony PlayStation community, for example, video-gaming enthusiasts exchange their thoughts on new games, provide tips and tricks, and support one another through hardware problems. Similarly, at eBay, members help one another with respect to security questions, setting up auctions, and irregular transaction evaluations. However, interaction per se, for example for entertainment purposes, does not lead to significant experiential value. Only the intended and targeted interaction provides brand community quality and thereby enhances memorable customer experiences. Similarly, brand–member interactions require the company to exhibit honest interest in its members, such as by responding to their requests. In addition to other methods, this goal can be accomplished by offering various feedback options. Figure 5.6 provides examples of possible measures for the six most relevant success factors that we derived from online surveys and interviews with brand community experts.

Fourth, a critical number of members must be reached to appeal to the broad majority of brand customers. In particular, retro marketing,[20] viral marketing,[21] and word-of-mouth marketing, in combination with public relations,[22] can be of great use. According to Gladwell, three relatively small groups of people should be identified to reach the brand community tipping point: connectors, mavens, and salespeople.[23] Connectors are brand fans with a vast social network and "a special gift for bringing the world together".[24] In their networking roles, connectors manage to occupy many different subcultures and niches, providing "social adhesive" among them. Connectors thus are people specialists, whereas mavens are information specialists. They accumulate vast amounts of knowledge about different brands. They like – and have the social skills – to help and educate others, not by persuading them but by providing them with relevant information, such as by initiating discussions and responding to requests. In essence, mavens are information brokers, sharing and trading what they know about a brand. Finally, salespeople have the appropriate skills to persuade others by the logic and appropriateness of their arguments.

1. Member – Member Support	4. Identification with Brand
▪ Thematically appropriate forums for purposeful information exchange ▪ Gratification of member support, e.g., via advancement in the community hierarchy	▪ Personal linkage with brand by supporting intense brand usage ▪ Brand personality establishment, e.g., lifestyle or way of living

2. Brand – Member Interaction	5. Need Fulfillment within Community
▪ Feedback alternatives, e.g., e-mail, telephone hotline, etc. ▪ Continuous contact between the brand company and members, e.g., via individually configured newsletters ▪ Member segmentation for better targeting, possibly including the establishment of sub-communities	▪ Broad information provision ▪ Extra offers or services for members, e.g., newsletters or specials } functional needs ▪ Offline events, e.g., regulars' tables, trips, or fun events } individual needs ▪ Online games and entertaining competitions

3. Enduring Brand Involvement	6. Commonalities among Members
▪ Brand differentiation ▪ Interest augmentation, e.g., by displaying new forms of brand usage ▪ Brand integration in the daily life of members, e.g., via offline events	▪ Facilitation of consistent brand perception by establishing a brand personality ▪ Formation of sub-communities based on common interests, e.g., via forums for specific topics or interests

Figure 5.6   Examples of the most relevant BCQ (brand community quality) success factors

This skill gets amplified by their positive thinking, energy, enthusiasm, and charm. With their charisma, salespeople get others involved with a brand; they light the fire, and the brand community keeps it burning!

Finally, activities should be aligned with the most interesting membership groups, which, according to Holt, often encompass less than one-third of the entire community. Two groups that he distinguishes are insiders and followers.[25] They encompass connectors, mavens, and salespeople and form the "inner circle" of brand-loyal customers. Furthermore, they often account for the vast majority of brand community members. Insiders give legitimacy to the brand community; followers function as the brand's magnets. Both groups in turn appeal to feeders, those brand customers who have only a superficial relationship with the brand. Thus, insiders and followers enhance the creation of memorable customer experiences for less-involved customers. Brand community management should focus on the two groups in the inner circle, who not only attract feeders but also initiate trends and provide valuable feedback for product improvements and innovations. In addition, they support the purchase process of new customers and create exit barriers for existing ones.[26]

Figure 5.7 summarises the different steps that we have identified through our literature review, expert interviews, and online surveys. These steps must be undertaken to create brand community management within a company. After the five initial steps for forming a company-run brand community and/or the four steps for monitoring and possible joint operation of unofficial brand communities have been taken, the two subsequent steps should be considered. These latter steps provide brand community management with a permanent foundation for undertaking regular evaluations to measure their impact on the brand. The brand community 7er, introduced at the beginning of this chapter, is an excellent example of a successful brand community. Currently, the brand community members are planning their next rally, which will lead them to Tuscany, Italy. The rally will be another event that brings together and creates memorable customer experiences for fans of the brand.

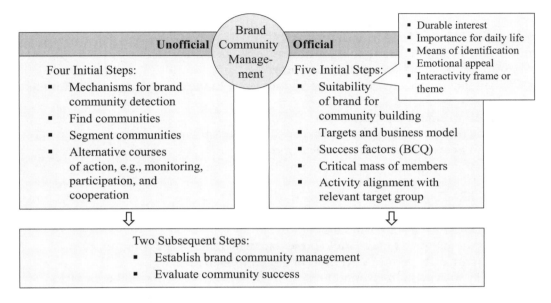

Figure 5.7   Brand community management

Appendix

CUSTOMER–BRAND RELATIONSHIP (C–B)

1. Enduring Brand Involvement (INV)
* Brand ___ is of great interest to me.
* I am always interested in news about brand ___.
* I enjoy keeping myself busy with brand ___.

2. Identification with Brand (IDE)
* I see similarities between my person and what the brand stands for.
* Brand ___ has an image that matches well my self-perception.
* Brand ___ is in line with me.
* I can identify myself with brand ___.

3. Brand–Member Interaction (INT)
* Brand ___ is responsive to my desires.
* Brand ___ is interested in its customers.

CUSTOMER–CUSTOMER RELATIONSHIP (C–C)

4. Commonalities among Members (COM)
- I have plenty in common with other community members.
- The community members have similar interests and needs.
- The community members are usually on the same wavelength.
- I can by and large identify with other community members.

5. Mutual Member Support (SUP)
- I gladly help other community members, as far as I can.
- Community members support each other.
- When looking for advice, I always find someone in the community who helps me.

6. Friendship among Members (FRI)
- In part, other community members are like friends to me.
- I found new friends by joining the community.
- Friendships in the context of the community are important to me.

CUSTOMER–COMMUNITY RELATIONSHIP (C–K)

7. Social Identity within Community (SOC)
- I consider myself a typical and representative member of the community.
- The community confirms my view of myself in many ways.
- I can identify with the community.
- The community raises positive feelings in me.
- I have the feeling of belonging to the community.
- It was a good decision to join the community.

8. Need Fulfilment within Community (FUL)
- The community entirely matches my expectations.
- The topics covered by the community exactly meet my interests.
- My needs are being fulfilled by the community.

9. Influence on Community (INF)
- I can have a share in the organization of the community.
- The individual community member has the opportunity to play a part in the community.

Notes

1. 7-forum.com (2008), available at http://www.7-forum.com (accessed 28 May 2008).
2. Muniz Jr., A.M. and O'Guinn, T.C. (2001), "Brand community", *Journal of Consumer Research*, Vol. 27, March, pp. 412–32.
3. Fournier, S. (1998), "Consumers and their brands: developing relationship theory in consumer research", *Journal of Consumer Research*, Vol. 24, March, pp. 343–73.

4. Cova, B. and Cova, V. (2002), "Tribal marketing: the tribalisation of society and its impact on the conduct of marketing", *European Journal of Marketing*, Vol. 35, No. 5, pp. 595–620.

5. Earls, M. (2003), "Advertising to the herd: how understanding the true nature challenges the ways we think about advertising and market research", *International Journal of Market Research*, Vol. 45, Quarter 3, pp. 311–36, at p. 319.

6. Raghunathan, R. and Corfman, K. (2006), "Is happiness shared doubled and sadness shared halved? Social influence on enjoyment of hedonic experiences", *Journal of Marketing Research*, Vol. 43, August, pp. 386–94.

7. Muniz, A.M. Jr. and Schau, H.J. (2005), "Religiosity in the abandoned Apple Newton brand community", *Journal of Consumer Research*, Vol. 31, No. 4, pp. 737–47.

8. Brown, S., Kozinets, R.V., and Sherry, J.F. Jr. (2003), "Teaching old brands new tricks: retro branding and the revival of brand meaning", *Journal of Marketing*, Vol. 67, July, pp. 19–33.

9. Algesheimer, R., Dholakia, U.M., and Herrmann, A. (2005), "The social influence of brand community: evidence from European car clubs", *Journal of Marketing*, Vol. 69, July, pp. 19–34.

10. Franke, N. & Shah, S.K. (2003), "How communities support innovative activities: an exploration of assistance and sharing among end-users", *Research Policy*, Vol. 32, January, pp. 157–78.

11. Holbrook, M.B. and Hirschman, E.C. (1982), "The experiential aspects of consumption: consumer fantasies, feelings, and fun", *Journal of Consumer Research*, Vol. 9, September, pp. 132–40, at p. 132.

12. Hirschman, E.C. and Holbrook, M.B. (1982), "Hedonic consumption: emerging concepts, methods and propositions", *Journal of Marketing*, Vol. 46, Summer, pp. 92–101, at p. 92.

13. Schouten, J.W. and McAlexander, J.H. (1995), "Subcultures of consumption: an ethnography of new bikers", *Journal of Consumer Research*, Vol. 22, June, pp. 43–61.

14. Harley-Davidson USA (2009), available at http://www.harley-davidson.com/wcm/Content/Pages/HOG/HOG.jsp (accessed 29 January 2009).

15. Algesheimer et al., "The social influence of brand community", p. 32.

16. Muniz & O'Guinn, "Brand community", p. 412.

17. McAlexander, J.H., Schouten, J.W. and Koenig, H.F. (2002), "Building brand community", *Journal of Marketing*, Vol. 66, January, pp. 38–54, at p. 38.

18. See for example, "The Microsoft boycott campaign", available at http://www.msboycott.com.

19. von Loewenfeld, F. (2006). *Brand Communities: Erfolgsfaktoren und ökonomische Relevanz von Markengemeinschaften*, doctoral dissertation, Johannes Gutenberg University Mainz. DUV, Wiesbaden, p. 281.

20. Brown, S. (2001), "Torment your customers (they'll love it)", *Harvard Business Review*, October, pp. 82–8.

21. Langner, S. (2007), *Viral Marketing: Wie Sie Mundpropaganda gezielt auslösen und Gewinn bringend nutzen*, Gabler, Wiesbaden.

22. Ries, A. and Ries, L. (2002), *The Fall of Advertising and the Rise of PR*, HarperCollins, New York.

23. Gladwell, M. (2000), *The Tipping Point: How Little Things Can Make a Big Difference*, Little, Brown, London, pp. 34ff.

24. Ibid., p. 38.

25. Holt, D.B. (2004), *How Brands Become Icons: The Principles of Cultural Marketing*, Harvard Business School Press, Boston, MA, pp. 139ff.

26. McAlexander et al., "Building brand community", p. 50.

6 Orchestrating the Experience: Authorship of the Soul. The Case of Mag Nation Melbourne

MICHAEL J. HEALY,* MICHAEL B. BEVERLAND,† AND
HARMEN OPPEWAL‡

Keywords

experience, retail, brand, sacred, soul, authorship, attachment, co-creation, ethnography

Abstract

Experiences consist of sacred meaning. They are holistic phenomena that shape who we are at an emotional, psychological, and cognitive level. Capitalising on this concept, retailers have adopted experiential designs, providing larger-than-life spectacles to build identity and presence for their brands. However, it is clear that "spectacle" alone may not be enough to sustain the authenticity of the brand; moments only become experiences if they hold lifelong meaning. For this reason, we turn our attention to Mag Nation – a new breed of small-scale experience stores, where adoption of the brand occurs at an intimate level. Using ethnographic research techniques, this chapter highlights the implications of sacred meaning found within the experience; the ability of authorship to empower brand attachment; and why providing a platform that nurtures lifestyle meaning is beneficial for the brand.

*   Michael J. Healy, Department of Management and Marketing, 4th Floor Alan Gilbert Building, 161 Barry St., The University of Melbourne, Parkville, Victoria 3010, Australia. E-mail: m.healy4@pgrad.unimelb.edu.au. Telephone: + 61 412 378 461.

†   Professor Michael B. Beverland, School of Economics, Finance and Marketing, Royal Melbourne Insititue of Technology University, GPO Box 2476V, Melbourne, Victoria 3001, Australia. E-mail: michael.beverland@rmit.edu.au. Telephone: + 61 416 102 492.

‡   Harmen Oppewal, Department of Marketing, Monash University, P.O. Box 197, Caulfield East, Victoria, 3145 Australia. E-mail: harmen.oppewal@buseco.monash.edu.au. Telephone: + 61 3 990 32360.

Introduction

"Everything in this store can be touched, felt, and browsed ... except for our staff!"

Experiential encounters are sacred. They are designed to inspire our imaginations through a holistic measure of tactile, sensory, and interactive cues for us as actors to play within. The retail experience is an exploration of ourselves, who we are, and what we wish to become.[1] Yet as popular as experiential marketing tools have become, their benefit remains uncertain, and the question of how these "big ideas" work has been left unresolved.[2] Although the experience has been thrust upon the podium of the flagship store, marketers are left with the challenge of translating their experiential concept into smaller retail spaces.

To address this challenge, we turn our attention to analysing a magazine lifestyle retail chain, Mag Nation. Mag Nation is presenting a new breed of small-scale experiential stores in Australia and New Zealand that have had an impact far greater than was expected, given the stores' small physical size compared with the large-scale shock-and-awe of American stores such as Prada, ESPN Zone, and Niketown. While creating experiential stores that are physically "larger than life" has been an assumed requirement to create interest and brand attachment,[3] it now appears important to reassess this belief. Is an experience merely about physical grandeur, or is it about nourishing the "sacred" places of the customer's lifestyle? Physical greatness is one end of the experiential equation, but are lavish spectacles enough to sustain customers' day-to-day nourishment? Experiential retailers often emphasise creating iconic events, whereas the focal retailer provides elevated forms of customer engagement by scripting meaning through permission and authorship – permission to engage with the total product, and authorship in correspondence with the customers' lifestyle desires.

Mag Nation is not a physical giant of established trends, nor is it a retail box for housing merchandise. Mag Nation is, however, a living "soul" for people to express their sacred desires within and embellish their escapist tendencies. Customers place themselves on display, lounge about in their own pseudo-private spaces, interact with neighbouring enthusiasts, and escape into seclusion provided by various nooks and crannies for hours on end. Customers do not pay to read; they pay to escape into a fantasyland of the mind, one where the price of admission is a contribution to the sacred rather than the traditional pressures of the service exchange.[4]

About Mag Nation

Mag Nation Melbourne, one in a series of five stores located in Australia and New Zealand, opened its doors in March 2006. Mag Nation stocks approximately 4,000 magazines sourced from around the world, focusing on specialist magazines and high-end niche journals ranging in price from A$10 to A$190. Celebrating the quality of their core product, the proprietors Sahil Merchant, Ravi Pathare, and Suchita Pathare have fashioned a two-level, art deco lifestyle space that shifts away from the tired conventions of detached retail settings. Mag Nation focuses on creating an experience that entices people to stay and linger for as long as they desire and to use their store as a place for self-creation. In principle, the permission to engage provides customers with an empowering sense of freedom and control, which makes Mag Nation a relevant brand for day-to-day interaction. The goal is not merely to wow customers in the short-term but to provide them with a meaningful level of intimacy that nourishes who they are and who they want to become.

Customers embrace Mag Nation's sense of empowerment, frequently articulating concepts of personal escapism that lead to alterations in their motivations for habitual spending behaviours, in which payment for consumption is merely the beginning of the relationship. Informants frequently describe their time at Mag Nation as "a fantasyland!" and an environment where there is "no pressure put on you to buy", while echoing feelings of attachment with variations of "I would probably spend the whole day if I had the time!" and "It made me feel like I could stay there. I just want to sit here!" inside what the informants often describe as "little places to withdraw away from the rest of the world". We found that it was common for shoppers to show an increased willingness to spend more time (45–90 minutes) than they normally would in the course of their historic retail behaviour when selecting and buying a magazine (10–15 minutes). Informants stated that a key characteristic of this change was an increased sense of "freedom" that enabled them to forgo their usual utilitarian behaviour.

Methodology

The ethnographic investigation took place inside Mag Nation between August 2007 and January 2008, allowing the researchers to absorb the natural events of the store using participant observations.[5] We experienced the events of the retail environment firsthand, while reflecting on our own thoughts and feelings as they occurred. In the context of our retail study, we focused on the store as the central link to triangulate the "truthfulness" between what our informants discuss and what we observed in the retail environment.[6] A collection of 20 in-depth interviews, of 45–60 minutes in length, took place at the informants' homes shortly after they had visited the store. Interviews were in-depth, with a short list of prompts and topics. What follows is a composite account of the experience based on photographic evidence, in-store conversations, and in-depth interviews.

Deconstructing the Experience

Mag Nation does not tell its customers that they need to buy; the company shows them why they should, leaving customers the freedom to make up their own minds. As a kind of club for magazine lovers, this breed of small-scale lifestyle store shows customers that consumption need not be a laborious affair and provides them with a place for playful indulgence. As we talked with informants about their activities inside the store, we received several analogies comparing the store to a place of personal worth rather than a mere retail store, such as:

> It was almost like a library – it was fun! The way the place was set up ... it wanted people to be! Just stay there, rather than come in, get what you need, and leave. I was only meant to be there for thirty minutes, yet I stayed for an hour and a half!

The majority of informants stated, nearly verbatim, that Mag Nation felt more like a "cool library", where time had no meaning as they ventured deeper into their "own little world". In addition, informants made special mention of a change in their spending behaviour, such that purchasing a product felt more like a side effect of their elevation. As one informant stated:

> It's because you're not necessarily handing over cash, so you're not thinking about "how much am I going to spend", and you're not just getting your purchase and going – it's like you're giving yourself a bit of a time out! You just step in there and there's nice music playing and you just go into your own fantasy world! I think they are creating an inner-sanctum group sort of feel. Like you're a part of the club! I always feel like I have to give them some money for their service. Not because I have to, but I feel I owe it to them ... I feel compelled to give something back.

Purchasing is a response to customers' clear sense of elevation towards their lifestyle goals. The first step in the process is feeling empowered by reduced sales pressures:

> You were warmed to browsing and they had, like, little cubicles and chairs, and stools, and whatever around. So it just felt like a nice environment to have a look around in. ... I felt like I was there to look around rather than just to buy! It was different to what I expected. It made me want to go in more. I will go back. ... I didn't expect it at all to be like that, nothing like that!

This informant illustrates how elevation from the service exchange favourably altered the perceptions of the retailer's brand. Mag Nation nurtures feelings of belonging and emotional enrichment, through a context of static and dynamic elements, which provide permissive aids and benchmarks for behaviour. To elaborate, static elements are "the cold, hard, tangible features of the store that facilitate the functional characteristics of the product(s), and the sensual and psychological benefits that emanate from the store's hard design features".[7] The static elements contribute to the sensory pleasures (the aesthetic), which are messages communicated to the customer to convey feelings of identity. These elements contribute to the physical "larger-than-life" epic that is characteristic of many existing experiential retailers.

However, these elements require balancing of the dynamic, "living narrative", that accounts for the human/warm/soft emotions that the store generates through intimate interactions with the customer–staff–store interface. Together, static and dynamic elements function as a holistic mechanism, driving the customer retail experience and creating sensations of flow among the various physical and psychological touch points of the store.[8] The activity enables the customer to become empowered and gain permission to move between areas of "role adoption" inside the store. In turn, customers shift from merely appreciating the physical evidence of the retail environment to feeling as if they belong to a space that is representative of their own ideals and behaviours and perceiving the place as helping them realise their private desires. Kozinets and colleagues[9] illustrate the necessity for symbiosis within the experiential retail design, because the personal interaction of customers allows them to adopt deeper levels of immersion within their fantasy roles. The result of this immersion is a context that guides the behaviours of customers like a conductor directs a musical ensemble – a subtle management of the lifestyle performance. Power and authority to play settles directly on the actors of the show, such that the core brand message becomes reinforced and provides customers with the ability to gain a sense of possession over their retail performance.

A parallel theme to this role-playing dynamic is the ability of the experiential platform to elevate the values of the brand. The sacredness of Mag Nation becomes attached to lifestyle meaning.[10] Leveraging the static and dynamic characteristic of the store, Mag Nation attains depth and breadth that customers can vocalise, consume, and identify with; the brand becomes a possession that exists in the physical, emotional, and psychological domain.[11] The authorship of the experience and the guided yet unbridled creation of the final product gives the consumption offering a personal relevancy, tied closely to the lifestyle behaviours of customers. In other words, the experience elevates the customer–brand relationship to one with greater symbiosis with customers' thoughts, feelings, and attitudes towards the brand.

By deconstructing these facets of the experiential design, this chapter provides insights into the workings of the experiential platform. By understanding the experiential impact from a contextual point of view, it is possible to show how the integration of static and dynamic elements facilitates customer authorship, which can be used to defuse the barriers associated with brand attachment.

Inside Mag Nation

Considering the space limitation, this ethnography is limited to describing select areas of the store, its touch points, and the activities deemed most memorable. The phenomena are discussed in sequential fashion, similar to the researchers' initial walkthrough of the store.

THE GROUND FLOOR

The knockout ring of an aged Melbourne tram echoes across the city sidewalk, resonating its way inside the store's entrance. It is a familiar sound heard throughout the streets of the city and evokes feelings common with the working week. Muting the sound of such occupational reminders, the distinct aroma of freshly poured coffee makes its way to our olfactory senses. Warm and soothing, the smell is pleasantly eclipsed by the familiar sounds of an epicurean latte culture. Upon first glance, we are greeted with an overload of signage – a collection of unified posters parade by with brightly coloured, yellow clocks beaming with smiling faces, telling entrants to "Take your time browsing. Don't worry, be happy!" Farther along, another sign reads, "Everything at Mag Nation can be touched felt and browsed … except for our staff." The sign conveys a provocative choice of words, certainly a little cheeky, and it tickles our funny bone while priming us for the unorthodox activities of the store. Additional memes catch our attention, such as the painted shadow of a figure reading a magazine, rising up from an oversized coffee cup. The image is slightly elongated and deceptive, as if its shadow is being cast from across the room. Two women sit below the shadowy figure, one looking out onto the city sidewalk while the other sits tucked in towards the wall. The store front is narrow, measuring approximately 15 feet across, but the internal, maze-like structure of Mag Nation heightens the illusion of depth with a winding collection of hideaway spaces.

Figure 6.1   A display from the ground floor

Continuing on from the shadowy figure is a high wall of magazines announcing the core product of the store: its own promotional editorial (Figure 6.1). Clean, neat, and decoratively positioned, the magazines are proudly displayed with poise and respect. A top-20 collection titled "Our Favourites" brands the opening showcase, with the latest niche collections: pop-fashion titles like *Curvy*, *Dumbo Feather*, *pass it on*, *Frankie*, and *Semi Permanent*. The covers of these magazines sell themselves with highly artistic renderings, adding their own unique texture to the wall space. They evoke feelings of individuality, intelligence, and inspiration; they are as much an assortment of light conversational aids as they are a collection of artefacts for the alternative trendsetter. There is a line of shoppers weaving their hands across the displays, often with a partner or friend. The magazines become a focal point for discussion, centrepieces for the journalese connoisseur.

Merchandise: buying a ticket to the show

Linda and Tom marvel at the magazine display at Mag Nation's entrance. Linda is dressed in a delicate white lace top, flowing over a solid white, bib-front cami, with a pair of thin black suspenders looping over her shoulders. The strap of a cushiony black handbag strikes a diagonal line across her upper body, meeting at her right hip. She leans slightly over to counter its weight, while playing with a set of dog tags hanging down around her neck. Her motion is quite lively, using her arms and fingertips to articulate the structure of every dialogued sentence. In contrast, the young man remains relatively silent, standing vertical and still, while gazing directly out upon the magazines in front of him. Tom is wrapped in a dark autumn jumper, dignified by a well-knotted emerald scarf. As Linda talks to Tom, almost contouring around his physical stature, he picks up a copy of *Ad!dict*. Linda leans in to watch Tom flick through the pages. "There are so many photos in here, there's barely any ads", Tom remarks. "Yeah it's really lovely", Linda agrees. The young couple pour over the pages, critiquing the photos canvassed within. "Shall I buy it?" Tom asks. "Oh yeah! Sure-sure! It looks fantastic." Linda moves back and forth for perspective. Her index finger circles around her right cheekbone, landing finally upon the corner of her mouth. She glances down at the rest of the magazines, while echoing back to Tom, "Do you want to buy it?" Tom's eyes return to the display. Locked in thought, he instinctively fans through the pages with his left thumb and forefinger, measuring his decision with tactile appreciation. Tom remarks, "Yeah, but it's fairly expensive", referring to the A$45 price tag. "But they are such ... passionate magazines", Linda replies. "They're absolutely beautiful!" Tom agrees and holds onto the magazine while wandering with Linda into the heart of the store.

In this vignette, Tom and Linda have found their "ticket to the show"; however, its price causes some hesitation. Bridging the gap between product search and decision making, the store permits Tom and Linda to familiarise themselves with the brand across every moment of their in-store journey; by defusing the pressures of the sale, the store gives customers time to identify with the product while overcoming their price sensitivity. Customers want to buy, but they require permission to do so; they find permission in a value that exceeds price. For many shoppers, the propensity to buy is increased by the store providing sacred meaning. In the following vignette, this sacred meaning involves the ability to belong to a group, attain a social presence, and become an actor within the lifestyle performance.

The experiential art of consumption

"Do you want this one?" Jane asks John, her hand stretched out across the table, extending her gaze from beneath a signature paper-doll crop, jet black in tone. Gingerly swirling a cup of coffee in his right hand, the young man accepts, and the two begin to browse through the pages of a magazine with brisk pace. "Oh, you should see this! These shoes are just like the ones Vanessa had last week", John declares. "Oh, really! I've wanted some of those for ages. You know I can't find any!" Jane replies. "I'd be a bit scared asking Vanessa...", John pauses for a moment. "These are on sale at the moment!" John holds the magazine out for Jane to view. "They're on sale for about $180, and I was looking at them ... and you know what?" "You get suckered in!" Jane replies with a bright shrill of laughter.

At this moment a third member of the group, Gemma, enters the discussion. "I just went to see if I could find the mag, but it was a dead loss. I couldn't recall the details of the cover." "It's probably lost somewhere in your bag!" Jane teases. Gemma looks up from a flaming red fringe, rolls her eyes, and snatches Jane's coffee cup before taking a deep drink, restoring balance to her misfortune. The three friends rummage through a collection of magazines using them for rest and reflection between bouts of conversation. Jane begins to nod and sway her head to the store's music, as it pipes over the conversations of neighbouring shoppers. The three friends continue to chat about topics of fashion and people sharing their social circle, while passing magazines to one another. The magazines seem to serve as a comfortable distraction from the pressing issues waiting for them back at the office. "I haven't progressed with my project all that much", Jane tells the group. "Yeah, I need to jump at some new ideas, too", John adds. "But, like, your ideas are taken and become popular", Jane remarks. "Yeah, but don't worry about that, just chuck anything you like into it and you can make it into a decent portfolio. Hey, do you think he looks too old wearing that?" John redirects the group's attention to another shopper. Gemma and Jane gaze up from their magazines and look in the direction of John's example. "No, of course not!" Gemma exclaims. Jane adds, "Daniel looks good in one of those. Have you seen him wear a vest?" "Yeah, I have, he looks really good. I'm just not sure how I'd look in one. I've had my eye on one, but they always seem to be too short, just way too short." John pauses and traces the movement of the shopper as if to imagine his own appearance.

After continued discussion, Jane announces that she is ready to move. "OK, shall we move this party back to the office?" "Yeah-yeah", John murmurs from a thoughtful gaze. Gemma laughs at his behaviour and provides him with a gentle jolt from her elbow. The three friends slowly rise from their seated positions. John pulls from under the table a Mag Nation shopping bag containing many magazines. Jane also grasps her own Mag Nation shopping bag but unsuccessfully tries to hoist it over her shoulder before it swings back down to her side with a thud. Rearranging their collection of emptied cups into a neat daisy chain, the three friends continue to chat as they leave the store.

For the three friends in this example, purchasing magazines was the beginning of their experience, followed by lengthy social exploration of other merchandise. The time spent after the transaction served as a platform for familiarising themselves with additional products for their next purchase event. Consumption becomes a lifestyle performance, defusing the pressures associated with pressured exchange.

Figure 6.2   Ground floor coffee bar

THE COFFEE BAR: DEFUSING THE SIDEWALK RUSH

Adjacent to the store's entrance is the coffee bar that doubles as a sales register (Figure 6.2). "One small latte!" an inviting voice calls out from behind a dark-wood counter. A large gleaming sign with the name "Mag Nation" beams out, swirling and rippling at random intervals. Everything at the bar is arranged in repetitive unison: jars filled with biscuits, juice bottles lined up like toy soldiers, and magazine covers framed in chromed steel. The back wall of the bar acts like a storyboard. Upon it are the writings of a mad poet in traditional script. Hanging from within an elevated mezzanine, a chandelier illuminates the bar with a warm glow. The coffee bar is a crucial introductory touch point for the store, readjusting the behaviour of the customer from the frenetic pace of the outside world to the exploratory brandscape of the store. The bar helps shoppers shift gears and warm their senses through the familiar comforts of the beverages it sells. In some ways coffee serves as an archetypal totem, reflecting the emotional comforts provided by the store. It is a moment of pause and introduction – a breath of new beginning.

THE ALCOVE: WATCHING ME, WATCHING YOU

Part hideaway, part podium for the social butterfly, the alcove consists of a plush booth with seating built for two (Figure 6.3). Cropped by pillars at each of its four corners, its back rests against the south wall adjacent to the coffee bar. Its design is reminiscent of a child's playhouse, decorated with stencilled patterns of the letter "M" and delicately highlighted with small red wedges etched along its surface. Its ambience is warm and secure and offers privacy from the buzz echoing throughout the store.

Figure 6.3   The alcove

Intimacy within the public performance

Brooke is seated within the centre of the alcove. Her right leg delicately poised over her left, she balances an open magazine with both hands. The woman is at incredible ease, hugged within the stalwart timbers of her private space. As she absorbs the pages of her magazine, she tips her head up from time to time, peering out upon the interactions of other shoppers. Brooke watches a group of young teenagers sitting in a circle upon the floor, shuffling magazines and discussing the highlights of their social life.

Brooke's partner, John, sneaks up to her. He gently caresses Brooke's head, as if to acknowledge his presence with a warm greeting. Brooke's reverie is distracted; she smiles and shuffles left to allow a space beside her. The couple quietly talk, without looking up from their magazines, nurturing their relationship in quiet intimacy.

Shoppers browsing neighbouring displays glance over at the couple, watching them while they comfort each other with gentle conversation and romantic affection. Customers approach the couple's performance, curiously watching as if glancing into a voyeuristic display of "reality" pop-culture: the couple laugh, joke, prod teasingly, her head resting upon his shoulder, followed by the consolation of quiet embrace. The alcove has become a living feature, displaying a relationship soap opera for other shoppers to absorb and the couple to explore. Their action is intimate but not out of place, and it brings warmth to the surrounding area.

The performance of customers watching one another is common behaviour within Mag Nation. The flow between public and private spaces provides an atmosphere that breaks down inhibitions about interacting in public. The experiential design facilitates the subtle interaction of people belonging to a place where everyone is brought together by a common interest – even something like magazines. Brooke and John are able to withdraw from the outside world while also conducting dual roles of actors within their own interpersonal relationship and spectators of the activities of other shoppers. Similarly, they become the performance for others to watch and cue messages.

OVERCOMING THE FRUSTRATIONS OF BROWSING

The back section of the ground floor displays a collection of magazines in a U-bend along the wall; heavy metal, information technology, games, business, house and living, and wine appreciation categories have their own dedicated displays. There is choice, heaps and heaps of choice. However, an abundance of choice may lead to situations of sensory overload, where too much of anything becomes a burden to process. To defuse potential frustration, Mag Nation gives its customers permission to forage and explore product selections, while simultaneously being able to withdraw, slowing things down as they privately assess their selections. As such, the pressure of the service exchange is eased by providing customers with a sense of authorship over how they go about solving their purchases. Customers have permission to take their time and play with magazines, carry them across the store, take momentary ownership, and empower their sense of control; the experience is possessive rather than reactive. By circumventing the pressures of utilitarian behaviour, shoppers maximise their selection process by spending intimate time with products.

Customers as sales agents: facilitating interpersonal decision-making

Judy and Kate have taken up residence on the floor just beside a mannequin wearing a ballroom gown of magazine covers. There is plenty of room, and comfortable chairs are positioned near their location; however, the two young women enjoy sitting on the floor, effortlessly picking out magazines from a neighbouring display. Sitting face-to-face, the women build a collection of magazines, placing them at their centre before sequentially sorting and discussing each one. Judy hands a magazine to Kate, highlighting the cover with a solidifying pat. Kate begins to flick through the pages, while Judy opens up a second, larger magazine, with an inlay of black and white photos; she flicks through until she finds a set of interesting prints. Eyes fixed, Kate opens the pages wide until the jacket is resting flat against the floor. After several minutes of quiet, Judy offers Kate her magazines: "Check out this one!" Kate gives it a quick glance while Judy assists with an inquisitive glance before both women agree it is not the right one. Kate hands the title back to Judy to be placed on the shelf. Kate, however, seems very pleased with a second magazine and hands it to Judy to place on top of the "keep" pile. They continue this process, whittling their pile down to a select few. "This one's got the latest stuff – the other one really doesn't cover the same style." "Hey yeah, look, we could really use that!" Both women study a final magazine with Judy turning each page. It is decided. Over a period of 30 minutes, the two women have reached an agreement over which magazines to keep for final purchase. The decision is a joint one, constructed of social deliberation and agreeable taste. Judy collects the magazines, and both women proceed to the counter.

The permission granted to shoppers to use the environment as a private space forwards them a sense of authorship over how they choose to spend their time inside the store. During this moment, the shopper takes ownership and gains suitable clarity over the decision process. As stated by an informant:

> The way the magazines are laid out, to have that many titles, it can sometimes be a hard thing to try and sort out. It is good the way Mag Nation has the couches, as it's sort of welcoming, and you feel that you can grab quite a few, sit down, and take your time to relax.

The context of the store is designed to liberate behaviour. The symbiosis between retail store and lifestyle means that shoppers become their own sales agents, finding and qualifying worthy product solutions. The contextual rule of being free to do and touch anything helps shoppers gain a sense of control over the interactive events of the experience, while providing behavioural direction. As expressed by many of our informants, it is common behaviour for customers to "find a stack of magazines and take them with [them]" across the various locations of the store, which adjusts their purchase criteria. It is a flexible and iterative process that allows customers to make decisions on the fly, which are best suited to their shifting goals and moment-to-moment expectations.

TOP FLOOR

Following an ascending set of wide, open stairs with chrome and wire railings, the customers continue to find comforting places, in which they can drift away into their own minds. At the top of the stairs, a long, black, leather, L-shaped couch seats multiple shoppers tucked in like sardines. They are all toting backpacks at their feet and notebook computers propped up on small circular tables. Above them, a bright electronic "Mag Nation" sign transiently ripples. A collage of illustrations and surrealistic characters, constituting a person made from Post-It notes, a large wireframe tower, and unusual patterns, fill the wall behind them; the walls arc in, contouring to the converted loft space. Paper coffee cups with the Mag Nation logo negotiate some of the table space – everyone has a cup within reach. It is the quietest location in the store, but there is plenty of activity going on, with shoppers chatting over instant messaging services and Internet browsing; their eyes are glued to the glow from their notebooks, while the warm tones of Michael Bublé bring warmth to a lack of dialogue. The patrons' electronic fixation is interrupted by the need for more caffeine or by watching the activities of other shoppers. With the addition of soft reflective lighting, the space feels very soothing – a rest stop for the weary looking to zone out for a while in a warm social slumber.

Adjacent to this serene spot is a wide, open-spaced void contained within a continuation of metallic railings that twist around at waist height. This space highlights passage to the floor below, as shoppers gently rest against the railing with their elbows while reading magazines from the displays covering the north and south walls of the room. Shoppers continue to meander up the staircase, gingerly placing a hand along the chrome railing as they survey the ascending servicescape, absorbing the soft ambience while touching the décor with tactile appreciation. They stroll quite leisurely, all the while looking at their surroundings rather than making a beeline to any specific location. A sumptuous red ottoman provides comfort for a couple conversing, slightly reclined on their elbows.

Near the couple's location, a slender return shelf for magazines sits in wait for readers to shed their completed magazines. The shelf is made of wood, varnished in a dark lacquer, and is reminiscent of a child's highchair. Branded into the wooden surface is the pictograph of an open magazine. Every now and then a staff member collects the magazines from the shelf, sorts them, and returns them to their appropriate location. Interestingly, staff are not the only people collecting magazines; shoppers occasionally take interest in the returned collections with a quick rummage:

> When you see the little piles of handled magazines that need to be put back like a library it's almost funny! I sometimes go back to them and look through just to see what other people have been reading, just to get some new ideas.

The room connects with another via a narrow walkway tunnelling its way between the two ends of the top floor's figure-eight design. Within the walkway is a second set of stairs that spirals down towards the ground floor like a secret passage; secluded and hidden, the walls inside are painted with bright orange rectangles with sequentially grouped spouts across a bright yellow wash.

Continuing this theme, the adjoining room displays a bright orange and yellow painting of a Second World War fighter plane. Its livid portrayal is reminiscent of a Mustang screaming across the backdrop of a rich blue sky. Magazine displays are positioned at each of the room's four corners: movies and TV, photography and writing, hobbies and crafts, and travelling. Sections of the walls depress by about a foot; distinguished by a coating of dark red paint, they create the illusion of privacy where there would otherwise be none. Within these spaces, pouffes are arranged, where shoppers sit, perched with their backs hugged by the wall. A young couple sits close together, deep in conversation. At the centre of the room a circular mezzanine drops down to the ground floor, revealing the presence of the coffee bar (Figure 6.4). Echoed sounds from the bar funnel up, articulating the buzz below.

A window along the top room allows natural light to flood in over a long leather couch neighbouring two single-seated armchairs, cushioned and separated by a coffee table. Two sisters sit in each armchair with sizeable pink handbags tucked at their sides. They read editions of *Vogue* while the recording of a South American pan flute plays in the background. They give their magazines considerable attention, only pausing momentarily to make comment to each other about their tastes in fashion and to critique the latest hot

Figure 6.4   Top floor, front end, with mezzanine

gossip. Both women balance several magazines in their laps. Upon finishing a magazine, one of the sisters shows it to the other for comment before swapping it over or placing it upon the adjacent coffee table. A staff member walks past to place some magazines back on the display, her arms completely full. One of the sisters lifts her head to watch her "librarian" performance.

Meanwhile shoppers continue to move around the circumference of the mezzanine's railing. Some pause to lean over, resting their weight upon the hand railing with the glow of a chandelier streaming across their faces. One customer stands on the other side of the room and watches another customer browse through a display. After watching him for a while, he walks over and begins to browse alongside him before selecting a title and taking it back to one of the small seats along the wall. As he sits down, a solo lamplight carves a shaft of soft light upon his magazine, creating a focal point of absorbed concentration. Another shopper intermittently sings the chorus of a song playing in the background, "it's the best you've ever had, the best you've ever had", while humming the unfamiliar sections. The two sisters, engrossed in their magazines, have slipped into a moment of timeless interaction, adjusted to the ambiance around them.

Mag Nation is a living world of discovery and orchestrated existence: a tapestry of physical objects, mood lighting, music, intimate performances, balanced buzz, and flow between public and private spaces. As shoppers engage with various touch points, moving between passive and active roles, the holistic product is reinforced as a lifestyle achievement. Customers can be who they want, can freely interact with one another, explore and try new things, all the while living out their unabridged fantasies. The authorship afforded to them makes Mag Nation's product offering just as much a result of the customer's creation as it is of the retailer's.

Dynamic Cues: Scripting the Behaviour

Critical to the authorship process is the scripting behaviour of the store's actors, which consists of dedicated (staff behaviour) and impromptu (customer behaviour) scripting. Both scripting techniques are used to maintain the core values of the brand, keeping in mind that staff and customers serve as promoters of the brand and have a direct impact on how the experience is perceived.[12] Dedicated scripting consists of the predefined behaviour of staff – the activities they perform to facilitate the experiential platform – which includes defusing barriers between the customer and the experience. In addition, the dedicated script provides the consistency of the value promise introduced by the static design cues. In the case of Mag Nation, staff reinforce the experiential promise by showing customers how to behave. This practice results in customers adopting a collaborative role that promotes empowering freedoms and responsibilities. Staff reinforce the store's core lifestyle message, which replaces the customers' perception of a "hard sell" stigma with an elevated sense of control and ownership.

Inside the store, staff are openly seen sorting magazine shelves, collecting items for return, and physically walking through the store with stacks of magazines hugged to their chests, which all contributes to the performance. Customers are sold levity rather than functional exchange. Shifting the role of staff to facilitators of the experience helps customers feel a sense of responsibility over their own behaviour. As highlighted in the following vignette, Jessica feels encouraged by the staff to stay in the store without being pressured to buy, which adds credibility to her experience. Furthermore, the low-pressure sales approach led to her belief that Mag Nation is an authentic brand, which reinforces the store's lifestyle value.

Staff: icons of the experiential promise

Says Jessica:

> The staff there seem to encourage people to sit and read magazines. They have couches, which are very comfortable, even more so than Borders. Like, at Borders you have to actually get your books and then go into Gloria Jeans, you know, and you do feel when you're going into Gloria Jeans that you have to buy something; whereas at Mag Nation it's a really relaxed, a very relaxed atmosphere. No one sort of says, "what can I get you?" like with Borders, and everyone seems fine with people sitting there. Staff seemed really cool, kind of, you know, pretty coolly dressed. You know, they all looked pretty cool, their look. And like they were friendly, but they weren't [elevates voice and changes demeanour to characterise a forced sales voice] "Hi!" You know? They weren't in your face! They weren't fake or over-the-top, they were just quite subdued, but friendly, which to me is a lot more real. Staff were not even looking up to see the people, you know! So you don't feel like "it's been half an hour, I better buy something, I better get another coffee," or whatever. I definitely didn't feel pressured.

In this example, staff members became a benchmark of behaviour and presentation for Jessica to learn from and clarify the behavioural position of the store. In short, Mag Nation's dedicated script provides a symbiosis between what the store's static elements promise and the values its customers identify as being associated with the brand. In addition, the impromptu scripting of customers is a reaction to the messages communicated from the static elements and dedicated scripting of staff. The result facilitates authorship attained by customers during their time spent within the experience. As identified from the data, authorship is the result of freedom, permission, and control, which allows customers to co-create the marketing effort. Co-creation is a result of the authorship process, which gives a degree of possession over the experience. It becomes a "sacred" part of their lifestyle behaviour, who they are, and what they want to become.

Elevating the Core Values of the Brand

The impact of the experience on the retail brand has remained unexplored, specifically in relation to how experiential strategies add value to a brand and affect the customer interaction with the brand. One of the main benefits identified from our research with Mag Nation is its ability to leverage qualities of "cool" and transfer them to its core product, while elevating consumer perceptions of its merchandise to social admiration and popularity.[13] As further expressed in the following vignette, by selling authorship, Mag Nation increases the relevancy of the products it sells to customers.

Leveraging the experience: overcoming customer inhibitions to engage

Says John:

> I felt like it wasn't embarrassing to be in a place like that. I usually feel uncomfortable at news agencies – I don't spend time there. But I was happy to be here! Like, it had the chrome stuff everywhere and it was very modern and it looked nice. Normally, I just go straight to what I want and leave. I always thought more nerdy people, into like figurines and stuff like that ... that's who I associate magazines with generally. People that are a little geeky. That's just how I see them; except for ... that's why I get them delivered because I don't want to go! However, at Mag Nation I was looking around. I would never look at DVD magazines or anything like that. They weren't even on the way out and I actually walked around the whole top level. So it wasn't like I was just looking for what I wanted, which is what I usually do. I didn't feel embarrassed to be in such a store. Normally I wouldn't want to be seen ... I normally feel awkward being in other types of stores – I wouldn't do it! Just the whole set-up of this store and so many people in there. I didn't feel awkward being at Mag Nation ... and for so long!

Mag Nation is able to create a consistent identity as a place that is cool and authentic, as well as free from the inhibitions associated with judgement of self-expression. Mag Nation's retail experience consistently reinforces the belief that customers exist in an environment that accepts people with a desire to explore private meaning: the sacred places of the soul. As such, the brand is elevated and attains authentic importance because it supports the life-sustaining meanings of its customers.

Conclusions

To complete our discussion and summarise the significance of Mag Nation's experiential platform, we return to the concept of authorship. Mag Nation evokes the multi-faceted environmental dialogue of play between spectators and actors – on display for a crowd of onlookers, enjoying the performance of enthusiasts, escaping into an ocean of popular intellect, embracing the numerous in-store cues that flow and weave across locations of intoxicating buzz and relaxed seclusion, breaking away from the conformities of the service exchange – this type of play empowers customers with control over the performance. Not only is the customer willing to engage with the retailer's brand, but they are elevated to a position in which they achieve personal investment with the ongoing lifestyle maintenance of the brand. Mag Nation gives its actors permission and control over the ongoing performance, as reflected in their adoption of the experiential environment as a place entwined with their lifestyle behaviours.

Mag Nation's experiential platform also provides a set of contextual rules and guidelines for customers to follow, providing its actors with liberty to fulfil their own desires in unconventional yet personally relevant ways. These rules are subtle but decisive enough to provide parameters for the overarching performance. The authorship process ensures that each performance is a self-guided event, specifically tailored to sacred meaning. One of the unique benefits of this platform is the ability to defuse barriers between the customers and their willingness to engage the retail brand. The immediate payoff is that actors become immersed in the brand's narrative as they are inducted through a sequence of meaningful touch points by exploring a greater range of goods and services; the offerings are enriched to a point that they ultimately become lifestyle aids rather than lifeless artefacts.

Staff members facilitate permission, adopting the role of conductor over the retail experience, rather than increasing pressure through the hard sell. They are there to maintain the rhythm of the performance, to set the stage and maintain its execution by setting an example for customers to follow. They circumvent the need for the hard sell by giving customers permission to debate and educate themselves about the merits of products through their collaboration with the experience. The retail environment becomes a possession of the actor. Customer interaction is liberated, no longer pressured by the traditions of the service exchange. The experience places responsibility in the hands of customers as they nurture their creation through interaction. As such, the authorship process establishes ownership well before the event of a monetary exchange occurs. Paying to play is simply a right of passage into the wider playing field of lifestyle enrichment.

Customers buy because the experience contributes to their private identity. The experiential process is not merely a single moment in time but an ongoing relationship in which the store becomes a living place of personal discovery, suited to lifestyle achievement. The store affords the customer an opportunity to express hidden intimacy based on a common core product. By elevating the core product through experiential messages, the product becomes an extension of customers' identity that orchestrates and reinforces their own perceptions. The retail experience does not emphasise money for services; the sale becomes a precursor to a much deeper form of consumption. Authorship and co-creation drive the interpersonal display through a sequence of escapist events, in which the customer gains control and ownership. Customers sell to other customers while also learning from the holistic mix of environmental cues and behaviours.

By cultivating intimate feelings that customers associate with their experiential encounter, Mag Nation illustrates some of the more fundamental principles of the brand at a sacred level. The sale becomes a process of building layered meaning through experiential exchange, to the point that a good or service is not merely the sum of its functional parts but a collection of introspective identities and narratives derived from the retail environment and the customers' co-authored extension of their personal creation. The merchandise thus attains depth and breadth reflective of the experiential context, the narratives of its actors, and the shared meaning of their unique encounter. The experience enables customers to explore their lifestyle dimensions. It is a process of promotion, performance, and learning, as customers nurture their identities through the freedom to create within a place of sacred meaning. The experience needs to engage, but to be sustainable it also must find lifestyle symbiosis by connecting with the sacred.

Notes

1. Schmitt, B. H. (2003), *Customer Experience Management: A Revolutionary Approach to Connecting With Your Customers*, John Wiley & Sons, New York.
2. Sherry, J.F. Jr. (1998), "The soul of the company store: Nike Town Chicago and the emplaced brandscape", in J.F. Sherry, Jr. (ed.), *Servicescapes: The Concept of Place in Contemporary Markets*, NTC Business Books, Lincolnwood, IL, pp. 109–46.
3. Peñaloza, L. (2000), "Consuming people: from political economy to theaters of consumption", *Journal of Marketing*, Vol. 64, No. 1 (Jan.), p. 106.
4. Pine, B. and Gilmore, J. (1999), *The Experience Economy: Work is Theatre and Every Business a Stage*, Harvard Business School Press, Boston, MA.
5. Kozinets, R.V., Sherry, J.F., DeBerry-Spence, B., Dushachek, A., Nuttavuthisit, K., and Storm, D. (2002), "Themed flagship brand stores in the new millennium: theory, practice, and prospects", *Journal of Retailing*, Vol. 78, No. 1, pp. 17–29.
6. Mariampolski, H. (1999), "The power of ethnography", *Journal of the Market Research Society*, Vol. 41, No. 1 (Jan.), pp. 75–86.
7. Healy, M., Beverland, M., Oppewal, H., and Sands, S. (2007), "Understanding retail experiences: The case for ethnography", *International Journal of Market Research*, Vol. 49, No. 6, pp. 751–78, at p. 754.
8. Csikszentmihalyi, M. (1997), *Finding Flow: The Psychology of Engagement with Everyday Life*, Basic Books, New York.
9. Kozinets et al., "Themed flagship brand stores in the new millennium".
10. Belk, R. (1988), "Possessions and the extended self", *Journal of Consumer Research*, Vol. 15, No. 2, p. 139.
11. Vargo, S.L. and Lusch, R.F. (2004), "Evolving to a new dominant logic for marketing", *Journal of Marketing*, Vol. 68, No. 1, pp. 1–17.
12. Schmitt, B.H., Rogers, D.L., and Vrotsos, K. (2004), *There's No Business That's Not Show Business: Marketing in an Experience Culture*, Prentice Hall, Englewood Cliffs, NJ.
13. Keller, K.L. (2003), "Brand synthesis: the multidimensionality of brand knowledge", *Journal of Consumer Research*, Vol. 29, No. 4, pp. 595–600.

Part III
Design of Customer Experiences

7 Balancing Act: The Impact of Rational and Emotional Designs on Memorable Customer Experiences

PETER C. HONEBEIN* AND ROY F. CAMMARANO†

Keywords

customer experience, emotional experience, rational experience, service-dominant logic

Abstract

In this chapter, we explore how customer experience designers must balance emotional customer experiences and rational customer experiences to create customer delight. By blending Pine and Gilmore's experience realms model[1] and the authors' coproduction experience model,[2] this chapter introduces the memorable experience model, which provides the foundation for this balancing act. In this chapter, we will explore the foundations of human experience; review models guiding the design of both emotional and rational experiences; introduce the four types of memorable customer experiences; and discuss the three key principles for good balance.

Introduction

Quick! What do you remember best about your last customer experience? The time you spent? The money you spent or that you saved? Did a store associate help you, or did you

* Peter C. Honebein, Customer Performance Group, LLC, and Adjunct Professor, University of Nevada, Reno and Indiana University. 5450 Wintergreen Lane, Reno, NV 89511, USA. E-mail: peter@honebein.com. Telephone: 775-849-0371.

† Roy F. Cammarano, Customer Performance Group, LLC. 3844 Milan St., San Diego, CA 92017, USA. E-mail: royedg@aol.com. Telephone: 619-993-6939.

have to fend for yourself? Did you accomplish your goal? Or do you remember the joy, surprise, disgust, or even anger of that experience?

These memories reflect two primary and expected responses to any type of human experience: the emotional response and the rational response. Many marketers, experience designers, brand managers, salespeople, and others who are in the business of persuasion for profit consider emotion the predominant force in establishing and maintaining customer relationships. Customers make decisions on the basis of emotion, and then defend those decisions with logic, so involving customers' emotions and intellect are critical to successful customer experiences.

Can customer experiences survive on emotion alone? Our research suggests that organizations must find a balance between the emotional and rational aspects of an experience. This idea receives support from examples culled from nearly 50 fieldwork studies conducted by our staff and students, exploring the balance between emotional and rational elements of an experience.

Starting at Disneyland

Discussions about memorable customer experiences typically start with Disneyland or Disney World – the prototypical examples of an emotional customer experience. But do consumers really look at the Disney experience through anything other than their emotional lens? The fun, the laughter, the rides, the treats! To help set a different stage, join us on a brief tour of the Hollywood Tower Hotel thrill ride.

At first glance, everything about this thrill ride reflects what anyone would consider a thrilling experience. The notion of entering this creepy hotel as a guest, a role that people play with much delight and some trepidation, triggers emotions of curiosity and joy. As the line wanders through the trappings of this old hotel, from the dingy walls, the cobwebs, and the "back of the house" passageways, curiosity begins to transition to fear, as the screams of other guests begin to grow louder and more frequent.

However, right before boarding the "falling elevator" part of the experience, visitors' emotions are interrupted with a rational experience. Groups of 24 "guests" get cued to stand on specific numbers embedded on the floor. When the door of the elevator opens, the number correlates with a numbered seat, and the expectation is clear: Sit in a seat with your number on it.

The emotional aspects of the Hollywood Tower Hotel create a memorable emotional customer experience. After all, we had this experience more than a year ago and still relish telling other people our memories of it whenever we hear someone is going to Disneyland. But without the rational elements of the experience – the numbers on the floor, the seating chart diagram on the wall, and the numbers on the seats that acted as necessary and supportive aspects to help create a *positive* memorable experience of delight – our memories of this experience might have been quite different. Our experience might have been easily replaced with a *negative* memorable experience involving dissatisfaction, dysfunction, or direction.

Similar customer experiences that we have all had make us either happy or sad. As illustrated, Disney has taken a great deal of time and exhibited deliberate purpose to create an experience that is scary yet safe, exciting, and enjoyable. Yet, it also has disguised the logic needed to be an active participant in a way that enhances the experience.

The Roots of Emotions and Rationality

To design memorable customer experiences, a designer must have a good grasp of the science behind emotions and rationality. These two concepts have long been the playground of philosophers, neuroscientists, biologists, psychologists, and even Hollywood. In the original *Star Trek* television series from the 1960s, the character of Mr. Spock was the epitome of rationality and logic. His pure logic and suppression of emotion formed one end of a continuum that was balanced on the other end with Dr. McCoy's emotional antagonism. From these popular culture examples, it is clear that emotions and rationality form the boundaries of human experience. And it is also clear that people's transition from emotional to rational beings has been evolutionary.

Long, long ago, when humans were less evolved creatures, emotions and instinct ruled our lives. Paul MacLean's[3] and Richard Ornstein's[4] ideas related to the brain and consciousness, respectively, introduced us to the neuroscience driving emotions and rationality. Their explanation is relatively simple. The brain has two key parts: the old brain and the new brain. The old brain operates as the centre of emotion. Consisting of the limbic system of the amygdale, hypothalamus, and hippocampus, this part of the brain is thought of as the source of emotion and instinct. Fight or flight, pleasure or pain, the old brain essentially influences what is agreeable or disagreeable. Obviously, in the very best behaviourist sense, people tend to migrate away from pain.

Fortunately, we evolved and so did our brain. The new brain, consisting of the cerebral cortex, controls our thinking and reasoning skills. Speech, math, reading, and problem solving – all the things we do that separate us from apes, dogs, and cats – occur in this part of the brain. Because of this, we humans are often referred to as *information processors*, with numerous theories of economics, consumer behaviour, and learning based on this cognitivist perspective.

This perspective suggests that we are instinctually and even genetically wired for both emotional and rational responses to various kinds of experiences, which may range from the beauty of a mountain vista or the price tag on a pound of pasta. So what is it that we want from these experiences that keeps us coming back for more?

Building on the basic premise of pain and pleasure, Robert Plutchik crafted a classification of primary human emotions.[5] Experiences can trigger positive emotions such as joy; negative emotions such as anger, fear, sadness, and disgust; and relatively neutral emotions like curiosity, surprise, and acceptance. Yet these emotions are not necessarily felt in isolation. In the span of minutes, or even seconds, a customer experience can take a person on an emotional rollercoaster ride, perhaps beginning with curiosity, transitioning into surprise, climaxing with fear, and resulting in joy.

Rational experiences, in contrast, are driven primarily by utility, which reflects the functional usefulness of an experience. For some customers, a visit to Disneyland can easily become an endeavour involving how many times one rides the rollercoaster and the subsequent calculation of the cost per ride, derived from the price of admission. Philosophers argue that rationality must be without emotion, focused on objectivity and logic. Stuart Rachels extends this point to incorporate concepts such as ethics, self-interest, and preference-maximization,[6] which all point to an experience from which customers can achieve what they calculate to be best.

This reasoning all sounds a bit like the paradox of the chicken and egg: Which is more important in a customer experience, the emotional or the rational? The answer may be found in the research that investigates the relationship between learning styles (visual, auditory, and kinaesthetic) and the design of learning experiences. Despite some evidence that humans favour visual representations, good teachers tend not to focus on one style.[7] Rather, they create learning experiences that blend and balance all three styles. The complexity of the human mind, its goals, and its context suggest that a memorable customer experience should blend both emotional and rational features in valuable combination.

Enlightened Eyes

Customers observe and participate in memorable customer experiences every day, whether in the brick-and-mortar walls of the shopping mall, the virtual world of the Web, or direct experience with goods and services. Two primary models enlighten our eyes to see the emotional and rational parts of an experience.

In 1999, Joseph Pine and James Gilmore offered experience designers a lens through which to see and design emotional customer experiences.[8] Using what they label the "experience realms model" (ERM) (Figure 7.1), Pine and Gilmore suggest that superior customer experiences have a well-balanced mixture of entertainment, education, escapism, and esthetics (Pine and Gilmore specifically call this "esthetics"). These qualities represent passive and active customer participation, as well as customer immersion and absorption.

Entertainment includes various passive activities, such as attending a concert, a movie, or even watching television. *Educational* involves the customer learning something,

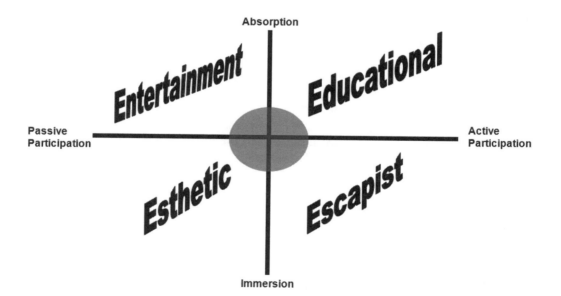

Figure 7.1   Four realms that drive emotional experiences

Source: Adapted from B.J. Pine and J.H. Gilmore (1999), *The Experience Economy*, Harvard Business School Press, Boston, MA, p. 30.

perhaps attending a class on laying tile at Home Depot or reading the instructions on a self-check-in kiosk at the airport. *Esthetic* reflects the nuances within an experience, such as the artwork on the walls of an airport or the aromas that waft from the bakery at the local grocery store. *Escapist* engages customers in an active role, whether as a checkout clerk at the grocery store (in the case of using a self-checkout system) or as a participant in a tricycle race at a local college bar.

Equipped and trained with this lens, an analyst can walk into virtually any customer experience and see it in action. For example, a team of our students used the ERM to investigate the experience of exercise classes. To conduct this fieldwork, members of the team took a boxing class, a kickboxing class, and a yoga class at local gyms. The analysis tool they used developed aspects of entertainment, education, esthetics, and escapism, rated on a 10-point scale.

The team discovered that the entertainment aspect of the exercise class focused on the instructor's personality and performance. The education aspect reflected not only the instructor's teaching ability but also the modeling and coaching provided by other students. The esthetics included such things as music, room temperature, lighting, and mirrors. And escapism reflected the overall level of involvement of the students who embraced certain roles, as captured in a customer quote that the team collected during the boxing class: "When I am in this class, I am no longer Nola Garcia, mother of four, practicing nurse ... but Nola Garcia ... THE BOXER."

What is most interesting about this fieldwork is not the connection of various experience elements to Pine and Gilmore's model but rather the deeper comparison of "violent" (boxing, kickboxing) and "nonviolent" (yoga) forms of exercise and the experience aligned with each. For the violent forms, every aspect of the experience, from the loud music to the instructor's policies (punishing all students if one student did something incorrectly), appeared consistently aligned with that form of exercise. In other words, listening to tranquil, soft music in a space with lavender walls and inhaling the aroma of incense while learning to kick the shit out of someone does not really go together (unless staged in a Quentin Tarantino film). All these consistent cues and clues are there for a purpose – to influence a student's emotions properly so that they are in tune with the skills being learned (i.e., the rational aspect of the experience).

Although the ERM is strong in evoking emotion, it lacks strength in guiding the design of the rational elements of a customer experience. In 2005, we created the coproduction experience model (CEM) (Figure 7.2) to provide a context for understanding and enhancing customer performance.[9] This model evolved from Steve Vargo and Robert Lusch's ideas surrounding the service-dominant logic of marketing,[10] which considers everything offered to customers services. For example, objects we typically consider tangible goods, such as a coffee cup, a computer, or even a car, must be thought of as services. A company can provide the labor to unlock the value these products offer, or customers themselves can provide the labor. In the latter case, the customer becomes a co-creator, or co-producer, of value, and the amount of value customers create correlates strongly with their ability to perform. To enable customer performance, an organization needs to provide a rational customer experience – the CEM.

To ensure customer performance, companies design experiences using the principles of vision, access, incentive, and expertise. *Vision* describes the goals, expectations, and feedback integrated into an experience. *Access* reflects the environment of the experience

Figure 7.2   The four realms of vision, access, incentive, and expertise

and the tools provided to customers, such as a self-service kiosk or silverware. *Incentive* is the motivator that drives the customer to perform in a certain way, whether that incentive is a reward or punishment. *Expertise* is the knowledge and skill customers acquire through specific customer education programs, like a product instruction manual.

Through these factors, companies can ensure that the conditions for customer performance are favorable. For example, when Southwest Airlines implemented its e-commerce strategy – southwest.com – in the mid-1990s, customers were set up for success. With regards to vision, various promotional channels communicated to customers an attractive, novel, achievable goal – book your own tickets. For access, the website itself provided the tool and a simple interface for completing transactions. The incentive to perform was the double Rapid Reward credit, which enabled customers to earn free flights twice as fast. Finally, expertise was provided through step-by-step booking instructions available on the site. By 2008, Southwest Airlines reported that more than 74 percent of its revenue was generated by self-service, online ticketing at southwest.com.[11] The customer conditioning was so successful that Southwest was able to transition the expensive Rapid Rewards incentive into a less expensive "Web Only" ticket price, without negatively affecting the site's revenue percentage.

Just as emotional and rational experiences overlap, so do the ERM and CEM. The most obvious overlap is education and expertise. Both these facets aim to enhance the knowledge and skills of customers. Yet in the ERM, education is seen as something from which a customer derives pleasure, whereas in the CEM, expertise provides the means to accomplish a specific goal.

Recipe for a Memorable Customer Experience

In our work analyzing, designing, and managing customer experiences, it is clear that the design of a customer experience has an impact on the type of memory the customer forms. Our recipe is that a great customer experience occurs when the emotional parts of an experience are memorable, but the rational parts of the experience are not. If the rational parts of the experience are memorable, it usually means a problem with the rational experience – lines are too long, services are not delivered, the staff are surly, and so on.

This framework is the foundation for the memorable experience model in Figure 7.3. From a rational perspective, customer performance may be either hindered or enabled. *Hindered* means that there are barriers in the experience that make it difficult for customers to accomplish goals or tasks. When customers encounter these barriers, that aspect of the experience becomes memorable in a negative way. *Enabled* means that customers accomplish goals and tasks without being impeded by flaws in the experience. If there are no flaws, nothing is really memorable about the rational experience. The customer essentially enters a flow experience in which challenge and ability are well balanced.

From an emotional perspective, an experience may evoke desired or undesired emotions. A *desired* emotion is one that the design of the experience intends to evoke. If an experience is designed to make customers laugh, and they do, then the emotion is evoked. An *undesired* emotion is one that the design of the experience does not intend to evoke or occurs when no emotion gets evoked. Continuing with the same example, if a customer does not laugh or becomes angry, the desired emotion has not been evoked.

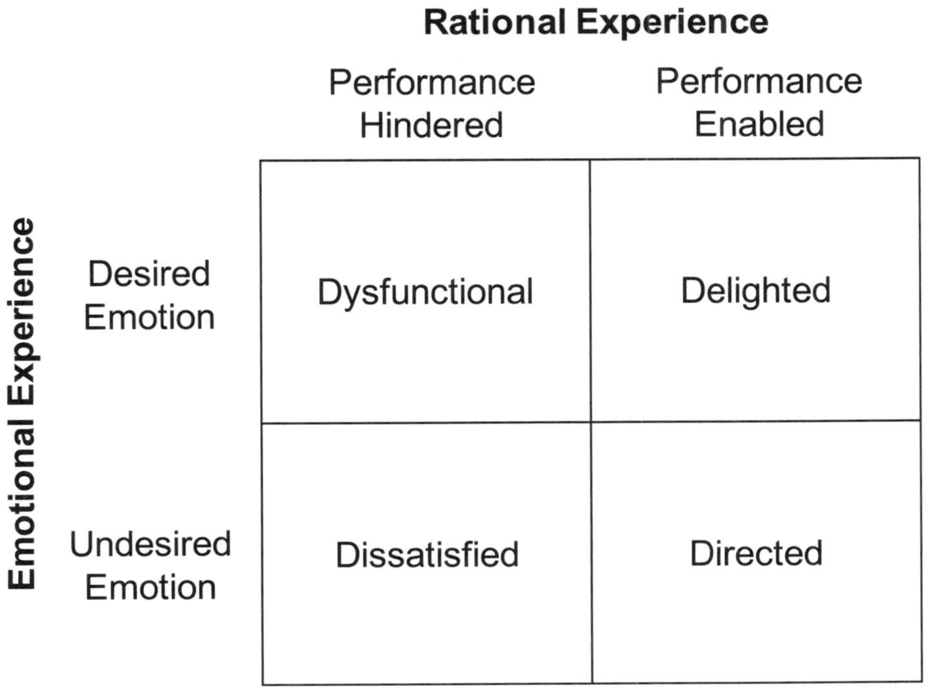

Rational Experience

	Performance Hindered	Performance Enabled
Desired Emotion	Dysfunctional	Delighted
Undesired Emotion	Dissatisfied	Directed

(Emotional Experience)

Figure 7.3   The memorable experience model

The memorable experience model illustrates four possible memories that customers can form, depending on the effectiveness and interaction of the emotional and rational experience: delighted, dissatisfied, dysfunctional, and directed. Ideally, a designer wants to achieve delight in an experience – which to us is what the phrase "memorable customer experience" means. However, if delight is not the memory that an experience achieves, the model helps identify which ingredients the experience needs to include.

DELIGHTED

We call the most desirable memory, in which the customer remembers being full of joy or pleasure, *delighted*. Customers form this memory when the experience evokes the desired emotion while enabling the customer's performance. The example of Disney's Hollywood Tower Hotel satisfies this test. Through various rational elements in the customer experience – the queuing path; the numbers on the floor and seats; the staff who direct, guide, and arrange guests; even the Fastpass reservation system – customer performance is enabled. Customers can get on and off the ride effortlessly, in a timeframe acceptable to them. The ride itself evokes the desired emotions of curiosity, fear, surprise, and, ultimately, joy. The result is that we expect customers to say, "Wow! That was great!" when the experience concludes. And then they go home and tell their friends how great it was.

Another illustration of delight comes from a student's fieldwork that examined experiences through the eyes of a child. For this fieldwork, the student brought her 3-year-old niece to two family-oriented casino experiences. One experience was the midway and circus act stage at the Circus Circus casino. The other was the arcade at the Sienna casino. The student videotaped the child's experiences in both settings. The results showed that the rational parts of the experience were well designed and, for the most part, invisible. Nothing hindered the child from participating in the many experiential activities available. Even more interesting were the desired emotions the experience evoked. The video shows an excited and joyous child as she enters an experience, an engaged and curious child as she watches the circus acts, and a sad and angry child who stamps her feet when told it is time to leave. This exhibit may be the true definition of an experience that causes delight: a customer is sad upon having to leave the experience.

DISSATISFIED

We call the least desirable memory, in which the customer remembers being appalled by the experience, *dissatisfied*. Customers form this memory when the experience evokes undesired or no emotions and hinders the customer's performance. For example, consider the following experience involving the upgrade of a cell phone:

> *Ordering the new phone was quite easy, and two days later it arrived in the mail. The packaging was gorgeous, and when we opened it a poster showing three steps seemingly provided the instructions we needed for success. Step 1 was easy. We charged the battery. So far, so good. Step 2 directed us to follow the online instructions to upgrade our phone. We entered the information into the form. Error. We tried again. Another error. We abandoned the website and called the optional telephone number. Once we got a live person on the line, we found ourselves being directed to take apart our phone to locate a code number on a teeny-weeny card.*

We found it, gave them the number, and were then directed back to the website to finish the process. Everything now worked. Step 2 complete. Step 3 involved setting up voicemail. Again, we followed the instructions on the poster – exactly. No luck. The feedback we received from the automated system did not provide a clue, so we went back to the support line. The first person we talked with had us change the voicemail access phone number. This resulted in our calling not the voicemail prompt, but a dear old lady who did not know the first thing about voicemail. Perplexed, our service representative put us on hold – and then she was gone forever. Our call luckily was bounced back into the queue. The second person provided us with a number that worked and now we had voicemail. But the damage was already done. The desired emotional excitement associated with the new phone had evaporated. The only thing keeping us from abandoning the service was the two-year service contract, which had no escape clause.

To explore the dissatisfied memory further, a group of students engaged in a study of obstructions in a shopping experience. The context was a large, big-box home improvement store. To conduct the study, students went to three different stores, grabbed shopping carts, proceeded to the far front corners of the stores, and then walked up and down each aisle. Any time they had to stop their cart, they recorded the event as an obstruction, which hindered their performance; obstructions included safety barriers, merchandise in the process of being stocked, and merchandise that had fallen into the aisles. Their conclusion was that the obstructions hindered customer performance and caused undesired emotions, thus resulting in dissatisfaction.

DYSFUNCTIONAL

When the experience hinders performance, yet the desired emotion is evoked, the resulting memory associated with the experience is *dysfunctional*. In other words, the experience does not function as it should. As an example, imagine going to a Broadway show in New York. Your experience starts with waiting in a long line at the theatre to pick up your tickets. You get to the will-call window, but the clerk cannot find your order. Fortunately, there are available tickets, but you have to pay again to get them. You then enter the theatre, and the usher seats you. Moments later, another couple who arrives informs you that you are in their seats – the usher seated you incorrectly. You finally get seated correctly and the show starts. It is a great show. You laugh, you cry, you are having a great time. Then at intermission, you get up to go to the restroom. Unfortunately, the line is long, and once you get into the restroom, you find it dirty, soiled, and smelly. You then try to purchase refreshments, but the line is too long. You return to your seat for the remainder of the show, and you once again laugh, cry, and have a great time. When the show is over, leaving the theatre is exasperating. The crowd is thick and slow, and it seems that everyone is either in your way or selling you something. When all is said and done, your memory is that the show was great, but everything else was a **p**ain **i**n **t**he **a**ss (which we call the "PITA factor"). If you hear the word "but" used when customers talk about an experience, you know that the experience is dysfunctional.

Another illustration of a dysfunctional experience emerges from one of the many wedding chapels in Reno, Nevada, that our research teams have investigated. The event of getting married is intended to evoke several desirable emotions, and for the most part, the design of a wedding chapel aims to support these emotions: the church-like atmosphere, the soft lighting, the simulated candles, the flowers, and the graciousness of the minister. But upon closer inspection, some rational elements of the experience potentially hinder customer performance. In one of the chapels was a sign that prohibited the throwing of rice, confetti, birdseed, and so on. Obviously, the presence of such a sign indicates that customers desire to engage in these rational performances to make the emotional experience complete. Prohibiting these performances detracts from the customer experience. In other words, customers leave the experience saying, "The wedding chapel was great, *but* they wouldn't let us throw rice." Rather than making the experience potentially punishing, a better solution for the chapel would be to offer customers a service option: for an additional US$50, guests of the wedding party can throw as much rice, confetti, and birdseed as they want. Instead of a dysfunctional experience, the couple would then enjoy a functional, but with cost, experience.

DIRECTED

When the experience enables performance yet the experience evokes undesired or no emotion, the resulting memory is one in which customers feel *directed*. The experience works, and the customer easily achieves the task or goal, but nothing else adds value to the experience or differentiates it from competing experiences.

The rise of self-service technologies for booking airline tickets and checking in for airline flights, whether online or through a kiosk, has become the epitome of a directed experience. When these technologies initially appeared, there was, of course, delight. Self-service technologies eliminated undesirable emotions associated with waiting on hold to speak to an agent or waiting in line to get a boarding pass. Customers were joyous! However, as it does for any innovation that becomes widely adopted and well used, the excitement waned as these self-service technologies matured. Using the technologies became routine, and the element of surprise that Pine and Gilmore speak of as the catalyst of desirable emotions disappeared.[12]

Experiences that result in customers feeling directed do not offer a competitive advantage. Virtually all airlines offer online ticket purchase and self-service check-in kiosks. Therefore, the point of differentiation is lost. Furthermore, these experiences no longer evoke unique, desirable emotions, reducing the potential for differentiation even further.

Our research teams have explored various such experiences, with generally the same conclusions regarding the absence of competitive advantage. One fieldwork study investigated the experience of teaching customers how to use contact lenses. Customers learned how to put the contact lenses in their eyes, remove them, clean them, and store them. Customer performance was enabled, and the memories from such an experience were very functional. Yet the experience evoked limited desirable emotions.

Similar results emerged from a fieldwork study that investigated the experience of buying cell phone services online. To conduct this fieldwork, the group set up a computer that not only recorded a subject's mouse movements and keyboard strokes but also video-recorded the subject engaging in the task. Although subjects were able to complete the task with little or no hindrances, the group observed limited desirable emotions.

Principles for Good Balance

Ensuring that a memorable customer experience is one of being delighted rather than being dissatisfied, dysfunctional, or directed, we offer three key principles. First, focus initially on the rational experience and then on the emotional experience. Second, involve the customer in designing the experience. Third, harmonize and balance the experience.

RATIONAL FIRST, EMOTIONAL SECOND

The overarching strategy for creating a memorable customer experience proceeds with rational first, emotional second. What this means is that it is very difficult to evoke and make memorable desirable emotions if the rational part of an experience does not work. As the preceding examples demonstrate, obstacles, poor policies, lack of customer education, and so on hinder the customer. This hindrance then causes the flaws in the experience to be more memorable than the emotions that differentiate the experience.

After the rational elements of an experience enable customer performance, then and only then does the investment in experience features that evoke desired emotions make sense. Consider the experience offered by Cold Stone Creamery, an ice cream shop where we take our students for their final exam. The rational elements of the experience include the scripted process for serving customers, from entry to consumption. The emotional elements begin with customers being able to co-produce their ice cream. Customers specify the type of ice cream and the various mix-ins they want, while the store associate puts on a show mixing the confection on a frosted cold stone. As the rational experience continues, additional emotional events get sprinkled in throughout, including the songs the staff sing when customers give them a tip or the jokes they tell when ringing up the sale. These aspects of the experience establish differentiation because they evoke desirable emotions. The resulting memory is one of delight rather than deprivation.

Our recommendation is that the design of any customer experience must first focus on the customer's goals and tasks. As co-producers, customers are the ones who will be creating much of the value that exists in an experience. Through the CEM, integrating elements of vision, access, incentive, and expertise will drive customer performance, setting the foundation for the emotional experience.

INVOLVE THE CUSTOMER IN DESIGNING THE EXPERIENCE

A customer experience that is well coordinated or even choreographed can have a distinct advantage, because the experience can be duplicated time after time with predictable outcomes. As we look at various customer experiences, we often wonder if the experience was crafted for the customer, if the customer crafted the experience, or if the experience blends the two crafts. In our experience, the latter is most desirable and the most profitable over time.

When the University of California, Irvine, was constructed, the buildings were erected using the best in architectural and engineering resources available. But when it came to landscaping and pathways between buildings, the university employed an innovative idea involving "desire lines", or the paths created by people that represent the shortest or easiest route to navigate. The university planted grass between the buildings in place of concrete sidewalks. Only after it became apparent by the repeated use of students did the natural pathways reveal themselves. The university then installed the concrete sidewalks and completed landscaping to enhance the students' experience.

The metaphor of desire lines as a foundation for the design of memorable customer experiences is a useful one. What this point reflects is that memorable customer experiences are created by design, not default, and that design comes from collaboration between company and customer.

HARMONIZE AND BALANCE THE EXPERIENCE

Understanding the balance between the operational realities of the company and the creation of the customer experience is a crucial component of creating customer loyalty. If an experience is too focused on the convenience of the company, it will lose the customers' creative input. Yet if a company only focuses on the customers' creative input, everything becomes customized and difficult to scale. This situation is fine for a do-it-yourself environment but not for a traditional service business.

Human nature and the desire for standardization threaten the emotional experience. Because customers value predictability in an experience, the surprises that constitute an emotional experience may be consciously or unconsciously eliminated. Emotional experiences are difficult to sustain because they are hard to achieve. They require specialized resources and a lot of effort. For example, if the labor market is tight, a shop like Cold Stone Creamery may not be able to recruit for attitude, which is what the experience needs to maintain its experiential advantage. Hiring solely for ability would be a potential threat to the viability of the experience.

Over time, the experience a company affords to customers may resemble a teeter-totter, with rational on one side and emotional on the other. One should avoid *experience volatility* (wild swings from one side to the other) and *experience weighting* (a sustained swing that results in performance or emotion being sacrificed). Experience managers must have a good vision of the balance between emotional and rational and measure the health of each on a regular basis. Such activities help effectively manage experience volatility and experience weighting.

Conclusions

Memorable customer experiences that deliver delight are wonderful things. They establish a competitive advantage and enable the customer to unlock the value that exists within a good or service. With an effective balance between the emotional and rational aspects of a customer experience, customers can not only achieve their goals but also experience delight. By combining the CEM and the ERM, experience designers gain a solid foundation for crafting memorable customer experiences that are valuable not only to the company but to the customer as well.

Notes

1.   Pine, J. and Gilmore, J. (1999), *The Experience Economy*, Harvard Business School Press, Cambridge, MA.

2.   Honebein, P.C. and Cammarano, R.F. (2005), *Creating Do-It-Yourself Customers*, Thomson Texere, Natorp, OH.
3.   MacLean, P.D. (1990), *The Triune Brain in Evolution: Role in Paleocerebral Functions*, Plenum Press, New York.
4.   Ornstein, R. (1992), *The Evolution of Consciousness*, Simon & Schuster, New York.
5.   Plutchik, R. (1980), "A general psychoevolutionary theory of emotion", in R. Plutchik and H. Kellerman (eds.), *Emotion: Theory, Research, and Experience*, Vol. 1: *Theories of Emotion*, Academic, New York, pp. 3–33.
6.   Rachels, S. (n.d.), "On three alleged theories of rational behavior", available at http://www.jamesrachels.org/stuart/rational.pdf (accessed June 14, 2008).
7.   Stahl, S. (1999), "Different strokes for different folks? A critique of learning styles", *American Educator*, Vol. 23, No. 3, pp. 27–31.
8.   Pine and Gilmore, *The Experience Economy*.
9.   Honebein and Cammarano, *Creating Do-It-Yourself Customers*.
10.   Vargo, S. and Lusch, R. (2004), "Evolving to a new dominant logic for marketing", *Journal of Marketing*, Vol. 68 (January), pp. 1–17.
11.   Southwest Airlines (2008). Fact Sheet, 16 May 2008, available at http://www.southwest.com/about_swa/press/factsheet.html#southwest.com (accessed June 14, 2008).
12.   Pine and Gilmore, *The Experience Economy*.

8 Reflections on Ultra-Fine Dining Experiences

MICHAEL BASIL* AND DEBRA Z. BASIL†

Keywords

experiential, fine dining, hedonic, luxury, restaurant

Abstract

Ultra-fine dining is a growing phenomenon. But how do people evaluate and remember these experiences? This chapter considers 352 online reviews of upscale dining experiences at Michelin three-star restaurants to investigate assessments of these luxury purchases. The reviews are primarily positive and focused on the aesthetics of the food, followed by service quality. Two evaluative frames emerge from the analysis. A hedonic frame that relates to the experience as special or a "splurge" frequently accompanied a positive review. Within this frame, sub-themes of holistic synergy and dream analogies were evident. The second theme is a more rational "value" perspective, more frequently related to negative reviews. Within this frame, a sub-theme referring to prior experience seemed to impact evaluations. With the value frame, whether the restaurant meets expectations provides the most important criterion for interpreting the experience, a finding consistent with service quality literature that demonstrates people often interpret experiences relative to their expectations. Finally, despite extensive service quality studies, these results suggest that the aesthetic and hedonic aspects of food are more important than service quality in an ultra-fine dining context.

*   Dr Michael Basil, Faculty of Management, University of Lethbridge, Lethbridge, AB T1K 3M4, Canada. E-mail: michael.basil@uleth.ca. Telephone: 403-329-2075.

†   Dr Debra Z. Basil, Faculty of Management, University of Lethbridge, Lethbridge, AB T1K 3M4, Canada. E-mail: debra.basil@uleth.ca. Telephone: 403-329-2164.

Introduction

Luxury purchases have been the subject of significant interest in marketing. Several recent books have examined the phenomenon of luxury purchasing and recommended it as an exploitable niche for marketers.[1] Generally these books argue for a sizeable and growing segment of the market to which luxury items can be targeted, whereas the "low price" category is extremely competitive, which should make luxury purchases an appealing strategic niche. Another argument for the viability of a luxury strategy is that luxury purchases often enjoy strong demand and customer loyalty.[2]

The term "luxury" has been defined in various ways,[3] including in very rational terms, such as prestige-seeking behaviour.[4] Prestige-seeking behaviour generally stems from social or self-expression motives that include a desire for conspicuousness, uniqueness, social interaction, emotions, and quality.[5] Other theorists frame luxury with an emphasis on aesthetic values related to uniqueness, quality, hedonics, and the extended self.[6]

Most of what we know about luxury purchases, however, has centred on durable goods,[7] so our knowledge of customer expectations may be distorted by a focus on the rational aspects of purchasing and specific product attributes, such as durability, which ignores many of the experiential aspects of consumption. Many rational models may not even apply to non-tangible goods and services. For example, research examining the purchase of luxury vacations notes that experiential aspects are critical to the evaluation of the service encounter.[8] Charters also observes that "Comparatively little work has been done within the discipline of marketing on the analysis of the aesthetic dimensions as a core component of a product."[9] We therefore adopt a relatively comprehensive definition of luxury purchasing that includes aesthetic qualities of the product or service, as well as brand identity and service quality.

As our research question, we ask how people evaluate and remember non-tangible luxury purchases in the specific domain of food. Food is becoming a popular form of luxury consumption. Whereas earlier followers of the food movement were termed "gourmets", such as Julia Child, a more current term is "foodie", a slang term for "a person who has an ardent or refined interest in food; a gourmet".[10] Some trace this new term to the *Official Foodie Handbook*.[11] Whatever the term or derivation, being a gourmet or a foodie is growing increasingly common.

The fine food industry was estimated to be worth US$62 billion in 2005, and premium food consumption is a major food trend, projected to grow during the next six years.[13] Citing the impact of the Food Network and increased health consciousness, *DSN Retailing Today* has identified 10 important consumer classifications, one of which is the gourmet foodie.[14] Numerous food groups, blogs, and television shows for foodies have emerged (e.g., www.foodies.ca, www.italianfoodies.blog.com, www.communities.canada.com). Although primarily hedonic or aesthetic, this movement also resonates with related factors such as consumers' increased awareness of food origins, ingredients, and the ethical aspects of food production.[15]

Restaurant Dining

An important aspect of the food experience is restaurant dining. Restaurants provide an important area for customer experiences. One of the primary differences between durable goods and restaurant dining is tangibility, which causes Muller to label restaurant dining an "experience good".[16] In this chapter, we attempt to understand how people evaluate luxury dining experiences.

From previous research on mainstream restaurants, we know a bit about how people evaluate the service aspects of restaurants. Kim, Lee, and Woo find that the "quality of the relationship" between the restaurant and diners provides the primary determinant of commitment, loyalty, and word of mouth.[17] Wall and Berry suggest that evaluations of a restaurant experience rest on three information categories: functional (technical quality of food and service), mechanical (ambiance), and humanic (employees), though humanic clues may be more impactful than mechanic ones.[18] IGD, a non-profit research organization for the food and grocery sector, suggests that when they eat out, consumers seek something new, a treat, time savings, and a pleasant experience.[19] Together, these studies imply that service and atmosphere play important roles in evaluations of restaurant experiences.

One frequently applied approach for evaluating restaurant experiences uses the expectancy disconfirmation model,[20] a seminal model for understanding consumer satisfaction and dissatisfaction. It suggests that consumers have expectations and evaluate products according to how well they meet these expectations. This model appears in the popular SERVQUAL scale as a means to assess service quality.[21] Although similar, these approaches generally are considered different in terms of how they conceptualise expectations. Assessments of consumer satisfaction tend to use predictive standards or the level of service that consumers believe will be provided, whereas assessments of service quality tend to use normative standards or the level of service they believe should be provided. For both conceptualizations, consumers form expectations, which they then use to assess satisfaction.

Service quality and satisfaction literature also offer useful perspectives for evaluating the restaurant industry.[22] People should be able to evaluate their experiences and may even have a priori expectations. Although people may not have eaten at many ultra-fine restaurants, they have eaten at a variety of restaurants. Drawing an analogy to product innovation, ultra-fine dining might represent a continuous innovation of the idea of restaurants rather than a drastically different discontinuous innovation.[23]

Yet other reasons suggest that an evaluation of ultra-fine dining may be difficult. First, expectations are based on similar past experiences. The cost and relative scarcity of ultra-fine dining indicates that the experience is likely to be very rare, so how can a customer evaluate a service encounter? Second, aesthetic and hedonic aspects may make dining experiences difficult to assess.[24] Research suggests that expectations about extraordinary experiences are likely to be vague, because they represent unusual events that involve high levels of emotional intensity. As such, expectancy disconfirmation may not be a sufficient evaluative tool. In their study of extraordinary experiences in the context of river rafting, Arnould and Price note the importance of affective, narrative, and ritual influences.[25] Expectations play an important role in their research, but another essential element is the idea that expectations tend to be vague, and many of the most valuable outcomes were unexpected. So despite experiences with restaurants in general, there may be other reasons consumers lack well-defined scripts or expectations for ultra-fine dining. Because of the exclusive nature, we expect that experiential aspects take on increased importance, similar to that detailed in "River magic".[26]

A critical question for ultra-fine dining is whether dining experiences are primarily aesthetic and hedonic or practical and utilitarian.[27] Certainly people do not use the same standard to evaluate a $250 per person meal that they would to evaluate a $5 fast-food meal. So what are the criteria for these exclusive and highly aesthetic experiences?

We contend that when considering an ultra-fine meal, the experience becomes more hedonic than that for lower priced meals.[28] One of the principle hedonic aspects of fine dining should revolve around the product, that is, the food, consistent with the categorisation of "haute cuisine" as "substantially aesthetic."[29] Food quality generally appears ignored in previous research, with the exception of a content analysis of restaurant critics' reviews.[30] According to that study, critics typically focus on the quality of food, ambience, and atmosphere in their reviews. Other research shows that taste is the most important factor in everyday food selection.[31] Yet some evidence suggests that taste may be more important in restaurant dining than in everyday food choice, and perhaps even more so in ultra-fine dining. Specifically, Lee and Cranage examine the relative importance of taste, appearance, price, and nutrition when selecting menu items and find that differences exist for high- and low-expenditure consumers; higher spenders place greater emphasis on taste and nutrition.[32] Given the very upscale nature of ultra-fine dining, these findings suggest that the taste of food should be particularly important for such experiences.

Atmosphere and service also should be critical, because fine dining represents an experiential purchase. Service and atmosphere help create an image of luxury.[33] According to a framework for brand luxury, service and atmosphere contribute to the elements of uniqueness, quality, and hedonics and therefore serve as vital factors in creating the image of luxury.[34] We propose that the intangible factors of service and atmosphere are very important in a luxury restaurant experience. Specifically, experiential aspects of restaurant dining are critical to customers' evaluations of the encounter and their desire to return or recommend the experience to others. People likely have some experience in restaurant dining and therefore should have some basis for applying a rational evaluation of the experience. We propose that hedonic aspects are also likely to be used to evaluate fine dining experiences.

The importance of memorable consumer experiences has been emphasised by Pine and Gilmore in their assertion that experience marketing is as distinct from services marketing as services marketing is from product marketing.[35] Memorable experiences are staged to provide sensations to the consumer that will be interpreted in a highly personal way, and ultra-fine dining should present a memorable consumer experience. The price and difficulty make it a high-involvement purchase. All of the consumers' senses are engaged – taste, smell, and appearance, all meticulously constructed. Restaurant service and ambiance, including music and noise levels, should be carefully constructed. The restaurant stages the experience to deliver an unfailingly consistent experience; consistency is such an important element in ultra-fine dining that it is a key criterion for highly coveted Michelin stars (http://www.michelinguide.com/us/ratings.html). The expense and difficulty of dining at some of the top restaurants makes it a rare and therefore memorable experience.

This chapter examines personal opinions about restaurant dining experiences using online consumer restaurant reviews. Previous research reveals that comments typically are positive; however, because people often provide online reviews to warn others about a negative experience, we expect negative evaluations as well.[36] This range of reviews should provide a thorough frame for understanding both positive and negative reactions. We examine each review's content, with specific attention to the experiential aspects of customers' recollections. In addition, we extract key themes that resonate with ultra-fine diners.

We focus on the five "three-star" Michelin-rated restaurants in the United States. Michelin is a French tyre company that provides maps and guides to various destinations worldwide; its "Red Guide" is commonly considered the industry standard in restaurant ratings.[37] Restaurants are included in the guide if they meet a reasonable standard; good restaurants receive one star, better restaurants are awarded two, and a very select number of restaurants achieve three stars. Michelin stars are highly coveted awards for chefs[38] and often serve as signalling devices among foodies and in the haute cuisine industry itself.[39] Because there are only five three-star restaurants in the United States, diners should have very high expectations for these experiences and remember them as unique and special.

Methods

For this chapter, we examine consumer recollections and evaluations of ultra-fine dining experiences in the five Michelin three-star rated restaurants in the United States: Alain Ducasse, Jean Georges, La Bernardin, and Per Se (New York City) and the French Laundry (Napa Valley). Some additional support for this selection appears in *Restaurant Magazine*'s 2008 list of the top 50 restaurants in the world, on which these restaurants appear among the top 20 in the world and represent the top US restaurants (French Laundry is at 3, Per Se at 7, Jean Georges at 9, and La Bernardin at 20; the list also includes Alain Ducasse but only the Paris location).

We examine existing reviews of these very upscale restaurants to investigate people's reactions to and recollections of these luxury purchases. The online reviews come from three sites with a sizeable collection of dining reviews: citysearch.com, epinions.com, and tripadvisor.com. Our analyses of the existing online reviews offer an understanding of the criteria that the reviewers brought to their evaluation of the experience. The research therefore also consists of a content analysis using both quantitative and qualitative approaches.

We found 355 reviews across the three websites, pertaining to La Bernardin (110), Jean Georges (92), Per Se (49), and the French Laundry (101). For some inexplicable reason, we found only three reviews for Alain Ducasse; therefore, we eliminated this restaurant from our analysis and retained a sample of 352.

After downloading and importing the reviews into a word processing program, we conducted coding and analysis. A student research assistant coded the reviews on the basis of several criteria. First, the overall ranking of the reviews was recorded; all three sites used a five-point rating scale. We subsequently recoded the ratings as either positive or negative (operationalised by whether the reviewer gave three or more (positive) or less than three (negative) stars). Second, a content analysis was conducted on the comments to develop the following coding categories: reservations process, food, beverages, service, atmosphere, whether they would recommend the restaurant, if they indicated they would recommend it, if they would return, and whether the reviewer used the term "splurge" or remarked that the visit was a special occasion. Third, the analyses compared the numeric review with the qualitative comments. Fourth, a textual analysis of the content was undertaken by both authors and reviewed by the original coder.

Results

QUANTITATIVE ANALYSES

Our analysis reveals that the restaurant reviews range between 10 and 1,521 words; the average review consists of 160 words. Although the number of words written differs among the four restaurants, this variation appears attributable to differences among the online review sites, such that epinions has significantly longer reviews (512 words compared with 200 on Trip Advisor and 109 for City Search).

The content analysis shows that the vast majority of reviews are positive. Of the ratings, 211 (60 per cent) give the restaurant the highest possible score of 5 points, 49 (14 per cent) achieve 4 points, and only 92 (26 per cent) of the ratings fall below 4. The average rating is 4.1 on a 1-to-5 scale, as we show in Table 8.1. A statistical comparison shows no significant difference in the overall evaluations across the four restaurants (F [3, 348] = 0.3, p = .81). This vast majority of positive ratings is somewhat reassuring, given the high standards expected of a Michelin three-star rated restaurant. However, the ratings do not seem to attain a ceiling effect, such that they all cluster at 5 points, which suggests that people were not comparing the restaurant to a "typical" meal. Instead, people appear to evaluate a US$250 meal according to very high standards, and though the restaurants often meet this standard, they do not always. Therefore, people may interpret an ultra-fine dining experience according to a relatively high standard. Several quotes illustrate that the experience does not receive comparisons to "standard" restaurants: "This is not your average restaurant. The service can be compared to no other"; "ABSOLUTELY the best meal I have ever had"; and "This meal is the benchmark for all future comparisons of restaurants."

Overall, almost everything about the experience was positive, as we show in Table 8.2. But what is the most critical factor in how people evaluate the restaurants? As an exploratory measure, we perform a correlation analysis, using comments about the food, beverages, service, atmosphere, and reservations process (rated by the research associate) to predict the restaurant evaluation (rated by the review writer). Because the experiences might be correlated, we use a multiple regression to control for all factors simultaneously.

Table 8.1   Restaurant, reviews, and overall rating

Restaurant	Number of reviews	Overall rating
French Laundry	101	4.0
Jean Georges	92	4.2
Le Bernardin	110	4.2
Per Se	49	4.1

Note: Ratings based on a 1-to-5 scale.

Table 8.2   Effects of various elements on overall evaluation

	Food	Service	Beverages	Atmosphere	Reservations process
Mean	4.4	4.3	4.1	4.0	3.0
Number mentioning	333	287	133	165	81
SD	1.1	1.2	1.2	1.1	1.0
Correlation	.85***	.77***	.63***	.56***	.50***
Beta	.57***	.30**	.02	.07	.14*

Note: Ratings based on 1-to-5 scale. Standardised beta reported here.

***p < .001. **p < .01. *p < .05.*

The results demonstrate that the evaluations of food and service are the significant predictors of the overall evaluation (food, r = .85, beta = .57; service, r = .77, beta = .30; both $p < .001$). The overall evaluation thus seems based primarily on the food and service. More accurately, the evaluations are primarily based on the food and only secondarily on the quality of the service.

The content analysis explicates which criteria people evaluated; most of the reviews mention food (333/352, or 95 per cent), such as "The meal started with a caviar course followed by the foie course (best we've ever had!) then a sea urchin course and finally a signature butter poached lobster tail", and "The food is everything it's said to be; Innovative. Interesting. Delicious. Noteworthy." The second most frequently mentioned aspect is service quality (287/352, or 82 per cent): "The service was incredible: warm, attentive, knowledgeable, and in great abundance" and "The service was stunning." Many reviews mention both food and service: "Fabulous food, impeccable service" and "Everything was perfectly done, from the execution of the food to the service." The atmosphere, beverage, and reservations process appear in 47 per cent, 37 per cent, and 23 per cent of the reviews, respectively.

To examine the impact of expectations, we compared the numeric restaurant evaluation with the measure of whether reviewers commented on having expectations. In this case, the numeric restaurant review (provided by the original review writer on a 1-to-5 scale) compared with written comments about how well the restaurant met expectations (judged on a 1-to-5 scale by the rater). The results in Table 8.3 show a very strong relationship to the overall evaluation (F [4, 157] = 222, $p < .001$, $eta^2 = .85$). Therefore, the bulk of the variability in the restaurant evaluation (85 per cent) depends on how well the restaurant met people's expectations. Even in the case of aesthetic and hedonic experience, expectations appear to come into play.

THEMATIC ANALYSIS

We conducted a deeper thematic analysis[40] and uncovered two common themes: extraordinary experience and value. The extraordinary experience theme suggests that the dining experience is a very special occasion or treat, often shown through words such

Table 8.3   Relationship between expectation satisfaction and overall evaluation

Met expectation	Overall evaluation	n
1 (poor)	1.7	28
2 (fair)	2.8	28
3 (moderate)	3.6	18
4 (good)	4.4	5
5 (excellent)	5.0	79

Notes: Overall evaluation, means on 1-to-5 scale. Expectations based on coder's judgement.

as "once in a lifetime" or "You only live once". For example, "All in all, [X Restaurant] is definitely a special occasion type of restaurant, catering to gourmets who appreciate a great meal as an almost spiritual celebration. You need to make this journey at least once in your life!"; "This is hands-down the best meal you will have IN YOUR LIFE"; "I really will remember it for a lifetime, and in that sense it was totally worth the price"; "It is expensive, but truly a once in a lifetime dining experience"; and "I am glad that I went there and can cross that 'experience' off my list, very much like the first and only time I ever made it down to Times Square on New Year's Eve."

Within this theme of extraordinary experience, two sub-themes frequently emerged in the reviews. First, there was frequently reference to a holistic evaluation, with an implication of synergy, so that the whole of the overall experience was more than the sum of its parts. For example, "To talk about how much it cost seems irrelevant when you're paying for a complete experience like this." Similarly, another respondent noted, "You need to go prepared to understand you're paying for the experience, ambience, service, name, as well as the food. (We were apparently sitting where Tyra Banks & Gisele Bundchen had parked their slight behinds weeks before!)." However there were others who clearly did not evaluate it as a holistic experience: "It's only food, not rocket science!!!"

A second sub-theme within this notion of extraordinary experience related to a dream analogy, used to describe both pre-dining expectations and post-dining memories: "When we arrived at the restaurant, it was literally like a dream come true." Another respondent commented, "will dream about the evening for a long time to come", and yet another noted, "what you will be given in return is a meal that you will remember, dream about and talk about for the rest of your life". Our analysis showed that the extraordinary experience theme was more frequently associated with a positive review.

The second major theme that emerged was a value theme, focused on whether the experience was worth the expense. The value theme often mentioned the cost of the meal or a comparison with similar restaurants (e.g., "not worth the price") and the reviewer's expectations. Thus, this theme appeared more frequently in association with a negative review: "Some wonderful tastes ... but not for the price tag. We had the 9 course lunch for $240 on a Sunday. The place was nice. The service was wonderful ... one server to each two people. We had the biggest plates with the smallest portions which I was expecting. I do remember the desserts and candy at the end which were quite nice. The wine was also great with the selection and the knowledge the wine servers had. The food was a little disappointing since only a couple of the courses were great ... the rest were just ok. I would not recommend this place unless you have an extra $500 laying around." Another reviewer acknowledged, "Yes, it was very good. But for over $1,200 for a party of four (dinner plus two bottles of decent ... not high-end ... wine), it should've been the best meal I'd ever had ... but wasn't." Finally, one complained, "Amazing wine list, with prices over the top. Will not return, will not recommend."

Within the value theme, experience emerged as an important sub-theme. Prior experience with other ultra-fine dining establishments served to help the respondent form his or her expectations: "Overhyped and overpriced. Dinner for six at almost $400 per with wines. Can easily name six restaurants where the food is better and prices lower. Had a California wine that retails for $40, which I drank in a top-end DC restaurant two weeks ago for $75 – at [X], paid a cool $240 for exactly the same wine." In this case, the respondent has other experiences he or she feels fall within the same comparative category. The respondent also has direct experiences with wines and thus has a point of comparison for evaluation. Speaking to the notion of experience, another reviewer wrote, "I'm a chef-proprietor of a 'fine dining' restaurant in New England ... What really left a very sour note in everyone's mouth was the outrageous wine list prices. Although the wine list is extremely extensive in CA offerings, the sticker shock is mind numbing. My establishment back East uses a mark-up average of 240 per cent on average. Compare that to an average m/u at [X Restaurant] of 600 per cent +. We all felt ripped-off at having to pay $300 for a $80 Cab Sauv, or $160 for a modest albeit suave Pinot Noir." Frequently greater experience and more potential points of comparison seemed to lead to a negative review: "We travel extensively & dine at some of the finest restaurants in the world/US ... A very expensive 'show', with food definately [sic] not on par with many restaurants, including others in [the area]. This was not worth the wait or the money."

Although there was a general tendency for the value perspective to result in a more critical review, there were plenty of instances in which reviewers evaluated the restaurants in terms of value, but the restaurants still fared well: "Can it possibly be worth it? It can. [X Restaurant] is better than I'd hoped – better even than that for which the Cookbook can prepare you. This experience changes you. It changes the way you think about food, cooking, and dining; and it extends to everything else as well." Perhaps the most insightful comment on the value proposition was "Is a meal, pre-wine, worth $240? I suppose that depends on your income status."

Overall, many reviews mentioned the reviewers' expectations. Although 194 of the reviews (55 per cent) did not mention expectations, a large minority (45 per cent) did. Several quotes from the thematic analysis reveal the importance of expectations: "I ate at the famous [X Restaurant] last weekend. I had great expectations." The reviewers also appear to evaluate their experience relative to their expectations: "A very expensive evening but it met all our expectations"; "All our expectations were met"; and "Exceeded my expectations in every way!" Sometimes though, very high expectations are not met: "We were expecting a sublime experience, we were disappointed"; "Zagats raved about [X Restaurant] – the best food, the best service, the best decor in [the area]. Maybe all the hype raised my expectations too much, but I did not find my experience at [X Restaurant] to be tres magnifique"; and "Without the hype, I would give the restaurant four or five stars. Relative to hype, I can only give it three." These comments suggest an expectancy disconfirmation approach, consistent with satisfaction literature rather than services quality literature. Specifically, consumers appear to assess their satisfaction on the basis of what they expect the service to be and also realise that their expectations depend on word of mouth.

Conclusions

This chapter provides insight into extraordinary consumer experiences in the context of ultra-fine dining. The dining experiences described herein are similar to those described by Arnould and Price,[41] in that both describe hedonic situations in which people enter the encounter with relatively vague expectations. In this instance, how should a person evaluate one of the five best restaurants in the United States, something that the vast majority of consumers have not experienced before? One of the key findings from our research is that people's reactions, at least as evidenced by the reviews, are generally positive. In addition, many people report life-changing experiences. Considering the cost of these restaurants and the difficulty of getting a reservation, their aim to provide a remarkable experience appears to be succeeding. People generally enjoy ultra-fine dining experiences and remember them very positively. Thus, the Michelin guides apparently provide a reasonable marker of restaurant quality for the majority of patrons, in support of the value of the star system.[42]

The evaluations of ultra-fine dining seem to be more about the quality of the food than the quality of the service, as observed through both the prediction of evaluations and the content of the reviews. Customers primarily care about the food. This interest should not be surprising, but we also note that most existing research on restaurant evaluations centres on service rather than food.[43] Although service is important, in the case of the fine dining experiences we examined here, the aesthetic and hedonic aspects of the meal are the most important aspects for customers. Research evaluating the dining experience cannot overlook the aesthetic and hedonic aspects of the experience,[44] even if they are more difficult to measure, because they are a critical element of the restaurant experience, and examining them helps clarify people's satisfaction. Although we gather this finding in very high-end dining situations, it is consistent with research that indicates quality and taste are the most important factors in food selection.[45]

People use a variety of frames to interpret, explain, and recall their experiences. In some instances, they frame the experience primarily in hedonic terms, so satisfaction with the upscale dining experiences is typically very high. Because hedonic experiences by nature are personally determined, fewer concrete criteria exist for comparison; therefore, perception is sufficient to determine satisfaction, without the need to succumb to rule-based or rational criteria. In more experiential, hedonic, and aesthetic consumer experiences then, customers' judgements may be more subjective and likely are based on more gestalt criteria.[46] The data support this gestalt notion, with frequent reference to the "overall experience". For many consumers, ultra-fine dining is an extraordinary experience, often likened to a dream analogy, achieved through the uniqueness and transformational qualities of the experience. In other cases though, satisfaction appears to depend on the experience meeting or exceeding people's expectations,[47] consistent with the expectancy disconfirmation model. In general, expectations provide frames that colour the experience.[48] Consistent with the more rational and cognitive approach, when expectations use a utilitarian frame, specifically addressing issues of value, satisfaction with upscale dining experiences tends to be lower. No matter how good the meal, it is still just a meal. If we consider the value of the meal, it becomes difficult to justify the high price tag, especially true when the consumer has concrete points of comparison, such as other, similar restaurant experiences.

Most of the experiences and comments are positive, consistent with previous findings that, at least for successful businesses, word-of-mouth comments tend to be more positive than negative.[49] Despite this general tendency towards the positive, several reviews also support the observation that people sometimes provide online reviews to warn others about negative experiences.[50] That is, most patrons are satisfied with their experience, but a few have negative experiences and write reviews to warn others. These findings are important for efforts to build customer loyalty in the Internet era, especially for high-involvement situations such as ultra-fine dining.

Overall, the evidence in this chapter suggests that people's expectations colour their experiences, especially as they remember them. This study of ultra-fine dining, similar to investigations of white-water rafting, also confirms that "there is a complex relationship between client expectations and satisfaction".[51] In our research, we cannot distinguish whether customers' expectations are (or could be expected to be) based on aesthetic standards versus value assessments. For example, prior similar experiences may encourage a more rational evaluation method, a topic worthy of further study. Whether the expectations occur in advance of the experience and colour the transaction while it is occurring, or whether they develop after the experience and help consumers interpret their experience (e.g., for the purpose of writing a review) is also worthy of further study. Finally, though our study is limited to ultra-fine dining, it suggests that any understanding of luxury purchasing should consider the added value of aesthetic factors. Estimating the value of the aesthetic aspects, or predicting which customers are most likely to pay for aesthetic qualities, also await further study.

Notes

1. Chada, R. and Husband, P. (2007), *The Cult of the Luxury Brand: Inside Asia's Love Affair with Luxury*, Nicholas Brealey, London; Danzinger, P. (2005), *Let Them Eat Cake: Marketing Luxury to the Masses – As Well as the Classes*, Kaplan Business, New York; Nunes, P. and Johnson, B. (2004), *Mass Affluence: Seven New Rules of Marketing to Today's Consumer*, Harvard Business School Press, Cambridge, MA.
2. Phau, I. and Prendergast, G. (2000), "Consuming luxury brands: the relevance of the 'rarity principle'", *Journal of Brand Management*, Vol. 8, pp. 122–38.
3. Beverland, M. (2004), "An exploration of the luxury wine trade", *International Journal of Wine Marketing*, Vol. 16, pp. 14–28.
4. Nueno, J.L. and Quelch, J.A. (1998), "The mass marketing of luxury", *Business Horizons* (November/December), pp. 61–8; Vigneron, F. and Johnson, L.W. (1999), "A review and a conceptual framework of prestige-seeking consumer behaviour", *Academy of Marketing Science Review*, p. 1.
5. Vigneron and Johnson, "A review and a conceptual framework of prestige-seeking consumer behaviour".
6. Ibid; Kapferer, J.N. (1997), "Managing luxury brands", *Journal of Brand Management*, Vol. 4, No. 4, pp. 251–60.

7.   Holbrook, M.B. and Hirschman, E. (1982), "The experiential aspects of consumption: consumer fantasies, feelings, and fun", *Journal of Consumer Research*, Vol. 9, pp. 132–40.

8.   Arnould, E.J. and Price, L.L. (1993), "River magic: extraordinary experience and the extended service encounter", *Journal of Consumer Research*, Vol. 20 (June), pp. 24–45.

9.   Charters, S. (2006), "Aesthetic products and aesthetic consumption: a review", *Consumption, Markets, and Culture*, Vol. 9, pp. 235–55, at p. 239.

10. Foodie. (n.d.), *The American Heritage® Dictionary of the English Language, Fourth Edition*, Answers. com website, available at http://www.answers.com/topic/foodie (accessed 7 May 2008).

11. Barr, A. and Levy, P. (1984), *The Official Foodie Handbook*, Olympic Marketing.

12. Wellman, D. (2005), "Gourmet to mainstream", *Retail Merchandiser*, Vol. 45, No. 10, pp. 20–22.

13. Lewis, H. (2007), "The 'magnificent seven' food trends to 2013 – Management briefing: Megatrend 3: 'Posh nosh'", *Just Food: The 'magnificent seven' food trends to 2013* (May), pp. 10–15; Quilter, J. (2008), "Premium food brands well placed for next recession", *Promotions & Incentives* (February), pp. 10–11.

14. Lisanti, T. (2002), "Consumer groups challenge retailers", *DSN Retailing Today*, Vol. 41, No. 23, p. 9.

15. IGD (2007), "Eating out", IGD Food & Grocery Information, Insight & Best Practice, 14 December, available at http://www.igd.com/CIR.asp?menuid=35&cirid=1137 (accessed 7 May 2008).

16. Muller, C.C. (1999), "The business of restaurants: 2001 and beyond", *International Journal of Hospitality Management*, Vol. 18, pp. 401–13.

17. Kim, W.G., Lee, Y.-K. and Yoo, Y.-J. (2006), "Predictors of relationship quality and relationship outcomes in luxury restaurants", *Journal of Hospitality & Tourism Research*, Vol. 30, pp. 143–69.

18. Wall, E.A. and Berry, L.L. (2007), "The combined effects of the physical environment and employee behavior on customer perception of restaurant service quality", *Cornell Hotel and Restaurant Administration Quarterly*, Vol. 48, No. 1, pp. 59–69.

19. IGD, "Eating out".

20. Oliver, R.L. (1980), "A cognitive model of the antecedents and consequences of satisfaction decision", *Journal of Marketing Research*, Vol. 14, No. 4, pp. 460–69.

21. Parasuraman, A., Zeithaml, V.A. and Berry, L.L. (1994), "Alternative scales for measuring service quality: a comparative assessment based on psychometric and diagnostic criteria", *Journal of Retailing*, Vol. 70, No. 3, pp. 201–30.

22. Bojanic, D.C. and Rosen, L.D. (1994), "Measuring service quality in restaurants: an application of the SERVQUAL instrument", *Hospitality Research Journal*, Vol. 18, pp. 3–14.

23. Moreau, C.P., Lehmann, D.R. and Markman, A.B. (2001), "Entrenched knowledge structures and consumer response to new products", *Journal of Marketing Research*, Vol. 38, pp. 14–29.

24. Chossat, V. and Gergaud, O. (2000), "Expert opinion and gastronomy: the recipe for success", *Journal of Cultural Economics*, Vol. 27, pp. 127–41.

25. Arnould and Price, "River magic".

26. Ibid.

27. Charters, "Aesthetic products and aesthetic consumption"; Hirschman, E.C., and Holbrook, M.B. (1982), "Hedonic consumption: emerging concepts, methods, and propositions", *Journal of Marketing*, Vol. 46, pp. 92–101.

28. Hirschman and Holbrook, "The experiential aspects of consumption".

29. Charters, "Aesthetic products and aesthetic consumption".

30. Titz, K., Lanza-Abbott, J. and Cordúra y Cruz, G. (2004), "The anatomy of restaurant reviews: an exploratory study", *International Journal of Hospitality & Tourism Management*, Vol. 5, pp. 49–65.

31. Glanz, K., Basil, M., Maibach, E., Goldberg, J., and Snyder, D. (1998), "Why Americans eat what they do: taste, nutrition, cost, convenience, and weight control concerns as influences on food consumption", *Journal of the American Dietetic Association*, Vol. 98, pp. 1118–26.

32. Lee, S.J. and Cranage, D. (2007), "The relative importance of menu attributes at point of menu selection through conjoint analysis: focused on adolescents", *Journal of Foodservice Business Research*, Vol. 10, pp. 3–18.

33. Arnould and Price, "River magic".

34. Vigneron, Franck and Johnson, L.W. (2004), "Measuring perceptions of brand luxury", *Journal of Brand Management, Vol. 11, No. 6, pp. 484–506.*

35. Pine, J.B. II and Gilmore, J.H. (1998), "Welcome to the experience economy", *Harvard Business Review, Vol. 76, No. 4, pp. 97–105.*

36. East, R., Hammond, K., and Wright, M. (2007), "The relative incidence of positive and negative word of mouth: a multi-category study", *International Journal of Research in Marketing*, Vol. 24, pp. 175–84; Wetzer, I.M., Zeelenberg, M., and Pieters, R. (2007), "'Never eat in that restaurant, I did!' Exploring why people engage in negative word-of-mouth communication", *Psychology & Marketing*, Vol. 24, pp. 661–80.

37. Harp, Stephen L. (2001), *Marketing Michelin: Advertising & Cultural Identity in Twentieth-Century France*, JHU Press, Baltimore, MD.

38. Ray, J. (2005), "Michelin Red Guide, cooked", Brandchannel.com, 7 March, http://www.brandchannel.com/features_profile.asp?pr_id=222 (accessed 6 May 2008).

39. Surlemont, B. and Johnson, C. (2005), "The role of guides in artistic industries: the special case of the 'star system' in the haute-cuisine sector", *Managing Service Quality*, Vol. 15, pp. 577–90.

40. Arnould and Price, "River magic".

41. Ibid.

42. Surlemont and Johnson, "The role of guides in artistic industries".

43. Bojanic and Rosen, "Measuring service quality in restaurants".

44. Hirschman and Holbrook, "Hedonic consumption"; Charters, "Aesthetic products and aesthetic consumption".

45. Lee and Cranage, "The relative importance of menu attributes at point of menu selection through conjoint analysis"; Glanz et al., "Why Americans eat what they do"; Titz et al., "The anatomy of restaurant reviews".

46. Arnould and Price, "River magic"; Chossat and Gergaud, "Expert opinion and gastronomy"; Holbrook and Hisrchman, "The experiential aspects of consumption".

47. Oliver, "A cognitive model of the antecedents and consequences of satisfaction decision".

48. Arnould and Price, "River magic".

49. East et al., "The relative incidence of positive and negative word of mouth".

50. Wetzer et al., "'Never eat in that restaurant, I did!'"

51. Arnould and Price, "River magic", p. 24.

9

Co-Production in Memorable Service Encounters: Three Hot Chocolates in Belgium

BEN WOOLISCROFT* AND ALEXANDRA GANGLMAIR-
WOOLISCROFT†

Keywords

memorable consumption experience, theatrical, co-production, quality

Abstract

What makes something as everyday as a hot chocolate memorable? Three case studies of memorable hot chocolates, all consumed in Belgium – a country well known for its quality chocolate – help uncover the essence of one route to creating memorable customer experiences. The consumer's involvement in co-producing hot chocolate in a theatrical and magical manner represents the central theme running through the three memorable hot chocolates. Other products that use, or could use, theatrical co-production also are discussed.

Memorable Consumption Experiences

This chapter pertains to positive memorable experiences. It is very easy to create a consumption experience that is memorable to consumers for all the wrong reasons – poor service, poor quality, poor hygiene. Memorable consumption experiences that delight the consumers are not everyday experiences; they require firms to go beyond normal

*   Ben Wooliscroft, Marketing Department, School of Business, University of Otago, Clyde Street, Dunedin 9054, New Zealand. E-mail: bwooliscroft@business.otago.ac.nz. Telephone: + 64-3-479-8445.

†   Alexandra Ganglmair-Wooliscroft, Marketing Department, School of Business, University of Otago, Clyde Street, Dunedin 9054, New Zealand. E-mail: aganglmair@business.otago.ac.nz. Telephone: + 64-3-479-8167.

levels of service and product provision. This chapter considers three hot chocolates, all consumed in Belgium, that were memorable consumption experiences.

It's Only Hot Chocolate

A hot chocolate is a normal, everyday drink purchased by millions of people in thousands of cities daily around the world. It is generally ordered at a counter or table, and it is delivered complete. Hot chocolate may have cream, spices, chocolate sprinkles, rum, or marshmallows added, and it is delivered as a finished product, apart from the possibility of adding sugar.

Although in most of the world, consuming chocolate is an everyday, or ordinary, experience, in Belgium, despite its ubiquity, chocolate is taken considerably more seriously. In Belgium (and Switzerland), the law defines what can and cannot be in chocolate. Most products sold as chocolate worldwide are not legally chocolate in Belgium (or Switzerland), where the only fat that chocolate may contain is cocoa butter. Other countries' chocolates typically include other fats for a variety of reasons, including production and ease of storage. Because cocoa butter melts at a very low temperature, Belgian (and Swiss) chocolate melts at 31°C, or lower than the temperature in a human mouth. This attribute leads to the widely regarded superior mouth feel of Belgian chocolate. For many consumers, chocolate of exceptional quality is one of the highlights of a visit to Belgium, making those visitors' involvement with chocolate higher than usual while in Belgium.

We use the experience of three memorable hot chocolates consumed in various cities in Belgium during 2007 to uncover one route – theatrical co-production – to creating memorable customer experiences. All three hot chocolates were enjoyable, but it was not the taste that stuck in our memory; it was the theatrical co-production of the hot chocolates that made them memorable, introducing an element of consumer involvement in the production and leading to a greater investment in its consumption and a memorable experience. It is well established in psychology literature that people remember unusual things as opposed to the things that surround us all the time – the wallpaper of our lives.[1] It is also acknowledged that emotional arousal enhances memory and enhances the chance of incidents being remembered in the long term.[2]

In recent years, customer participation in the production of goods and services has been increasingly encouraged.[3] However, until recently, consumer participation in production has been explored mainly from an economic point of view, and only some research has looked at the psychological responses of consumers.[4] Recent recognition indicates that: "In the experience space, the individual consumer is central, and an event triggers a co-creation experience. The events have a context in space and time, and the involvement of the individual influences that experience. The personal meaning derived from the co-creation experience is what determines the value to the individual."[5]

Three Belgian Hot Chocolates

To explore the way in which three, normally mundane, consumption experiences were memorable, brief narratives on three memorable Belgian hot chocolates follow, before suggesting central themes leading to their memorability. The three hot chocolates were all consumed in the European café tradition – relaxed, un-rushed consumption of beverages and food in comfortable surroundings.

THE GENT HOT CHOCOLATE EXPERIENCE: TWIST YOUR OWN

The first hot chocolate was consumed in the Grote Markt (Main Square) in Gent, a beautiful area surrounded by historic buildings, very much the centre of the city.

We sat in the outside section of a café on a cool summer day, looking out on the historic square and one of the old churches of the city with tourists and locals bustling all around. The café was tidy and clean but unspectacular, apart from its view of the Grote Markt. In the slightly cool weather a hot chocolate felt appropriate, so when the waiter came around I ordered one. It was an unexceptional encounter – a friendly waiter and a customer struggling with the local language (Flemish). But when the hot chocolate was brought out it was very unusual. It consisted of a cup of hot milk and a strange lollipop-like stick with chocolate on the end of it (Figure 9.1). It was quickly clear that the customers

Figure 9.1   Chocolate sticks from Gent[7]

were meant to "make their own" hot chocolate by putting the stick in the hot milk. The chocolate, being Belgian, melted at around 31°C, but to get the chocolate to melt fully into the milk required twisting the stick repeatedly in the hot milk to maximise the exposure of the chocolate's surface to the hot milk. The experience was fun, like a child making something for him- or herself for the first time. The novelty was delightful.[6]

THE BRUGGE "FAMOUS" HOT CHOCOLATE EXPERIENCE: POUR YOUR OWN

Brugge is a leading Belgian tourist attraction, a medieval historic settlement surrounded and dissected by canals. The centre of Brugge has World Heritage status. To serve the hordes of tourists, Brugge has many chocolate retailers and cafés selling hot chocolate.

There is one café that stood out, advertising "famous hot chocolate".[8] How could we resist? We entered the café, sat, and saw the menu: €3.50 for a hot chocolate. That seemed like an awfully high price, but we had already sat down and felt that we could not leave, so we ordered two. The hot chocolates arrived with one chocolate praline and three pieces of chocolate with nougat beside each! The price did not seem so steep after all. The hot chocolate was also served in an interesting way. The cup of hot milk had a saucer on top of it, which contained molten chocolate (Figure 9.2). The customer was meant to tip the molten chocolate into the hot milk and stir. This extra touch was nice and made the whole drink into a bit of theatre. It didn't hurt that the hot chocolate was stunningly good, made with great chocolate, and presented in very civilised surroundings.

Figure 9.2 "Famous" hot chocolate in Brugge

THE OUDENAARDE HOT CHOCOLATE EXPERIENCE: ADD YOUR OWN

Oudenaarde is a town not often visited by tourists, though it is famous for its gin production, tapestries, and as the centre of the Ronde van Vlanderren (the Tour of Flanders bicycle race and museum).

We had stayed overnight in the Steenhuyse Gastenverblijf,[9] and, as is the custom in most of Europe, breakfast was included. The hotel was in a converted sixteenth-century mansion, which had been renovated in a Danish minimalist style by its new owners. Breakfast was a luxury buffet, with hot drinks brought to the table according to the customer's wishes. I asked whether a hot chocolate – often available in Europe at breakfast – was possible. "Of course" it was, but I was not ready for the extraordinary hot chocolate that arrived (Figure 9.3) – a collection of premium chocolate buttons and a mug of hot milk. The customer could choose how many buttons, or which type (dark or milk chocolate), to add to the milk. Once more it was time for me to make my own hot chocolate, in the third different way.

Figure 9.3   Oudenaarde hot chocolate

What Made These Three Hot Chocolates Memorable?

Hot chocolate, for adults, is often associated with childhood, a nostalgic experience. Nostalgic experiences are "affective experiences associated with those cognitive memories of days gone by and with associative links of these feelings to objects of the past",[10] with the concept primarily relating to experiences and objects that have somewhat been lost.

Scents, fragrances, or tastes related to foods associated with one's childhood can elicit memories of hedonic experiences but also relate to a feeling of security and belonging.[11] But the fact that the hot chocolates hark back to childhood memories does not make these hot chocolates memorable; only hot chocolates as an experience set are memorable. And these hot chocolates were very different from the hot chocolates of childhood.

Differentiation has been at the centre of the marketing process, as a source of competitive advantage, for many years.[12] But differentiation is more than a potential source of competitive advantage; it is essential for memorable consumption experiences. As consumers, we do not remember the mundane or ordinary; we remember what is different from the norm.[13] These three hot chocolates were different from the normal hot chocolate that we have encountered. They are also different from one another in some significant respects. The uniqueness of the hot chocolates is an important factor in their being memorable. Uniqueness is, obviously, person-dependent; for many Belgians, the hot chocolates we sampled would be "ordinary" hot chocolates and not memorable in any manner.

Although novelty and surprise are different concepts, with the former being characterised as a mismatch between present and past experiences and the latter being something contrary to existing expectations,[14] in consumption literature, these concepts are frequently combined. In existing literature, novelty and surprise are mainly discussed in the pre-consumption context, such as their role in the decision-making process,[15] with the suggestion that attention gets directed to novel and surprising stimuli. In this situation, with a "low-involvement" purchase, the novelty of the hot chocolates and the associated surprise factor, unexpected as they were, contributed to the memorability of the consumption experiences.

Surprise is a post-consumption reaction related to consumer satisfaction.[16] If surprise is experienced in combination with joy, it leads to delight,[17] a post-consumption emotion that has received some attention in marketing literature.[18] Delighted customers have received the unexpected, and they therefore experience a highly positive emotional state.[19] The psychological stage of delight and pleasant surprise has been linked to more memorable experiences.[20]

There is no question that the three hot chocolates were of good quality, but that is the minimum expectation when ordering a hot chocolate in Belgium. Consumers expect all products to be of a satisfactory quality, meaning that quality alone is unlikely to provide a memorable consumption experience, unless the quality is considerably better than the usual product encountered by the consumer.[21] Given the high quality of the hot chocolates, they were all purchased at good value, despite the initial surprise at the price of one of them. But had they been served, as hot chocolate is generally served, pre-mixed and delivered in a mug/glass/cup, they would have been "normal" hot chocolates at higher-than-normal prices. Value was added by the unusual elements of the consumption experience. When firms produce a "good value" exchange, consumers are not likely to feel that they have been involved in an unjust transaction, which is one of the easiest ways to create a negatively memorable experience.[22] Although fair exchange and good value are necessary for a positive memorable consumption experience, these factors are not enough in and of themselves.

The hot chocolates were all experiences, not simple exchanges followed by consumption. The idea of experience within a consumption context first appeared in marketing and consumer literature in 1982 with Holbrook and Hirschman's pioneering paper on "The experiential aspects of consumption: consumer fantasies, feelings and fun"[23] and has since become a key element in understanding the behaviour of consumers.

Multi-sensory perceptions and emotive aspects are essential components of a multitude of consumption situations[24] whose outcomes are heavily determined by the fun and enjoyment that consumers experience.[25] Experiences therefore emphasise emotions and the inclusion of senses when consumers immerse themselves in activities rather than the cognitive, rational side of consumption.[26]

Experiences allow consumers to seek and find meaning rather than utility, with meaning being a more memorable concept.[27] Engaging in an experience, being engaged and creative, and taking an active role in the production and consumption process also reflects consumers' desire for authenticity.[28]

All of the hot chocolates involved the consumer co-producing the finished product. Co-creation emphasises the interaction between companies and customers in the construction of unique experiences.[29] Here, the sellers of the hot chocolates put the consumer at the centre of the co-production of the hot chocolate experience. All of the co-productions also involved a theatrical, or dramatic, element, with the twisting of the chocolate stick, the pouring of molten chocolate, and the addition of the chocolate buttons to the hot milk. During a theatrical experience, consumption turns into a performance, in which consumers act as participants.[30] All of this activity was experienced in the midst of the Belgian culture, with its reverence for enjoyable and memorable eating, drinking, and socialising.

The consumer changed the white milk into dark hot chocolate in a transformation with magical elements. Having consumers make the transformation allowed them to attribute more of the hot chocolate's quality to themselves. Satisfying experiences are generally linked to intrinsic attribution,[31] so having the consumer involved in and invested in the production made the hot chocolates more satisfying and memorable experiences than they would have been had the "finished product" arrived at the table. By participating in co-production, consumers gain intrinsic benefits such as play and fun, as well as extrinsic values like self-expression.[32]

This finding, however, does not mean that the co-production model of hot chocolates is appropriate for all markets and all consumers. Those consumers who wish to take away their beverage will not want to deal with a mug of hot milk and a chocolate lollipop, a handful of chocolate buttons, or a second smaller mug with molten chocolate in it. But the takeaway customer is purchasing a hot chocolate product, not a hot chocolate experience.

The three hot chocolates were straightforward in their co-production, but the same co-production created the opportunity for product (experience) failure, should the chocolate be spilt, melted, or dropped during the co-production of the hot chocolate. The cafés selling these co-produced hot chocolates may have an elevated rate of product (experience) failure, which requires a service recovery strategy to be in place for consumers who fail with their part of the co-production process. To minimise the likelihood of a service failure of this nature, the chocolate lollipop came in a wrapper to avoid melting; the Brugge famous hot chocolate came in a convenient saucer that was easy to pour from; and the chocolate buttons in Oudennarde were in a convenient container to make it easy and safe to pour them into the hot milk.

Conclusions

The list in Table 9.1 provides elements that firms can use to create memorable consumption experiences. Quality, value, and differentiation are givens for a positive memorable

Table 9.1   Elements that can be used to create positive memorable consumption experiences (required elements emboldened)

- Co-creation/co-production
- Differentiation/uniqueness/novelty
- Magic/transformation
- Quality
- Surprise/delight
- Theatricality
- Value

consumption experience, but the other elements can be used together, as in the cases with the hot chocolates, or individually.

Other examples of theatrical co-production might include table-top cooking in a restaurant (e.g., fondue, stone grill), and any form of kitset, be it a model plane, a car, or a house. For example, the process of assembling the flat pack from IKEA into the bed or cabinet or kitchen, when managed properly – with clear instructions and the correct parts, plainly marked and easily assembled (but not too easily, or it becomes boring) – has the opportunity to create a memorable experience. What can firms add to this co-production process to enhance the experience for consumers? The items in the list suggest way consumers can consider the offerings and potential offerings.

If firms decide to pursue this type of co-production in the search for memorable consumer experiences, they must accept that they are giving up control over the final form of their product; consumers may not complete their side of the co-production as the firm intends. The firm also must consider who its (potential) consumers are and what their ability levels are. The co-production experience should be challenging without being too difficult, easy without being boring.

The implication for managers is that they should go beyond current firm-centric models of co-production and investigate how far consumers can be involved in co-production of experiences that will be satisfying and memorable. Even a product as ordinary as hot chocolate can stand out by involving the consumer in its production. The appropriate use of some of or all of the elements listed in Table 9.1 can make a mundane product a memorable consumption experience, allowing the consumer to become an advocate for the product.

Notes

1.   Kishiyama, M. and Yonelinas, A. (2003), "Novelty effects on recollection and familiarity in recognition memory", *Memory & Cognition*, Vol. 31, No. 7, pp. 1045–51; Tulving, E. and Kroll, N. (1995), "Novelty assessment in brain and long-term memory encoding", *Psychonomic Bulletin & Review*, Vol. 2, No. 3, pp. 387–90.
2.   McGaugh, J. (2000), "Memory – a century of consolidation", *Science*, Vol. 287, No. 5451, pp. 248–51.

3.	Bendapudi, N. and Leone, R. (2003), "Psychological implications of customer participation in co-production", *Journal of Marketing*, Vol. 67, No. 1, pp. 14–28; Vargo, S. and Lusch, R. (2007), "Service-dominant logic: continuing the evolution", *Journal of the Academy of Marketing Science*, Vol. 36, No. 1, pp. 1–10.

4.	Ibid.

5.	Prahalad, C. and Ramaswamy, V. (2003), "The new frontier of experience innovation", *MIT Sloan Management Review*, Vol. 44, No. 4, pp. 12–18, at p. 14.

6.	Choc-o-lait (2007), "Choc-o-lait website", available at http://www.choc-o-lait.com (accessed 15 January 2009).

7.	Stadt Gent (2008), "Stadt gent", available at http://www.gent.be/ (accessed 15 January 2009).

8.	Chocolaterie Sukerbuyc (2008), "Chocolaterie sukerbuyc", available at http://www.sukerbuyc. be/ (accessed 15 January 2009).

9.	Gastenverblijf Steenhuyse (2008), "Steenhuyse gastenverblijf", available at http://www. steenhuyse.info/ (accessed 15 January 2009).

10.	Holbrook, M. and Schindler, R. (2003), "Nostalgic bonding: Exploring the role of nostalgia in the consumption experience", *Journal of Consumer Behaviour*, Vol. 3, No. 2, pp. 107–27, at p. 108.

11.	Ibid.

12.	Alderson, W. (1957), *Marketing Behavior and Executive Action: A Functionalist Approach to Marketing*, Richard D. Irwin, Homewood, Ill.

13.	Kishiyama and Yonelinas, "Novelty effects on recollection and familiarity in recognition memory"; Tulving and Kroll, "Novelty assessment in brain and long-term memory encoding".

14.	Bianchi, M. (1998), "The active consumer: introduction", in M. Bianchi (ed.), *The Active Consumer: Novelty and Surprise in Consumer Choice*, Routledge, London, pp. 1–17.

15.	Bettman, J., Luce, M., and Payne, J. (1998), "Constructive consumer choice processes", *Journal of Consumer Research*, Vol. 25, No. 3, pp. 187–217; Bianchi, "The active consumer".

16.	Oliver, R.L. (1997), *Satisfaction: A Behavioral Perspective on the Consumer*, Irwin McGraw-Hill, Boston, MA; Vanhamme, J. and de Bont, C. (2008), "'Surprise gift' purchases: customer insights from the small electrical appliance market", *Journal of Retailing*, Vol. 84, No. 3, pp. 354–69.

17.	Plutchik, R. (1960/80), *Emotion: A Psychoevolutionary Synthesis*, MESA Press, Chicago.

18.	Oliver, *Satisfaction*; Rust, R. and Oliver, R. (2000). "Should we delight the customer?", *Journal of the Academy of Marketing Science*, Vol. 28, No. 1, pp. 86–94.

19.	Oliver, R., Rust, R., and Varki, S. (1997), "Customer delight: foundations, findings, and managerial insight", *Journal of Retailing*, Vol. 73, No. 3, pp. 311–36.

20.	Pine, B. and Gilmore, J. (1999), *The Experience Economy: Work is Theatre & Every Business a Stage*, Harvard Business School Press, Boston, MA.

21.	Zeithaml, V., Berry, L., and Parasuraman, A. (1996), "The behavioral consequences of service quality", *Journal of Marketing*, Vol. 60, No. 2, pp. 31–46.

22.	Bolton, L., Warlop, L., and Alba, J. (2003), "Consumer perceptions of price (un)fairness", *Journal of Consumer Research*, Vol. 29, No. 4, pp. 474–91.

23.	Holbrook, M. and Hirschman, E. (1982), "The experiential aspects of consumption: consumer fantasies, feelings, and fun", *Journal of Consumer Research*, Vol. 9, No. 2, pp. 132–40.

24.	Carù, A. and Cova, B. (2003), "Revisiting consumption experience: a more humble but complete view of the concept", *Marketing Theory*, Vol. 3, No. 2, pp. 267–86; Holbrook and Hirschman, "The experiential aspects of consumption".

25. Hirschman, E. and Holbrook, M. (1982), "Hedonic consumption: emerging concepts, methods and propositions", *Journal of Marketing*, Vol. 46, No. 3, pp. 92–101.

26. Carù and Cova, "Revisiting consumption experience"; Carù, A. and Cova, B. (2007), "Consuming experiences: an introduction", in A. Carù and B. Cova (eds), *Consuming Experiences*, Routledge, London, pp. 3–16.

27. Carù and Cova, "Consuming experiences".

28. Sherry Jr., J.F., Kozinets, R.V., and Borghini, S. (2007), "Agents in paradise: experiential co-creation through emplacement, ritualization, and community", in Carù and Cova, *Consuming Experiences*, pp. 17–33.

29. LaSalle, D. and Britton, T. (2002), *Priceless: Turning Ordinary Products into Extraordinary Experiences*, Harvard Business School Press, Boston, MA; Prahalad, C. and Ramaswamy, V. (2004), "Co-creation experiences: the next practice in value creation", *Journal of Interactive Marketing*, Vol. 18, No. 3, pp. 5–14.

30. Arnould, E.J. (2007), "Consuming experiences: retrospects and prospects", in Carù and Cova, *Consuming Experiences*, pp. 185–94.

31. Oliver, *Satisfaction*.

32. Etgar, M. (2008), "A descriptive model of the consumer co-production process", *Journal of the Academy of Marketing Science*, Vol. 36, No. 1, pp. 97–108.

Part IV
Management
of Customer
Experiences

10 Oh Yeah, I Remember That Store! Memory, Experience, and Value

BARRY J. BABIN* AND ADILSON BORGES†

Keywords

shopping value, consumer memory, hedonic value, retailing

Abstract

Retail memory refers to knowledge accumulated through repeated retail and service experiences that influences consumer preferences. The framework presented here describes retail memory as instrumentally affecting hedonic and utilitarian shopping value. The purpose of this chapter is to describe a framework that will be useful for understanding the mechanisms by which retail memories create shopping value and by which value shapes memories. The framework is not intended to be complete but rather provides some practical and theoretical insights that may stimulate more thought and research. Memory is pervasive in the consumer experience; however, memory is far from pervasive in retailing research. This chapter attempts to bring more attention to this shortcoming.

Introduction

The capacity for consumers to remember things, just as is any human endeavor involving memory, is truly remarkable in many ways. So many memories involve consumption. The memories impressed on a child can remain vivid and continue to shape the value of

* Professor Barry J. Babin, Max P. Watson Professor of Business and Department Head, Marketing & Analysis, College of Business, Louisiana Tech University, Ruston, LA 71272, USA. E-mail: bbabin@latech.edu.

† Professor Adilson Borges, IRC Professor of Marketing, Auchan Chair of Retailing, Reims Management School, 59 rue Pierre Taittinger, BP 302, Reims, France. E-mail: adilson.borges@reims-ms.fr.

consumption experiences. For instance, the special memories that surround childhood Christmas experiences endure, create nostalgia, and largely drive adult consumption behavior related to Christmas rituals. The fact that *White Christmas* by Bing Crosby, originally recorded in 1942, remains the bestselling Christmas single and is among the most popular musical recordings ever exemplifies people's desire to recapture, in some way, their pleasant experiences.

Many consumption memories involve retail experiences. The memories may be of recent events, such as recalling a difficult and frustrating experience when the consumer was unable to buy the items that he or she wanted most and had to settle for something less. Alternatively, the memories may tap into past experiences and the sights, sounds and smells of Christmas shopping done long ago. In either case, memories determine value, either in the form of the recall of the previous events or in the way the past memories affect patronage decisions and behavior in the present.

Retail scholars and retail managers have an important stake in understanding the role that memory plays in shaping value and the role that value plays in shaping memory. For scholars, retail memory research can allow for greater theoretical development. For managers, retail memory research can emphasize that the retail shopping experience is not just a "here and now" phenomenon. Present events are very much influenced by past events, a point that few would argue, but managers would benefit from knowing more precisely the mechanisms by which present, past, and future come together. With such knowledge, they could direct the experience through retail design, merchandising, and management in a way that creates more positive and effective consumer memories.

The purpose of this chapter is to provide some introspective reflection on connections between consumer memory and the value of consumption experiences. In particular, the focus here is on the retailing context and the mechanisms by which shopping memories create shopping value and by which value shapes memories. In presenting and elaborating on a broad theoretical framework, the intended contribution of this chapter lies not in providing a comprehensive review of all memory research that may be relevant to consumer behavior. Such a review would indeed be extensive. Instead, because relatively little memory-related research directly involves retail shopping contexts specifically, the contribution of this chapter lies in provoking further thought and motivating research aimed at developing, correcting, and refining this body of knowledge further.

Shoppers and Memory

Should retailers attempt to build shopping experiences that will make a lasting impression on a shopper's memory? The intuitive response is that they should do so only if the experiences are positive. But is that view too narrow? Are shoppers' memories driven primarily by the products that they purchase or by the totality of the interactions that constitute the whole shopping experience? The following example provides a frame of reference for discussing the way that memory can shape a retail consumption experience.

ILLUSTRATION

Sandy enters the store with a bit of apprehension. She needs to find a dress for her friend's wedding, and she wants something really special. Just two weeks ago, she went to Nordstrom's while on a lunch break and purchased a black dress that she wore to the company Christmas party. In thinking about her friend's wedding, she recalls this event and also the name of Kathy, a helpful salesperson who fortunately encouraged her to accent the black dress with just the right belt and shoes. Never before did she receive so many compliments on her looks. She also thinks back to a childhood experience when she served as a maid of honor in an uncle's wedding. She remembers how special she felt and seems to recall visiting Nordstrom's with her mother on a mom-and-daughter excursion to find the dress and shoes she wore that day. All those events come to her like a flash. She calls her mom and invites her to come along on the shopping trip, and she actually feels comfortable, relaxed, and quite certain that she will have a successful shopping adventure with her mother in a store about which she has many fond memories. The occasional instances of less than prompt service or out-of-stock merchandise get overwhelmed by the numerous high-value experiences she has had.

A Quick Reminder (No Pun) of Basic Memory Theory

Memory functions generally are well understood. Although many variations exist when it comes to the details of memory functioning, the general theory, which states that memory exists in multiple forms and is processed in multiple stages, is generally accepted. This very brief overview provides context for the subsequent material. Human memory consists of three main storage systems: sensory memory, short-term memory, and long-term memory.

SENSORY MEMORY

Sensory memory involves the very brief way that people mentally maintain sensations from any sensory mechanisms while waiting for other memory processes to take over. Sensory memory is very brief in duration, usually fading away in less than a second. When Sandy gets to the store, her sensory memory will be highly engaged as she takes in all the sensations and touches, sees, feels, and even smells the dresses on display or tries on a few. Stronger stimuli are more likely to lead to elaboration and alter the value of an experience. However, with sensory memory alone, she will not develop a meaningful and lasting impression.

SHORT-TERM MEMORY

Short-term memory, also known as working or workbench memory, stores small pieces of information for short periods of time. Past research suggests that working memory can store at most about seven pieces of information – or "chunks" – at a time (with a standard deviation of about two).[1] All the work gets performed in short-term memory, which means that incoming stimuli get processed by attaching them to other stimuli pulled from long-term memory in an effort to give something meaning. When Sandy recognizes the need to go shopping, the information about the upcoming wedding becomes active in her working memory, and her recent shopping experience comes to mind, including the meanings associated with Nordstrom's. After being processed in working memory, information may or may not end up as useful knowledge, depending on the process of meaningful encoding. Sandy was able to code the name of the salesperson effectively on her earlier visit to Nordstrom's, as indicated by her ability to remember the salesperson's name.

LONG-TERM MEMORY

Long-term memory stores information permanently, together with meaning. Associative networks form in long-term memory to link concepts together with varying strength and allow consumers to form rules about specific behaviors. These associative networks also provide the pool of schemas that fuel short-term memory. Each time a concept goes from long- to short-term memory, it becomes malleable again. Therefore, whenever someone interacts with a retailer in some way, the schema that represents that particular retail information in long-term memory is subject to adjustment. The better known that retailer is and the more familiar is a customer with a retailer, the less its schema will change. If Sandy is unable to find a dress for the wedding, her memory will make adjustments to the Nordstrom's schema, but given her long history with Nordstrom's, more than one unsuccessful shopping trip will be needed to alter the cognitive rules that become active when she associates Nordstrom's with shopping.

RETAIL SHOPPER MEMORY

In most ways, there is nothing particularly special or unique about retail consumer memory compared with general memory. However, the focus on the retail shopping context is what makes this topic most unique, in addition to the inevitable focus on value and exchange that coincides with shopping. Furthermore, the brief review of memory presented makes clear that retail shopper memory is both a process and a result. In other words, the term memory serves as both a noun and an action. In noun form, memory refers to the results or exactly what things get stored as knowledge. In verb form, memory means the process by which these results are created. Succinctly, we define retail shopper memory as all the psychological processes by which consumers store knowledge related to their retail shopping experiences. The processes of developing, adjusting, and coding, and the results of these processes in the form of associative networks and schemata are all included in this conceptual domain. Retail shopper memory is both an antecedent and an outcome for explaining shopping experiences. Memory is necessary to function as a retail consumer, but it also is a result of functioning as a retail consumer. In this chapter, the phrase retail memory will be interchangeable with retail shopper memory or retail consumer memory.

A Framework for Exploring Retail Memory

Figure 10.1 provides the proposed retail memory framework. Although we use retail memory here, our intention is to account for common service experiences as well. The framework suggests that retail shopper memory directly affects retail meaning, shopper perceptions, and the affect shoppers experience when they shop with or contemplate various retail options.

Affect includes emotional elements such as pleasure, satisfaction, excitement, warmth, and more attitudinal elements, which could be represented simply by liking.

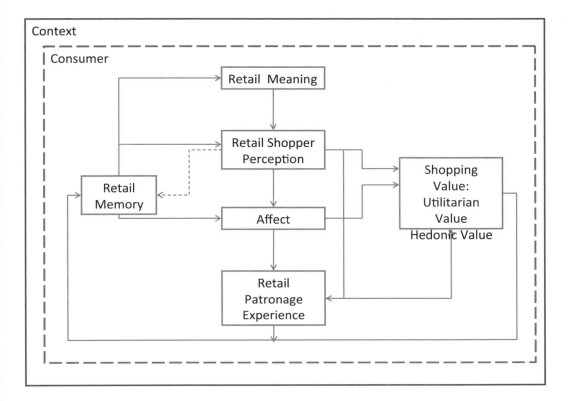

Figure 10.1 Retail memory framework

Note: Dashed arrows represent implicit memory.

Source: Developed by the authors.

The retail patronage experience includes behavioral aspects of shopping-related events, such as shopping in a store, making purchases, and approaching salespeople, among other things.

Similar to marketing activities in general, the key outcome of shopping-related activities is value – or more specifically, personal shopping value.[2] Personal shopping value represents the overall perceived worth of a shopping activity, considering all costs and benefits. The basic measure of shopping value captures two encompassing dimensions: utilitarian value represents how well a shopping instance allows some task to be completed, and hedonic value represents how much experiential gratification a shopping instance delivers. These two dimensions provide common outcomes of behavioral, personal, and environmental variables, especially the affect associated with a retail atmosphere, and they drive loyalty-related behavior.[3] In the following sections, we explain the individual paths that constitute the framework in detail.

MEMORY AND MEANING

Practically all meaning is relative in some sense. A shopper's past gives meaning to what he or she sees and experiences today. Retailer efforts to position themselves in the mind of the consumer depend upon how consumer memory processes retail stimuli. Deciding between a low-end or high-end store is possible only because past information retrieved from memory enables the consumer to "know" how a store fits in the appropriate category. Consumers who view themselves as "high-end" will tend to seek out "high-end" alternatives.

All meaning is attached to stimuli in short-term memory. Consumers interact with a retailer, associations become processed and meaningfully encoded, and the resulting nodes of knowledge end up representing retail phenomenon. Thus, memory represents human knowledge and is developed in a cognitively inductive way as confirming experiences reinforce meaning and disconfirming instances make knowledge less certain or can even change meaning.[4] Thus, many children develop positive perceptions of McDonald's and come to learn what a "fast-food" experience is through the activities they experience and associate with a McDonald's visit. The good feelings associated with a Happy Meal and joining friends on the playground reinforce this concept. In contrast, a restaurant without a playground and without toys may end up representing an entirely different concept, even if the food items are quite the same.

Over time, consumers develop cognitive stereotypes, or in the language of social cognitive psychology, prototypes or exemplars, against which they compare all retail types. For example, the prototypical fast-food restaurant is characterized by bright colors, a menu board, and, indeed, a playground.[5] Assuming McDonald's is the exemplar stored in long-term memory, consumers perceive whether a restaurant is a fast-food restaurant to the extent that it shares associated characteristics with McDonald's. An automobile dealership is judged to match or not match the stereotype based on the appearance of the showroom but also largely on the appearance and demeanor of the salespeople who approach customers.[6] Generally speaking, the more a schema gets reinforced, the stronger it becomes, the more resistant the meaning is to change, and the more predictable shopper behavior becomes in turn, because the rules for engagement get pre-programmed over time. When a retail schema representing a store type becomes very vivid, well defined, and representative of a shopping category, better than any other schema, it becomes the category exemplar. Seldom is a retailer that becomes a category exemplar unsuccessful.

Thus, the meaning of the store type, store brand, and store itself are shaped by memory processes. In addition, active concepts can shape meaning. For instance, situational factors may change the meaning of some concept temporarily or shift the rules for the shopper. Shoppers who visit stores with friends, with their mothers, or with other relatives, as in Sandy's case, may have to adjust rules about shopping behavior, at least temporarily. For instance, they may shop in a store for which they have a negative meaning because they would be uncomfortable saying no to their shopping partner. This point brings us more specifically to perceptions.

MEMORY AND SHOPPER PERCEPTIONS

The schemas that exist in long-term memory provide bases for comparisons that shape meaning. Long-term memory is structured within an associative network that links all schemas together in a huge cognitive net. Each schema provides a way for consumers to develop expectations for a store. These expectations become integral in determining shopper satisfaction with the retail experience. For example, Nordstrom's is a category exemplar for an upscale department store for many consumers like Sandy. The Nordstrom's schema is very vivid, and her expectations for what will happen during a visit are well developed and somewhat resistant to change. Sandy expects to find a wide arrangement of acceptable dresses on her shopping trip. Her expectations do not guarantee a successful shopping trip, but the fact that she is a loyal customer with a strong schema will likely shape her in-store perceptions to some extent. This shaping may become more obvious in a comparison with a shopper who has heard of Nordstrom's and knows that it is high-end department store but has no actual experience shopping there.

Assimilation–contrast effects

What consumers perceive in a given situation depends considerably on assimilation–contrast processes.[7] Sandy, being loyal to Nordstrom's, may be more likely to have assimilation effects than a consumer shopping there for the first time. The meaning of Nordstrom's, captured by the active schema, may frame the shopping experience. Thus, to some extent, anything that Nordstrom's sells will benefit from a very positive schema because categorization processes in memory affect in-store product evaluations.[8] The same dress that Sandy might see at another store is likely to be evaluated more favorably at Nordstrom's, and chances are, her expectations for the product assortment are likely to be met. In contrast, assuming the unfamiliar consumer shares similar tastes with Sandy, her opinions are likely more subject to change. If her expectations are not met, she has no loyalty-based psychological need to maintain balance in memory. Thus, unless she is very excited about her first trip to Nordstrom's, she is more likely to experience a contrast effect, even with the same product assortment.

One particular area in need of further research is the way the actual retail environment and the subsequent meaning that develops alter shoppers' price perceptions. Consider a nicely decorated grocery store located in a high-end shopping center. Over time, its customers develop the impression that a consumer gets rewarded with a pleasant experience by visiting this store, which may seem like a good thing. However, along with this impression is an equally as strong impression that prices are high. In an attempt to bring customers back and generate traffic, the store manager decides to reduce prices by an average of 10 percent, which positions the store objectively (as measured by a price-scan institute) as the lowest price store in its trade zone. However, the price perceptions (i.e., price image) do not change, nor does the traffic level. This particular store's retail schema proved very resistant to change, and the upscale meaning continued to create perceptions of high prices. In fact, the idea that an upscale store would have very low prices is inconsistent with consumer memory. Thus, the retailer may be better off building on the idea of superior service and trying to create differentiation in this way, because competing on price may prove difficult in the face of a persistent "non-discount" schema.

An active schema can even affect consumer tastes – literally. The very same steak will have a different flavor when served in a beautiful steak house as opposed to a simple roadside drive-in. This phenomenon is sometimes called the rose-colored glass effect, and store atmosphere may be one factor that can frame the way we perceive and experience the product. Similarly, prior research shows that consumers spend more time looking at, and are willing to spend three times the amount for, wine when they were listening to classical music as opposed to Top 40 music.[9] Not only do price perceptions change, but the entire shopping experience becomes more enjoyable and thus higher in value.

The meanings shaped by memory influence perceptions in many ways. Ultimately, these perceptions drive the retail experience, affecting store choice decisions, brand choice decisions, and subsequent reactions to the retail experience – including shopping value.

Implicit memory

Figure 10.1 displays a dotted line from shopper perception back to memory, because processes like the mere exposure effect are in play. Consider an online shopping experience. An online shopper is exposed to dozens of banner advertisements in a single browsing experience. However, after shopping, he or she probably cannot remember any of the banner advertisements, and a normal shopper does not click through any of these advertisements, according to the average click-through rate of less than 2 percent. Nonetheless, the background banner ads have some effect on memory, and these effects are even stronger the less attention a consumer pays to the banner ads.[10] Although no real perception of the banner ads may be obtained consciously, implicit memory processes the background information, which eventually creates small traces that affect the meaning of things. Similarly, do virtual backgrounds produce the same implicit memory effects as real backgrounds? If so, the more involved a consumer is with a shopping task, the more he is likely to be cognitively and affectively affected by non-focal environmental elements. Whether real or virtual, the area of implicit memory in a shopping context is ripe for further study.

Virtual memory

A shopper's behavior leaves behind a memory trace in the form of not only episodic memory but, more and more, virtual memory, which includes electronic records of purchase behavior. Companies can keep profiles of what preferred customers like to do and tailor customized packages of benefits that are more likely to lead to satisfaction and a positively valued experience. Thus, virtual memory can work together with a customer's actual memory to shape the shopping experience.[11] Clearly though, virtual memory can induce perceptions into the mind of a consumer who otherwise may have difficulty successfully retrieving past behavior: "What was the Champagne that I purchased last May?" Furthermore, websites can use past behavior to suggest other shopping and buying opportunities. The interaction between virtual and shopper memory is ripe for further research and offers opportunities to leverage technology for retailers.

MEMORY AND AFFECT

Sensory memory and affect

One factor playing a key role in the process of encoding the information into long-term memory is emotion. Emotionally intense events are better recalled than more neutral events. The amygdala seems to play an important role in modulating the strength of conscious memory, according to its emotional valence.[12] These findings support the view that amygdala activation reflects moment-to-moment subjective emotional experience and that this activation enhances memory in relation to the emotional intensity of an experience.[13] Retailers that want to be remembered should strive to create pleasant emotions during the consumer's shopping experience, and perhaps even more important, they should react quickly to critical incidences that may cause strong negative emotions among shoppers.

Even low-level perceptions can alter a shopper's feelings, perhaps in a direct link from sensory memory. For instance, environmental stimuli such as lighting, colors, and odors can change the way shoppers feel. Citrus scents can produce more pleasant emotions than the ambient scents that would exist in shopping environments otherwise. The scents also become a basis for changing recall and even mood-congruent recall, as well as feeding back through value to leave emotional memory traces that in turn can affect retail meaning.[14]

Schema-based affect

Every retail schema develops a schema-based affect associated with it. Schema-based affect not only changes the feelings a person has when the schema becomes active, but the affect also gets tagged with the concept in a way that alters subsequent reactions.[15] Thus, a child traumatized by a clown in a Sears store may well develop negative affect that persists and becomes active to some degree each time he or she encounters or even thinks about a Sears store. Whatever the source, once a shopping experience changes the affective state of a shopper, this change directly alters the shopping value that results.

Nostalgia

In the preceding illustration, Sandy seems to experience nostalgia when considering her shopping trip. Nostalgia is based on memories of the past and produces a variety of emotions, generally centered around feelings of warmth. The feelings that accompany nostalgia create approach behaviors that may lead to shopping value, but the feelings themselves also create value directly in the form of hedonic shopping value. More and more, retailer and service environments are designed intentionally to evoke memories of the past. The walls of restaurants are often covered with artefacts of bygone eras. Furthermore, consumers have a desire for things that created pleasure long ago to remain as they were – or at least to have the appearance of remaining as they were.[16] Even the experience of a scent associated with a past, pleasant experience, such as the smell of a Christmas tree in a retail store, can evoke nostalgia and create value.[17]

Important questions remain regarding the pervasiveness of positive effects due to nostalgia. Are there some situations in which nostalgia does not create a positive experience? In particular, a consumer's memory may create expectations that are impossible for a retailer to attain. A childhood memory gets framed by the experience of being a child, such that when the same experience is framed by adulthood, things that seemed so pleasant may not be particularly pleasant after all. Are certain segments of the market then turned off by nostalgia? Perhaps certain segments are so future oriented that they consciously try to suppress the past. Certainly though, nostalgia is one way in which memory clearly links to shopping emotion, experience, and value.

MEMORY AND PATRONAGE EXPERIENCE

The framework proposed in Figure 10.1 links memory to actual patronage experience. Although memory could be linked directly to behavior, as might be the argument following from classical conditioning, the indirect mechanisms are the focus in this chapter. Memories are necessary to create meaning and adjust and create new perceptions. Inevitably, human perception evokes appraisals, and these appraisals have affective content. These processes come together to affect the entire retail experience.

This chapter defines the retail experience broadly and includes multiple dimensions. Store choice is perhaps a key patronage decision, and until a consumer decides to patronize a retailer, that retailer has no chance of gaining sales from that particular consumer. Memory certainly influences store choice as previous experiences become stored and drive the schemas and scripts that come to mind when consumers recognize a need to go shopping. The processes shape the affective reactions that not only color attitudes about shopping with a given retailer but also frame the actual shopping experience. The retail experience also includes brand choices and selections made within the environment. Again, these choices are framed by the meaning and feelings evoked by the retail concept. The social interactions that take place in the social environment are also part of the retail experience. For instance, we come to have certain expectations for what a "Nordstrom" or "Carrefour" shopper looks like. When these expectations are confirmed or disconfirmed, consumers have different reactions that may change their behavior and even cause small adjustments to the retail schema. The behavior that retail shoppers exhibit will precipitate further evaluations and further affect, perhaps in the form of consumer satisfaction or dissatisfaction. Ultimately, this discussion brings us to value.

ALL RESULTING IN VALUE

Ultimately, consumers all pursue value. Shopping activities are and were worth doing to the extent that they provide value. Memory, meaning, and perception are important parts of the shopper's pursuit of value. The retail memory framework outlines a process by which memory primarily influences value indirectly. Affect and the actual retail shopping activities that form the retail experience facilitate memory's influence. A few ways that memory and personal shopping value may be linked have been illustrated; the following list outlines a few other specific mechanisms by which a shopper's memory may link to value:

- A loyal consumer who has often before found a good cheese selection at Auchan visits Auchan and purchases several different cheeses for a small party. In this way, one key meaning associated with Auchan is a good place to buy cheese, and after the shopping experience is complete, the consumer realizes utilitarian shopping value.
- Sandy from our illustration enjoys the shopping excursion with her mother, and they relive some good times of the past. She also tries on at least half a dozen new dresses and gets her mother's reaction to each one of them. All in all, the afternoon adventure was much better than working! In this way, the trip creates high hedonic value through all the pleasant feelings evoked through multiple processes involving memory. The fact that she was successful in making a purchase means that Sandy realizes utilitarian shopping value as well.
- An American consumer recounts a visit to Harrods of London. He recalls the orchestra playing in the store and the indulgences of the food halls and enjoying a glass or two of wine with his friend from London. The activation of this memory and the feelings

associated with these perceptions influence the consumer's mood in a positive way and create hedonic shopping value.

- Another consumer moves to a new town and visits Java Town, a chain of upscale coffee shops. Each time she purchased a bag of fresh roasted coffee beans at her old Java Town, she received a free espresso. On her first visit to the new Java Town, the clerk charges her for the espresso. In this case, the expectations created by previous experiences have led to an unfavorable emotional reaction, which diminishes both value dimensions.

- Even false memories may create value. For example, autobiographical advertising can modify memories about the past. Two experiments show that subjects express greater confidence that something happened in their childhood when the event was suggested by the ad (e.g., shaking hands with Mickey Mouse), even if the event is impossible (e.g., shaking hands with Bugs Bunny at Disney).[18] However, it seems that to be planted successfully in memory, the event should be plausible and the script relevant.[19] In this case, retrospective but constructed memories may still alter feelings and thereby create value. They also may end up feeding back into memory and changing the schema associated with the retailer, which is important particularly when the consumer has an actual bad experience with the retailer. The bad experience reinforces a rule in memory discouraging patronage. However, if the consumer can be coaxed into constructing a positive but imaginary experience, the rule becomes reframed in a way that will encourage further store visits.

THE FULL CIRCLE: SHOPPING VALUE MAKES MEMORIES

When talking about memorable shopping experiences, we do not imply that only one shopping visit will decide if the consumer will or will not vividly remember (though it might happen in some cases) this shopping experience in the future. Moreover, retail memory is probably better understood as a dynamic concept that results from multiple encounters between a retailer and shopper. Many of the experiences are mundane but accumulated and thus become prominent in an associative network. Over time, a retailer that produces value through these experiences will be remembered in a good way. Cognitively, the consumer develops rules that go with that particular retail brand schema that motivate and encourage further patronage behavior. The rules can become pronounced, such that the consumer comes to identify strongly with the particular retailers and a positive halo builds up in the form of positive schema-based affect. When this happens, the retailer becomes distinct in the mind of the consumer, who sees few substitutes for that particular store.

The relationship between value and memory is not typically linear, because the experiences that leave the least effect on memory are the mundane – those that provide only a small amount of value. In contrast, those that provide substantial amounts of value – or perhaps especially those that provide negative utilitarian and hedonic value – are likely to have the greatest effect. Such a rationale is theoretically consistent with the role of heightened arousal in human experience. Arousal plays an important role on both short- and long-term memory. In a picture recall task, pictures rated as highly arousing are better remembered both immediately after the presentation and in a free recall task performed a year later.[20] Retailers can try to enhance memory by creating excitement (which combines pleasure and arousal) and avoiding anger or anxiety (which may be arousing but are unpleasant) in their stores. Arousal and emotional experiences in particular are assessed through hedonic value, which then ties back to memory.

Good and bad outcomes in terms of value are likely not recalled in the same way. People will list more positive shopping outcomes than negative when prompted, because positive experiences are likely to be both more frequent and more easily retrieved/ processed. Psychologically, positive experiences are considered more cognitively dense in that they share more connections with each other than with negative events.[21] However, negative events, including critical incidences, are likely charged with emotion and stand out distinctly; thus, though more difficult to process in memory, they may have greater effects on behavior. If so, retailers' efforts at disproportionately redressing bad experiences may be wise. One tool in addressing consumers who have built a firewall in memory that prohibits them from patronizing a store is to make other consumers' experiences so valuable that their patronage experiences become matters of conversation. The credibility that another consumer brings may cause information to have greater impact than would information coming directly from the retailer. Thus, customers spreading positive word of mouth may be more effective than discounts in enticing a jilted customer into returning.

Simply put, value plays the key role in consumer learning. The impact on learning is a derivative of experienced value. Consumers will sometimes intentionally repeat experiences that they have known to produce less than high satisfaction or quality. However, consumers are not likely to repeat experiences coded in memory as offering no value.

Closing Memories

This chapter is intended to stimulate thought on how the retail experience interacts with human memory. Clearly, many of the relationships can be developed in far more detail, and eventually, the framework presented herein should be elaborated upon and developed further. However, the framework presents several basic premises that have implications for further research and retail practice.

HOW TO BUILD A MEMORABLE SHOPPING EXPERIENCE

Store choice is one of the most basic though sometimes overlooked types of decisions that consumers face. Although brand choice tends to receive more recognition, consumers often first decide on which retailer to patronize and then decide on brands from among those that the retailer offers. Retailers should take steps that cause customers to bring them to mind when they recognize a relevant need. Considering the way customers process, store, and retrieve information from memory, three interrelated, focal questions that retailers should consider to maintain their place in consumers' minds and hearts are:

- How can we be noticed?
- How can we be remembered as performing our function better than any other retailer?
- How can we create an arousing and positive experience for our customers?

Noticeable

To be remembered, the target must be noticed. New retailers that want to stand out from the crowd should provide a different and unique experience. This differentiation should be perceived, or noticed, by the consumer. Many elements provide avenues for differentiation. For example, the store atmosphere is one of the more visible aspects of the shopping experience. The design, the colors, light, scents, and various other environmental elements come together to convey a meaning to the consumer and help consumers meaningfully encode this experience in long-term memory. At the Maldives Hilton Hotel, the main restaurant is actually built below sea level, where diners can eat as exotic fish, marine turtles, or other sea animals swim by. That is different, that is noticeable, and that creates a memorable retail experience.

Meaning and value also may be heightened by creating a stronger sensory experience. Several upscale restaurants offer a blind dinner, in which diners eat in a completely dark room while wearing blindfolds. The restaurants sometimes go to the extreme and use wait-staff who are legally blind and trained to serve customers. The consumer can then focus on non-visual senses while eating, which heightens the taste experience. That is, they can truly learn what food and wine taste like. The unique experience is likely to create value and leave a lasting impression of not only the event but also the food and wine consumed.

Performance

A retail name can become synonymous with some function, generally over time as the combination of repeated utilitarian value and store performance create a lasting impression. Office Depot is extremely salient among shoppers who need basic office supplies. In many parts of the United States, Wal-Mart is synonymous with the need for common consumer goods in general. Time and time again, consumers go to Wal-Mart and return with bags and bags of merchandise. Many consumers believe that Wal-Mart performs better on the convenience and price functions than any other retailer. However, Wal-Mart shoppers typically report low satisfaction with the shopping experience, yet the utilitarian value constantly brings them back.

Be exciting

Highly arousing experiences are better recalled than low arousal experiences. Consumers wait in line outside the American Girl stores in Chicago for the unique and emotional experience. Mothers and daughters enter the store together with their dolls, and all can have their hair styled together (including the doll). Another example comes from Asia: just before the summer season, Carrefour, the world's second-largest retailer, painted all the external walls of its Shanghai store with beaches and holiday motifs. Of course, the store attracted a huge amount of publicity for this unusual décor, but the initiative also created excitement and curiosity among consumers.

Become valuable

Delivering value is one of the best ways to build a memorable experience. Both types of value, utilitarian and hedonic, can contribute to create a memorable shopping experience.

Utilitarian value can help consumers associate with feelings of accomplishment. Hedonic value can create an inert desire to relive an experience. Retailers and service providers should focus on delivering value. When consumers believe the value equation is balanced in their favor, they will develop rules in memory that bring them back, time and time again. Retailers that can provide high levels of both utilitarian and hedonic value are likely to be recalled most easily. Both theory and practice will benefit from greater insights derived from testing, developing, and extending our proposed retail memory framework.

Notes

1   Miller, G.A. (1956), "The magical number 7 plus or minus two: some limits on your capacity for processing information", *Psychological Review*, Vol. 63, No. 2, pp. 81–97.

2   Babin, B.J., Darden, W.R. and Griffin, M. (1994), "Work and/or fun: measuring utilitarian and hedonic shopping value", *Journal of Consumer Research*, Vol. 20 (March), pp. 644–56.

3   Babin, B.J. and Darden, W.R. (1995), "Consumer self regulation in a retail environment", *Journal of Retailing*, Vol. 71 (Spring), No. 1, pp. 47–70; Babin, B.J. and Attaway, J.P. (2000), "Atmospheric affect as a tool for creating value and gaining share of customer", *Journal of Business Research*, Vol. 49 (August), pp. 91–9; Carpenter, J.M. (2008), "Consumer shopping value, satisfaction and loyalty in discount retailing", *Journal of Retail and Consumer Services*, Vol. 15 (September), pp. 358–63.

4   Holland, J.H., Holyoak, K.J., Nisbett, R.E., and Thagard, P.R. (1989), *Induction: Processes of Inference, Learning, and Discovery*, MIT Press, Cambridge, MA.

5   Ward, J.C., Bitner, M.J., and Barnes, J. (1992), "Measuring the protypicality and meaning of retail environments", *Journal of Retailing*, Vol. 68 (Summer), pp.194–220.

6   Babin, B.J., Darden, W.R., and Boles, J.S. (1995), "Salesperson stereotypes, consumer emotions, and their impact on information processing", *Journal of the Academy of Marketing Science*, Vol. 71 (Spring), pp. 94–105.

7   Babin, B.J. and Harris, E. (2009), *CB: A Value Based Approach*, Cengage, Mason, OH.

8   Babin, B.J. and Babin, L.A. (2001), "Seeking something different? A model of schema typicality, consumer affect, purchase intentions and perceived shopping value", *Journal of Business Research*, Vol. 54, No. 2, pp. 89–96.

9   Areni, C.S. and Kim, D. (1993), "The influence of background music on shopping behavior: classical versus top-forty music in a winestore", *Advances in Consumer Research*, Vol. 20, pp. 336–46.

10 Yoon, H.S. and Lee, D.H. (2007), "The exposure effect of unclicked banner advertisements", *Advances in International Retailing*, Vol. 18, pp. 211–29.

11 Jones, M.Y., Spence, M.T., and Vallaster, C. (2008), "Creating emotions via B2C websites", *Business Horizons* (March), pp. 419–28.

12 Hamann, S.B., Ely, T., Grafton, S., and Kiltz, C. (1999), "Amygdala activity related to enhanced memory for pleasant and aversive stimuli", *Nature Neuroscience*, Vol. 2, No. 3, pp. 289–93.

13 Canli, T., Desmond, J.E., Zhao, Z., and Gabrieli, D.E. (2000), "Event-related activation in the human amygdala associates with later memory for individual emotional response", *Journal of Neuroscience*, Vol. 20, No. 19, pp. RC99 1–5.

14 Herz, R.S., Eliassen, J., Beland, S. and Souza, T. (2004), "Neuroimaging evidence for the emotional potency of odor-evoked memory", *Neuropsychologia*, Vol. 42, pp. 371–8.

15   Jones, Spence, and Vallaster, "Creating emotions via B2C websites".

16   Holbrook, M. and Schindler, R.M. (1996), "Market segmentation based on age and attitude toward the past: concepts, methods, and findings concerning nostalgic influences on customer tastes", *Journal of Business Research*, Vol. 42 (September), No. 3, pp. 27–39.

17   Orth, U.R. and Bourrain, A. (2008), "The influence of nostalgic memories on consumer exploratory tendencies: echoes from scents past", *Journal of Retailing and Consumer Services*, Vol. 15, No. 4, pp. 277–87.

18   Braun, K.A., Ellis, R., and Loftus, E.F. (2002), "Make my memory: how advertising can change our memories of the past", *Psychology and Marketing*, Vol. 19, No. 1, pp. 1–23.

19   Pezdek, K., Finger, K., and Hodge, D. (1997), "Planting false childhood memories: the role of event plausibility", *Psychological Science*, Vol. 8, No. 6, pp. 437–41.

20   Bradley, M.M. (1992), "Remembering pictures: pleasure and arousal in memory", *Journal of Experimental Psychology: Learning, Memory, & Cognition*, Vol. 18, No. 2, pp. 379–90.

21   Unkelbach, C., Fiedler, K., Bayer, M., Stegmuller, M., and Danner, D. (2008), "Why positive information is processed faster: the density hypothesis", *Journal of Personality and Social Psychology*, Vol. 95 (July), No. 1, pp. 36–49.

CHAPTER 11

Managing Hospitality Experiences: Las Vegas Style

KATHRYN A. LATOUR,* LEWIS P. CARBONE,† AND
SUZIE GOAN‡

Keywords

memory, perception, sensory, framing, research methods

Abstract

Whether or not a hospitality organization considers the nature of its customers' experience, customers leave with an impression of that experience – good, bad, or indifferent. The customers' experience is important and inescapable – surveys show that customers base their decision to revisit or recommend on their impressions and "assessment" of that experience. Fortunately (or not, for some organizations) the customer experience can be highly malleable and managed by hospitality organizations. The purpose of this chapter is to identify how hospitality organizations can systematically manage their customers' experiences so that they will be both perceived and remembered in more favorable ways. We take examples from Las Vegas – a city renowned for its use of experiential marketing – to demonstrate our findings. We discuss how the new "science of the mind" may have implications for framing and researching the nature of the customer experience and suggest several techniques for hospitality researchers to consider.

*   Kathryn A. Latour, Associate Professor of Hospitality Marketing, William F. Harrah College of Hotel Administration, Department of Tourism and Convention, University of Nevada, Las Vegas. 4505 Maryland Parkway, Box 456023, Las Vegas, NV 89154-6023, USA. E-mail: kathryn.latour@unlv.edu.

†   Lewis P. Carbone, President and CEO, Experience Engineering™. Experience Engineering™ is a systematic methodology for developing insights into the subtleties of product and brand experience and the design, creation, and management of experience clues that mold and reinforce consumer perception. E-mail: lcarbone@experienceengineering.com.

‡   Sizie Goan, Marketing Director, Experience Engineering™. E-mail: sgoan@experienceengineering.com.

Engineering Hospitality Experiences: Las Vegas Style

The future of this industry is not going to be decided by new product on the casino floors. It will be achieved by the resort atmospherics that are produced by the most innovative operators. The customer's loyalty is to our product or brand, and that loyalty is determined by resort ambience, quality of service, consistency of experience and the value of total packaging – the amount of entertainment and experience the customer gets at a certain price point. That's what makes Las Vegas, for example, so unique. That value proposition isn't truly rivaled anywhere else in the world right now.

Glenn Schaeffer, (former) President and CEO, Mandalay Resort Group[1]

Customer experience and the framing of the "experience economy" are the current buzz in marketing,[2] and for good reason. According to a July 2004 American Express survey[3] on luxury trends, for the first time in over 20 years, consumers say they prefer new experiences such as travel and fine dining over material items like new cars and jewelry. Perhaps no other destination reflects this shift, or is as well known for the myriad of experiences offered, as Las Vegas, Nevada. Upon setting foot into McCarran International Airport, the tourist is bombarded by the sights and sounds of flashing slot machines with the dramatic skyline of the famous Las Vegas Strip, with its numerous landmarks – such as Paris's Eiffel Tower, the Excalibur castle, the Stratosphere tower – all illuminating the background. The "clue-laden" setting is intoxicating and can set the tourist almost into a different emotional state. From the speeding rush of the Coney Island roller coaster to the stimulating, glowing walls of rum in Mandalay's Rumjungle to the relaxing and inspiring waters dancing outside the Bellagio, Las Vegas resorts and casinos appear to understand the importance of experiential marketing. But do they really understand experience management? Have companies grasped the differentiation and value that comes from thinking and executing experientially at every level of interaction?

What happens in Vegas does not necessarily have to stay in Vegas. There are learning opportunities that those in the hospitality industry interested in experience as a value proposition can draw from Las Vegas – both good and bad. After all, one cannot *not* provide an experience. One can, however, avoid managing experiences in enlightened and systematic ways that utilize leading-edge research applications and experience management disciplines. The purpose of this chapter is to move hospitality managers to recognize the importance of the experience offering as the value proposition and understand how they can, on a day-to-day basis, manage their customer experience in a manner that will build preference and instill customer loyalty. Although the importance of the customer experience has become a hot topic in business periodicals, one should ask: How many hospitality companies really know how to design and consistently deliver a total experience? And how they can create the systems to steward and support the effort? Where are the management research tools for capturing and meeting the experiential preferences of individual customers? And what are the business implications of research findings that suggest that experiences, and memories of those experiences, can be malleable and constructed with managers' guidance?

An Ode to the Past and a Look to the Future

James Gilmore and Joseph Pine have been instrumental in delivering the message that experience is foremost in the hospitality product offering.[4] One of their take-aways is that by offering a theme to one's hospitality offering, one can charge for the experience, thereby creating an additional source of revenue. The authors cite the examples of American Girl and Niketown as success stories.

Viewing the hospitality experience as a thematically organized production is one way to organize the various customer contact points and offer a unique product to the customer. Walt Disney is best known for the development of themes, and Las Vegas has been heralded as the adult Disneyland. (And perhaps not coincidentally, former Disney CEO Michael Eisner and Las Vegas whiz Steve Wynn are neighbors.) The skyline of the Strip includes a 1930s view of Manhattan, the Eiffel Tower, and the Luxor Pyramid, and each of these properties' themes are driven by the exteriors. Such a theme approach is product-centered rather than customer-centered, however, and may not be applicable to restaurants or hotels that do not have such discretion in their choice of architecture. The Strip (and off-Strip) properties are evolving to become more customer-centered, considering the needs of the customer first and designing the property with the customer in mind. As examples, the newest properties are not themed. The Palms, for example, has been very successful in appealing to the 18–24-year-old crowd, and the new Wynn Resort and the Palazzo also are not themed but have created plenty of positive press and expectations. Even the themed properties are attempting to move beyond their original themes; for instance, New York, New York is creating a sophisticated atmosphere of New York City through its product offerings, such as the risqué show Zumanity. Treasure Island (now called "TI"), which was built during the "family friendly" era of Las Vegas, is becoming more provocative, touting its various bars and its US$100 margarita.

Moving away from the thematic branding does not mean moving away from experience management. On the contrary; as stated in a recent brand metrics study related to the integration of brand, perceptions, and experience, "the delivery of branded customer experiences requires [an understanding] of what defines the optimal customer experience that spans the customer lifecycle through all touch points of the experience".[5] Customers *always* get an experience. It can be good or bad, lasting or fleeting, a random phenomenon or an engineered perception. Managers have the opportunity to imprint customers' experiences with thousands of clues ranging from a simple gesture like a handshake to the design, layout, and even smell and temperature of the environment. Knowing and understanding how the customer experiences a hospitality destination at every touch point is critical in developing a plan to manage those encounters effectively. Experiences can be embedded with highly specific and detailed experience clues that effectively create the "brand edges" that foster solid customer preferences and thereby cultivate customer loyalty. The first step, however, is to understand the nature of the customer experience and how the hospitality provider can influence the expectation, perception, and memory of that experience.

The Nature of Experiences

For the great majority of mankind are satisfied with appearances, as though they were realities and are often more influenced by the things that seem than by those that are.

Machiavelli

Experience is *noeic*, from the Greek *nous*, meaning intellect or understanding – knowledge as experienced directly with a feeling of certitude. Experiencing a hotel, restaurant, or casino imparts a different sort of knowledge than simply reading or hearing about it. Customers genuinely believe that their experiences drive their choices. An interesting paradox exists, however, that though customers believe that their experiences are direct, unbiased, and diagnostic, research in marketing and psychology suggests experiences are easily malleable (both as a perception and as a memory[6]). One classic example that demonstrates this malleability is the blind taste test. Customers cannot discriminate the taste of a private label from that of a national brand, but, once labels are attached to cola samples, customers suddenly perceive dramatic differences between the brown fuzzy waters. Although objectively the experience remains the same, subjectively the experience changes greatly due to their prior knowledge and expectations about the brand.

To understand the impact of marketing cues on the customer's experience, one must consider the difference between sensation and perception. Traditionally, sensation has been thought of as the taking in of information from the outside world – the sights, smells, tastes. It was once thought that sensations were a "pure" representation of reality.[7] But psychologists now concur that even at this very basic level, our top-down processes influence our experiences through perceptual processes:

Perception is not a one-directional process in which stimuli received by our sense organs cause "brain events" that in turn get converted into an internal experience of an outside occurrence. Stimuli cause "brain events," but the way in which those events are coded depends partly on what the brain expects and remembers. The old proverb "Seeing is believing" would read more accurately as "Believing is seeing." We tend to see what we expect to see ... We tend to look for familiar patterns in what we see, filling in the blanks in such a way as to make sense of them, and we discriminate between those elements that are essential and those that are dispensable for our understanding of the whole.[8]

Our brains constantly try to make sense of incoming sensory information to form a meaningful representation; for instance, upon entering a hotel lobby we feel like we are "taking in" the entire room. Most of the time, the brain corresponds pretty well with the reality of the outside world. Sometimes, though, we know we are seeing only an illusion. Figure 11.1 contains the Muller-Lyer illusion: the lengths of the two lines look longer or shorter depending on how

Figure 11.1 Muller-Lyer illusion

the "fins" point. These fins serve as visual depth cues. Researchers find that there are some cultures that are less susceptible to this illusion, such as the Bushmen of the Kalahari Desert. Their environment lacks architectural verticals that set the expectations for "seeing" the different lengths.[9]

The knowledge that influences our perception of the line lengths is embedded in our minds. We probably cannot verbalize why the lines appear different to us, and our experience of the difference in line lengths may feel very real. Architects have made use of these types of biases; for instance, consider the design of the Venetian Casino Mega-Resort's marble floors in its grand entryway in Figure 11.2. Not only do these tiles exude an unusual optical illusion for the visitor, but the tactile sense of walking on such a huge expanse of marble offers a unique experience as well.

Within marketing, a forward frame theory has been offered to account for how prior information acts as schema and influences the perception of a current experience.[10] These forward framing effects are likely to have their intended impact when they are consistent with assumptions and help shape the emergent expectations about a service outcome.[11] The hospitality operator can attempt to influence these schemas by being more deliberate and purposeful about organizing clues in advertising, website, and word of mouth that the customer receives prior to visiting.

Once the customer is at the establishment, the management of the customer experience as a perception continues. As clues grow in consistency, number, and sensory diversity, the imprinting potential of the experience is heightened. For example, researchers have found that music can change the pace at which people eat (they eat to the tempo of the music), smells can evoke strong emotions (men prefer a spicier smell, such as cinnamon), and color can

Figure 11.2 The Venetian Casino Mega-Resort's tile floors

alter the taste experience (skim milk naturally has a bluish tint that, when removed, causes people to rate the taste as richer).[12] These atmospherics can alter the nature of the consumer experience, and the consumer might not be aware of such influences. We refer to these non-human elements as "mechanics."[13] The advantage of utilizing mechanics in the engineering of a customer perception is that they can be uniform, planned, and consistent.

The understanding of sensory management is critical in creating an experience that is unique, emotional, authentic, and memorable. These sensory elements should not be considered in isolation, however. It is equally important to understand the interdependencies that exist with other elements in the experience. Synesthesia, which refers to the crossing of the senses, finds that sensory components can be felt in a very direct, emotional manner. Synesthesia is a neurological condition in which a stimulus in one sense modality is involuntarily elicited in another sense modality. For instance, someone with synesthesia (called a synesthete) may be able to see sounds, taste shapes, or read black-and-white printed words in color. While only one in several thousand synesthetes experience full-blown synesthesia, researchers suggest that, according to the way in which the human brain has evolved, we are all to some degree synesthetes, as most children experience some aspect of synesthesia.[14] In terms of managing the experience, this neurological condition suggests that the way to trigger an emotional response to an experience offering is through different sensory elements. Smell, for example, has long been associated with bringing forth emotional memories.[15] In addition, memory researchers find that information that is delivered through multiple sensory layers is more likely to be remembered later on, and emotional experiences are also more likely to be retained.[16]

What distinguishes a hospitality experience is the role of humans, which we call "humanics".[17] We have all probably had the experience of a skilled waiter or waitress guiding us during a pleasurable meal, as well as the opposite, when even the most skilled chef could not compensate for a rude waiter or hostess. Ideally, mechanics and humanics should not compete but should work in concert to create a preferential customer experience.

Once the experience has been had, it continues in the customer's mind as a memory. It was once believed that experiences were remembered intact; at a later time, they could be called up, similar to cuing a video on the VCR. Indeed, when we recollect an experience, we may feel that we are watching a tape of ourselves, like watching a video in our mind. But human memory works very differently than computer or digital memory; it is a reconstructive process that neurologists assert is hardly ever complete or exact. The rememberer has been likened to a paleontologist who attempts the reconstruction of a dinosaur from fragmentary fossil remains: "out of a few stored brain chips we remember a dinosaur".[18]

Both marketing and hospitality literature are replete with examples of customers "forgetting" important information about their product or service. For instance, in one study, researchers asked customers as they left their hotel what their room rate was. Only one-fifth were able to give a correct response.[19] Similar findings appear in marketing literature, where researchers have inquired about the cost of grocery items customers have just purchased, but very few could correctly recall the price. Price may be an important dimension in considering a hotel or restaurant, but it is not the type of information customers generally retain. A rule of thumb is that people remember what is interesting, personally relevant, unique, and surprising. The customer may be bombarded with thousands of messages and information during their stay, and what he or she retains or remembers about the experience is important for future visits. We refer to that bundle of information as "sticktion" (literally, what "sticks" or is remembered later).

However, even in situations when customers recall a past visit to a restaurant or travel destination, their memories can be merely illusions. For instance, Braun, Ellis, and Loftus look at customers' memories of a childhood visit to Disney World, and then attempt to alter some memories through advertising.[20] Those who received the advertising report more favorable memories of their childhood experiences at Disney and indicate they would be more likely to visit again. But even more important, the researchers could alter the childhood memory and even create a false memory using advertising information. Sixteen percent of participants recalled meeting Bugs Bunny during their childhood stay (Bugs was featured in the experimental ad); Warner Brothers owns Bugs Bunny, and there was no way the customers could have met Bugs during their childhood stay. This finding is consonant with the work of cognitive psychologists who find that post-experience suggestion can lead to the creation of totally new, different memories of experiences.[21]

The take-away from this discussion for the hospitality manager is that the customer experience starts far before they enter the establishment and continues long after they leave. The marketer can direct the experience during these different touch points (featured in Figure 11.3) by consistently managing the mechanics and humanics. For instance, the hotel's website can send confidence and style clues for the type of experience the customer might expect to receive. Linking the site to favorable reviews (from a third party) would add credibility to the hotel's positioning. Or the hotel might consider making an employee list of "favorites" to be listed on the hotel (similar to what Barnes & Noble does with book recommendations) – which should of course include some of the hotel's

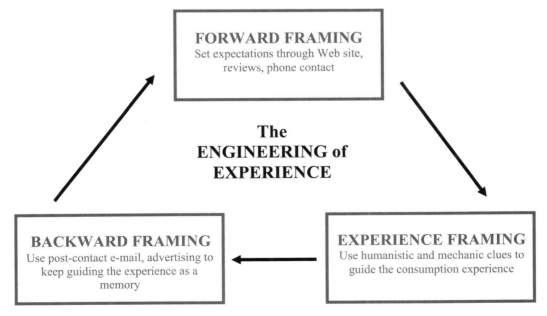

Figure 11.3 The engineering of experience

own dining or experiences but also provide tourists with other things they might do while in town. At the time of the customer experience, the hotel can set the mood with humanic and mechanic clues, such as having the bellperson ready to collect the bags, providing easy check-in, lighting the reception area, offering easy access to the rooms, and so on. Once the experience is finished and the customer checks out (which should be an easy process as well) and leaves the hotel, the hotel can continue the dialogue with the customer through mementos or souvenirs. Think about the small shampoo bottles that many guests take from their hotel rooms. The distinctive scent of the Hyatt Hotel's Malibu Spa at Lake Las Vegas can transport the guest to recollect images of the sunshine poolside while showering in her own bathroom in January.

The error in interpretation would be in looking at these touch points as independent. Research from cognitive psychology on memory processes finds robust effects of what is known as "encoding specificity".[22] Encoding specificity means that when the encoding and retrieval conditions match, successful memory retrieval is more likely. Ideally, the hotel finds a means to connect the forward, concurrent, and backward framing.[23] As an example, the Palms Hotel has a live camera on its website of the pool area. Guests going to the site before their visit can get an idea of the Palms experience. During their visit, they can "play" for the camera, and afterward, they can revisit their experience by going back to that website. Or one could follow the Disney model, where the hotel or destination is sprinkled with designated spots for "photographing memories" that frame the property and the guest in visually pleasing surroundings. When back home viewing the photo and recalling their experience, guests are reminded of the beautiful space, the pleasing Disney icons, and time with family – not irrelevant backgrounds or unintended visual violations on the property (like construction or garbage).

Characteristics of a Well-Managed Experience

In a recent tour of the Las Vegas Strip, we found some examples of well-managed experiences, and some that did not quite measure up. We identify critical aspects needed in the "engineering of experiences" and use our Las Vegas tour as a means to bring them to life.

FUSE HUMANIC AND MECHANIC CLUES SO THEY ARE INDISTINGUISHABLE

Our experience at Sheldon Adelson's Venetian (Steve Wynn's biggest competitor) was first-rate, and that property will be used throughout this section. What makes the Venetian stand apart is its integration of its architecture (mechanics) – the hand-painted murals, the bell tower modeled on the Campanile in St Mark's Square, the reproductions of Tiepolo and Tintoretto – and the humanics – the people in costume singing at the entrance, playing the accordion, walking the streets of the shopping area. Both worked together to create an authentic, engaging and total experience.

In contrast, the Bellagio (now owned and operated by MGM Mirage) has some great mechanics, such as the Chihuly glass lily structure on the lobby's ceiling. But there was no corresponding human element in the lobby – nobody to be seen, ask for directions, or direct questions about the property.

MAKE THE GUEST AN INTEGRAL PART OF THE EXPERIENCE

The Venetian understood the guest experience. We were greeted immediately upon entrance to the lobby; in fact, one employee who saw us admiring the hall came up to talk to us and give us the background on the design (including references to the real gold leaf used), and then invited us to see the hotel's new tower. We immediately felt we were an active part of the Venetian experience. The eye contact, emotive gesturing, and engaging interaction with all employees we encountered continued that involvement.

The Bellagio, because it was lacking that human presence, seemed exclusive and made us feel more like gawkers or outsiders to the experience. Intentional humanic clues like simply talking to or observing the needs of guests make them feel included and may provide the opportunity to entice them into experiencing other offerings available (though there is a fine line between hawking and providing information).

CREATE INTIMACY WITH THE CUSTOMER

Having personal contacts when there are thousands of people walking through an establishment each day may sound like a lofty goal. But understanding how to put customers at ease and make them feel comfortable can have great payoffs. For instance, one casino found its great halls, though architecturally pleasing, made the customer "stick out" too much, so the slot machines in the grand hall went unused until the casino added trees to make the customer feel more rooted in the experience and connected. Las Vegas has struggled to incorporate touristy elements into its hospitality offerings, such as the Conservatory at the Bellagio (which draws thousands of visitors each day), and a relationship with hotel- and casino-paying customers.

CONSIDER EVERY ENCOUNTER FROM THE CUSTOMER BACK

Operations that truly understand the customer experience are evidenced in their attitude toward customer problems. Do they embrace the problem through the customers' eyes, or do they try to diminish or dismiss it, or do they send it to another co-worker? When we were leaving the Venetian, we asked an employee delivering water to customers under the canopy (it was 109°F) directions to the monorail. She did not know the way but immediately brought over Mario, who did, and he walked with us over a half mile toward Harrah's to the station. Bear in mind – we were not paying guests, not even gamblers or big tippers. But he embraced the problem and showed us a special shortcut through the parking garage to the monorail.

As a test, we asked for the same directions at Harrah's, Monte Carlo, and the Bellagio. At Harrah's, we were pointed in the wrong direction. At the Monte Carlo, we were simply motioned to look across the street toward the MGM. At the Bellagio, the bell cap at first looked like he did not want us to approach him (we were obviously not guests and probably not tippers). Ultimately though, he provided the necessary information, though not in the same extraordinarily involving manner as the Venetian employee.

UNDERSTAND THE EMOTIONAL ASPECT OF THE CUSTOMER'S EXPERIENCE

A restaurant or hotel may have a specific theme in mind for the customer, but it probably has not considered the emotion it wants customers to take away from their stay, such as feeling privileged, relaxed, or energized. Once the emotion is understood (through various research methods described later) the experience can be engineered to support those key emotions. In January 2004, the Bellagio came under fire when its for-profit art gallery charged guests a fee to see the Claude Monet exhibit, even though it was on loan from the Museum of Fine Arts in Boston, a public institution.[24] The criticism likely would have been avoided altogether had management investigated the emotional value to guests of feeling privileged and somewhat exclusive in their ability to visit Vegas during the renowned Monet tour.

Smell also can be a driver of emotional memories. The magnolia scent in the Venetian lobby is an example of how smell can effectively bring the guest back in time or to another place. Of course, these sensory clues also can be used to help imprint the experience as a memory; for instance, a follow-up mailing with the scent and a picture of the guest can evoke past fond remembrances of a visit. Furniture can also be used to send clues. In Caesar's, we found all the chairs were captain's chairs with arms – a way to give the gambler a feeling of power at the tables or slots, perhaps. The whole energy and emotion created by Caesar's was that this place was for serious gambling, novices not allowed.

USE ATMOSPHERIC ELEMENTS TO CREATE AN AUTHENTIC REPRESENTATION

The terms "authentic" and "Las Vegas" do not on the surface seem to fit; Vegas is the master of creating illusions. In our visit to the Bellagio's lobby, we observed two huge floral bouquets, each approximately two feet in diameter and four feet high. We noticed several passers-by touch them to see if they were in fact real (they were). But within those illusions, one that is truly transformative is one that takes customers to a different place so that they feel they are experiencing something authentic. For instance, in the long marbled entrance of the Venetian, carefully crafted holes appear in the ceiling so that light hits the floor, just like in a European cathedral. The smell of candles in the air, the setting, and the people are reminiscent of being in Venice.

In contrast, the scent management system at the Monte Carlo (also called "smoke suppression") renders the experience manufactured – it is a heavy detergent smell, like Downy [brand of US fabric softener]. The only element that appears unique within that property is the usage of huge glass chandeliers, and though in any other city, those chandeliers may make a statement, in Las Vegas, they seem generic. There is no sense of being in the city of Monte Carlo when one enters the casino or hotel. Caesar's, the granddaddy of Strip hotels, seems to accentuate its inauthenticity by having staff members dressed like Caesar yell trivia questions at customers through a handheld microphone. Certainly the mechanics could have been integrated so that Caesar did not have a handheld microphone, but even the trivia game seemed force-fit rather than integrated in the offering, as the Venetian had done.

PAY ATTENTION TO THE LANGUAGE OF SIGNAGE

Beyond the glow of Las Vegas neon, secondary signage can send subtle but important hospitality signals to customers. We were surprised, however, that in this hospitality mecca, the language used on the signs tended toward the inhospitable. In Caesar's, construction was underway on the casino floor with "caution" signs right near the slots. But isn't caution the last thing a casino manager would want the gambler to exercise? Also in Caesar's, there were "Do Not Enter" signs and locked doors around the Celine Dion theatre – not exactly a welcoming introduction for potential concertgoers. The Venetian again reigned above the others with much more friendly, accessible language: "Team members only please" replaced "Do Not Enter" signs.

SHOW CUSTOMERS YOUR BEST FACE

There is nothing more distracting from an illusion than the sound of jackhammers. There is a difference between seeing the chef make a pizza and seeing construction in progress. The latter does not work. Disney, the master of creating illusions, used to mandate that its customers have no contact with any construction onsite (though that is no longer the case). Las Vegas is a 24/7 city (as are most hotels), and there is no "off-time" to do construction. However, we were dismayed that the upscale Bellagio had construction workers in plain sight (no curtains) working on a retail extension project in the middle of the day right near the very touristy Conservatory. Caesar's fared slightly better: it had large curtains hiding most of its construction areas. Hospitality providers should always try to make sure the face they show customers is their best; they may not get another opportunity to make an impression.

PAY SPECIAL ATTENTION TO ENTRANCES AND EXITS

Because of forward and backward framing effects, the impressions a hotel or restaurant makes at arrival and upon leaving can influence how the experience is perceived and remembered. The driveway to the Bellagio sets high expectations for the visitor – one has the feeling of driving to an elegant Italian manor house while turning off Las Vegas Boulevard. Little details, such as the chirping of birds in the trees lining the drive, help give the experience an authentic feel. Unfortunately, the exit is not as well managed; we saw departing guests sitting on the ground waiting for rides to the airport. The lobby only had seating for about 8 people, and we saw at least 100 milling around, in addition to the guests on the ground.

The Venetian, for all the positive experiential elements discussed previously, really missed an opportunity in its driveway entrance. First, the entrance itself is set back from Las Vegas Boulevard, so there is not the same presence as other hotels have. Second, the gondolas, a "signature" clue for the hotel, do not travel near the entrance, so there is no immediate, exciting entry point (which could have easily been accomplished by extending the gondolas several hundred feet). The Venetian's exit though, with water attendants, taxi services, and revelers, is superb and very well managed.

MANAGE THE EXPERIENCE BEFORE CUSTOMERS ARRIVE AND AFTER THEY LEAVE

This aspect may seem to go without saying, considering the aforementioned forward and backward frame effects, but because we were not guests at the hotels we visited, we did not experience the reservation, check-in, or check-out procedures, or any follow-up correspondence. Many operations outsource some of these activities, which places a very important aspect of the customer experience in others' hands, which may not be the best choice.

OFFER CUSTOMERS VALUABLE ADVICE

From social and cognitive psychology research, we know that customers are most influenced by what they perceive as "unbiased" sources of information, that is, information from someone who does not appear to have a vested interest in the outcome. Critic and customer reviews are therefore important (but not always manageable). MGM Mirage companies have had a successful venture with Zagat's guide. They packaged Zagat's reviews of restaurants in their Las Vegas properties and handed them out to customers. They have a hard time keeping the guides in stock. Posting positive reviews has always been popular in restaurants, but people may make their decision to visit prior to coming to the restaurant or through the hotel doors. In this internet-savvy era, why not scan and post those positive reviews on the company's website? The content "brags" about the company, the company gets to pick the reviews (which should deter customers from seeking perhaps less favorable information), and the customer feels he or she is getting an unbiased source of information.

Finding the Right Cues/Clues for a Hospitality Business

Organizations that simply tweak design elements or focus on the customer experience in isolated pockets of their business will probably be disappointed in their results. The "me-too" factor in Las Vegas is high – some properties seem to work on the belief that if something worked in one property, it will work in another (the current fad is the ultra lounge). But copycatting elements from other properties is not the way to be distinctive, nor is it a focus on what the customer really wants.

Research might help clarify the experiential dimensions that have the potential to make a company's offering distinctive, memorable, and attractive enough to entice the customer to revisit again and again. Experiential tools also are needed to act on such research insights. But how does a manager tackle these feats? An experience audit involves four basic steps: (1) scanning the current experience offering; (2) researching what customers truly desire from their experience; (3) implementing an experience blueprint that addresses customers' emotional needs; and (4) testing the effectiveness of the implementation.

THE EXPERIENCE CLUESCAN

The first step involves a ClueScan, which enables managers to visit their own experience destination and identify what signals – or clues – they see, feel, taste, smell, and hear as they have their experience (see Figure 11.4). What emotion do they feel as they experience the offering? What clues, whether humanic (people) or mechanic (architecture), are present that enhance or diminish the experience? What is the "take-away" impression from the experience? The managers can then ask themselves: Is this the emotional impression that

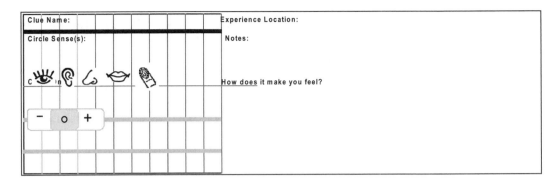

Figure 11.4 ClueScan

I want my customers to have? The purpose of this scan is to demonstrate how managers can themselves assess the current state of their experiential offerings.

DEPTH RESEARCH

Hospitality offerings, because of their intangible nature, are subject to even more constructive processing than the cola example provided previously in this chapter. Even though these experiences are malleable, customers are not always aware of how external communications or clues alter how they experience the service. Therefore, traditional surveys of customer satisfaction or even more in-depth focus group interviews may not uncover what truly drives the customer or which types of clues would be most effective. According to Gerald Zaltman, Professor Emeritus at the Harvard Business School, customers' preferences and motivations are far less influenced by the functional attributes of products and services than the subconscious sensory and emotional elements derived by the total experience.[25]

Cues and clues can affect customers at unconscious levels, so they may not be able to verbalize why they like what they experience. What may be most troubling to the hospitality researcher is what psychologists have found with respect to explicit and implicit memory:[26] what people remember may be quite different than what people actually do. Thus, asking people to retrospectively report on their past experiences not only will be biased by the context and the manner of the survey (or the focus group researcher) but sometimes may contradict what is really driving the customer's choices. In addition, the drivers of a managed customer experience may be most effective when they are not noticed.[27] Unfortunately this dilemma can leave the hospitality manager in the difficult position of not knowing how to "listen" to customers and then apply the research effectively to manage the experience. Our suggestion is to incorporate methods that dig deeper into customers' minds to uncover their emotional and sensory reactions to hospitality offerings. Zaltman has developed an interview technique called the Zaltman metaphor elicitation method (ZMET), which uses pictorial images, the "language of the brain", to drive the interviews.[28] This type of depth interview can move beneath customers' more conscious rational processes and uncover emotional connections that the hospitality manager might want to encompass with the company's service offerings. This idea ties in with the importance of understanding the emotional take-away managers want the customers to retain. Other in-depth interview procedures, such as the Early Childhood Memory Elicitation Method, can help managers find the emotional connection that drives how consumers perceive hospitality experiences.[29]

Implicit research methods can indirectly assess the effectiveness of cues and clues. Customers might not be able to indicate that a certain scent makes them hungrier or prompts them to linger longer over a bottle of wine, but designing an experiment that tests the different cues may show that one scent is more effective than another. Computer software and other implicit measures can be designed as well to incorporate different elements and determine how the customer responds.[30]

IMPLEMENTING THE DESIRED EXPERIENCE

After the emotional elements of the desired experience are understood, the manager must determine how to create that experience. This step requires meeting with company personnel involved in delivering the experience and identifying how they might consistently impart the desired emotion (experience motif) through their use of humanic (people) and mechanic (environmental) clues. For example, if research reveals that feelings of safety are most important to hotel guests, the personnel might make security cameras very visible, train the check-in staff on various safety procedures, and feature clues in the environment that it is a safe establishment (e.g., lights in the parking lot, security guards available to walk guests to their cars). The manager also might want to design an experiment to test the effectiveness of various implementation strategies on customer behavior. In Las Vegas, much of the experience design has been left to architects, not marketers or psychologists.

TESTING THE IMPLEMENTATION

The process does not stop after the implementation process. The manager returns to the first step of performing the experience scan: Does the current experience now meet the customer's emotional needs? If so, the manager can continue on the path to executing an experience that meets customers' needs. To avoid the Rainforest Café trap, in which the experience becomes passé, the manager should continually refine the experience offering as customer needs develop and change. If a discrepancy remains between the experience offering and the customer-desired offering, additional clues may need to be incorporated into the experience.

Future Directions

In a city that keeps reinventing itself and even relishes the demolishment of the past (i.e., the Dunes drew thousands of spectators to its implosion[31]) it will be an interesting adventure to see the next phase of development. The core to Las Vegas will be its unique experience offering. Hotel casino executives keep one-upping one another. Wynn's Encore expansion was highly anticipated and likely will offer even more cues or ideas for experience engineers. On a tour of the Wynn Las Vegas with other casino executives, Gary Loveman, CEO of Harrah's Entertainment, proclaimed, "This is the kind of place that God would build if he had the money."[32]

Another trend in Las Vegas, driven in part by the mayor's interest in revitalizing the downtown area, is the resurgence of more nostalgically themed properties, such as the Golden Nugget. Will this trend continue, and will Las Vegas return to its authentic roots? Or will Lady Luck and the Stardust become dinosaurs that wither away as the new era enters Las Vegas? The razing of the Sands in 1996 made way for the Venetian; the Hacienda's demolition in 1996 became the site of Mandalay Bay; the Landmark was replaced by a parking lot in 1995; the Dunes created space for the Bellagio in 1993; and the destruction of the Desert Inn in 2002 made room for Wynn Resorts. MGM Mirage spokesperson Alan Feldman realizes the implosions make impressive images: "I think the images send a message that Las Vegas moves forward in a dramatic way, a beneficial message outside Las Vegas. But for some Las Vegas residents, I think there's growing concern about how disposable our history is, how quickly we demolish historic structures."[33]

This chapter has focused on what other hospitality operators may learn from the Las Vegas experience, but it also will be interesting to see if Las Vegas takes stock of industry research. For instance, the typical hotel/casino forces guests to walk at least 500 feet through the casino before check-in – a cumbersome clue for travelers accustomed to the intimate hotel lobby experiences of typical hotels. Might this design standard change as Vegas Strip businesses move to even more concentration on the customer?

Another finding in hospitality literature has been the fallacy of "loyalty" programs, designed to encourage repeat business.[34] Companies have been so driven by the value of the customer for their business that they seem lost as they enter an era that demands a focus on what the company offers to the customer. The casino industry has always worked under the assumption that loyal gamblers receive something back for their patronage: "You are in the business of slowly taking players' money from them. At least you could be pleasant about it."[35] As Las Vegas continues its growth, getting in tune with the individual customer will continue to be a challenge. Some customers have complained that they used to be recognized at the door, their drink and table known, whereas now they are just a number in the company's large database.

Notes

1. Schaeffer, Glenn (2002), interview *The Wall Street Transcript*, 25 November, available at http://twst.com/notes/articles/mac200.html (accessed January 1, 2009).
2. Gilmore, James H. and Pine, Joseph B. II (2002), "Differentiating Hospitality Operations via Experiences", *Cornell Hotel and Restaurant Administration Quarterly*, Vol. 43, pp. 87–97.
3. Thrasher, Paula Crouch, "Travel Replacing Toys for Affluent; Luxury Shift: New Experiences are more Satisfying than Cars and Jewelry, Survey Shows", *Atlanta Journal Constitution*, Sec. C1, July 24, 2004.
4. Gilmore, James H. and Pine, Joseph B. II (2002), "The Experience IS the Marketing", *Strategic Horizons Special Report*.
5. Canadian Marketing Association (2004), Brand metrics study, *Today's Brand Measurement: The Integration of Perceptions, Behaviors & Environments*.
6. Hoch, Stephen J. (2002), "Product Experience is Seductive", *Journal of Consumer Research*, Vol. 29 (December), pp. 448–54.
7. John Locke and his empiricist views were first discussed in his *Essay Concerning Human Understanding* (1690).

8. Cohen, David (1996), *The Secret Language of the Mind*, Chronicle Books, San Francisco, p. 47.

9. Ibid.

10. Alba, Joseph W. and Hasher, Lynn (1983), "Is Memory Schematic?", *Psychological Bulletin*, Vol. 93 (March), pp. 203–31. The forward framing view perpetuated most of consumer research on how prior knowledge biases experience, such as Anderson, Rolph E. (1973), "Consumer Dissatisfaction: The Effect of Disconfirmed Expectancy on Perceived Product Performance", *Journal of Marketing Research*, Vol. 10 (February), pp. 38–44; Boulding, William, Kalra, Ajay, Staelin, Richard, and Zeithaml, Valarie (1993), "A Dynamic Process Model of Service Quality: From Expectations to Behavioral Intentions", *Journal of Marketing Research*, Vol. 30 (February), pp. 7–27; Hoch, Stephen J., and Deighton, John (1989), "Managing What Consumers Learn From Experience", *Journal of Marketing*, Vol. 53 (April), pp. 1–20.

11. Stayman, Douglas M., Alden, Dana L., and Smith, Karen H. (1992), "Some Effects of Schematic Processing on Consumer Expectations and Disconfirmation Judgments", *Journal of Consumer Research*, Vol. 19 (September), pp. 240–55.

12. A number of researchers in various fields have described how senses can influence how we experience the world; for instance, Adrian North looks at how music influences the perception of experience and time: North, Adrian, Hargreaves, David J., and McKendrick, Jennifer (1997), "In-store Music Affects Product Choice", *Nature*, Vol. 390, p. 132; North, Adrian and Hargreaves, David J. (1999), "Can Music Move People? The Effects of Music Complexity and Silence in Waiting Time", *Environment and Behavior*, Vol. 31, pp. 136–49. Marketers also realize the importance of smell in influencing experience: Miller, Cyndee (1991), "Research Reveals how Marketers Can Win by a Nose", *Marketing News*, 4 February, p. 1+. Casinos, with their smoke suppression systems, use different scents, and research suggests some might be more influential than others: Hirsch, Alan R. (1995), "Effects of Ambient Odors on Slot-Machine Usage in a Las Vegas Casino", *Psychology & Marketing*, Vol. 12, pp. 585–95. Agricultural engineers have found that the color of milk can influence its taste; see http://www.news.cornell.edu/general/Nov95/Skimmilk.bpf.txt (accessed May 1, 2008).

13. Carbone, Lewis P. (2004), *Clued In: How to Keep Customers Coming Back Again and Again*, Financial Times/Prentice Hall, Upper Saddle River, NJ.

14. Cytowic, Richard (1998), *The Man Who Tasted Shapes*, Bradford Books, Cambridge, MA.

15. Proust, Marcel (trans. 1932), *Remembrances of Things Past*, Random House, New York.

16. Schacter, Daniel L. (1996), *Searching for Memory*, Basic Books, New York.

17. Carbone, *Clued In*.

18. Neisser, Ulric (1967), *Cognitive Psychology*, Appleton-Century-Crofts, New York. The reconstructive view of memory is widely recognized by psychologists, biologists, and neuroscientists. Daniel Schacter provides a good review in *Searching for Memory*.

19. Kotler, Philip, Bowen, John and Makens, James (2003), *Marketing for Hospitality and Tourism*, 3rd ed., Prentice Hall, Upper Saddle River, NJ, p. 455.

20. Braun, Kathryn A., Ellis, Rhiannon and Loftus, Elizabeth F. (2001), "Make My Memory: How Advertising Can Change our Memories of the Past", *Psychology & Marketing*, Vol. 19 (January), pp. 1–23.

21. Loftus, Elizabeth F. (1982), "Memory and Its Distortions", from the G. Stanley Hall lecture series, American Psychological Association, Washington, DC.

22. Tulving, Endel (1983), *Elements of Episodic Memory*, Clarendon Press, Oxford.

23. Braun, Kathryn A. and Zaltman, Gerald (1998), "Backward Framing: A Theory of Memory Reconstruction", MSI Working Paper Series, No. 98-109.

24. Holson, Laura M. (2004), "What's Doing in Las Vegas", *New York Times*, October 3, p. 14.

25. Zaltman, Gerald (2003), *How Customers Think: Essential Insights into the Mind of the Market*, Harvard Business School Press, Boston, MA.

26. Neurologists have discovered two types of memory systems, which are controlled by different brain regions. Schacter's *Searching for Memory* offers a thorough review of the neurological evidence supporting distinct implicit and explicit memory systems.

27. Ellin, Abby (2004), "True Hospitality: At Your Service, then Invisible", *New York Times*, August 24.

28. Zaltman, *How Customers Think*.

29. See Braun-LaTour, Kathryn A., LaTour, Michael S., and Zinkhan, George (2007), "Using Childhood Memories to Gain Insight into Brand Meaning", *Journal of Marketing*, Vol. 71, pp. 45–60.

30. There is a disassociation between implicit and explicit memory, which means that what is revealed through an explicit test may tell a different story when an implicit measure is utilized. For example, marketers have found that people may not consciously recall seeing a product advertised on the Internet but that exposure implicitly influences their choices. See Shapiro, Stephen, MacInnis, Deborah, and Heckler, Susan (1997), "The Effects of Incidental Ad Exposure on the Formation of Consideration Sets", *Journal of Consumer Research*, Vol. 24, pp. 94–104. People also might not recall a product placement in a television show, but that placement has an influence on what they choose (an implicit measure); see Law, Sharmistha and Braun, Kathryn A. (2000), "I'll Have What She's Having: Gauging the Effectiveness of Product Placements", *Psychology & Marketing*, Vol. 17, No. 12, pp. 1059–75. Researchers use reaction time software to study implicit effects; visit http://www.empirisoft.com (accessed January 1, 2009) for a demonstration.

31. Douglass, William A. and Raento, Pauliina (2004), "The Tradition of Invention: Conceiving Las Vegas", *Annals of Tourism Research*, Vol. 31, No. 1, pp. 7–23.

32. Clarke, Norm (2004), "The Punch Line", *Las Vegas Review Journal*, Sec. 4A, 5 September.

33. Simpson, Jeff (2004), "Next DI Implosion Planned", *Las Vegas Sun*, April 27.

34. Skogland, Iselin and Sigauw, Judy (2004), "Are Your Satisfied Customers Loyal?", *Cornell Hotel and Restaurant Administration Quarterly*, Vol. 45, pp. 221–35.

35. Bourie, Steve, quoted in Simpson, Jeff (2001), "Panel of Experts Rate Best, Worst of Las Vegas Casinos", *Las Vegas Sun*, October 7.

12 *Considerations in Creating Memorable Tour Experiences*

FRANK M. GO* AND ROBERT GOVERS†

Keywords

customer, destination, experience, packaged tour

Abstract

This chapter proposes that rapid tourist growth has begun to interfere with the holiday plans of customers, causing them to reject many intensively developed destinations. In the face of deteriorating environmental conditions, how can the world's largest tour operator, TUI Travel plc, apply packaged tour innovations to create memorable customer experiences in future? We will examine what requirements TUI Travel plc must consider in creating packaged travel experiences that customers experience as special; chronicle the growth of the packaged tour business, its complexity, its emerging forms, and how it may represent the antithesis of mass tourism; refer to the significant role that physical reality plays – particularly the spatial features of the destination – in relation to delivering packaged travel experiences and the potential decline without deliberate steps to manage natural resources in a sustainable manner; and draw conclusions regarding the need for environmental reporting as a pre-condition to ensure pristine environments and create memorable customer experiences.

*   Frank M. Go, Professor and Director of the Centre for Tourism Marketing, Department of Marketing Management, Rotterdam School of Management, Erasmus University, P.O. Box 1738, 3000 DR Rotterdam, the Netherlands. E-mail: fgo@rsm.nl. Telephone: + 31 10 408 2753.

†   Robert Govers, Catholic University of Leuven, Sint Jobseweg 57, Brasschaat, 2930 Belgium. E-mail: rgovers@geo.kuleuven.be. Telephone: + 32 70 426 942.

Introduction

The theme of this chapter marks an important shift of focus: away from finished objects and towards the holistic processes through which experiences may be generated and remembered. Therefore, the "objectness" of a product, superior design, or service delivery method, by itself, represents a research question rather than an assumed entity. Likewise, rather than thinking about consumer experiences as objects of knowledge, the goal becomes connecting the processes of "knowing" and "making" consumer experiences. How then can the theme of this book, in the overlap of these processes, be considered in the context of packaged travel experiences as opposed to a vicarious customer experience drawn from secondary sources, such as books or television?

With the emergence of the service marketing field, and more recently the "experience economy", social scientists and practitioners alike have realised that judgements about *intangible* characteristics (e.g., quality, speed of service, quality of atmospherics, ambience, user experience, employee competencies) represent important decision criteria for understanding consumer choices within both temporal and spatial contexts.[1] Few, if any, consumption contexts are self-contained and separate from the exponential growth in communications. In particular, the spontaneous, technology-mediated interactions, from web pages to air traffic,[2] contribute to the expansion of tourism. The United Nations World Tourism Organization projects that the annual number of international tourist visits will double from 800 million in 2008 to 1.6 billion by 2020.[3]

Against this backdrop, this chapter examines the requirements that TUI Travel plc, the world's largest tour operator, must consider in creating packaged travel experiences that customers will experience as special. As chronicled in three sections, several aspects can either constrain or contribute to the company's goal of creating special travel experiences in a sustainable manner. The first section focuses on the growth of the packaged tour business, its complexity, and emerging forms that supposedly represent the antithesis of mass tourism. The second section refers to the significant role that physical reality, particularly the spatial features of the destination, plays in relation to the delivery of packaged travel experiences and the decline that appears possible without deliberate steps taken to manage natural resources in a sustainable manner. The third section concludes with an overview of the aspects that may either benefit or hinder TUI Travel plc from transforming its vision into reality.

Complexity in the Value Chain

In January 1994, Michael Frenzel, who had been a member of the management board for six years, became CEO of Preussag, a diversified conglomerate whose portfolio comprised logistics, mining, oil exploration, metal production, shipbuilding, engineering, and trading activities. Between 1997 and 2004, Preussag, a diversified German conglomerate of "old economy" businesses, transformed itself into TUI, a company focused almost entirely on tourism and logistics.[4]

HORIZONTAL AND VERTICAL INTEGRATION

Marked by intense competition, the European tour operator industry has witnessed many mergers and acquisitions in recent decades. The sector therefore can be characterised as dominated by a few large corporations. However, the real balance of power has hardly altered in the last decade. There are approximately 1,000 tour operators registered with the Civil Aviation Authority's Air Travel Organiser's License (ATOL). By the end of December 2006, the top five tour operators claimed roughly 45 per cent of the total number of passengers carried: TUI Travel (4.6 million), First Choice Holidays Group (2.5 million), Thomas Cook Group (2.5 million), MyTourTravel (2.5 million), and Expedia (1.0 million).[5]

For TUI Travel, integration occurs in two directions: horizontal, such as when it takes over another group (e.g., First Choice Holidays Group) at the same level of the supply chain, and vertical, as in its takeover of organisations through backward integration, such as airlines and hotels, or forward integration, such as retail travel agencies. Practical reasons have supported such integrations. Frenzel's efforts focused on consolidating and restructuring Preussag's tour operating business while also exiting from previous business lines. On 26 June 2002, Preussag changed its name to TUI, a former tourism subsidiary. By the end of 2004, almost three-quarters of TUI's sales were generated by tourism. Horizontal integration offers economies of scale, increased market share, the opportunity to grow through further organic expansion, and an opportunity to leverage its diversification in the marketplace. In addition to these economics of scale advantages, vertical integration provides TUI Travel with a greater sense of control over supply and the ability to control quality, deal with over-distribution, and create synergies across the multiple businesses it owns.[6] Vertical integration also is based on an industrial model, which places great significance on rationalised, centralised management as the solution to the irrational chaos and disorder of market activities and relationships within its legal boundaries. Despite positive developments though, such rationalisation also involves irrationalities that may result in dehumanisation and homogenisation,[7] or manufactured customer experiences.

On 3 September 2007, TUI Travel merged with First Choice Holidays. The key contributions of TUI Travel included distribution through travel agencies and direct sales channels, such as call centres and the Internet; leading tour operators that offer both inclusive tours and modular travel products; airlines, which offer seats available as components of inclusive package tours or through a "seats-only business"; and incoming agencies that organize accommodation and daytrips for a broad range of holiday destinations and hotels, from exclusive hotels to family-oriented club holiday venues.[8] However, information and communication technologies have reduced the dependency of principals and customers on such contributions.

Simultaneously, budget airlines have removed some of the price advantages enjoyed by tour operators. Under the pull of blurring boundaries, decentralising markets, and enabling technologies, a whole new arena for undertaking experiences is emerging. On the one hand, "consumers are reacting with more and more urge to try and experience new things. They are going to greater lengths to experience greater things".[9] On the other hand, professional providers recognise that memorable customer experiences are less tied to the depth, relevance, and merging of various expertise-driven contributions and more related to particular parameters of action, such as the time spent in a theme park or museum.

CHARACTERISTICS OF THE PACKAGED TOUR EXPERIENCE

The delivery of the TUI Travel experience largely determines the company's success by influencing the customer's decision to remain loyal or defect to a competitor. This decision largely depends in turn on the corporate capability to consider holistically a complex set of requirements. The following list summarises the key characteristics of the packaged tour experience:[10]

- It consists of a package of services rendered by third parties; only a small share of services is provided by the tour operator itself.
- It is composed largely of service components, which are intangible in nature.
- The purchase of the travel experience takes place before the "goods" can be inspected. This act implies that the customer pays the price on the basis of a "promise" in the TUI Travel brochures. Only after arrival and during the stay in the chosen destination will the customer learn whether his or her experience meets his or her expectations and whether the confidence granted in advance to the TUI Travel brand has been justified.
- The extent to which travel experiences seem special or memorable, according to customers, depends largely on individual assessments and perceptions and does not necessarily correspond with the description in the TUI Travel brochures.

Accordingly, to deliver memorable customer experiences, TUI Travel first must be capable of effectively coordinating the complex, transnational network of relationships[11] involving hotels, car rentals, cruises, financial services, national tour operators, airlines, policy-makers, and reservation operators. Second, the company must constantly assess the intentions, actions, and reactions of its customers and various other stakeholders who provide component services. Third, TUI Travel must share critical requirements, as opposed to limited insights, so stakeholders can effectively contribute to the process of co-creating memorable customer experiences.[12]

RESPONDING TO THE THREAT OF DISINTERMEDIATION

Presently:

> TUI Travel PLC, a FTSE 100 Company, is a leading international leisure travel group, which operates in approximately 180 countries worldwide and serves more than 30 million customers in over 20 source markets. By becoming the only tourism company in the world to be listed in the Dow Jones Sustainability Index (DJSI) World, TUI Travel PLC demonstrates its commitment to sustainable development. The Group mainly serves the leisure travel consumer [and its vision is to offer] special travel experiences.[13]

TUI Travel employs approximately 48,000 people and operates a pan-European airline consisting of 155 aircraft. Although it holds a relatively dominant position within the tourism supply chain, it faces several challenges, including the threat of disintermediation due to advances in information technologies, competition from no-frills airlines and the subsequent growth of independent travel, debates about the process of concentration and integration and concerns for meeting personalised customer desires in future, and growing pressure for greater environmental responsibility in tour operations. Accordingly, the question arises: Has the tour operating sector run its course and slipped into decline? Having considered potential ways to respond to these challenges and maintain its position in the supply chain, TUI Travel has chosen to attempt to inject greater quality in its holiday packages by following a vision focused on delivering memorable customer experiences.

This proposal may be easier said than done; TUI Travel contains more than 200 products and brands, each offering a different holiday experience.[14] The company attempts to match personalised customer demands, when appropriate, to services offered by its four sectors: mainstream; specialist and emerging markets; activity; and online destination services. For example, TUI Travel plc positions its mainstream sector as follows:

> *The largest sector in the Group in terms of size ... and employee numbers, serves over 25 million customers each year. It comprises a number of vertically integrated tour operators, a fleet of 156 aircraft and about 3,500 retail shops. We operate within two key segments of the leisure travel market: Mainstream holidays which include the sale of differentiated and exclusively available content such as our HolidayVillages hotels and long-haul travel as well as more traditional mainstream holidays. Components, which includes sales of flights, accommodation, car hire, transfers and excursions either as separate components or together as part of customer assembled mainstream holidays usually through our branded web portals such as Thomson.co.uk.[15]*

Whereas the mainstream sector builds on a standardized approach, it is nevertheless a complex business because it still depends on the locations of power, control, and decision-making, which differ from country to country.[16] In contrast, Disney's theme park division can exercise strict and consistent standard controls over its various themes, rides, costumed characters, souvenirs and merchandise, trash removal, and security – anything that might disturb the coherence of each themed story. Therefore, guests at Disney invariably feel the "magic" of its parks.[17]

The specialist and emerging markets sector within the TUI Travel Group offers a wide range of holiday products, beyond holiday packages, featured on the corporate website as follows:

> *Operating in North America, Europe and a number of emerging markets, including China and Russia, this sector has over 40 specialist travel companies and services over 2 million customers annually. The companies within this Sector operate with business models that are flexible and cost efficient with shared characteristics: flexibility in aircraft and accommodation contracts; typically a reverse charter model with third party airlines (aircraft based in destination not source market) and less than 50% of seat capacity contracted; low overhead infrastructure; administration and management are maintained at the optimum level to support the business but maximise margins.[18]*

The corporate website projects the activity lifestyle travel sector as follows:

> *The Activity sector operates in the market segments of Marine, Adventure, Ski, Student and Sports. It comprises circa 60 businesses, operating out of 8 countries, reaching worldwide source markets. We operate with a mix of flexible and capital intensive business models to suit the travel experience offered. Selective asset ownership delivers competitive advantage with the businesses able to invest in new technology and content, maintain operational control of the experience and seek to optimise asset utilisation.[19]*

Finally, the online destination services portion consists of two divisions. The business-to-business divisions (Hotelbeds and Portfolio Incoming) provide accommodation, transfers, and excursions online and offline through a portfolio of destination agencies in 48 countries. Its customers are tour operators, travel agents, cruise lines, and other corporate customers. In contrast, the business-to-consumer division sells accommodation directly to customers through LateRooms, Hotelopia, and AsiaRooms.[20] In this collection of business units, organisational complexity becomes further exacerbated on the hedonic level. We return to this issue in the conclusion.

From a global value chain perspective[21] lead firms such as TUI Travel market tourist experiences in the home country and therefore help define how tourists perceive a particular destination,[22] at least in symbolic terms. In the latter half of the twentieth century, managerial thinking focused on processes unfolding in time and the cognitive domain, not "concrete spatial and material" ideas,[23] which in turn caused organizations to ignore the material reality – to the peril of society. Tourism development has positive effects, including the creation of jobs and income, but it also has negative consequences such as overexploitation of natural resources and environmental deterioration. Increasingly, tourists are turned off by dense traffic, polluted beaches, and landscapes disfigured by a surplus of service facilities. The next section explores such spatial and temporal contexts. In particular, we explore the building blocks for memorable customer experiences in destination travel, namely, demand specifications, tourism service delivery, and tourism development strategy.

Spatial and Temporal Contexts

Holiday travel-related consumption is a fact of life for large sections of the population in Europe, North America, Australia, and parts of Asia. In the global market, tourist attractions, events, and destinations represent the cultures from which the consumer's dreams emerge, leading to an anticipated doubling of the number of international tourist arrivals by 2020.[24] Assuming the inevitability of continued growth, the consequences of ever-increasing traffic and over-exploitation of natural resources may lead to overcrowding and environmental deterioration. These factors have caused increasing public concerns, particularly regarding the by-products of human movement, such as greenhouse gas emissions, and their impact on the environment and nature.[25] Thriving in a global market requires looking closely at the tourism effects that endanger the grounds for its existence, especially on a local scale. Just such an examination led TUI Travel to adopt a philosophy dedicated to balancing economics with ethics and ecology,[26] as follows:

> The high substantial expectations of the financial markets, policy makers, media, and non-governmental organizations emphatically demand – particularly from publicly-quoted, multinational companies – quantified and qualified reporting on the extra-financial aspects and risks, and the associated inherently-linked presentation of concrete facts concerning corporate responsibility (CSR) for employees and society, and the environment and nature.[27]

The considerable negative externalities, such as social, economic, and environmental costs, typically are excluded from the market prices of tour packages. However, such costs may explode when tens of millions of middle-income consumers from the emerging markets of Brazil, Russia, India, China, and so forth go in search of relatively cheap, commoditised, packaged tours. Such tours often are characterised by simulated interactions, particularly by Disney-style service providers, who are trained to recite memorised scripts in their encounters with guests. In contrast, TUI Travel envisions a memorable customer experience that depends on "real" human interactions and "authentic products".[28] To offer these services and products in a sustainable manner, TUI Travel plc must bridge three gaps: tourist demand specifications, tourism delivery and supply, and tourism development strategies, as we examine in the next sections and depict in Figure 12.1.[29]

TOURIST DEMAND SPECIFICATIONS

Customers who originate from industrialised countries and parts of Asia are increasingly spoiled and have high expectations of their travel experiences. Through more than 200 products and brands, TUI Travel affords customers a wide choice of differentiated, flexible travel experiences to meet their changing needs. The increasing expectations of customers have also pushed TUI Travel to provide travel beyond mass-production and customised experiences. Moreover, the delivery of memorable customer experiences is complex,[34] in that they relate on one level to multi-sensory, fantasy, emotive aspects of product experiences in the form of "hedonic consumption".[35] On another level though, customers display different needs and perceptions, often depending on their country segments. In that regard, the travel market demonstrates a national-orientation and idiosyncrasies, including marked differences in preferred accommodation types.

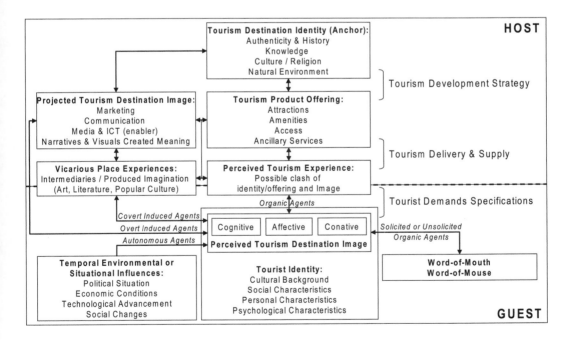

Figure 12.1 The 3-gap image formation model

Source: The GAPS service quality analysis model by Parasuraman,[30] with major contributions from Baloglu and McCleary,[31] Fesenmaier and MacKay,[32] and Gartner.[33]

For example, approximately 90 per cent of Scandinavians prefer apartments to hotel accommodation; 90 per cent of Germans prefer hotels over apartments; in Britain, this choice becomes a 50/50 proposition.[36]

It thus appears relevant to define customer requirements clearly and then interpret how the identified attributes likely contribute to delighting the customer. These results might be accomplished, for example, by classifying the power of the attributes of a product or service, including the extent to which they contribute to satisfying specific customers' needs.

Basic needs, also known as "must-be needs", reflect the features that must exist before a potential customer will consider a product or service for purchase. Performance or one-dimensional needs provide customers with a direct comparision between competing products, such that their perceptions of the attribute's strong performance lead to higher customer satisfaction. The third category includes excitement or attractive needs, also called delighters. Including these features in the travel experience will likely delight customers, even if they do not ask for such features – they give customers a "wow" or special feeling and afford travel companies such as TUI Travel a means for differentiation.[37] However, this model merely classifies, without providing a measurable quantification of the weight of different levels of customer experience attributes, such as variety, safety, quality, price, and exclusivity.[38]

TOURISM DELIVERY AND SUPPLY

Customer engagement, a prerequisite for memorable customer experience, involves sensation or knowledge acquisition and happens on two levels: the personal level, whether through active or passive customer participation, and the environment level, through either absorption or immersion.[39] Within this context, it becomes important to note that the majority of TUI Travel's customers consider the environmental quality of their holiday destinations an important determinant of the quality of their holiday experience. For example, 59 per cent of the company's surveyed respondents said that "holidays with a low impact on the environment would influence their decision in making a holiday purchase", and 77 per cent of customers conveyed that "holidays with a fair deal for local people would influence their holiday purchase choice".[40] Accordingly, TUI Travel must build an overall capability to turn the vision of memorable customer experiences into reality, as delivered by its stakeholders and experienced by customers. The implementation of quality function deployment (QFD) would afford TUI Travel a means to transform extensive data gathered about customer requirements into a concrete design for delivering memorable customer experiences. However, this transformation requires overlap between two fields of expertise, namely, marketing and environmental science. The next section therefore considers the urgent need to establish a critical mass for effective decision-making between domains. Although closely linked in conduct and remit, these domains remain managerially isolated.

TOURISM DEVELOPMENT STRATEGY

TUI Travel plc demonstrates its commitment to sustainable development according to its listing on the Dow Jones Sustainability Index (DJSI) World. But customer perceptions about the environmental quality of their holiday destinations represent the major determinant of the quality of holiday experience. Against this backdrop, environmental management priorities in holiday destinations count for a great deal. The aim thus becomes safeguarding the natural foundations, including crystal-clear water, clean beaches, unsullied countryside, viable ecosystems, and high species diversity, as well as pedestrian precincts, organised waste disposal, and animal protection measures.

Traditionally, the main role of TUI Travel has been direct involvement in the marketing of holiday destinations, with a base outside the destination. In contrast and due to its commitment to effective environmental protection, TUI Travel today has established its own global TUI Environmental Network (TEN) with the multi-pronged aim "to integrate staff, international affiliates, contractual partners and external partners; [and] promote networking, dialogue and cooperation".[41] For example, Europark Federation, an independent non-governmental organisation (NGO), seeks to protect Europe's unique variety of wildlife, habitats, and landscapes. Across the TUI Travel Group, several subsidiary companies engage in partnerships with ECPAT (End Child Prostitution, Child Pornography and Trafficking of Children for Sexual Purposes).

Without the support of a network of stakeholders, TUI Travel plc would be unable to achieve its sustainability objectives effectively. Stakeholders consist of primary and secondary stakeholders. The former include customers, employees, and investors, whereas secondary stakeholders include the local government (elected), local public sector policy-makers, local residents, the private sector, media, competitors, the general public, the national government, professionals and consultants, and NGOs. Achieving its main environmental management priorities no longer depends solely on its relations with primary stakeholders; rather, it depends increasingly on TUI Travel plc's capabilities to assess collaborative tourism marketing, particularly in the relationship between the Destination Management Organisation (DMO) and local enterprises. Such an analysis is relevant because, to be effective, TUI Travel must continuously assess its relationships and understand its stakeholders to gain insights that may help answer key questions: What are our stakeholders' intentions and interactions within the network? How responsive are stakeholders to our environmental management priorities?[42]

Factors that Help or Hinder the Creation of Memorable Travel Experiences

This chapter has introduced an emerging shift in the perspective of the customer, not as one who receives a finished object or provides a source of business but rather as a co-creator of experiences that are memorable. Particularly, this chapter investigates the mechanics of and their more salient consequences for TUI Travel plc in relation to its efforts to sustain its competitiveness.

TRANSLATING PERFORMANCE REQUIREMENTS INTO MEMORABLE EXPERIENCES PRIORITIES

To make significant and sustainable gains in the marketplace, TUI Travel must compete on both its service outcomes and its memorable customer experiences. Implicit in this notion is that TUI Travel must strive to capture a "world-class position", from which it is universally recognised as the best in complying with high standards for memorable customer experiences, compared with both competitors and the standard of environmental sustainability. As we have seen, TUI Travel operates in a rather complex value chain. Therefore, decision-makers might find that the company's services and customer experiences are world class, whereas competitors are at best average. It is important to distinguish among the experiences, perhaps through the application of a critical incident technique.

The service concept design identifies the customer experience to be provided, whereas the performance objectives define the competitive priorities for TUI Travel and, by extension, its network partners. TUI Travel must outperform its rivals on many criteria. Two dimensions, importance and performance, provide a good means to prioritise objectives and thus identify which aspects warrant expenditures of time, money, and effort.

To assess the importance of a factor, one method, the Kano method, attempts to understand what customers regard as important. For example, research findings indicate that most customers of TUI Travel regard the environmental quality of their holiday destinations as important. To help judge this relative importance on a personal level, we must gain more insight into customers' expectation priorities, perhaps according to TUI Travel's mainstream versus specialist or emerging markets sectors and brands.

PERFORMANCE

Performance measurement involves an assessment of the conduct objectives of TUI Travel plc versus those of its competitors. This approach assesses the factors that are critical to TUI Travel's competitive position, according to its relative environmental management and "experience-centric" service performance.[43] The QFD technique combines the specifications of customers' desires about performance requirements, thereby linking marketing strategy to performance metrics. By applying this importance–performance matrix, TUI Travel can translate its strategic intentions into clear priorities for implementation and identify how to spend its scarce resources to achieve its objectives. The strategy development and implementation is driven by both an external force ("keeping nature intact") and an internal force (visionary leadership). Dr Michael Frenzel, the CEO of TUI Travel, recognises that the so-called "middle market ground" is giving way to increasing polarisation. He also observes that demand for tailor-made packaging has increased, warranting an appropriate response. Moreover, Frenzel recognises that the company's performance is influenced by its service orientation.[44] To cope with the intense competition in vertically and horizontally integrated tourism businesses, product and process innovation is not just an option but a must.

But can Frenzel galvanise internal and external stakeholders to realise his vision of "Making travel experiences special"? The unique appeal of this vision is its holistic approach, which requires balancing economics with ethics and ecology. The approach assumes that harmony and symbiosis, as reflected in the ethics of environmental quality, have major impacts on the economics of memorable customer experiences and furthermore that TUI Travel can use its market power to improve sustainability in the tourism sector. However, in reality, decision-making in support of a sustainable environment requires expertise in the domains of marketing management and environmental science, which in the travel destination context may be linked to conduct and remit, whereas on an administrative level, they are isolated. Therefore, to make a difference, public and private stakeholders require common criteria for sustainability reporting, as well as compliance with policies pertaining to service performance.[45] In Table 12.1 we suggest some particular criteria for sustainable reporting and their possible implications for the creation of memorable customer experiences. Currently, compliance or lack thereof may be the single greatest factor that can help or hinder.

Concluding Remarks

Arising from massive tourist flows, the natural environment of destinations is coming under threat, which has compelled TUI Travel plc to establish collaborative relationships with its public and private partners. In comparison with other tour operators, TUI Travel provides more extensive reports of its sustainability initiatives, monitoring, and compliance than the industry average. However, it ranks well behind the average in sustainability reporting practices compared with companies in the pharmaceutical, forestry, pulp and paper, and automotive sectors. Small operators are able to operate in a more sustainable fashion because their tour products tend to be locally embedded.[47] In contrast, TUI Travel

Table 12.1 Sustainability: pre-condition for creating memorable customer experiences

Criteria for sustainability reporting	Implications for creating memorable customer experiences
1. Product management and development	Anticipating, considering, measuring, and monitoring the impacts of tourism services, including the number of visitors, building destination infrastructure, and transportation.
2. Internal management	Policy considerations of all operations in the headquarters or country offices of personnel training.
3. Supply chain management	Policies relating to the selection and contracting of service providers to improve sustainability performance in the destination.
4. Customer relations	Informing customers about and raising consumer awareness of sustainable issues.
5. Cooperation with destinations	Efforts to engage in dialogues with destination operators and local stakeholders regarding the impacts of tour packages and philanthropic activities.
6. Information source on issues	Collecting information about the performance of suppliers, resources, and knowledge.
7. Monitoring systems	Quantification of sustainability activities and specificity about time horizons.
8. Memberships	Participation in memberships and certification schemes.
9. Sustainability reporting	Publishing a separate report about sustainability issues.

Source: Van Wijk and Persoon[46]

has inflexibilities built into its complex supply chain. This limitation raises questions about TUI Travel's voluntary measures and their impact on pristine destinations, as well as the creation of memorable customer experiences.

Customers give meaning to their own experiences. In the physical context, they do so by leveraging a tourist destination as a source of information. Through enactment, the tourist's dream turns into reality. In other words, the creation of tourist experiences is impossible without the dimensions of time and space.[48] How a tourist perceives and experiences a particular destination ultimately depends on his or her personal interpretation of the situation, based on his or her cultural background, prior experience, mood, sensation-seeking personality traits, and so on. As customer experiences gain in richness, customisation, and complexity, TUI Travel has introduced its Platform Strategy Y-model.[49] The model enables the company to manage its source markets separately and create synergies among airline, destination services, and accommodation facilities. In summary, creating memorable customer experiences entails holistic considerations that contribute to the portrayal of TUI Travel's symbolic brand as a visually appealing and elegant (sense), hospitable tour operator oriented towards sustainable principles (feel), innovative and creative (think), service and action-oriented (act), and simultaneously thinking and acting locally and globally (relate).[50]

Notes

1. Personal communication with Ad Pruyn, University of Twente (2007).
2. Eriksen, T.H. (2001), *Tyranny of the Moment Fast and Slow in the Information Age*, Pluto Press, London.
3. Nunes, P.F. and Spelman, M. (2008), "The tourism time bomb", *Harvard Business Review*, Vol. 10 (April), No. 2, pp. 20–22.
4. Dittmann, I., Maug, E., and Schneider, C. (2008), "How Preussag became TUI: a clinical study of institutional blockholders and restructuring in Europe", *Financial Management*, Vol. 10 (Autumn), No. 4, pp. 571–98.
5. *ATOL Business*, Summer 2006, No. 29, available at http://www.caa.co.uk/docs/33/ATOL_Business_Issue_29.pdf (accessed 9 October 2008).
6. Witt, R. and Meyer, R. (1998), *Strategy: Process, Content, Context*, Thompson International Press, London.
7. Ritzer, G. (1998), *The McDonaldization Thesis: Explorations and Extensions*, Sage, London.
8. TUI Travel PLC, Annual Report 2006, p. 27.
9. O'Dell, T. and Billing, P. (2004), *Experiencescapes: Tourism, Culture and Economy*, Copenhagen Business School, Copenhagen.
10. Ihlau, G. (1997), "TUI: an example for quality and quality assurance", paper presented in Venice, 12 December 1997.
11. Go, F.M. and Ritchie, J.R.B. (1990), "Tourism and transnationalism", *Tourism Management*, Vol. 11, No. 4, pp. 287–90.
12. Obenour, W., Patterson, M., Pederson, P., and Pearson, L. (2006), "Conceptualization of a meaning-based research approach for tourism service experiences", *Tourism Management*, Vol. 27, No. 1, pp. 34–41.
13. TUI Travel PLC website, available at http://www.tuitravelplc.com/tuitravel/ (accessed 15 November 2008).

14. TUI Travel PLC, "Investors FAQs", available at http://www.tuitravelplc.com/tuitravel/investors/faqs/ (accessed 15 November 2008).
15. TUI Travel PLC, "Mainstream Sector", available at http://www.tuitravelplc.com/tuitravel/structure/mainstream/ (accessed 15 November 2008).
16. Orbasli, A. (2001), *Tourists in Historic Towns: Urban Conservation and Heritage Management*, E. & F.N. Spon, London.
17. Pine, B.J. and Gilmore, J.H. (1999), *The Experience Economy: Work is Theater and Every Business is a Stage*, Harvard Business School Press, Boston, MA.
18. TUI Travel PLC, "Specialist & Emerging Markets Sector", available at http://www.tuitravelplc.com/tuitravel/structure/specialist (accessed 15 November 2008).
19. TUI Travel PLC, "Activity Sector", available at http://www.tuitravelplc.com/tuitravel/structure/activity/ (accessed 15 November 2008).
20. TUI Travel PLC, "Online Destination Services Sector", available at http://www.tuitravelplc.com/tuitravel/structure/online/ (accessed 15 November 2008).
21. Clancy, M. (1998), "Commodity chains, services and development: theory and preliminary evidence from the tourism industry", *Review of International Political Economy*, Vol. 5, No. 1, pp. 122–48.
22. Lanfant, M.F. (1980), "Introduction: tourism in the process of internationalization", *International Social Science Journal*, Vol. 32, No. 1, pp. 14–43.
23. Clegg, S.R. and Kornberger, M. (2006), "Introduction: rediscovering space", in S.R. Clegg and M. Kornberger (eds), *Space, Organizations and Management Theory*, Liber & Copenhagen Business School Press, Malmo.
24. Ibid., p. 3.
25. TUI Travel PLC, "Mobility and the Environment", available at http://www.tui-group.com/en/nachhaltigkeit/environment/mobilitaet_umwelt/ (accessed 15 November 2008).
26. Bennis, W., Parikh, J., and Lessem, R. (1994), *Beyond Leadership: Balancing Economics, Ethics and Ecology*, Blackwell, Oxford.
27. TUI Travel sustainability report (2006–2007).
28. Ibid., p. 7.
29. Based on the GAPS service quality analysis model by Parasuraman, A., Zeithaml, V., and Berry, L.L. (1985), "A conceptual model of service quality and its implications for future research", *Journal of Marketing*, Vol. 49, No. 4, pp. 41–50.
30. Ibid.
31. Baloglu, S. and McCleary, K.W. (1999), "A model of destination image formation", *Annals of Tourism Research*, Vol. 26, No. 4, pp. 808–89.
32. Fesenmaier, D. and MacKay, K. (1996), "Deconstructing destination image construction", *Revue de Tourisme*, Vol. 51, No. 2, pp. 37–43.
33. Gartner, W.C. (1993), "Image formation process", *Journal of Travel and Tourism Marketing*, Vol. 2, Nos 2 and 3, pp. 191–215.
34. Kotler, P. (1984), "'Dream' vacations: the booming market for designed experiences", *The Futurist*, Vol. XVIII, No. 5, pp. 7–13; Lawer, C. (2006), "Eight styles of firm–customer knowledge co-creation", OMC Group Insight, available at http://www.theomcgroup.com/insightseries.htm (accessed 9 October 2008).
35. Hirschman, E.C. and M.B. Holbrook (1982), "Hedonic consumption: emerging concepts, methods and propositions", *Journal of Marketing*, Vol. 46, No. 3, pp. 92–101.
36. TUI Travel PLC, "Mobility and the Environment", 25, p. 5.

37. Kano, N., Seraku, K., Takahashi, F., and Tsuji, S. (1984), "Attractive quality and must-be quality", *Hinshitsu (Quality, The Journal of Japanese Society for Quality Control)*, Vol. 14, No. 2, pp. 39–48.

38. These are the features that give customers an unexpected excitement and satisfaction – the "wow" factor – according to Kano et al. "Attractive quality and must-be quality", p. 33.

39. Kano et al. "Attractive quality and must-be quality".

40. Whittingham, J., Environment Manager, TUI Travel PLC, "Climate change adaptation & mitigation in the tourism sector: Framework, tools & practices", 9 April 2008.

41. TUI Travel PLC, "TUI Environmental Network", available at http://www.tui-group.com/en/nachhaltigkeit/environment/kon_u_sys/ten/index.html (accessed 15 November 2008).

42. d'Angella, F. and Go, F.M. (2009). "'Tale of two cities' collaborative tourism marketing: toward a theory of destination stakeholder assessment", *Tourism Management*, Vol. 30, No. 3, pp. 429–40.

43. Prahalalad, C.K. and Ramaswamy, V. (2004), *The Future of Competition: Co-Creating Unique Value with Customers*, Harvard Business School Press, Boston, MA.

44. Lytle, R.S. and Timmerman, J.E. (2006), "Service orientation and performance: an organizational perspective", *Journal of Services Marketing*, Vol. 20, No. 2, pp. 136–47.

45. Cohen, M., Agrawal, A., and Agrawal, V. (2006), "Achieving breakthrough service delivery through dynamic asset deployment strategies", *Interfaces*, Vol. 36, No. 3, pp. 259–71.

46. van Wijk, J. and Persoon, W. (2006), "A long haul destination: sustainability reporting among tour operators", *European Management Journal*, Vol. 24, No. 6, pp. 381–95.

47. Ibid.

48. Gartner, W.C. and Hunt, J.D. (1987), "An analysis of state image change over a twelve-year period (1971–1983)", *Journal of Travel Research*, Vol. 25, No. 2, pp. 15–19.

49. Brackenbury, M. (2002), "Has innovation become a routine practice that enables companies to stay ahead of the competition in the travel industry?", unpublished OECD paper, Paris.

50. Schmitt, B.H. (1999), *Experiential Marketing: How to get Customers to Sense, Feel, Think, Act, Relate to your Company and Brands*, Free Press, New York.

Part V
Methodological Issues

13 *Made it More Memorable? Evaluating the Customer's Emotional Experience*

ADAM FINN* AND LUMING WANG†

Keywords

emotional experience, self-report emotions, generalisability theory, variance components

Abstract

Numerous marketing gurus urge firms to deliver a more memorable customer experience by managing the customer's emotional experience, not just the functional and physical experience. But managing the emotional experience assumes access to a reliable method of evaluating what is being experienced. Although enthusiasts advocate the use of behavioural or physiological measures of emotions, the only current practical option is structured self-reports. This chapter investigates the self-report measures of emotions provided by a random sample of consumers for a crossed, random sample of online service providers. The results indicate that very little of the variance in self-reported emotions is due to service providers. Rather, the substantial sources of variance in reported emotions are consumers and the interaction between consumers and service providers. This evidence calls into question the managerial usefulness of self-reported emotion measures and the assumption that service providers can measure and manage the emotions that make for memorable service experiences.

*   Adam Finn, R.K. Banister Professor of Marketing, 3-23, University of Alberta School of Business, Edmonton, Alberta, Canada T6G 2R6. E-mail: adam.finn@ualberta.ca. Telephone: 780-492-5369, Fax: 780-492-3325. Support for this research was provided by a Social Sciences and Humanities Council of Canada Initiative on the New Economy Research Grant.

†   Luming Wang, doctoral candidate in Marketing, 2-24, University of Alberta, School of Business, Edmonton, Alberta, Canada T6G 2R6. E-mail: luming@ualberta.ca. Telephone: 780-492-5816, Fax: 780-492-3325.

Introduction

A well-designed product for a specific target group, a strong brand, and good customer service are still necessary but no longer sufficient to ensure market success. According to marketing gurus, firms must now deliver a "memorable customer experience".[1] Commoditised markets are a real concern. Modern consumers often face choices between physically and functionally similar products that are available from a wide range of suppliers. To meet their short-term performance objectives, more firms rely on sales promotions, both customer-directed (e.g., couponing, rebates) and trade-directed (e.g., wholesale case discounts), that decrease differentiation and shrink realised margins.[2] But do the marketing gurus really know how to help companies to design, sell, and deliver "memorable customer experiences"?

Pine and Gilmore identify the experience economy as "a new economic era in which every business is a stage, and companies must design memorable events for which they charge admission."[3] Moreover, they offer five principles for designing memorable experiences, namely, creating a consistent theme, laying the theme with positive cues, eliminating negative cues, offering memorabilia, and engaging all five senses to heighten the experience. However, this prescription appears to be based on anecdotal evidence, and it fails to address the consumer psychology that makes products or services into memorable experiences. The novelty in this new enthusiasm for creating memorable customer experiences would appear to be the focus on the customer's emotional experience, not just the customer's functional or physical experience.[4] Shaw even quantifies that more than 50 per cent of a customer experience is about emotions.[5]

The experience economy and memorable customer experiences are new terminology, but their roots lie in extant literature pertaining to emotional responses to products and services. Marketing traditionally has focused on the instrumental part of the consumer–product relationship. But a congenial part,[6] which generates subjective, emotional benefits, also has long been discussed. For example, Havlena and Holbrook note, "instrumentally, an individual might buy an automobile in order to drive to work, but congenially, s/he might draw a picture for the sake of having fun".[7] Thus emotional benefits may determine the choice between instrumental alternatives that are functionally equivalent. Many brand choices confer few objective or tangible benefits while producing many subjective or emotional reactions in the consumer. Aesthetic products such as music and creative activities such as drawing fall into this category of emotion-laden experience, as do spiritual responses and religious activities. Hence, any examination of behaviour involving these product categories must begin with an understanding of their hedonic benefits. Moreover, some forms of consumption, such as eating or dressing, that provide objective, tangible benefits also involve a substantially subjective, hedonic, or symbolic component.[8] In short, proponents argue that consumption experiences vary in their mix of utilitarian/hedonic, tangible/intangible, or objective/subjective components,[9] and that the latter, more emotional aspects of consumption experiences occur to a greater or lesser degree in almost all consumption situations.[10]

The new gurus generally assume that the "Opportunity to emotionally connect with your customers is everywhere, no matter what your business."[11] But managing these emotional connections requires a way to gauge the emotional experiences that are being generated reliably, not just traditional customer satisfaction. Shaw claims organisations can be characterised by a profile of their customers' experience on four clusters of emotions: advocacy, recommendation and attention clusters are presented as drivers of value, the eponymous final cluster as destroyers of value.[12] The attention emotions, such as stimulated, energetic, and interested, are reported to encourage increased customer spending. The recommendation emotions, such as cared for, safe, and valued, may drive customers to recommend the organisation. Pleased and happy, the only advocacy emotions, reportedly prompt customers to promote the organisation proactively. Finally, the destroying emotions, such as unhappy, irritated, and disappointed, not only destroy future value but also cost the organisation money in dealing with complaints and returns. Organisations can build a great customer experience by focusing on evoking value driver emotions and eliminating value destroying emotions.[13]

But how can the emotions as experience be measured by managers? Enthusiasts advocate the use of behavioural or physiological measures of emotions, such as facial action coding.[14] However, behavioural and physiological methods are not currently feasible in most consumption environments, leaving structured self-reports as the only practical and popularly employed alternative. This research investigates whether self-reported measures of emotions can provide the information necessary to manage customer emotional experiences in typical consumption environments.

To investigate this question, this chapter reflects two methodological choices. First, we examine self-reports in the domain of e-commerce. E-commerce is growing more and more important, and the competition is increasing concomitantly. Online US retail sales are expected to increase from US$172 billion in 2005 to US$329 billion in 2010, representing 13 per cent of total US retail sales. Because of low search costs, the threat of being "commoditised" is even more serious online than it is in a brick-and-mortar setting. Moreover, online shoppers are both shoppers and computer users. This "double identity" gives website managers more scope to make the shopping process memorable. Second, this chapter examines variation across service providers while accounting for variation between customers and the interaction between service providers and customers. Using a generalisability study, we attempt to determine how much of customers' reported emotional response to service provider websites can be accounted for by differences between websites, which managers have (or have not) designed to make memorable for their online shoppers. In contrast, more common research practice focuses on one service provider and its customers. Although simpler in terms of both data collection and analysis, that common practice can only examine whether customers who visit the same service provider's website exhibit varying emotional responses. It cannot determine how much of the emotional response is due to the website versus the customer's mood or temperament, let alone whether websites may have substantially different emotional profiles than their competitors.

EMOTIONS

In psychology, emotion differs from mood, though they are closely related, because both refer to feeling states that reflect what is happening within the organism and are controlled by similar processes.[15] Emotions are associated with specific events or stimuli and are intense enough to disrupt thought processes,[16] whereas moods are generalised feeling states that are not associated with a particular stimulus and are not sufficiently intense to interrupt ongoing thought processes.[17] An emotional episode may last seconds, or minutes at the most, whereas moods can last for hours or even days. Emotion and mood are both transitory states, unlike temperament, a related trait that is defined as a person's average emotional state across a representative sample of life situations.[18]

SELF-REPORT MEASURES

A common approach to emotions assumes a small set of discrete, basic, primary, or fundamental emotions, often held to be the building blocks from which other emotions emerge. Izard, on the basis of facial muscle responses, proposes interest, enjoyment, surprise, distress (sadness), anger, disgust, contempt, fear, shame/shyness, and guilt as ten hardwired fundamental emotions.[19] Plutchik suggests a circular pattern of eight basic emotions, namely, fear, anger, joy, sadness, acceptance, disgust, expectancy, and surprise, which combine to generate more numerous second-level emotions.[20] Ekman, Friesen, and Ellsworth use the universality of facial expressions to identify anger, disgust, fear, joy, sadness and surprise as the basic emotions.[21] These discrete emotions commonly are assessed using adjective checklists.

An alternative approach suggests emotions are interrelated and that a small number of dimensions provide a sufficiently comprehensive description of all emotions.[22] In their pleasure–arousal–dominance (PAD) model, Mehrabian and Russell identify the three nearly orthogonal dimensions of emotion as pleasure–displeasure, arousal–non-arousal, and dominance–submissiveness.[23] Combinations of different levels of pleasure, arousal, and dominance are necessary and sufficient to describe any emotional state. These three basic dimensions even account for almost all the reliable variance in other verbal measures of emotional states.[24] Watson, Clark, and Tellegen also develop two 10-item scales to measure nearly orthogonal positive affect and negative affect dimensions,[25] which can also be interpreted as a rotation of the first two PAD dimensions.[26] Two-dimensional structures commonly are represented as a circumplex in which emotion adjectives are systematically arranged around the perimeter of a circle.

In psychology, self-report scales originating in both approaches measure emotions, moods, and temperament.[27] As Laros and Steenkamp show in their Table 1,[28] such scales have been used to characterise the emotions generated by marketing stimuli or contexts, such as ads,[29] products,[30] retail shopping environments,[31] consumption situations,[32] and satisfaction assessment environments.[33]

CUSTOMER DELIGHT

One emotional response that could be of particular relevance for experiential marketing is customer delight. Bitner, Booms, and Tetreault first identified customer delight by applying the critical incident technique to services,[34] but it was popularised in the 1990s as a performance goal beyond mere customer satisfaction.[35] Oliver, Rust, and Varki identify customer delight, resulting from surprising and positive levels of service performance, as a key emotional response to a service.[36] They propose and find support for a model of the antecedents and consequences of customer delight, in which customer delight and customer satisfaction are distinct concepts that both influence intention. This model has been corroborated for business-to-consumer websites and online retailers.[37]

Empirical Study

For this chapter, we investigate the emotions self-reported by consumers immediately after an online shopping experience.

SAMPLES OF WEBSITES AND RATERS

To capture all sources of variance and covariance for e-services, we employ a G-study data collection design, in which we cross a sample of consumers with a sample of e-services. The stratified sample of e-services consists of the 20 online retailers shown in Table 13.1. Twelve smaller retailers were randomly sampled from a list of 1,588 Canadian

Table 13.1   List of websites included in the study

Retailer	Web site	Lines of trade
Major Canadian chain store retailers		
A&B Sound	absound.ca	Audio and video electronics
Canadian Tire	canadiantire.ca	Auto parts and general merchandise
Chapters-Indigo	chapters-indigo.ca	Bookstore
Club Monaco	clubmonaco.com	Unisex clothing
The Bay/Zellers	hbc.com	Major and discount department stores
Radio Shack	radioshack.com	Electronics
Roots Canada	roots.com	Unisex clothing
Staples	staples.ca	Office supplies and equipment
Randomly sampled		
Ampal Flowers	yyzflowers.com	Flower arrangements and gift baskets
Basket of Wishes	basketofwishes.ca	Gift baskets
Bear St. Canada	bearst.com/canada	Stuffed animals
The Body Shop	thebodyshop.ca	Soaps and cosmetics
Direct Video	directvideo.ca	VHS and DVD movies
Earth Cool Cottons	earthcool.com	Casual clothing
Forest City Surplus	fcsurplus.com	Military, electronic and general surplus
House of Tools	houseoftools.com	Hand and power tools and accessories
Laserland	laserland.com	DVD software and hardware
Pasha Gourmet	pasha-gourmet.com	Gourmet foods and condiments
Renouf Books	renoufbooks.com	International and government agency books
Velotique	velotique.com	Cycling clothes and accessories

retail websites, and the remaining eight were randomly chosen from 20 well-known Canadian retail chain websites. The simple user search tasks created for each of the sites require, for example, selecting a suitable gift or determining the total cost of purchasing the gift from the site. The respondents replied to a job posting for part-time marketing research assistants on a Canadian university campus. Interested applicants were briefed and then assigned a pre-test travel website to visit and evaluate. Among the applicants who performed satisfactorily on the pre-test – which meant they provided appropriate answers, completed all the structured response questions, provided a sensible response to the unstructured questions, and returned the material to the research office on time – 20 were randomly assigned to this research project rather than an alternative project.

EMOTION ITEMS

The 20 specific emotion items in Table 13.2 comprise 15 items selected by Oliver to capture Larsen and Diener's affect circumplex,[38] supplemented by five items from

Table 13.2 Principal components rotated matrix

| Emotion Items | Factors | | | |
	Customer Delight	Positive Affect	Negative Affect	Surprise
Joy	.88			
Elated	.86			
Gleeful	.80			
Cheerful	.79	.34		
Lucky	.79			
Delighted	.78	.32		
Excited	.68	.42		
Enthused	.65	.36		
Relaxed		.72		
Happy	.46	.71		
Pleased	.39	.68		
Stimulated		.67		.44
Content	.41	.65		
Grouchy			.85	
Annoyed			.84	
Bored			.78	
Distressed			.73	
Sad	.32		.56	
Astonished				.80
Surprised		.37		.73

Notes: Principal component analysis following Varimax rotation with Kaiser normalisation. Loadings below .3 not reported to aid in interpretation.

customer delight literature, namely, delighted and stimulated,[39] gleeful,[40] and joyful and lucky.[41] We investigate the dimensionality and sources of variation in these consumption emotions, as experienced during online shopping.

DATA COLLECTION PROCEDURE

Data for the 400 combinations of 20 websites and 20 raters were collected by the raters, who made one website visit per day for 20 successive weekdays. The study design began by randomly assigning websites and consumer raters to two factors in a 20-level Latin square design. The third factor is days, so each website gets evaluated once per day by a different rater. To control for possible order effects, we randomly reordered the days for the analysis. The consumer raters had 24 hours to visit an assigned website, use the site to answer the assigned questions, complete their evaluation, and then return it to the research office. The emotion question asked, "During this visit to the website, how frequently did you feel each of the following?" followed by the list of 20 emotion items, with never, hardly ever, sometimes, quite often, and always as the five ordered response categories. The website evaluation also included website quality, satisfaction, and intentions questions. The satisfaction item, to be used for comparison purposes, requests, "Please indicate whether you agree, disagree, or neither agree nor disagree with the following statements about the website you just visited: This site was satisfying to me." Data collection commenced on 22 September 2003, and concluded on 23 October 2003. The resulting crossed data allow for the estimation of variance and covariance components of emotions over websites, over raters, and over their interaction. Thus, the methodology is similar to that employed by Finn,[42] but here, we address a broad range of emotions, not just customer delight.

ANALYSIS

Before examining the sources of variability in the emotion data, we employed two traditional forms of analysis to examine the dimensional and spatial structures derived from the data for the 20 emotion items.

Dimensional structure

Table 13.2 reports the results of a principal components analysis of the data for the 20 emotion items, treating the 400 observations as if they were independent. The Varimax-rotated loading matrix for a four-component solution accounts for 69.9 per cent of variance in the 400 observations. On the basis of the loadings, we can label the four components delight, positive affect, negative affect, and surprise. The positive affect and negative affect components, always found in such analyses, appear to match the advocacy and destroying emotion clusters identified by Shaw.[43] The delight and surprise components reflect two constructs in Oliver, Rust, and Varki's model of the foundations of customer delight.[44] However, some emotions show substantial loadings on more than one component; for example, happy cross-loads on customer delight (.46) and loads strongly on positive affect (.71).

Multidimensional scaling

Multidimensional scaling (MDS) can identify emotional items that give similar coordinates in a reduced space representation of emotion data.[45] We calculate the Euclidean distance between each pair of emotions and subject the resulting distance matrix to metric MDS analysis using ALSCAL in SPSS. The Kruskal stress coefficients for the two- and three-dimensional solutions are .094 and .060, respectively. The variance in distance accounted for by the solutions is .97 and .98, respectively. In Figure 13.1, we plot the MDS stimulus coordinates in two dimensions. A greater differentiation occurs on Dimension 1, which appears to be a pleasure–displeasure dimension, than on Dimension 2, which appears to be an arousal–non-arousal dimension. The third dimension, which provides only a minor improvement in fit, separates stimulated (1.10), astonished (0.80), and surprised (.78) from joy (−.62), bored (−.60), and relaxed (−.57), which implies it may be related to the surprise dimension identified by the principal components analysis.

The principal components analysis and MDS analysis could be generated from any set of emotion rating data. We next turn to generalisability analyses that take advantage of our unique data, resulting from the crossing of websites with raters. A generalisability study uses random-effects ANOVA to estimate the magnitude of various sources of measurement variation and identify the most efficient strategy for achieving desired measurement precision.[46] It addresses the relationship between the "true" variance in what is being measured (e.g., emotions) within the objects of measurement (e.g., websites) and the other unwanted main effect, interaction, or random error variances. Univariate generalisability theory provides a superior approach for achieving measurement precision

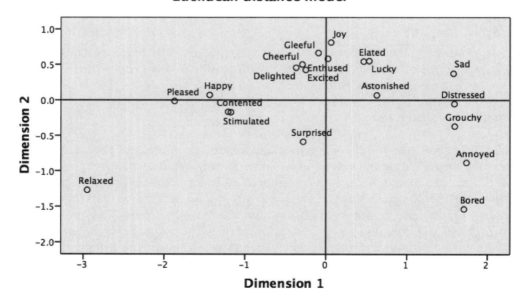

Figure 13.1 Derived stimulus configuration

in marketing.[47] It has been used to analyse daily mood data,[48] but it has not been used to assess emotion data collected over consumption situations. Multivariate generalisability theory has also been used in marketing,[49] following the work of Brennan,[50] who provides useful estimation software.[51] However, it has not been used to analyse emotion data.

Variance components

We use univariate generalisability analysis to estimate the variance components for each of the 20 emotions. Estimates of the variance components for the three sources of variability appear in Table 13.3. To aid in interpretation, we group the emotion items based on the results of our previous principal components analysis. Table 13.3 also lists

Table 13.3   Variance components for emotion items grouped by dimension

	Variance Components						
Dimensions							
Emotion item	**Websites**		**Raters**		**Websites by Raters**		**Total**
	Estimate	**%**	**Estimate**	**%**	**Estimate**	**%**	
Customer delight							
Joy	.046	3.7	.772	62.7	.413	33.6	1.231
Elated	.028	3.1	.517	57.0	.362	39.9	.908
Gleeful	.056	4.5	.655	52.4	.538	43.1	1.249
Cheerful	.085	6.9	.567	44.8	.611	48.3	1.264
Lucky	.043	5.8	.375	50.4	.326	43.8	.744
Delighted	.075	6.1	.523	41.8	.653	52.1	1.252
Excited	.050	4.6	.372	33.1	.702	62.4	1.125
Enthused	.051	4.8	.344	32.5	.664	62.7	1.059
Positive affect							
Relaxed	.110	6.3	.818	46.4	.835	47.3	1.765
Happy	.170	11.1	.684	44.0	.699	44.9	1.556
Pleased	.185	12.1	.461	29.8	.896	58.0	1.545
Stimulated	.181	12.6	.577	39.9	.685	47.4	1.445
Content	.146	10.1	.705	48.0	.616	41.9	1.469
Negative affect							
Grouchy	.083	9.5	.212	23.9	.591	66.6	.887
Annoyed	.170	14.0	.174	14.4	.868	71.6	1.212
Bored	.236	16.0	.305	20.6	.940	63.5	1.481
Distressed	.042	6.0	.161	22.8	.503	71.2	.706
Sad	.009	2.4	.161	41.8	.215	55.8	.386
Surprise							
Astonished	.013	1.4	.410	43.3	.525	55.3	.948

the total variance and percentage of variance due to websites, raters, and websites × raters to facilitate comparisons across the emotions. Note that considerable variation exists in the total variance observed for different emotions. Whereas a high level of total variance appears for relaxed (1.765), happy (1.556), and pleased (1.545) – positive affect items – there is a low level of total variance for distressed (.706), lucky (.744), and, particularly, sad (.386).

Substantial differences also appear in the proportion of variance due to the three sources for different emotions. The proportion of variance due to websites is very small for the surprise items (average 2 per cent) and the customer delight items (average 5 per cent). It is somewhat larger for some of the positive affect and negative affect items, reaching as high as 14 per cent for annoyed and a maximum of 16 per cent for bored. The proportion of variance due to raters is generally much more substantial, accounting for more than 50 per cent of the variance for half of the customer delight emotions. The interaction between websites and raters is usually the largest source of variance. The variance components for the five-category, single-item measure of satisfaction, estimated for comparison purposes, reveal that 26.3 per cent of the variance is due to websites, 6.0 per cent to raters, and 67.7 per cent to the interaction.

Covariance components

We use multivariate generalisability analysis to estimate covariance components for the 20 emotion items. The data collection process ensured each response was complete, providing the balanced data necessary for an analysis using mGENOVA.[52] Conceptually, this analysis treats the 20 measures as fixed, whereas the websites, raters, and interaction are random. The websites and raters are fully crossed, and their levels reasonably are treated as randomly sampled from an infinite population. The items are linked in the sense that measures of all 20 items for each combination of rater and website come from a single visit. Therefore, we could obtain covariance components for websites, raters, and the websites by raters interaction, confounded with error.

Estimates of the covariance components for the three sources of variability appear in the three sections of Table 13.4. The 20 emotions are shown in sequence, based on the size of their loadings on the rotated principal components. The variance components (from Table 13.3) are along the diagonal, whereas the covariance component estimates are below the diagonal. Corresponding disattenuated correlations, computed by dividing the covariance component by the square roots of the two variance components,[53] are reported above the diagonal to help interpret these covariance values. For the websites component, the magnitude of some of the disattenuated correlation estimates exceeded 1, which may occur as a result of sampling error, particularly when the sample size for a facet is small,[54] as was the case for websites and raters in our study, or it may be indicative of a hidden facet, not explicitly represented in the design.[55]

The majority of disattenuated correlations over websites are close to 1 (or –1), which suggests most of the emotion items cannot really be distinguished over websites. The customer delight and positive affect emotion items correlate close to perfectly to form a single dimension over websites. All the negative affect emotion items except annoyed also correlate perfectly negatively with that dimension. Astonished and surprised are the only two emotion items that clearly represent a second dimension across websites; a

Table 13.4 Variance-covariance component for scaling websites, raters, and websites × raters

Websites	Joy	Elated	Gleeful	Cheerful	Lucky	Delighted	Excited	Enthused	Relaxed	Happy	Pleased	Stimulated	Content	Grouchy	Annoyed	Bored	Distressed	Sad	Astonished	Surprised
Joy	.046	1.036	1.123	.957	.984	.990	.983	.946	.992	.946	1.004	.858	.912	-.873	-.854	-.890	-1.196	-1.009	.440	.819
Elated	.037	.028	1.067	.946	.878	.980	.875	.902	.861	.850	.913	.948	.914	-.751	-.762	-.926	-1.039	-.722	.994	.919
Gleeful	.057	.043	.057	1.109	.992	1.086	1.117	.972	.981	1.076	1.091	1.029	1.071	-.955	-.843	-.992	-1.045	-.780	.695	.884
Cheerful	.060	.047	.078	.087	1.007	1.081	1.016	.828	1.041	1.064	1.057	1.009	1.039	-1.014	-.834	-1.082	-1.001	-.729	.586	.789
Lucky	.044	.031	.049	.062	.043	1.030	.963	.884	.868	.881	.927	.773	.995	-.914	-.818	-.863	-1.017	-.801	.225	.727
Delighted	.058	.046	.071	.088	.059	.076	1.061	.839	1.049	1.093	1.086	1.061	1.124	-1.085	-.989	-1.114	-1.101	-.887	.434	.584
Excited	.048	.033	.060	.068	.045	.066	.051	.964	1.036	1.030	1.100	1.097	1.116	-.920	-.734	-1.086	-1.004	-.743	.542	.892
Enthused	.046	.034	.052	.055	.041	.052	.049	.051	.865	.713	.886	.912	.908	-.841	-.693	-.893	-1.082	-.818	1.069	1.089
Relaxed	.071	.048	.078	.102	.060	.096	.078	.065	.111	.995	1.033	.932	.961	-.993	-.864	-1.009	-1.035	-.854	.302	.575
Happy	.084	.060	.106	.130	.076	.125	.097	.067	.138	.173	1.002	.921	.961	-.934	-.790	-.984	-.950	-.732	.505	.674
Pleased	.093	.067	.112	.135	.083	.129	.108	.086	.149	.180	.187	.968	1.023	-.934	-.841	-.959	-1.039	-.798	.433	.802
Stimulated	.078	.068	.105	.127	.069	.125	.106	.088	.133	.163	.179	.182	.981	-.915	-.753	-1.001	-.901	-.643	.623	.732
Content	.075	.059	.098	.118	.080	.119	.097	.079	.123	.154	.171	.161	.149	-.988	-.849	-.953	-.993	-.790	.341	.668
Grouchy	-.054	-.037	-.066	-.087	-.055	-.087	-.060	-.055	-.096	-.113	-.117	-.113	-.110	.084	1.008	1.089	1.057	1.087	-.350	-.338
Annoyed	-.075	-.053	-.083	-.101	-.070	-.112	-.069	-.064	-.119	-.135	-.150	-.132	-.135	.120	.170	.917	1.088	1.207	-.295	-.190
Bored	-.093	-.076	-.115	-.155	-.087	-.149	-.120	-.098	-.164	-.199	-.202	-.208	-.179	.154	.184	.237	1.016	.889	-.664	-.587
Distressed	-.053	-.036	-.051	-.061	-.043	-.062	-.047	-.050	-.071	-.081	-.092	-.079	-.079	.063	.092	.102	.042	1.230	-.350	-.546
Sad	-.021	-.012	-.018	-.021	-.016	-.024	-.016	-.018	-.028	-.029	-.033	-.027	-.029	.030	.048	.042	.024	.009	-.226	-.009
Astonished	.011	.019	.019	.020	.005	.014	.014	.028	.012	.024	.021	.030	.015	-.012	-.014	-.037	-.008	-.002	.013	.752
Surprised	.029	.026	.035	.039	.025	.027	.034	.041	.032	.047	.058	.053	.043	-.016	-.013	-.048	-.019	.000	.014	.028

Table 13.4 Continued

Raters	Joy	Elated	Gleeful	Cheerful	Lucky	Delighted	Excited	Enthused	Relaxed	Happy	Pleased	Stimulated	Content	Grouchy	Annoyed	Bored	Distressed	Sad	Astonished	Surprised
Joy	.772	.841	.939	.894	.866	.931	.806	.771	.407	.598	.510	.239	.540	.286	-.017	-.147	.475	.666	.468	.333
Elated	.532	.517	.858	.887	.937	.897	.855	.903	.288	.529	.502	.296	.600	.526	.256	.052	.731	.863	.695	.526
Gleeful	.667	.500	.655	.933	.870	.932	.806	.844	.388	.683	.523	.361	.611	.456	.165	.073	.605	.688	.582	.462
Cheerful	.591	.480	.568	.567	.933	.979	.917	.870	.468	.750	.599	.343	.636	.478	.253	-.037	.652	.643	.566	.566
Lucky	.466	.413	.431	.430	.375	.965	.926	.860	.340	.611	.542	.353	.591	.344	.142	-.081	.678	.711	.625	.595
Delighted	.592	.467	.545	.533	.428	.523	.928	.882	.547	.760	.617	.421	.700	.419	.154	-.062	.637	.668	.605	.603
Excited	.432	.375	.398	.421	.346	.410	.372	.887	.508	.814	.603	.502	.622	.487	.290	-.003	.778	.654	.649	.714
Enthused	.397	.381	.400	.384	.309	.374	.317	.344	.510	.754	.631	.457	.679	.547	.355	.278	.789	.731	.669	.670
Relaxed	.324	.187	.284	.319	.188	.358	.280	.270	.818	.687	.647	.516	.585	.058	-.188	-.135	.106	.101	.306	.552
Happy	.435	.315	.457	.467	.310	.455	.411	.366	.514	.684	.804	.715	.780	.543	.358	.224	.570	.323	.517	.765
Pleased	.304	.245	.288	.306	.225	.303	.250	.251	.397	.451	.461	.538	.642	.408	.228	.142	.326	.364	.548	.600
Stimulated	.159	.162	.222	.196	.164	.232	.232	.204	.354	.450	.277	.577	.758	.432	.238	.246	.378	.174	.474	.641
Content	.398	.362	.415	.402	.304	.425	.319	.334	.444	.542	.366	.483	.705	.618	.443	.334	.579	.394	.646	.747
Grouchy	.116	.174	.170	.165	.097	.140	.137	.148	.024	.207	.127	.151	.239	.212	.794	.698	.789	.649	.780	.571
Annoyed	-.006	.077	.056	.079	.036	.046	.074	.087	-.071	.124	.065	.075	.155	.153	.174	.678	.802	.402	.588	.560
Bored	-.071	.021	.032	-.016	-.027	-.025	-.001	.090	-.067	.102	.053	.103	.155	.177	.156	.305	.427	.152	.341	.314
Distressed	.168	.211	.196	.197	.167	.185	.190	.186	.038	.189	.089	.115	.195	.146	.134	.095	.161	.769	.899	.819
Sad	.235	.250	.224	.195	.175	.194	.160	.172	.037	.107	.099	.053	.133	.120	.067	.034	.124	.161	.811	.440
Astonished	.264	.320	.302	.273	.245	.281	.254	.251	.177	.274	.238	.231	.348	.230	.157	.120	.231	.209	.410	.797
Surprised	.182	.236	.233	.266	.227	.272	.272	.245	.311	.394	.254	.303	.391	.164	.146	.108	.205	.110	.318	.388

Table 13.4 Concluded

Websites x Raters	Joy	Elated	Gleeful	Cheerful	Lucky	Delighted	Excited	Enthused	Relaxed	Happy	Pleased	Stimulated	Content	Grouchy	Annoyed	Bored	Distressed	Sad	Astonished	Surprised
Joy	.413	.512	.401	.436	.486	.438	.382	.392	.223	.390	.369	.301	.376	-.121	-.129	-.128	-.117	-.157	.134	.156
Elated	.198	.362	.471	.510	.410	.488	.520	.516	.194	.475	.360	.424	.332	-.164	-.159	-.142	-.191	-.194	.050	.199
Gleeful	.189	.208	.538	.378	.290	.494	.416	.393	.193	.431	.340	.352	.350	-.100	-.104	-.196	-.181	-.136	.229	.260
Cheerful	.219	.240	.217	.611	.355	.596	.610	.421	.259	.452	.411	.430	.402	-.196	-.185	-.235	-.243	-.146	.102	.284
Lucky	.178	.141	.121	.158	.326	.308	.317	.360	.222	.232	.281	.255	.323	-.061	-.067	-.063	-.165	-.161	.200	.257
Delighted	.228	.237	.293	.376	.142	.653	.529	.343	.203	.438	.379	.425	.311	-.151	-.148	-.220	-.160	-.139	.182	.316
Excited	.206	.262	.256	.399	.152	.358	.702	.547	.192	.480	.477	.481	.364	-.218	-.140	-.189	-.127	-.113	.096	.326
Enthused	.206	.253	.235	.268	.167	.226	.374	.664	.119	.429	.399	.495	.422	-.197	-.170	-.222	-.113	-.069	.077	.256
Relaxed	.131	.107	.129	.185	.116	.150	.147	.089	.835	.317	.455	.181	.290	-.330	-.336	-.182	-.237	-.200	-.056	-.021
Happy	.210	.239	.265	.295	.111	.296	.337	.292	.242	.699	.493	.491	.367	-.295	-.298	-.363	-.202	-.177	.128	.217
Pleased	.225	.205	.236	.304	.152	.290	.378	.308	.394	.391	.896	.444	.437	-.331	-.394	-.441	-.212	-.174	-.012	.161
Stimulated	.160	.211	.214	.278	.120	.284	.333	.334	.137	.340	.348	.685	.396	-.244	-.234	-.353	-.197	-.062	.285	.402
Content	.190	.157	.201	.246	.145	.197	.239	.270	.208	.241	.324	.257	.616	-.241	-.286	-.308	-.170	-.121	.162	.257
Grouchy	-.060	-.076	-.056	-.118	-.027	-.094	-.141	-.124	-.232	-.189	-.241	-.155	-.145	.591	.604	.391	.427	.304	-.036	-.038
Annoyed	-.077	-.089	-.071	-.134	-.036	-.112	-.109	-.129	-.286	-.232	-.348	-.180	-.209	.433	.868	.517	.377	.336	-.042	.024
Bored	-.080	-.083	-.139	-.178	-.035	-.172	-.153	-.175	-.161	-.295	-.404	-.283	-.234	.291	.467	.940	.327	.339	-.064	-.148
Distressed	-.053	-.081	-.094	-.135	-.067	-.092	-.076	-.065	-.154	-.120	-.142	-.116	-.094	.232	.249	.225	.503	.392	.052	.042
Sad	-.047	-.054	-.046	-.053	-.043	-.052	-.044	-.026	-.085	-.069	-.077	-.024	-.044	.108	.145	.153	.129	.215	.081	.116
Astonished	.056	.020	.109	.052	.074	.095	.052	.041	-.033	.069	-.008	.154	.082	-.018	-.025	-.040	.010	.025	.423	.471
Surprised	.082	.098	.155	.181	.120	.209	.223	.170	-.016	.148	.125	.271	.165	-.024	.018	-.117	.024	.044	.250	.665

Notes: Diagonal elements are variance components, lower diagonal elements are covariances, and upper diagonal elements are disattenuated correlations.

lower dimensionality to the data over websites occurs than would have been suggested using principal components.

Only very few of the disattenuated correlations over raters come close to 1, and none equal −1. Many of the correlations for the negative affect items that we might expect to be negative actually were positive over raters. In particular, all the correlations for grouchy, distressed, and sad with customer delight and positive affect items are positive instead of negative. The disattenuated correlations over websites by raters generally are much smaller and reveal the expected sign.

Discussion

The initial results we obtained when employing traditional methods to analyse self-report emotion data produce the expected findings. The component analysis identified four dimensions, readily interpreted as positive affect, negative affect, delight, and surprise, as previously found in academic literature. However, some cross-loading of items occurs, particularly between positive affect and delight. The two-dimensional MDS derived space also is generally consistent with the circumplex commonly found in psychology, with pleasure–displeasure and arousal–non-arousal dimensions. Adding a third dimension provides a minor improvement in fit by accounting for what appears to be surprise. Thus, there is little reason to think our emotion data are unique; in turn, the generalisability results likely are not attributable to the specific set of emotion items that we chose for use in this chapter.

Univariate generalisability results show that very little of the variance in consumer emotions when shopping online depends on differences among the websites, even though our sample includes both popular websites of major retailers and lesser-known sites by small retailers. Whereas websites account for 26 per cent of the variance in a measure of customer satisfaction, they constitute only a fraction of that share of variance for emotion items. In 2003, when this research was conducted, Canadian retail websites varied little in their ability to generate a consistent emotional response across respondents. When the responses varied a little more due to websites, it was not in desirable emotions but rather for bored and distressed, hardly the type of memorability that marketing gurus had in mind. It seems unlikely that any websites actually were creating the memorability advocated by marketing gurus.

Far more of the variance in emotions results from differences among the consumers who participated in the research. The substantive explanation for such differences could be consumer trait differences in temperament, in that they represent something that remains consistent over the four weeks of data collection. A more methodological explanation for these differences is response effects in the self-reporting of emotions that vary across persons. Such response effects are the most likely explanation for the unexpected positive relationships between emotion items loading on positive affect and emotion items loading on negative affect observed over raters in the multivariate generalisability analysis.

Variance due to the interaction between websites and raters also is generally quite substantial, which might be considered evidence that websites generate strong emotional responses and thus can create memorable experiences for segments of consumers. However, these differences are either due to inconsistency in how consumers react to the same website on different occasions (day to day) or because what makes one consumer feel an emotion more strongly makes another feel the same emotion less strongly. Distinguishing between these two explanations requires data collected over multiple occasions.[56]

The emotions measured in self-reports provided by consumers visiting these websites thus seem highly idiosyncratic, beyond the differences among customers. One online shopper's feelings about the website appear almost independent of how other customers feel about it. If managers use self-report measures to profile the emotional component of shopping experience and try to improve their service to generate more positive emotions, they will be taking on a greater challenge than trying to use satisfaction scores to improve customer satisfaction. The greater variance due to raters suggests there could be more potential for success if managers are more selective about the temperament of the consumers they try to attract.

LIMITATIONS

One limitation of this chapter is that the universe of generalisation that it addresses is a relatively mundane service domain rather than an obviously more memorable domain, such as entertainment or adventure holidays.[57] However, it still has relevance for managers of a broad range of services. A second limitation is our reliance on traditional self-report measures at a time when enthusiasts are advocating the use of behavioural measures,[58] such as eye tracking and facial action coding,[59] or tracking activity in the autonomic nervous system (ANS) that accompanies emotions, such as IBM's emotion mouse[60] or the wearable sensors designed by the Affective Computing Group at MIT.[61] We also employ time-inclusive reports that can be biased by peak and recency effects that plague retrospective reports.[62] However, the time-inclusive questioning at the conclusion of the experience is probably the least biased option available to service managers. Finally, we employ a somewhat arbitrary subset of the more extensive list of adjectives that have been used to capture self-reported emotions. However, this subset captures variation along four dimensions commonly identified when emotion data are analysed.

IMPLICATIONS FOR PRACTITIONERS

Companies are being urged to respond to the threat of commoditisation by striving to deliver a memorable customer experience, managing the emotional customer experience, not just the physical customer experience. But if companies collect data on the emotions reportedly experienced by their customers, much of the variance they observe will be due to the emotional set point of the customers, which have nothing to do with the service provided to the customer. Another substantial proportion of the variance will come from idiosyncratic responses to a common customer experience or idiosyncratic customer experiences. It may not be realistic to think companies can measure and control what creates memorable customer experiences for most of their customers. If little of the variation in emotional responses to the customer experience actually is due to differences in their services, managers likely cannot make the service experience much more memorable for all their customers.

Our data suggest managers should give more thought to identifying and attracting customers who are predisposed to respond with more positive emotions. Practitioners also might implement more sophisticated one-to-one marketing, aimed at increasing the value of the customer base by establishing a learning relationship with each customer. This strategy suggests managers should encourage input from customers about their idiosyncratic needs and contradictory emotional responses, then try to customise their products or services to meet those needs on a one-to-one basis, rather than think they can provide a common experience that will be memorable for all.

Conclusions

The marketing gurus urge companies to respond to the threat of commoditisation by delivering memorable customer experiences. This effort requires managing the emotional, not just the physical, customer experience. But how realistic is it to think companies can measure and control the emotions that their customers experience? Our results show that measures of consumption emotions using self-report items generate data that when analysed with principal components analysis and MDS appear consistent with previous reports in psychology and consumer research literature. However, when examined more closely from a generalisability theory perspective, it becomes clear that very little of the variance in the reported emotional response to the consumption experience is attributable to the service provider. Our results for the service domain of online shopping in 2003 further demonstrate that very little of the variation in emotional responses to the customer experience is due to differences between websites, especially with regard to the positive emotions that figure so prominently in the emotional profile promoted by the pundits and their consulting services.[63] Most of the variance in customers' emotional response comes from differences between people rather than differences between service providers. It seems it will be difficult for many firms to create distinctive emotional customer experiences that are both memorable and sustainable, because very little of the variation in emotions experienced by customers depends consistently on the service provider.

Notes

1. Pine, B. Joseph and Gilmore, James H. (1999), *The Experience Economy: Work Is Theatre and Every Business a Stage*, Harvard Business School Press, Boston, MA; Shaw, Colin and Ivens, John (2002), *Building Great Customer Experiences*, Palgrave Macmillan, Basingstoke; Smith, Shaun and Wheeler, Joe (2002), *Managing the Customer Experience: Turning Customers into Advocates*, Prentice-Hall, Englewood Cliffs, NJ.
2. Pine and Gilmore, *The Experience Economy*; Aaker, David A. (1991), *Managing Brand Equity*, Free Press, New York.
3. Pine and Gilmore, *The Experience Economy*, p. 4
4. Shaw and Ivens, *Building Great Customer Experience*.
5. Shaw, Colin (2007), *The DNA of Customer Experience: How Emotions Drive Value*, Palgrave Macmillan, Basingstoke.
6. Alderson, Wroe (1957), *Marketing Behavior and Executive Action*, Richard D. Irwin, Homewood, IL.
7. Havlena, William J. and Holbrook, Morris B. (1986), "The varieties of consumption experience: comparing two typologies of emotion in consumer behaviour", *Journal of Consumer Research*, Vol. 13, pp. 394–404, at p. 394.

8. Hirschman, Elizabeth and Holbrook, Morris B. (1982), "Hedonic consumption: emerging concepts, methods, and propositions", *Journal of Marketing*, Vol. 9, pp. 92–101.

9. Holbrook, Morris B., Lehmann, Donald R., and O'Shaughnessy, John (1986), "Using versus choosing: the relationship of the consumption experience to reasons for purchasing", *European Journal of Marketing*, Vol. 20, pp. 49–62.

10. Holbrook, Morris B. (1986), "Emotion in the consumption experience: toward a new model of the human consumer", in Peterson, Robert A., Hoyer, Wayne D., and Wilson, William R. (eds), *The Role of Affect in Consumer Behavior: Emerging Theories and Applications*, D.C. Heath, Lexington, MA.

11. Shaw, *The DNA of Customer Experience*, quoting Maxine Clark, founder of Build-A-Bear Workshop, p. xiv.

12. Shaw, *The DNA of Customer Experience*.

13. Ibid.

14. Cohn, Jeffrey F., Ambadar, Zara, and Ekman, Paul (2007), "Observer-based measurement of facial expression with the facial action coding system", in James A. Coan and John J.B. Allen (eds), *Handbook of Emotion Elicitation and Assessment*, Oxford University Press, Oxford, pp. 203–21; Hill, Dan (2007), "Face value", *Marketing Research: A Magazine of Management and Applications*, Vol. 19 (Fall), pp. 8–14.

15. Parkinson, Brian, Totterdell, Peter, Brinner, Rob B., and Reynolds, Shirley (1996), *Changing Moods: The Psychology of Mood and Mood Regulation*, Addison-Wesley Longman, London.

16. Zajonc, Robert B. (1998), "Emotions", in Daniel T. Gilbert, Susan T. Fiske, and Gardner Lindzey (eds), *Handbook of Social Psychology*, McGraw-Hill, Boston, MA, pp. 591–632.

17. Clark, Margaret and Isen, Alice (1982), "Towards understanding the relationship between feeling states and social behavior", in Albert Hastorf and Alice Isen (eds), *Cognitive Social Psychology*, Elsevier, New York, pp. 73–108.

18. Mehrabian, Albert (1996), "Pleasure-arousal-dominance: a general framework for describing and measuring individual differences in temperament", *Current Psychology*, Vol. 14 (December), pp. 261–92.

19. Izard, Carroll E. (1977), *The Psychology of Emotions*, Plenum, New York.

20. Plutchik, Robert (1980), *Emotions: A Psychoevolutionary Synthesis*, Harper & Row, New York.

21. Ekman, Paul, Friesen, Wallace V., and Ellsworth, Phoebe (1982), "What emotion categories or dimensions can observers judge from facial behavior?", in Paul Ekman (ed.), *Emotion in the Human Face*, Cambridge University Press, New York, pp. 39–55.

22. Mehrabian, Albert and Russell, James A. (1974), *An Approach to Environmental Psychology*, MIT Press, Cambridge, MA; Watson, David, Clark, Lee Ann, and Tellegen, Auke (1988), "Development and validation of brief measures of positive and negative affect: the PANAS scales", *Journal of Personality and Social Psychology*, Vol. 54, No. 6, pp. 1063–70.

23. Mehrabian and Russell, *An Approach to Environmental Psychology*.

24. Mehrabian, "Pleasure-arousal-dominance"; Russell, James A. and Mehrabian, Albert (1977), "Evidence for a three-factor theory of emotions", *Journal of Research in Personality*, Vol. 11 (September), pp. 273–94.

25. Watson et al., "Development and validation of brief measures of positive and negative affect".

26. Mano, Haim and Oliver, Richard L. (1993), "Assessing the dimensionality and structure of the consumption experience: evaluation, feeling, and satisfaction", *Journal of Consumer Research*, Vol. 20 (December), pp. 451–66.

27. Gray, Elizabeth K. and Watson, David (2007), "Assessing positive and negative affect via self-report", in Coan, James A. and Allen, John J.B. (eds), *Handbook of Emotion Elicitation and Assessment*, Oxford University Press, Oxford, pp. 171–83.

28. Laros, Fleur J.M. and Steenkamp, Jan-Benedict E.M. (2005), "Emotions in consumer behavior: a hierarchical approach", *Journal of Business Research*, Vol. 58, pp. 1437–45.

29. Edell, Judie A. and Burke, Marian Chapman (1987), "The power of feelings in understanding advertising effects", *Journal of Consumer Research*, Vol. 14 (December), pp. 421–33; Holbrook, Morris B. and Batra, Rajeev (1987), "Assessing the role of consumer response to advertising", *Journal of Consumer Research*, Vol. 14, pp. 404–19; Holbrook, Morris B. and Westwood, Richard A. (1989), "The role of emotion in advertising revisited: testing a typology of emotional responses", in Caffereta, Patricia and Tybout, Alice M. (eds), *Cognitive and Affective Responses to Advertising*, Lexington Books, Lexington, MA, pp. 353–71.

30. Philips, Diane M. and Baumgartner, Hans (2002), "The role of consumption emotions in the satisfaction response", *Journal of Consumer Psychology*, Vol. 12, No. 3, pp. 243–52; Westbrook, Robert A. (1987), "Product/consumption based affective responses and postpurchase processes", *Journal of Marketing Research*, Vol. 24 (August), pp. 258–70.

31. Machleit, Karen A. and Eroglu, Sevgin A. (2000), "Describing and measuring emotional response to shopping experiences", *Journal of Business Research*, Vol. 49 (August), pp. 101–11.

32. Richins, Marsha L. (1997), "Measuring emotions in the consumption experience", *Journal of Consumer Research*, Vol. 24 (September), pp. 127–46.

33. Mano and Oliver, "Assessing the dimensionality and structure of the consumption experience"; Westbrook, Robert A. and Oliver, Richard L. (1991), "The dimensionality of consumption emotion patterns and consumer satisfaction", *Journal of Consumer Research*, Vol. 18 (June), pp. 84–91.

34. Bitner, Mary J., Booms, Bernard M., and Tetreault, Mary S. (1990), "The service encounter: diagnosing favorable and unfavorable incidents", *Journal of Marketing*, Vol. 54 (January), pp. 71–84.

35. Keiningham, Timothy L. and Vavra, Terry G. (2001), *The Customer Delight Principle: Exceeding Customer's Expectations for Bottom-Line Success*, McGraw-Hill, New York.

36. Oliver, Richard L., Rust, Roland T., and Varki, Sajeev (1997) "Customer delight: foundations, findings, and managerial insight", *Journal of Retailing*, Vol. 73 (Fall), pp. 311–36.

37. Finn, Adam (2005), "Reassessing the foundations of customer delight", *Journal of Service Research*, Vol. 8 (November), pp. 103–16; Finn, Adam (2006), "Generalizability modeling of the foundations of customer delight", *Journal of Modeling in Management*, Vol. 1 (May), pp. 18–32.

38. Larsen, Randy J. and Diener, Edward (1992), "Promises and problems with the circumplex model of emotion", in Margaret S. Clark (ed.), *Review of Personality and Social Psychology*, Vol. 13, Sage, Newbury Park, CA, pp. 25–59; Oliver, Richard L. (1997), *Satisfaction: A Behavioral Perspective on the Consumer*, McGraw-Hill, New York.

39. Oliver et al., "Customer delight".

40. Finn, "Reassessing the foundations of customer delight".

41. Kumar, Anand, Olshavsky, Richard W., and King, Maryon F. (2001), "Exploring alternative antecedents of customer delight", *Journal of Consumer Satisfaction, Dissatisfaction and Complaining Behavior,* Vol. 14, pp. 14–26.

42. Finn, "Generalizability modeling of the foundations of customer delight".

43. Shaw, *The DNA of Customer Experience*.

44. Oliver et al., "Customer delight".

45. Richins, "Measuring emotions in the consumption experience".

46. Cronbach, Lee J., Gleser, Goldine C., Nanda, Harinder, and Rajaratnam, Nageswari (1972), *The Dependability of Behavioral Measurements: Theory of Generalizability for Scores and Profiles*, John Wiley & Sons, New York.

47. Finn, Adam and Kayandé, Ujwal (1997), "Reliability assessment and optimization of marketing measurement", *Journal of Marketing Research*, Vol. 34 (May), pp. 262–75; Peter, John P. (1979), "Reliability: a review of psychometric basics and recent marketing practices", *Journal of Marketing Research*, Vol. 16 (February), pp. 6–17; Rentz, Joseph O. (1987), "Generalizability theory: a comprehensive method for assessing and improving the dependability of marketing measures", *Journal of Marketing Research*, Vol. 24 (February), pp. 19–28.

48. Cranford, James A., Shrout, Patrick E., Iida, Masumi, Rafaeli, Eshkol, Yip, Tiffany, and Bolger, Niall (2006), "A procedure for evaluating sensitivity to within-person change: can mood measures in diary studies detect change reliably?", *Personality and Social Psychology Bulletin*, Vol. 32 (July), pp. 917–29.

49. Finn, "Generalizability modeling of the foundations of customer delight"; Finn, Adam (2004), "Assessment of the dimensionality of retail performance: a multivariate generalizability theory perspective", *Journal of Retailing and Consumer Services*, Vol. 11, No. 4, pp. 235–45; Finn, Adam and Kayande, Ujwal (2005), "How fine is COARSE? A generalizability theory perspective on Rossiter's procedure", *International Journal of Research in Marketing*, Vol. 22, No. 1, pp. 11–21.

50. Brennan, Robert L. (2001), *Generalizability Theory*, Springer-Verlag, New York.

51. Brennan, Robert L. (2001), *Manual for mGENOVA*, University of Iowa, Iowa Testing Programs Occasional Papers No. 50.

52. Ibid.

53. Brennan, *Generalizability Theory*.

54. Hox, J.J. (2000), "Multilevel multivariate and structural equation modeling: some missing links", paper presented at Social Science Methodology in the New Millennium, Fifth International Conference on Logic and Methodology, Cologne, October.

55. Brennan, *Generalizability Theory*.

56. Finn, Adam (2007), "Doing a double take: accounting for occasions in service performance assessment", *Journal of Service Research*, Vol. 9 (May), pp. 372–87.

57. Arnould, Eric J. and Price, Linda L. (1993), "River magic: extraordinary experience and the extended service encounter", *Journal of Consumer Research*, Vol. 20 (June), pp. 24–45; Holbrook, Morris B. and Hirschman, Elizabeth C. (1982), "The experiential aspects of consumption: consumer fantasies, feelings and fun", *Journal of Consumer Research*, Vol. 9 (September), pp. 132–40.

58. Gray and Watson, "Assessing positive and negative affect via self-report".

59. Cohn et al., "Observer-based measurement of facial expression with the facial action coding system"; Hill, "Face value".

60. Ark, W., Dryer, D.C., and Lu, D.J. (1999), "The emotion mouse", *Proceedings of HCI International '99*, Munich Germany, August.

61. Picard, R.W. (2000), "Toward computers that recognize and respond to user emotion", *IBM Systems Journal*, Vol. 39, Nos 3 & 4, pp. 705–19.

62. Robinson, Michael D. and Clore, Gerald L. (2002), "Belief and feeling: evidence for an accessibility model of emotional self-report", *Psychological Bulletin*, Vol. 128, No. 6, pp. 934–60.

63. Shaw, *The DNA of Customer Experience*.

CHAPTER **14** *The Surprise–Delight Relationship Revisited in the Management of Experience*

JOËLLE VANHAMME*

Keywords

delight, surprise, experiential, satisfaction

Abstract

Practitioners firmly believe that customer delight, through surprise, offers a source of competitive advantage. Yet competing conceptualisations, methodologies, and stimuli in existing studies of delight leave the relationship between surprise and delight ambiguous. This chapter will assess the different conceptualisations of delight; offer an overview of existing empirical evidence regarding the surprise–delight relationship; show that during highly hedonic experiences, surprise indirectly influences satisfaction (through joy) and can increase satisfaction overall; and propose further research avenues.

Introduction

There has been an evolution in marketing theories since the hegemony of models depicting the consumer as a rational being in which emotions and senses have either little or no place. Experiential marketing – which has its origins in the pioneering studies of Holbrook and Hirschman[1] – is considered by some as the new era in the development of marketing

*   Joëlle Vanhamme, Assistant Professor, Rotterdam School of Management, Erasmus University (ERIM Research Institute), Department of Marketing, Room T10-09, Burg, Oudlaan 50, 3062 PA Rotterdam, The Netherlands. E-mail: Jvanhamme@rsm.nL; and Associate Professor at the IESEG School of Management (LEM, UMR CNRS 8179), Rue de la Digue 3, Lille, France. Note: this chapter is an abridged version of the article J. Vanhamme (2008), "The surprise–delight relationship revisited in the management of experience", *Recherche et Applications en Marketing*, Vol. 23, No. 3, pp. 113–39. An English translation of that article is available on ABI-Inform and Business Premier databases.

thought, a new paradigm[2] (for a critical discussion on experiential marketing also see Carù and Cova[3] and Marion[4]). This emphasis on the "production of experience" has been very pronounced since the end of the last decade, both in the world of business and in the heart of the academic milieu. There are numerous articles and studies published in the literature on the subject.[5] Experiential marketing is aimed at immersing the consumer in memorable, unforgettable experiences,[6] and one of the tools available to companies to help achieve this objective – perhaps *the* most important tool according to some[7] – is to surprise customers.[8]

In the literature that examines customer satisfaction and loyalty/retention, the concept of surprise is often associated with that of delight.[9] The concept of "delight" appeared as a source of competitive advantage in the mid-1980s and was rapidly adopted in professional circles as the new strategic objective to achieve, rather than and in place of mere customer satisfaction.[10] The reason for this change of direction lies in the fact that several studies have revealed that customers who are merely satisfied are not loyal, whereas customers who are completely satisfied, also known as "delighted customers", are loyal.[11] Moreover, it has been argued that surprising customers is a way to delight them.[12] However, surprising the client or the consumer is not always desirable, or even possible, in the context of every transaction, or at least every aspect of the exchange (e.g., online credit card payment is a type of service in which the consumer would no doubt prefer to avoid any element of surprise).

The first studies published on the subject of the causal "surprise → delight/extreme satisfaction" relationship date from the end of the 1990s. Ten years later, however, there are still a certain number of points that need to be clarified in terms of the nature of delight – due to the existence of competing conceptualisations – and its relationship with surprise. When one weighs the results of all the studies published, the results clearly are mixed and do not all point in the same direction. Moreover, none of these studies demonstrates the existence of this type of causality. One of the reasons for this divergence is the lack of experiments involving surprise manipulation. Most studies focus on surveys (varied forms and methodologies) whose results are analysed using correlations, regressions, or structural equations. To date, only one published experiment uses manipulation of (positive) surprise and analyses its post-consumption effect.[13] The results of this study indicate that there is no significant difference between the control group and the experimental group. However, the type of consumption episode used in this experiment involved a decidedly small experiential dimension, which would appear to show little promise if the goal is to discern a quantifiable effect of surprise.

This chapter proposes a critical assessment of the concept of delight and its link to surprise – an assessment that relies on an analysis of empirical studies relating to delight – and shows the relevance of the experiential component in surprising experiences through an experiment that reproduces the (positive) surprise manipulation by Vanhamme and Snelders[14] (referred to as V&S hereafter), using a product/service with a more dominant experiential component. This experiment determines whether it is possible to show that surprise has a causal post-consumption effect for this type of product/service.

Assessment

Before presenting the studies carried out on the surprise–delight tandem, this chapter presents what the concept of delight encompasses and the methodological issues that characterise it.

DELIGHT: TWO CONCEPTUALISATIONS

Literature recognises two delight conceptualisations. The first, *delight-as-surprise-and-joy*, defines delight as an emotional response.[15] This "extreme positive emotion"[16] is a combination of the emotions of surprise and joy. For example, Plutchik describes delight as a secondary emotion that combines two primary emotions: surprise and joy.[17] The critical incident study by Arnold et al.,[18] which aimed to provide a "thick description" of the "delightful experiences" encountered by their respondents, effectively illustrates this conceptualisation. The interview guide they developed recommends that researchers provide the following definition of delight to respondents: "feelings of joy or happiness and surprise". Concurrently, Verma defines delight as: "joy and surprise mix to create a feeling of delight in consumption situations".[19] This conceptualisation implies that an absence of surprise (or joy) leads to an absence of delight (which is questionable, as discussed in the next section). For example, re-watching a film that delighted us the first time might not delight us the second time around, because it is unlikely that the film will surprise us again. When defined as an emotion in accordance with the first conceptualisation, delight is ephemeral,[20] which raises the question of its ability to provide a lasting competitive advantage.

Authors who subscribe to the first conceptualisation of delight tend to measure the concept using scales of emotions. However, to date, there is no consensus as to the measurement of delight in accordance with this conceptualisation,[21] which poses certain methodological problems, as detailed in the next section. Moreover, proponents of the first conceptualisation claim that delight is a construct distinct from satisfaction.

The second conceptualisation of delight, *delight-as-extreme-satisfaction*, is derived from the well-known concept of satisfaction. Satisfaction is defined as a psychological state resulting from a purchase and/or consumption experience[22] that emanates from cognitive and affective processes.[23] Authors who share this second view of delight define the concept as an extreme level of satisfaction (e.g., "outstanding high level of satisfaction", "exceptional level of satisfaction", "completely satisfied"), a kind of "super-satisfaction".[24] Therefore, the zone of delight is located on the extreme right of the satisfaction continuum,[25] and delight is simply measured in terms of satisfaction.[26] Authors occasionally divide their respondents into delighted/not delighted using the most extreme score of satisfaction. For example, "delighted" respondents include those with a score of 5 on a scale with 5 levels of intensity (e.g., Estelami[27]). This conceptualisation largely originates from the studies of Jones and Sasser,[28] who demonstrate that satisfied consumers are not necessarily loyal consumers, whereas completely satisfied consumers are generally much more loyal. Therefore, these authors emphasise the importance of aiming for something more than "mere" satisfaction. Westbrook's D-T satisfaction scale[29] illustrates this second conceptualisation: the positive levels of the scale range from "neither satisfied/nor unsatisfied" to "delighted", with an intermediary degree of "mostly satisfied". In contrast with the first conceptualisation, the experience of surprise (and joy) is not a necessary ingredient of delight (level of extreme satisfaction) in the second conceptualisation; surprise is just one possible antecedent amongst others. Moreover, the second conceptualisation of delight relies on the concept of satisfaction, which is not as ephemeral as an emotion. Its competitive advantage stems from its capacity to induce greater loyalty.[30]

The existence of these two conceptualisations undoubtedly could be perceived as an outcome of a criticism of traditional satisfaction scales, namely, that they do not permit a fine differentiation between the positive satisfaction levels experienced by consumers (because the distribution of satisfaction scores is skewed to the left and there is a ceiling effect), nor do they correctly capture the affective dimension of satisfaction.[31] This criticism becomes even more significant when trying to establish the added value of surprise, because it gets detected at the highest levels of satisfaction and likely in its most affective component. From this point of view, Westbrook's D-T scale offers an advantage: it refers explicitly to the affective dimension, permits a finer graduation of this component, and allows improved differentiation of the extreme positive levels.[32] Nonetheless, this single-item measure contains only one anchor that refers to delight.

DELIGHT-AS-SURPRISE-AND-JOY: VALIDITY AND TAUTOLOGY ISSUES

The delight-as-surprise-and-joy conceptualisation poses problems regarding the validity of the construct. Existing studies suggest, on the one hand, that in consumers' minds "delight" is not necessarily a combination of surprise and joy;[33] it can also result from joy on its own or surprise on its own. Moreover, Kumar, Olshavsky, and King,[34] replicating the results of Plutchik's first study,[35] offer evidence that a combination of joy and surprise does not unequivocally lead to the term "delight"; respondents also mention terms such as "ecstatic", "pleased", "thrilled", "excited", and so forth, whose content is not always identical to that of delight (in this study, respondents had to identify the most appropriate term to describe a series of combinations of primary emotions, including surprise and joy). Along the same lines, St-James and Taylor,[36] in their interpretive study of experiences of delight, bring two forms to light, only the first of which relates to surprise and joy (delight-as-pleasant-surprise). The second (delight-as-magic) relates to experiences with a strong emotional intensity and a rich symbolic content.

On the other hand, studies that use the delight-as-surprise-and-joy conceptualisation exhibit discriminant validity problems among the measures of delight, joy, and surprise. Items typically used to measure delight are, for example, "delighted", "gleeful", and "elated".[37] However, Izard's DES-II scale,[38] the scale of emotions most widely used in consumption experience studies,[39] includes "delighted" as an item for measuring joy. The same is true of Plutchik's scale, which is also frequently used.[40] The issue of discriminant validity appears clearly in the results of the factorial analysis carried out by Oliver, Rust, and Varki,[41] which places the "delighted" item (the only measurement item they used to capture delight) on the same factor as those measuring positive emotions (*high positive affect*). Similarly, in his replication of the study by Oliver, Rust, and Varki, Finn[42] shows that the discriminant validity between delight and joy is unsatisfactory. In other studies, delight is measured by one or several items normally used to measure joy. For example, Tokman, Davis, and Lemon[43] measure delight using two items: *how frequently do you feel happy* [item 1] or *delighted with the level of service* [item 2] (see also Hicks et al.[44]).

Because delight is defined as a combination of joy and surprise, it is inevitable that discriminant validity issues systematically appear in studies subscribing to the delight-as-surprise-and-joy conceptualisation. Furthermore, in this kind of delight conceptualisation, it would seem tautological to test the existence of a causal relationship between surprise and delight or between joy and delight, because, by definition, surprise combined with joy equals delight.

These difficulties can be avoided in the delight-as-extreme-satisfaction conceptualisation, which measures delight with a traditional measure of satisfaction, whose discriminant validity has been widely demonstrated. Because it relies on an existing concept of satisfaction, this conceptualisation is also more parsimonious; it avoids a multiplication of concepts that are very closely related (and thus whose discriminant validity poses a problem).

The second conceptualisation therefore appears to be the most acceptable, particularly given that – as N'Gobo[45] emphasises – no study has demonstrated the superiority of the measure of delight (as distinct from the measure of satisfaction) in terms of its predictive validity. Oliver, Rust, and Varki's[46] study and its replication by Finn[47] systematically show that delight (measured as "delighted" and "delighted", "elated", and "gleeful", respectively) has a non-significant impact on purchase intentions, or at the very most, a weaker impact than the measure of satisfaction.

In the interest of avoiding any terminological confusion in the remainder of this chapter, I use the term "delight" only when the measure chosen to determine the concept is composed of items such as "delighted", "gleeful", and "elated", not as a traditional measure of satisfaction, such as "delight-as-surprise-and-joy". The term "satisfaction" will appear in other cases, in references to "delight-as-extreme-satisfaction". However, this chapter does not linger on the results related to the causal influence of surprise in the delight-as-surprise-and-joy conceptualisation, due to its inherent methodological and conceptual problems.

SURPRISE–SATISFACTION CAUSALITY: CRITICAL SYNTHESIS OF EMPIRICAL RESULTS

In reviewing various studies dedicated to the surprise–satisfaction link (see Vanhamme's[48] Table 1 for an overview), four main points emerge. First, there is some confusion between measurements. For example, in Mano and Oliver and Oliver, Rust, and Varki,[49] the concept of "arousal" is measured using surprise items, namely, "astonished" and "surprised"; in Oliver, Rust, and Varki,[50] the concept of surprising consumption is measured using a disconfirmation item. Other studies[51] are much more coherent in terms of measurements, measuring surprise with surprise items (Izard's DES-II) and disconfirmation with disconfirmation items. V&S also use non-verbal measures of surprise (coding facial expressions and behaviour).

Second, most studies tend to show, using correlation analysis (i.e., regressions, structural equation models), a causal effect of surprise, as in empirical studies by Mano and Oliver; Oliver, Rust, and Varki; and Finn and Vanhamme. These studies do not permit a definitive conclusion of the causal link between surprise and satisfaction, nor do they show a net surprise-induced satisfaction gain that is discernible in absolute figures.

Third, studies that attempt to demonstrate a positive gap in satisfaction between positively surprised consumers and others lead to results that are not significant[52] or do not emanate from an experimental design (and therefore do not permit a valid determination of the extent to which surprise is truly the source of this increased satisfaction). Such is the case, for example, in the typological studies carried out by Westbrook and Oliver and Oliver and Westbrook. The latter present a group of consumers exhibiting very high surprise and joy scores ("delighted consumers"); these consumers also have higher scores than other groups on the satisfaction scales.

Fourth, the results remain mixed. Some studies suggest a direct link between surprise and satisfaction;[53] others suggest an indirect link through positive emotions; and still others find both a direct *and* an indirect link.[54] In addition, V&S's experiment suggests the absence of any effect of surprise manipulation on the level of satisfaction attained (i.e., no satisfaction gain in absolute figures when consumers are positively surprised). The type of consumption episode hardly seems the most adequate to reveal a net effect caused by surprise though. A consumption episode with a greater experiential component may have been a more judicious choice. In V&S's experiment, pleasant surprise was created during a taste test by the consumer finding a small folding spoon in the packaging of a strawberry yoghurt (the consumer was not previously aware of the existence of this spoon). Filser[55] indicates that there is an experiential component, of greater or lesser dominance, involved in the consumption of any product or service, but that enriching the positioning of a product/service by developing its experiential component is easier when this component is dominant. When a consumption/purchase episode is essentially utilitarian (with "a non-dominant experiential component"), evaluation takes place mainly at the functional and cognitive levels and essentially pertains to satisfaction of the consumer's instrumental expectations,[56] which leaves little or no room for the positive appraisal of any more hedonic or emotion-based element. Studies by Oliver, Rust, and Varki; Westbrook and Oliver; and Oliver and Westbrook all focus on products or services with an important experiential component (concert, theme park, purchase/use of a car). The experiential component inherent in a taste test for strawberry yoghurt in a laboratory seems considerably less dominant. A positively surprising experience created during the consumption of a product/service with greater experiential dominance is no doubt more typical of the type of positively surprising experiences encountered by consumers and might reveal a net surprise-induced satisfaction gain. To shed light on these propositions, this chapter describes a pre-test and an experiment replicating the V&S manipulation using a service consumption episode with a strong experiential component.

Experiment

PRE-TEST

Prior to conducting the experiment, a demonstration that positively surprising consumption experiences most often involve products and services with a dominant experiential component is necessary. Therefore, a convenience sample of 71 respondents, aged between 30 and 50 years (average age 42 years), was recruited (49 per cent of participants were female) and asked to remember a positively surprising consumption/ purchase episode – as recent as possible – with a product or service and then describe it. Two independent judges, unaware of the specific aim of the study, coded the 71 surprising episodes into two categories: consumption/purchase experience with a dominant experiential component versus consumption/purchase experience with a non-dominant experiential component (the level of inter-judge reliability was very acceptable at PRL[57] .95 > .7). As expected, positively surprising experiences were most often experiences with a dominant experiential component (62 per cent, $\chi^2 = 4.070$; $p = .044$), and the majority involved experiences that are cultural or linked to the pleasures of eating. Positively surprising experiences with a non-dominant experiential component were considerably less frequent (38 per cent) and generally linked to a "good deal" or "surprising effectiveness". The consumption episode used by V&S[58] does not correspond to any of the categories of surprising experience with a non-dominant experiential component found herein.

EXPERIMENT

Because consumption episodes with a dominant experiential component yield the greatest number of positively surprising experiences, the experiment aims to test V&S's hypotheses on this type of episode to verify the extent to which one can detect a significant surprise effect on satisfaction. The V&S hypotheses are as follows: during a consumption experience, a positively perceived attribute of a product/service will be perceived even more positively if it is surprising (H1); positively surprised consumers are more satisfied than non-surprised consumers during the same consumption experience (H2); during a positively surprising experience, surprise has a direct and indirect positive influence – through the amplification of joy – on satisfaction; and this influence of surprise remains significant when disconfirmation is taken into account in the model (H3).

STIMULI AND EXPERIMENTAL SETTINGS

The service consumed in this experiment is a visit to a virtual museum, which has a dominant experiential component. The "visit service" was pre-tested on 20 consumers of the same type as the respondents in the target group to ensure that it offered a performance that was at least satisfying. Pine and Gilmore and Rust, Zahorik, and Keiningham[59] emphasise that one can only delight consumers if the product or service itself is capable of a satisfactory performance. The attribute of the service used in the surprise manipulation is a voucher for a free comic book. In other words, the voucher for the comic book and the virtual museum visit correspond respectively to the folding spoon and the yoghurt taste test in the study by V&S.

EXPERIMENTAL DESIGN

The design involved an experimental group, a control group, and a reference group, as per V&S:

Experimental group: A positively surprising experience generated by an unannounced element – the inclusion of a voucher for a comic book in the service purchased – discovered during consumption of the service.

Control group: A non-surprising control experience, identical to that of the experimental group. The surprising element (the comic) for the experimental group is presented from the outset as part of the service and appears as expected during consumption of the service.

Reference group: A non-surprising experience permitting verification that the visit's performance is at least satisfying. The voucher for the comic book is not mentioned at any time and does not appear during consumption of the service.

EXPERIMENTAL PROCEDURE AND MANIPULATION

On arrival at the laboratory, each respondent received 12 euros, which they could use to purchase a subscription to a service that provided a virtual visit to a museum. They filled out a short questionnaire relating to their current mood and read a document presenting the service they were going to purchase and consume for the experiment. The service was a subscription for 20 virtual museum visits, with or without a voucher for a free comic book, depending on the conditions. After allowing respondents to read the presentation document for the service, the experimenter demonstrated the software for the visit.

The visit program began with a welcome page allowing access to the virtual visit and stipulating that payment would be made after the visit. It also mentioned to the control group that the comic book voucher would be printed after the visit. At the end of the visit, respondents viewed a page on a screen explaining the methods of payment. After paying, they were thanked for their visit. Finally, depending on the conditions, a message appeared on the screen with one of the three following possibilities: notification that the respondent would receive a comic book, instructions on how to print the voucher and leave the visit program (experimental group); instructions on how to print the voucher and leave the visit program (control group); or instructions on how to leave the program (reference group). After they had left the program, respondents completed the questionnaire. The experimenter interviewed each respondent about the experience (for all respondents, the experience was very real, and their reactions would not have been different in reality), explained the aim of the study, advised them of the camera behind the two-way mirror, and asked their permission to analyse the videotape recorded (none of the respondents guessed a camera's presence, and all gave their permission). The experiment lasted a maximum of 1 hour and 15 minutes. A pre-test of the stimuli and settings was carried out on 20 respondents prior to the experiment.

SELECTION OF RESPONDENTS

A convenience sample of 104 respondents was recruited from a population of consumers aged between 25 and 60 years. They were informed – before their arrival – that the study would focus on a service that was a visit to a virtual museum. After being grouped into identical profiles in terms of their involvement with regard to virtual museums, enjoyment of museum visits, gender, and age, respondents in each profile were randomly assigned to the three groups. Eight respondents had to be eliminated due to technical problems with the visit program, lack of attention during the demonstration, problems that arose during manipulation, or not following the instructions given.

MEASURES

The same measurements as those used by V&S were collected, using the same procedure. Izard's DES-II[60] multi-item scale was used to collect a verbal measure of the subjective experience of surprise and other emotions felt whilst viewing the page containing the manipulation (five-point scale). Facial expressions and behaviours were filmed by the camera and coded by the three judges (three women of around 25 years of age), in accordance with the procedure developed by Ekman and Friesen[61] and adapted for surprise by Reisenzein.[62] In addition to facial expressions, the judges were asked to note the appearance of the other components – *behavioural* (focus of attention, exploratory behaviour, interruption of ongoing activities) and *subjective* (exclamation of surprise) – of surprise. These non-verbal measures have the advantage of being taken in real time and are exempt from the influence of rationalisation, introspection, and retrospection. The three judges carried out the coding independently, on an ad hoc form.

In addition to the emotion-related measures, a three-item disconfirmation measure,[63] three measures of satisfaction, and one three-item measure were used to evaluate the idea of adding a comic book to the service (adapted from V&S). The scales used for satisfaction were Westbrook's D-T single-item scale, the twelve items of Oliver's scale, and three of the five items of Aurier and Evrard's SATEXP scale.[64]

Approximately three months before the experiment, respondents had completed a questionnaire relating to their involvement in virtual museums, their experience of museums, and their personality (eight items measuring introverted/extroverted character from Saucier's personality scale).[65] On the day of the experiment, respondents initially replied to the four items from Peterson and Sauber's mood scale.[66] These measures were used either for distribution into profiles prior to the random assignment of respondents or as control measures (cf. V&S[67]).

RESULTS

Verification of the manipulation and of the experimental setting

Thirty-two valid questionnaires were collected for each group. As expected, the average scores of the verbal and facial/behavioural measures obtained for the emotion of surprise, when they appear on the manipulated page, are all significantly higher in the surprise group than in the control and reference groups ($p < .01$). In addition, the verbal surprise scores in the control and reference groups are both very close to the minimum score, which reflects an absence of emotional experience (1.2 and 1.1, respectively). In terms of non-verbal measures of surprise, the results also indicate a significantly higher number of observable elements of surprise in the experimental group than in the control and reference groups (z proportion tests; $p < .05$). Also as expected, when the manipulated page for the experimental group appeared, the polarity of surprise felt by respondents was positive (mean score of 8.2/10 on the scale that ranged from "totally negative" [1] to "totally positive" [10]). The manipulation seems therefore to have functioned correctly.

Reliability, uni-dimensional character, and type of variable distributions

The uni-dimensional character of each multi-item verbal variable was verified, as well as its reliability level. The Cronbach's alpha coefficients were acceptable (>.7), so the items of each variable were aggregated and the variable distributions analysed to verify the validity of the assumption of normality (which did not hold for several variables). The judges' agreement on the facial coding of surprise and joy, as well as the other components of surprise observed, is very acceptable (PRL indices > .7). In addition, no significant difference appeared between the different groups regarding the control variables (i.e., mood, expertise, and extraversion/introversion). Finally, analysis of the reference group's satisfaction scores indicates that the performance of the museum visit was satisfying (mean scores greater than 8 on all 10-point scales and greater than 5.5 on the D-T 7-point scale). The satisfaction scores do not differ significantly between the control group and the reference group.

Hypothesis 1

In accordance with H1 and V&S's results, the idea of adding a comic book to the visit is evaluated more positively in the experimental group than in the control group (see Table 14.1).

Hypothesis 2

Our data indicate that all satisfaction scores are systematically higher in the experimental group than in the control group. These differences, however, are only marginally significant ($p \leq .10$) for SATGLO, SATEXP, and SAT. However, for D-T, the difference is significant at the traditional threshold of 5 per cent if comparing the percentage of respondents who circled the highest level of the scale, "delighted" (see Table 14.1). As a reminder, V&S conclude that there is no significant difference for H2 ($p > .10$); the satisfaction scores observed in the experimental group are sometimes lower (not higher, as predicted in H2) and sometimes equal to those of the control group. Therefore, even if our data only offer weak support to H2 due to the marginal significance of several results, they corroborate H2 to a greater extent than does V&S.

Table 14.1   Comparison of means in the experimental and control groups: H1 & H2 test

	Experimental group mean	Control group mean	Mean differences (Wilcoxon's paired t test and rank test)
TOTAL (10-point total satisfaction: aggregation of SAT, D-T, and SATEXP scales)	8.25	7.83	$t(31) = 1.352°$ $z = -1.356°$
D-T (7-point satisfaction scale)	5.84	5.50	n.s.
% of "delighted" participants (based on D-T scale: 7 = "delighted")	35 %	19 %	$z = 1.79*$
SAT (Oliver's 10-point satisfaction scale)	8.22	7.79	$t(31) = 1.277^{(p=.105)}$ $z = -1.262^{(p=.103)}$
SATEXP (Aurier and Evrard's 10-point satisfaction scale (1998)	8.33	7.97	$t(31) = 1.332°$ $z = -1.373°$
Comic (10-point appreciation scale for the free comic)	8.03	7.19	$t(310) = 1.911*$ $z = -1.903**$

Note: ** $p < .01$; * $p < .05$; ° $p < .1$; unilateral tests.

Hypothesis 3

The small sample size, types of data (ordinal at the very most for certain variables), and the types of variable distributions in this study (non-multinormality) do not permit the use of structural equation modelling with maximum likelihood estimation procedure (e.g., LISREL). The PLS structural modelling approach with latent variables, which is an alternative to the maximum likelihood approach, is advised by Fornell and Bookstein[68] when there is a deviation from the underlying assumptions. H3 therefore was tested using the PLS approach with reflective indicators (i.e., estimation mode A[69]), in accordance with V&S.

Measurement model

The full model for the experimental group, including all the possible indicators for each latent variable, was first estimated and evaluated using reliability criteria, convergent validity, and discriminant validity.[70] Reliability was evaluated with Jöreskog's internal coherence *rho* and the average variance extracted criterion.[71] The results of the completed model are presented in Table 14.2. As the convergent validity of surprise was not satisfactory, the model required re-evaluation, using only those indicators of surprise whose correlations with the estimate of the latent surprise variable were sufficiently high (in practice ≥ .65), as Wold[72] advises. The results are shown in Table 14.2 and indicate that the second model (which is very similar to the first) satisfies all the criteria related to reliability and discriminant and convergent validity.

Structural model

The coefficients of the structural model are reviewed at the bottom of Table 14.2. Their statistical significance was estimated using a t-test, as recommended by Tenenhaus.[73] The predictive validity of the final model estimated using the Stone-Geisser Q^2,[74] as well as the R^2 coefficient,[75] is completely satisfactory. The results of the model (which takes disconfirmation into account) indicate that the influence of surprise on satisfaction is only manifested indirectly through joy. H3 is therefore only partially verified by the data. Our results are relatively different from those of V&S, in that these authors demonstrated a direct rather than an indirect effect of surprise on satisfaction. Conversely, they corroborate the results of Mano and Oliver and of Oliver, Rust, and Varki.[76]

Conclusions, Discussion and Areas for Further Research

The results of the pre-test field study indicate, as expected, that positively surprising experiences are most often consumption or purchase episodes with a dominant experiential component. The experiment itself, using a consumption episode with a dominant experiential component, indicates that surprised consumers are indeed more satisfied than non-surprised customers. However, except for the significant difference in terms of the percentage of respondents who say they are delighted, most of the results are only marginally significant. Moreover, the differences are not very great in absolute

Table 14.2 Structural and measurement models (lvpls 1.8 (Lohmöller)): H3 test

Latent Variable (VL)[5]	Indicator[4]	FULL MODEL					FINAL MODEL				
		Conv. Validity[1]	Reliability		Discriminant validity		Conv. Validity	Reliability		Discriminant validity	
		Loadings	Rho[2]	AVE[3]	Loading > Cross loading?	√(AVE)> correlation with other LVs?	Loadings	Rho	AVE	Loading > Cross loading?	√(AVE)> correlation with other LVs?
Surprise			.84	.44		OK		.90	.59		OK
	VSUR	.72			OK		.76			OK	
	EYE	.77			OK		.77			OK	
	EYEB	.77			OK		.78			OK	
	FS	.74			OK		.73			OK	
	EXCL	.00			KO		-			-	
	EXPL	.44			OK		-			-	
	BEHS	.59			OK		-			-	
	OBSS	.83			OK		.78			OK	
Joy			.80	.67		OK		.80	.67		OK
	VJ	.85			OK		.87			OK	
	FJ	.78			OK		.75			OK	
Satisfaction			.97	.91		OK		.97	.91		OK
	D-T	.94			OK		.94			OK	
	SAT	.95			OK		.95			OK	
	SATEXP	.97			OK		.97			OK	

PATHS	PATH COEFFICIENTS FULL MODEL	PATH COEFFICIENTS FINAL MODEL
Surprise→Joy	.551***	.570***
Joy→Satisfaction	.428**	.436**
Surprise→Satisfaction	n.s.	n.s.
Disconfirmation→Satisfaction	.664***	.662***

PREDICTIVE VALIDITY FOR SATISFACTION	FULL MODEL	FINAL MODEL
Q^2	.55 (t = 6.67)	.55 (t = 6.78)
R^2	.638 (R^2adj. .599); $p < .001$	.640 (R^2adj. .601) ; $p < .001$

Notes: Coefficients are standardized coefficients. The distribution of latent variables is normal.

*** $p < .001$; ** $p < .01$; * $p < .05$; • $p < 0.07$; unilateral tests.

[1] Acceptable convergent validity if loading ≥ , 6 (conservative criterion).

[2] Rho = Jöreskog's composite reliability rho (Rho > .7 for a reliable measure).

[3] AVE = Average variance extracted (AVE > .5 for a reliable measure).

[4] EYE = eyes open; EYEB = eyebrows raised; FS = total judgement of facial expression of surprise (takes into account EYE, EYEB); EXCL = spontaneous exclamation of surprise; STOP = interruption of activities; EXPL = focus of attention/exploration; BEHS = overall judgement of the different aspects of behaviour with the exception of facial expression (takes into account EXCL, STOP, and EXPL); OBSS = overall judgement of the surprised behaviour (includes all of the previous aspects); VSUR = verbal surprise; VJ = verbal joy; FJ = facial expression of joy.

[5] The multi-item verbal disconfirmation scale is the only indicator of the latent disconfirmation variable (loading in the structural model = 1).

figures. There are three possible explanations (either alone or in combination) for this phenomenon.

The first is simply that surprise is not capable of having a significant effect on satisfaction levels. In other words, a great deal of energy may have been expended on a marketing tactic that, in reality, does not make a great deal of difference.

The second concerns the type of surprising element. Whether in the V&S experiment or in the experiment presented in this chapter, the surprising element is a peripheral element of the total offer and is relatively marginal; the yoghurt and the virtual visit are the central elements of the total offer. The slight gap demonstrated in the experiment could stem from this marginality, which would also explain the more pronounced effects of surprise on the evaluation of the surprising object. It would therefore be interesting to study the variation of the gap in terms of this degree of marginality/centrality (e.g., is surprise more effective when it is integrated into the central offer?). However, true integration of the surprising element, to make it part of the central offer (e.g., totally new shape for a car, new taste for a food product), brings about managerial challenges. Such integration can prove very costly, in that it could lead to a simultaneous increase in consumers' expectations.[77] The effect of surprise would therefore not be lasting and may barely be profitable. Rust and Oliver[78] term this effect "assimilated delight". It would also be relevant to evaluate satisfaction in terms of the total offer, the central element of the product/service, and the peripheral elements to determine the impact of surprise better. An additional point in common with the V&S study is the congruence between the type of surprising stimulus and the product/service consumed (comic book and museum are cultural products/services). The impact of a surprising stimulus that is not congruent with the type of episode could be more pronounced and should be examined in future studies.

The third explanation is that satisfaction scales are the reason for such weak results. If these scales do not permit sufficient differentiation between high levels of satisfaction or do not correctly capture the affective dimension of satisfaction, it is possible that the slight differences are just a foretaste of the more consistent differences that would be recorded by more appropriate satisfaction scales. In other words, the existing scales may provide over-conservative results. This problem with satisfaction scales was recognised in the literature in the 1990s, yet to date, no scale has been proposed to resolve the issue. Use of "delight" as a new and distinct construct from that of satisfaction (i.e., delight-as-joy-and-surprise) is, no doubt, a step in this direction. However, in view of the methodological problems linked to this approach, the use of satisfaction scales seems the lesser evil. One explanation for the problem of satisfaction scales is the use of the term "satisfaction" in the wording of the scale. There are many scales of the type "to what extent was X experience satisfying to you?" and in general terminology, satisfaction is the equivalent of "doing enough". Moreover, even though from the outset and well thereafter, research into satisfaction defined it as a purely cognitive concept, the current conception holds that it is both cognitive and affective.[79] However, in analysing the measurement scales used for satisfaction, it appears clear that no real attempt has been made to distinguish the two components. One might have expected to find measuring scales with two dimensions, one cognitive and the other affective, according to other constructs present in marketing literature (e.g., "affective commitment", "calculative commitment"[80]).

Literature conceptualises satisfaction as a construct consisting of an affective and a cognitive component, so developing a two-dimensional measurement might offer a solution to the conceptual and methodological problems highlighted herein and reunite proponents of both conceptualisations. Supporters of the delight-as-surprise-and-joy approach also emphasise the need to develop better measurements of delight.[81] The model by Oliver, Rust, and Varki,[82] completed and/or improved by Finn,[83] V&S, and this study (Figure 14.1, model a), would thus become model b in Figure 14.1.

In terms of the way surprise affects satisfaction, it seems that the results of the experiment, according to the studies by Oliver, Rust, and Varki and by Mano and Oliver,[84] point towards an indirect relationship through an increase in joy. Conversely, these results contradict V&S, who suggest a direct (not indirect) link between surprise and satisfaction. Several accounts can be proposed to explain this difference. The academic history of satisfaction has shown that the formation processes tend to vary according to the type of product or service.[85] Consumption experiences with a strong experiential component (e.g., virtual museum, concert, theme park) could give rise to an indirect link, whereas consumption experiences with a weak experiential component (e.g., yoghurt test) could lead to a direct link. Further studies are required to test this possibility. Surprise also may have no direct or indirect impact on either the affective or the cognitive dimension of satisfaction (see Figure 14.1, model b).

The task used in the V&S experiment was a taste test, which may have forced participants to focus their attention on this particular attribute, favouring a cognitive evaluation of satisfaction, whereas the participants in this chapter (and the study by Oliver, Rust, and Varki[86]) probably evaluated their consumption experience in a more holistic and hedonistic manner, favouring an affective evaluation of satisfaction. This difference in evaluation processes could explain the differences in the results. The use of satisfaction measures that better represent both dimensions would provide a more definitive response to this question.

One final aspect worth mentioning is the mnemonic traces left by emotions experienced during the positively surprising episode. According to Cohen and Areni,[87] emotions felt, though ephemeral, leave strong mnemonic traces that can remain long after the emotions have gone. In addition, when an emotional episode is remembered, it potentially can revive the same emotions,[88] which is likely to influence subsequent satisfaction judgements, such as satisfaction with a similar episode or accumulated satisfaction. It would be interesting to determine how influential the reactivation of the mnemonic trace of a positively surprising episode might be, as the results could constitute a lasting competitive advantage. Rust and Oliver[89] term this reactivated trace "reenacted delight".

Before concluding, a gap still exists between managerial assumptions and the conclusions that may be drawn from this chapter. Many companies launch themselves into an experiential adventure and attempt to surprise customers in the hope of delighting them and creating certain loyalty. The introduction to this chapter emphasises that not all transactions or all aspects of exchanges necessarily lend themselves to this type of practice. In addition, this chapter notes that certain aspects of the surprise–satisfaction/ delight relationship are obscure, and the net effects of surprise may not be very extensive. These statements highlight the importance of conducting a realistic cost–benefit analysis. However, ensuring that surprise will be experienced positively constitutes an additional challenge companies must face. This task requires a very sound knowledge of customers'

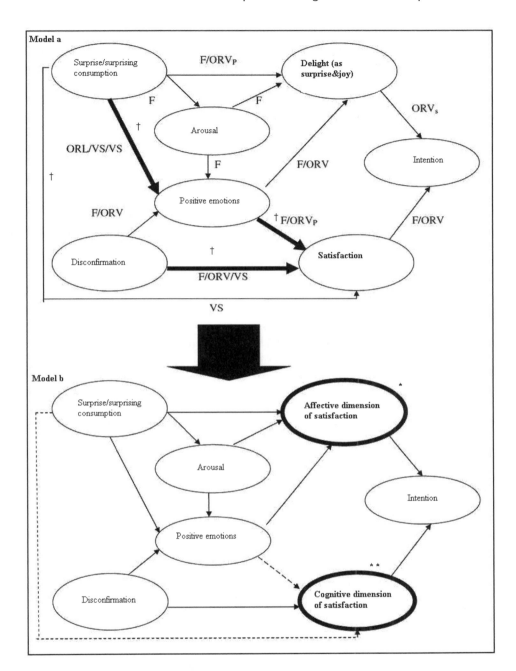

Figure 14.1 Revised model of "delight"

Note: This model includes the results of Oliver, Rust, and Varki (1997) (ORVp represents a theme park-based study; ORVs represents a concert/symphony-based study), Vanhamme and Snelders (2003) (V&S), and Finn (2005) (F), as well as the author of the present study (darker arrows). The Positive Emotions/Surprise-Cognitive Dimension relationships of satisfaction are represented by dotted lines since they may no longer be significant in the context of this model.

* Replaces the "delight" construct in the models by Oliver, Rust, and Varki (1997) and Finn (2005).

** Replaces the 'satisfaction' construct in the models by Oliver, Rust, and Varki (1997) and Finn (2005).

† This section of the model corresponds to Vanhamme and Snelder's H3 and H4 (2003) and H3 in this chapter.

characteristics and behavioural patterns. For example, offering a disposable toiletries bag to airline passengers could be experienced as a negative surprise if they are sensitive to environmental issues. Conscientious segmentation must therefore be recognised as a condition *sine qua non* prior to any tactic involving surprise. Furthermore, for companies to measure the effects of their delight campaigns, adequate measures must be available. Current satisfaction measures may fail to detect the effects of surprise at all.

Notes

1. Holbrook, M.B. and Hirschman, E.C. (1982), "The Experiential Aspects of Consumption: Consumer Fantasies, Feelings and Fun", *Journal of Consumer Research*, Vol. 9, No. 2, pp. 132–40.
2. Carù, A. and Cova, B. (2006), "Expériences de consommation et marketing expérientiel", *Revue Française de Gestion*, Vol. 32, No. 162, pp. 99–115; Hetzel, P. and Volle, P. (2003), "L'expérientiel: de la théorie à l'action", *Décisions Marketing*, Vol. 28 (Oct.–Déc.), p. 5; Schmitt, B.H. (1999), *Experiential Marketing: How to Get Customers to Sense, Feel, Think, Act, and Relate to Your Company and Brands*, Free Press, New York; Schmitt, B.H. (2003), *Customer Experience Management: A Revolutionary Approach to Connecting with Your Customers*, John Wiley & Sons, Hoboken, NJ.
3. Carù and Cova, "Expériences de consommation et marketing expérientiel".
4. Marion, G. (2003), "Le marketing expérientiel: une nouvelle étape? Non de nouvelles lunettes", *Décisions Marketing*, Vol. 30 (Avr.–Juin), pp. 87–91.
5. Bouchet, P. (2004), "L'expérience au cœur de l'analyse des relations magasin-magasineur", *Recherche et Applications en Marketing*, Vol. 19, No. 2, pp. 53–71; Carù and Cova, "Expériences de consommation et marketing expérientiel"; Honebein, P.C. and Cammarano, R.F. (2005), *Creating Do-It-Yourself Customers: How Great Customer Experiences Build Great Companies*, Thomson Higher Education, Mason, OH; Lasalle, D. and Britton, T.A. (2002), *Priceless: Turning Ordinary Products into Extraordinary Experiences*, Harvard Business School Press, Boston, MA; Pine, J.B. and Gilmore, J.H. (1999), *The Experience Economy: Work is Theatre and Every Business a Stage*, Harvard Business School Press, Boston, MA; Wheeler, J. and Smith, S. (2002), *Managing the Customer Experience: Turning Customers into Advocates*, Prentice Hall, NJ.
6. Pine and Gilmore, *The Experience Economy*; Carù and Cova, "Expériences de consommation et marketing expérientiel".
7. Pine and Gilmore *The Experience Economy*, p. 96.
8. Hetzel, P. (2002), *Planète conso: marketing expérientiel et nouveaux univers de consommation*, Editions d'Organisation, Paris; Pine and Gilmore, *The Experience Economy*; Schmitt, *Experiential Marketing*.
9. Berman, B. (2005), "How to Delight Your Customers", *California Management Review*, Vol. 48, No. 1, pp. 129–51; Finn, A. (2005), "Reassessing the Foundations of Customer Delight", *Journal of Service Research*, Vol. 8, No. 2, pp. 103–16; Hicks, J., Page, T.J. Jr., Behe, B.K., Dennis, J.H., and Fernandez, R.T. (2005), "Delighted Customers Buy Again: An Investigation into the Impact of Consumer Knowledge on Consumer Satisfaction and Delight of Flowering Potted Plants", *Journal of Satisfaction/Dissatisfaction, and Complaining Behavior*, Vol. 18, pp. 94–104; A. Kumar, R.W. Olshavsky, and M.F. King (2001), "Exploring Alternative Antecedents of Customer Delight", *Journal of Consumer Satisfaction/Dissatisfaction and Complaining Behavior*, Vol. 18, pp. 14–26; Oliver, R.L., Rust, R.T., and Varki, S. (1997), "Customer Delight: Foundations, Findings and Managerial Insight", *Journal of Retailing*, Vol. 73, No. 3, pp. 311–36; Rust, R.T. and Oliver, R.L. (2000), "Should We Delight the Customer?" *Journal of the Academy of Marketing Science*,

Vol. 28, No. 1, pp. 86–94; Rust, R.T., Zahorik, A.J., and Keiningham, T.L. (1996), *Service Marketing*, Harper Collins, New York.

10. St-James, Y. and Taylor, S. (2004), "Delight-as-Magic: Refining the Conceptual Domain of Customer Delight", in B.E. Kahn and M. Frances Luce (eds), *Advances in Consumer Research*, Vol. 31, Association for Consumer Research, Valdosta, GA, pp. 753–58.

11. Jones, T.O. and Sasser, W.E. (1995), "Why Satisfied Customers Defect", *Harvard Business Review*, Vol. 73, No. 6, pp. 89–99; Verma, H.V. (2003), "Customer Outrage and Delight", *Journal of Services Research*, Vol. 3, No. 1, pp. 119–33.

12. Oliver, Rust, and Varki, "Customer Delight "; Rust and Oliver, "Should We Delight the Customer?"

13. Vanhamme, J. and Snelders, D. (2003), "What If You Surprise Your Customer … Will They Be More Satisfied? Findings from a Pilot Experiment", in P.A. Keller and D.W. Rook (eds), *Advances in Consumer Research*, Vol. 30, Association for Consumer Research, Valdosta, GA, pp. 48–55.

14. Ibid.

15. Arnold, M.J., Reynolds, K.E., Ponder, N., and Lueg, J.E. (2005), "Customer Delight in a Retail Context: Investigating Delightful and Terrible Shopping Experiences", *Journal of Business Research*, Vol. 58, No. 8, pp. 1143–5; Finn, "Reassessing the Foundations of Customer Delight"; Oliver, Rust, and Varki, "Customer Delight"; St-James and Taylor, "Delight-as-Magic"; Verma, "Customer Outrage and Delight".

16. Rust and Oliver, "Should We Delight the Customer?", p. 88.

17. Plutchik, R. (1980), *Emotion: A Psychoevolutionary Synthesis*, Harper & Row, New York.

18. Arnold et al., "Customer Delight in a Retail Context".

19. Verma, "Customer Outrage and Delight", p. 124.

20. Rust and Oliver, "Should We Delight the Customer?"

21. Berman, "How to Delight Your Customers".

22. Aurier, Ph. and Evrard, Y. (1998), "Elaboration et validation d'une échelle de mesure de la satisfaction des consommateurs", in B. Saporta and J.F. Trinquecoste (eds), *Actes de la Conférence de l'Association Française du Marketing*, Vol. 14, No. 1, IAE, Bordeaux, pp. 51–71; Vanhamme J. (2002), "La satisfaction des consommateurs spécifique à une transaction: définition, antécédents, mesures et modes", *Recherche et Applications en Marketing*, Vol. 17, No. 2, pp. 55–85.

23. Oliver, R.L. (1997), *Consumer Satisfaction: A Behavioural Perspective on the Consumer*, McGraw-Hill, New York; Price, L.L., Arnould, E.J., and Deibler, S.L. (1995), "Consumers' Emotional Responses to Service Encounters", *International Journal of Service Industry Management*, Vol. 6, No. 3, pp. 34–63.

24. Berman, "How to Delight Your Customers".

25. Ibid.; Schneider, B. and Bowen, D.E. (1999), "Understanding Customer Delight and Outrage", *Sloan Management Review*, Vol. 41, No. 1, pp. 35–45.

26. Biyalogorsky, E., Gerstner, E., and Libai, B. (2001), "Customer Referral Management: Optimal Reward Programs", *Marketing Science*, Vol. 20, No. 1, pp. 82–95; Estelami, H. (2000), "Competitive and Procedural Determinants of Delight and Disappointment in Consumer Complaint Outcomes", *Journal of Service Research*, Vol. 2, No. 3, pp. 285–300; N'Gobo, P.V. (1999), "Decreasing Returns in Customer Loyalty: Does It Really Matter to Delight the Customers?", in E.J. Arnould and L.M. Scott (eds), *Advances in Consumer Research*, Vol. 26, Association for Consumer Research, Provo, UT, pp. 469–76; Rust, Zahorik and Keiningham, *Service Marketing*; Vanhamme and Snelders, "What If You Surprise Your Customer …".

27. Estelami, "Competitive and Procedural Determinants".
28. Jones and Sasser, "Why Satisfied Customers Defect".
29. Westbrook, R.A. (1980), "A Rating Scale for Measuring Product/Service Satisfaction", *Journal of Marketing*, Vol. 44, No. 4, pp. 68–72.
30. Jones and Sasser, "Why Satisfied Customers Defect".
31. Gardial, S.F., Clemons, D.S., Woodruff, R.B., Schumann, D.W., and Burns, M.J. (1994), "Comparing Consumers Recall of Prepurchase and Postpurchase Product Evaluation Experiences", *Journal of Consumer Research*, Vol. 20, No. 4, pp. 548–60; Oliver, *Consumer Satisfaction*; Vanhamme, "La satisfaction des consommateurs spécifique à une transaction"; see also Finn, "Reassessing the Foundations of Customer Delight".
32. Westbrook, "A Rating Scale for Measuring Product/Service Satisfaction".
33. Kumar, Olshavsky and King, "Exploring Alternative Antecedents of Customer Delight".
34. Ibid.
35. Plutchik, *Emotion*.
36. St-James and Taylor, "Delight-as-Magic".
37. Finn, "Reassessing the Foundations of Customer Delight"; Oliver, Rust and Varki, "Customer Delight".
38. Izard, C. (1977), *Human Emotions*, Plenum Press, New York.
39. Richins, M.L. (1997), "Measuring Emotions in the Consumption Experience", *Journal of Consumer Research*, Vol. 24, No. 2, pp. 127–46.
40. Havlena, W.J. and Holbrook, M.B. (1986), "The Varieties of Consumption Experience: Comparing Two Typologies of Emotion in Consumer Behavior", *Journal of Consumer Research*, Vol. 13, No. 3, pp. 394–404.
41. Oliver, Rust and Varki, "Customer Delight".
42. Finn, "Reassessing the Foundations of Customer Delight".
43. Tokman, M., Davis, L.M., and Lemon, K.N. (2007), "The WOW Factor: Creating Value Through Win-back Offers to reacquire Lost Customers", *Journal of Retailing*, Vol. 83, No. 1, pp. 47–64.
44. Hicks et al., "Delighted Customers Buy Again".
45. N'Gobo, "Decreasing Returns in Customer Loyalty".
46. Oliver, Rust and Varki, "Customer Delight".
47. Finn, "Reassessing the Foundations of Customer Delight".
48. Vanhamme, J. (2008), "The Surprise–Delight Relationship Revisited in the Management of Experience", *Recherche et Applications en Marketing*, Vol. 23, No. 3, 113–39.
49. Mano, H. and Oliver, R.L. (1993), "Assessing the Dimensionality and Structure of the Consumption Experience: Evaluation, Feeling, and Satisfaction", *Journal of Consumer Research*, Vol. 20, No. 3, pp. 451–66; Oliver, Rust and Varki, "Customer Delight".
50. Oliver, Rust, and Varki, "Customer Delight".
51. Finn, "Reassessing the Foundations of Customer Delight"; Vanhamme J. (2001), "L'influence de la surprise sur la satisfaction des consommateurs: étude exploratoire par journal de bord", *Recherche et Applications en Marketing*, Vol. 16, No. 2, pp. 1–32; Vanhamme and Snelders, "What If You Surprise Your Customer …"; Westbrook, R.A. and Oliver, R.L. (1991), "The Dimensionality of Consumption Emotion Patterns and Consumer Satisfaction", *Journal of Consumer Research*, Vol. 18, No. 1, pp. 84–91; Oliver, R.L. and Westbrook, R.A. (1993), "Profiles of Consumer Emotions and Satisfaction in Ownership and Usage", *Journal of Consumer Satisfaction/Dissatisfaction and Complaining Behavior*, Vol. 6, pp. 12–27.
52. For example, Vanhamme and Snelders, "What If You Surprise Your Customer …".
53. For example, Vanhamme and Snelders, "What If You Surprise Your Customer …".

54. For example, Vanhamme, "L'influence de la surprise sur la satisfaction des consommateurs".
55. Filser, M. (2002), "Le Marketing de la production d'expérience: statut théorique et implications managériales", *Décisions Marketing*, Vol. 28 (Oct–Déc.), pp. 13–18.
56. Mano and Oliver, "Assessing the Dimensionality and Structure of the Consumption Experience".
57. Rust, R.T. and Cooil, B. (1994), "Reliability Measures for Qualitative Data: Theory and Implications", *Journal of Marketing Research*, Vol. 31, No. 1, pp. 1–14.
58. Vanhamme and Snelders, "What If You Surprise Your Customer ...".
59. Pine and Gilmore, *The Experience Economy*; Rust, Zahorik, and Keiningham, *Service Marketing*.
60. Izard, *Human Emotions*.
61. Ekman, P. and Friesen, W.V. (1975), *Unmasking the Face*, Prentice Hall, Englewood Cliffs, NJ.
62. Reisenzein, R. (2000), "Exploring the Strength of Association between the Components of Emotion Syndrome: The Case of Surprise", *Cognition and Emotion*, Vol. 14, No. 1, pp. 1–38.
63. Oliver, *Consumer Satisfaction*.
64. Westbrook, "A Rating Scale for Measuring Product/Service Satisfaction"; Oliver, *Consumer Satisfaction*; Aurier and Evrard, "Elaboration et validation d'une échelle de mesure de la satisfaction des consommateurs".
65. Zaichkowsky, J.L. (1985), "Measuring the Involvement Construct", *Journal of Consumer Research*, Vol. 12, No. 3, pp. 341–52; Ohanian, R. (1990), "Expertise", in W.O. Bearden and R.G. Netemeyer (eds) (1999), *Handbook of Marketing Scales: Multi-Item Measures for Marketing and Consumer Behavior Research*, Sage , Thousand Oaks, CA, p. 302; Saucier, G. (1994), "Mini-Markers: A Brief Version of Goldberg's Unipolar Big Five Markers", *Journal of Personality Assessment*, Vol. 63, No. 3, pp. 506–16.
66. Peterson, R.A. and Sauber, M. (1983), "A Mood Scale for Survey Research", in P. Murphy et al. (eds), *American Marketing Association Educators' Proceedings*, American Marketing Association, Chicago, pp. 409–14. See also Bearden and Netemeyer, *Handbook of Marketing Scales*, pp. 250–51.
67. Vanhamme and Snelders, "What If You Surprise Your Customer ...".
68. Fornell, C. and Bookstein, F.L. (1982), "Two Structural Equation Models: LISREL and PLS Applied to Consumer Exit-Voice Theory", *Journal of Marketing Research*, Vol. 9, No. 4, pp. 440–52.
69. Wold, H. (1980), "Model Construction and Evaluation when Theoretical Knowledge is Scarce: Theory and Applications of Partial Least Squares", in J. Kmenta and J.B. Ramsey (eds), *Evaluation of Econometric Models*, Academic Press, New York, pp. 47–74.
70. Chin, W.W. (1998), "The Partial Least Squares Approach for Structural Equation Modeling", in G. Marcoulides (ed.), *Modern Methods for Business Research*, Lawrence Erlbaum Associates, Hillsdale, NJ, pp. 295–336.
71. Ibid.; Fornell, C. and Larcker, D.F. (1981), "Evaluating Structural Equation Models with Unobservable Variables and Measurement Error", *Journal of Marketing Research*, Vol. 18, No. 3, pp. 39–50.
72. Wold, "Model Construction and Evaluation".
73. Tenenhaus, M. (1998), *La régression PLS : théorie et pratique*, Editions Technip, Paris.
74. Fornell and Bookstein, "Two Structural Equation Models".
75. Tenenhaus, *La régression PLS*.
76. Mano and Oliver, "Assessing the Dimensionality and Structure of the Consumption Experience"; Oliver, Rust, and Varki, "Customer Delight".
77. Rust and Oliver, "Should We Delight the Customer?"
78. Ibid.

79. See Vanhamme, "La satisfaction des consommateurs spécifique à une transaction", for a review.
80. Gundlach, G.T., Achrol, R.S., and Mentzer, J.T. (1995), "The Structure of Commitment in Exchange", *Journal of Marketing*, Vol. 59, No. 1, pp. 78–92.
81. Ibid.
82. Cf. Kumar, Olshavsky, and King, "Exploring Alternative Antecedents of Customer Delight".
83. Oliver, Rust, and Varki, "Customer Delight".
84. Finn, "Reassessing the Foundations of Customer Delight".
85. Oliver, Rust, and Varki, "Customer Delight"; Mano and Oliver, "Assessing the Dimensionality and Structure of the Consumption Experience".
86. Churchill, G.A. and Surprenant, C. (1982), "An Investigation into the Determinants of Customer Satisfaction", *Journal of Marketing Research*, Vol. 19, No. 4, pp. 491–504.
87. Oliver, Rust, and Varki, "Customer Delight".
88. Cohen, J.B and Areni, C.S. (1991), "Affect and Consumer Behavior", in T.S. Robertson and H.H. Kassrjian (eds), *Handbook of Consumer Theory and Research*, Prentice Hall, Englewood Cliffs, NJ, pp. 188–240.
89. Ibid.
90. Rust and Oliver, "Should We Delight the Customer?"

Part VI
Critique of
Experiential
Marketing

CHAPTER 15

Please Hold, Your Call is Important to Us: Some Thoughts on Unspeakable Customer Experiences

STEPHEN BROWN*

Keywords

salutary reminder, unpleasant experiences, shopper stories, Starbucks shocker

Abstract

There has been much talk in recent years about "experiential marketing". It is widely regarded as a radical, some say revolutionary, approach that'll change the face of business forever. This may be so, but experiential marketing is not new. In fact, it's been around since the earliest days of organised trade. The Elysium it envisages is not really attainable either, though it's nice to have something utopian to aspire to. Most importantly perhaps, the experiential marketing "paradigm" ignores the brute reality of everyday service encounters. The experiences most consumers experience are anything but pleasant. As this chapter shows, many "memorable" customer experiences are memorable in a *very bad way*. Consider, for example, the less than enthralling everyday experience of hanging on a menu-driven customer helpline – premium rate, naturally – which eventually connects to a functionary with a script in a benighted call centre several thousand miles distant. Please hold? My call is important? Yeah right!

Press 1 for Introduction

There has been much talk in recent years about "experiential marketing". A slew of books – some aimed at academics, most targeted towards practitioners – has made the case for

---
*   Professor Stephen Brown, Department of Marketing, Entrepreneurship & Strategy, Ulster Business School, University of Ulster, Jordanstown, Co. Antrim, BT37 0QB, Northern Ireland. E-mail: sfx.brown@ulster.ac.uk. Telephone: + 44 28 9036 6130.

compelling customer experiences, broadly conceived.[1] Contemporary consumers, we are told, crave nothing less than awesome, astonishing, ideally unforgettable experiences that they'll treasure till the end of time. Or until senile dementia kicks in, at least. According to one of the paradigm's leading exponents, in fact, we are "in the middle of a revolution. A revolution that will render the principles and models of traditional marketing obsolete. A revolution that will change the face of marketing forever. A revolution that will replace traditional feature-and-benefit marketing with experiential marketing."[2]

Setting aside the boosterism and the BS, it is necessary to note three crucial caveats about the recent rapid rise of experiential marketing. First and foremost, it is not new. Awesomely overwhelming commercial spectaculars have been around since the earliest days of organised trade.[3] Whether it be the bread and circuses of Ancient Rome, the massive fairs and markets of the Middle Ages, P.T. Barnum's mind-boggling museums in the mid-nineteenth century, or the nauseating Nuremberg Rallies of the 1930s, astute marketers have long recognised that stupendous sensory experiences sell stupendously well. The magnificence of Whiteley's department store at its 1900 apogee, or the Eiffel Tower-enriched *Exposition Universelle* during 1889, make today's Niketowns and Rainforest Cafes and Louis Vuitton flagship stores look feeble by comparison.

Second, it is aspirational rather than attainable. The books and articles that advocate this emerging experiential Elysium are the management equivalent of gourmet cookbooks and/or guaranteed diets. They describe an ideal, almost Utopian, world where customers are enchanted, employees are enthusiastic, stakeholders are supportive, and day-to-day management is an effortless breeze (nay, a susurrating zephyr that plucks melodiously on the Aeolian Harp of prodigious profitability). They are execu-porn, in short, titillating texts that contain seductive promises of orgiastic organisational abandon involving consenting consumers and concupiscent CEOs. Or something like that.

Third, it is highly likely to end in failure. Would it were otherwise, but the brute reality is that the vast majority of business ventures fail.[4] Most companies collapse, most CEOs flop, most start-ups stop, most mergers misfire, most innovations implode, most R&D founders, most long-range forecasts flub, most new products flatline, most brand extensions crater, most advertising campaigns are ignored, and most business success stories have a back story full of botches, blunders, clangers, and catastrophes.[5] Memorable customer experiences are unlikely to be any different, unfortunately.

Press 2 for Rationale

Now, none of this means that memorable experiences aren't worth pursuing. On the contrary, unattainably utopian targets are vitally necessary for organisational motivation, and in the workaday world of blue-suited business a little bit of bliss never goes amiss. Likewise, the fact that experiential marketing is rather old hat is no reason to rule it out of court. The vast bulk of "new-fangled" business concepts – CSR, CRM, viral-cum-buzz marketing, and so forth – have been around for a very long time, albeit they have been rebooted and retrofitted and (expensively) repackaged to suit contemporary circumstances.[6] Failure, moreover, may be probable, but it's by no means inevitable. History consistently shows that those who hang in there despite repeated failure, abject failure, heart-rending failure, are those who win through to success in the end.

That said, it is arguable that an experiential reality check is sorely needed. The overwhelming majority of business books focus on success – how to attain it, how to sustain it, how to unearth it, how to unleash it – and they thus convey an unrealistic impression, especially when failure is the default setting of commercial life. Analogously, our search for unforgettable customer experiences mustn't blind us to the often unpleasant reality – namely, that many "memorable" customer experiences involve surly shop assistants, extortionate bank charges, couldn't-care-less utility companies, thieving ticket touts on eBay, traffic wardens with wheel-clamps akimbo, grasping insurance companies who refuse to honour critical life cover, unconscionable health trusts that deny customers' life-saving cancer treatments on account of a grotesque postcode lottery, and (lest we forget) being forced to queue all night outside Toys 'R Us in order to get our hands on a Wii, or whatever this year's must-have Christmas toy happens to be.[8] And then there's the less than enthralling everyday experience of hanging on a menu-driven customer helpline, premium rate, naturally, which eventually connects to a functionary with a script in a benighted call centre several thousand miles distant. Please hold? My call is important? Yeah right!

In this regard, consider the following quote, plucked at random from this weekend's newspapers. It refers to one customer's experience with a high-flying company that is often featured in puffs for the experiential marketing paradigm: Virgin Atlantic. After ranting about the hell on earth that is Heathrow Airport, the *Financial Times* columnist continues:

Just in case I needed reminding of the bliss that it is to avoid Heathrow, I flew out of there just after Christmas, to spend the New Year in the Caribbean.

This was a lot less glamorous than it sounds and Heathrow, to be fair, was the least of the problems. Virgin Atlantic's exhortation to cut down on time spent at the airport by checking-in online proved impossible three times over – remotely on my computer (the website just refused, even after half an hour on the phone to Virgin); at the airport automatic check-in desk ("Sorry, we cannot print at the moment"); and then even when a helpful assistant took me off to her terminal, which promptly jammed. So we stood in line for an hour for the so-called "bag drop" which wasn't functioning as a bag drop at all, but as an old-fashioned check-in.

By the time [my husband's] in-seat entertainment had failed to function in spite of repeated re-setting by the cabin crew, any appearance by Sir Richard Branson would have resulted in my husband being arrested for assault.[9]

As someone who has gone through the exact same experience on Virgin Atlantic, I can personally testify to the veracity of this account. Actually, the *Financial Times'* correspondent fails to mention the woeful lack of legroom in Cattle Class (or whatever Virgin currently calls it), which is significantly worse than some of the lowest low-cost carriers. I know one should never say never, but I never intend flying Virgin Atlantic again.

Such critiques can of course be dismissed as churlish or pettifogging. They are either the ravings of professional dyspeptics with column inches to fill or the grumblings of middle-aged misanthropes with too much time on their hands. This may be so, but as someone who makes a point of visiting the places praised in articles and books about experiential marketing, I've been disappointed more often than not.[10] Niketown? Don't do it. Disneyland? Long lines, short rides. Guinness Storehouse? Brewing is boring. South St. Seaport? North-west passage. Irvine Spectrum? Only in California. Mall of America? Wall of death. Whole Foods Market? Bare-faced rip-off. Citroën's Parisian flagship? Great story, badly told. Caesars Palace? Which way to the vomitorium?

As a card-carrying marketer, admittedly, I'm conscious that raised expectations (such as mine) are difficult to satisfy, let alone surpass. I'm equally conscious that expectations management is a delicate balancing act (because they have to be raised to attract the punters, but if customers are led to expect too much, nothing is ever good enough). I'm happy to admit, furthermore, that not all my encounters with pre-packaged experiences have been of the Virgin Atlantic variety. The Bellagio's dancing fountains are fantastic. The BCE galleria in Toronto is an airy delight. Bilbao's Guggenheim is two parts breathtaking, one part barking. The underground bunkers in Nuremberg are chilling. The touring *Titanic* exhibition is awe-inspiring. Japanese department stores, during the Christmas shopping season, are nothing less than breathtaking.

Press 3 for Method

Yet, I suspect that when all the caveats are introduced and all the excuses are accepted, my experiences with experiential offerings are far from exceptional. Indeed, I *know* that they aren't. For some time now, I've been building a database on consumer experiences. This database is not derived from questionnaire surveys or longitudinal observations or sophisticated tracking studies or even free-wheeling focus groups. It's much, much simpler – and, hence, more meaningful – than that. As a firm believer in storytelling, I ask my informants to tell their own, unprompted stories about good, bad, and indifferent everyday encounters with brands, retail stores, advertising campaigns, and various other aspects of the marketing environment. These encounters range from sipping frappuchinos in Starbucks, Howard Schultz's celebrated "third place", to attending Harry Potter Halloween parties in full Hogwarts regalia, broomsticks included. They include the horrors of waiting in never-ending line at Universal Studios to holidaying in a timber wolf-themed hotel in the watery wilds of backwoods Wisconsin. For the purposes of the present chapter, however, I'll be focusing on retail store stories, if only because retailing environments are regarded as the crucible of the experiential paradigm.[11]

Press 4 for Findings

Although my collection of consumer stories offers a bracing corrective to the enraptured proselytisation of experiential evangelists, as we shall see, it's necessary to stress one thing from the outset. Many consumers *adore* the retail encounter. The glitz, the glamour, the gleaming goods, the grovelling sales assistants, the gloriously gleeful gotta-have-it sensations are never less than intoxicating. Countless informants, in fact, freely describe themselves as hopelessly addicted "shopaholics". True, this tends to be said with a wink and a smile and an ironic acknowledgement of their personal susceptibilities, rather than any overt reference to the distressing clinical condition. This tendency, what is more, is much less marked among males of the species, substantial numbers of whom claim to "hate" shopping, but it lurks below the linguistic surface all the same. When it comes to, say, CDs and books and power tools and plasma screen TVs and classic cars and prestigious wrist watches, men are just as deliriously shopaholic as the distaff half of the population. Except they don't call it "shopping". Other words are used instead: "hobby", "pastime", "work", and, my personal favourite, "an investment".

Be that as it may, attractive retail environments undeniably exert a quasi-hypnotic power on some customers, as do especially desirable objects on alluring display:

> Swerving past the queues of trolleys, I just can't resist a quick glance at Masquerade next door. Masquerade is a delightfully small space rather than a shop, with fascinating bits and pieces. Sensual aromatherapy oils, scented candles, floating candles, burners, vases, miniature clocks and coveted jewellery are all carefully aligned into this Pandora's Box. I snatch a quick smell from the erotic Ylang Ylang (purported to be an aphrodisiac). Enraptured, I drift into Wellworths. Is there such a thing as an aphrodisiac for shopping, I wonder.
>
> 23-year-old female

> Then I saw it. I walked over to it in a dream-like state, scared stiff of seeing it up close. My legs were like jelly as I approached it. As I stretched out my hand to hold the dress I thought I would faint. It was the most perfect dress in the whole world. I had to try it on. The next few minutes passed in a haze. The dress was perfect. But I couldn't afford it, could I? I looked at the price tag. My mind started to work overtime, I knew that I couldn't let an opportunity like this pass me by. I would regret it for the rest of my life.
>
> 20-year-old female

However, for every irresistible store environment, which draws consumers in against their better judgement, there are retail experiences that are not only less than pleasant but the nearest thing to hell this side of the grave. My consumer stories are replete with words like "angry", "frustrated", "vexed", "irritated", "anguish", "torture", "gutted", "disgusted", "fed-up", "flustered", "bothered", "dread", "hatred", "horror", "annoyed", and others that are pretty much unprintable in works of scholarship.[12] Sometimes, in fact, words don't do full justice to the sheer awfulness of the retail encounter:

> As I walked back to the holiday apartments with my girlfriend, after another gruelling and fruitless shopping expedition in that revolting heat, the only thing that made me feel better was the reflection that, had I had a gun on me, I would by now have shot at least three people.
>
> 25-year-old male

Retail rage, clearly, is alive and kicking – kicking being the operative word on occasion – and it is triggered by many and varied experiential occurrences. For the purposes of explication, these can be divided into three main categories: those pertaining to the *physical* setting; those caused by the *social* setting; and those attributable to the *situational* setting.

PHYSICAL FACTORS

As the experiential marketing literature leads us to expect, the physical environment is a major influence on consumer activities and attitudes. Badly designed or poorly laid out retail stores are particularly annoying, as are overpowering smells, oppressive heat, obtrusive background music, and, not least, shopkeepers' infuriating tendency to rearrange the merchandise without prior warning:

> *I frantically run up and down the aisles, running round in circles. Typical, they have moved all the stuff around again. I hate the way they change everything around so you can't find anything. It is so frustrating.*
>
> 22-year-old female

Of all the elements of the physical environment, though, perhaps the most frustrating are changing rooms, shopping trolleys, and checkouts. Communal changing rooms, for example, are universally reviled, and even when individual cubicles are provided, these are unfailingly small, cramped, and overheated, with trick mirrors, a dearth of pegs, and curtains that conspire to leave a yawning gap through which passing voyeurs can catch a less than titillating glimpse of threadbare underwear, unshaven legs, and unsightly rolls of fat …

> *When shopping for clothes I might look round for hours and chat about clothes till I am blue in the face. But when it comes to trying them on in the shop I tend to be in and out of the changing rooms in five seconds. It seems strange but I have a kind of fear of changing areas. It's like the curtain doesn't pull the whole way across, I might have smelly feet without shoes on, and more times than not start to feel intense heat and sweat like mad. I don't think I can get my original clothes on quick enough, no matter how nice the new ones are. I can take a guess and say I bought a lot of clothes without actually seeing them on me in the shop.*
>
> 30-year-old male

Similarly, shopping trolleys are an alien species intent on the extermination of humankind through an epidemic of twisted backs, bruised ankles, crushed feet, and coronary thrombosis induced by decades of raised blood pressure. It is generally acknowledged that trolleys are not only sentient creatures but are temperamental to boot. They slow down, speed up, won't stop, swerve suddenly, block aisles, and ram innocent bystanders amidships:

> *We eventually get our trolley and it seems to be quite co-operative. As soon as we enter the supermarket, the trolley begins to squeak and, yes you've guessed it, the wheels have minds of their own, oblivious and uninterested in what way I may wish to go – Oh no, we've hired the trolley from Hell … The next stop is the meat counter. As we go towards our destination, the trolley from Hell seems to have its own ideas and veers off in the direction of the cereal display. Just missing by inches, we gently persuade the trolley to come round to our way of thinking by giving it a good hard kick. I don't know if this treatment did the trolley any good but it sure made me feel better.*
>
> 21-year-old female

The horror of horrors, however, is the checkout. Apart from the familiar, frequently observed, profoundly irritating fact that the "other" queue always moves faster, checkout psychosis is redoubled when the line is long, the store is busy, the tills are understaffed (or manned by the terminally ignorant), and the person in front has eleven items in their basket when the sign clearly states ten items or less!

> *It was my brother's birthday last month and I remember when going in to purchase a card for him, I really didn't want to spend long in there. So I grabbed one that looked quite cheap and slightly funny, and brought it to the till. To my astonishment the card I selected was well over a fiver, and it was already too late to leave it back, because the shop assistant had already scanned it through. With the queue behind me becoming more hostile, I was searching through my pockets for coins, then realized I had forgotten the envelope and had to go back to get it. So I dumped my money on the counter, marched to the other end of the shop and back, to get the envelope and then with great relief I took my change and left the shop, getting dirty looks from everyone in the queue.*
>
> 28-year-old male

SOCIAL FACTORS

The above, it must be stressed, are but a few of the many physical factors that impinge on the consumer's retail experience.[13] Yet even if such things are carefully managed by retainer fee-enriched exponents of the experiential paradigm, the social side of things can derail even the most brilliantly designed store environments. My consumer stories consistently show that overcrowded retail outlets are a major source of customer frustration. Heaving crowds of "bloody people", most of whom don't look where they're going, are especially hateful, as is the associated hustle and bustle, pushing and shoving, and all-round chaos and disorder:

> *After that, we went to another nearby shop, which was packed full of people of all sorts, in what was a cramped and very hot atmosphere, in what could only be described as a cattle market. It was doing my head in. So, after choosing a suitable gift, we proceeded to the front desk which was crammed full of people grabbing their goods and then pissing off as soon as they could, to get out of the bollocks of a mess they were standing in. It was a mad scramble with people from all backgrounds going absolutely mad.*
>
> 23-year-old male

Alongside the overall madness of the marketplace, there is the inexplicably infuriating behaviour of specific individuals. These are people who cause delays when everyone else is in a hurry, who imperiously block the aisles with their prams or trolleys or revolting offspring, who can't make up their minds what they want, and who act at all times as though the whole store is their oyster:

> *The top of my hate list is parents, especially mothers with prams. They think they have the right to walk straight ahead and that myself and every other shopper has to move and twist their way round them. If I don't move for them and accidentally collide with them, I can be 100 percent sure I will get tutted at and told to "watch where I'm fucking going". They think they own the place.*
>
> 21-year-old male

Above and beyond "other people", there's one's own shopping companions. Shopping with friends or relatives may seem like a good idea, especially if a second opinion is required, but it can quickly descend into a Herculean ordeal that makes the Augean Stables look like Planet Hollywood. Indeed, there's only one thing worse than shopping with friends, and that's shopping with mother. What's more, there's only one thing worse than shopping with mother, and that's shopping with one's significant other:

Flanked by a protesting James, who is either on the verge of murder or exploding, I try to calm him down with those three soothing, tender words "Oh shut up!" Sensing another outburst, I dive into the shop, select and pay for the jacket and appear before James has realised I've gone! "WHY COULDN'T YOU HAVE DONE THAT TWO HOURS AGO?" Here we go again, the usual rant, "We could have been out of here in five minutes! When I go shopping I get what I want in one shop and go home – inside half an hour. You have to go into every shop and then back to the first one and pick the first thing you saw. We could have been home ages ago!" Are all men the same? Why is it they have to apply this macho, chauvinistic image to everything? Men are better at this. Men are better at that. We can do our shopping in five minutes!

23-year-old female

SITUATIONAL FACTORS

Bad as the male/female shopping imbroglio is, there are certain "situational" scenarios that run it close in the customer meltdown stakes. Christmas shopping is a case in point, as are similar special occasions (e.g., weddings, birthdays, christenings, dinner parties, job interviews, Mother's Day, Father's Day, Valentine's Day). Not only are everyday shopping frustrations exacerbated at these particular junctures, but when things go awry (as they often do), the price of failure is astronomical. Failing to get what one set out for is one of the most annoying consumption experiences of all, especially when it's being given as a gift. The merchandise that's in stock invariably turns out to be the "wrong" colour, size, style, fit, brand, model, specification, price, and so forth. Grrrrrr.

Another essentially situational factor is consumers' prior physical or financial state. Shopping is much more irritating when one's in a foul mood or feeling poorly or when wallets are empty and payday's a long way away. The weather is another important influence too, since there is a world of difference between browsing bargain bins on a sunny summer's afternoon and trying to buy a last-minute gift during a downpour in December:

The total button is activated and the cashier's uninterested voice drones out, "£52.67 please". My eyes shoot open in an instant and I can feel the heat of embarrassment cover my face in a flash. Immediately, I realise why the phrase "I wish the ground would open up and swallow me" was coined. My feelings range from downright embarrassment to panic to humiliation, as I sheepishly explain to the cashier that I've only got £38.75.

21-year-old female

If there is one situational element that is capable of turning even the most amenable, easy-going consumer into a cantankerous, foul-mouthed misanthrope, it is travel conditions en route. Traffic jams, overcrowded buses, inadequate parking facilities, inconsiderate road users, dictatorial traffic wardens, and analogous killjoys are considered by many to be the very worst part of the entire shopping experience, checkout psychosis notwithstanding:

> *As we headed out of the car park towards the attendant in his little booth, I realised that I didn't have any loose change. I handed over the parking ticket to the attendant and was duly asked to pay the exact amount. I only had a ten pound note. The attendant took a look and immediately started tearing strips off me, shouting about the correct fucking change and how I was holding up the rest of the motorists behind me. At this point I replied with a stream of equally colourful language, while my girlfriend sat behind me telling me to shut up and stop arguing. When we eventually left the car park with wheels spinning, my temper had moved into the red face with bursting headache stage and stayed like that until we were halfway down the motorway.*
>
> 32-year-old male

Press 5 for Discussion

The foregoing stories are far from unusual. Not only could they be repeated till the cows come home, humming "I'm lovin' it" but, in the interests of brevity, I've even omitted some of the most horrid consumer accounts.[14] No doubt spokespersons for experiential marketing regard such incidents as opportunities rather than threats. If only, one can imagine them saying, all retail stores embraced the experiential paradigm, then everyone would be so much better off, sweetness and light would prevail, and we'd all shop happily ever after. However, the problem with experiential solutions and similar one-word panaceas – excellence, relationships, co-creation, *keiretsu*, and so on – is that they're much less successful in practice than they are in principle. This doesn't mean they're worthless; it means that they need to be treated with caution. Big Pharma may have a pill for every ill, but let's not forget that management consultants sell sugared water, with lashings of added snake oil.[15]

Indeed, even if we concede that the experiential paradigm is an honourable exception to the Nostrums-R-Us rule, three related problems remain. The first of these concerns sustaining and maintaining the original vision. As experiential offers are scaled up and rolled out (and, moreover, imitated by competitors), the experience itself becomes less and less unique, more and more mundane. The seen-one-seen-'em-all curse kicks in, as Starbucks sadly illustrates. When Starbucks started out, it really was the much-vaunted Third Place, a welcoming home from home that was unlike any other coffee shop then available. Starbucks and its surrogates have since taken over the world – the third place has become *every* third place – and the quality of the experience has deteriorated alarmingly, to the point that revenues are slipping, like for like sales are declining, and Howard Schultz himself has come out of retirement to save the organisation.

Some of course will say that Starbucks has never been anything other than a grotesque rip-off, a triumph of marketing over mocha, as in this extract from the trenchant critic A.A. Gill:

> *Have you ever been to a Starbucks? … Of course you've been to a Starbucks. Starbucks is your second living room. The question I should have asked is: why?*

I'm not a habitué of these West Coast coffee shops. Not for any snobbish reason – just because I like coffee … Anyway, I did go to a Starbucks recently. And I'm still reeling. I can't remember the last time I was served something as foul as its version of cappuccino. I say "version," but that's a bit like saying Dot Cotton's a version of Audrey Hepburn.

To begin with, it took longer to make than a soufflé. I was the only customer, and asked the girl for a cappuccino. There followed an interrogation that would have impressed an SS Scientologist. What size did I want? Did I need anything in it? Was I hungry? By the time she'd finished, I felt like sobbing: "You've found Tom, and Dick's under the stove in D Hut, but I'll never give away Harry – he's got Dickie Attenborough up him." Suspiciously, she passed the order, written in Serbian, to another girl standing all of three inches away, who, in turn, slowly morphed into Marie Curie and did something very dangerous and complicated behind a counter, with a lot of sighing and brow-furrowing.

An hour and a half later, I was presented with a mug. A mug. One of those American mugs where the lip is so thick, you have to be an American or able to disengage your jaw like a python to fit it in your mouth. It contained a semi-permeable white mousse – the sort of stuff they use to drown teenagers in Ibiza, or pump into cavity walls. I dumped in two spoonfuls of sugar. It rejected them. Having beaten the malevolent epidermis with the collection of plastic and wooden things provided, I managed to make it sink. Then, using both hands, I took a sip. Then a gulp. Then chewed. I had the momentary sense of drowning in snowman's poo, then, after a long moment, a tepid sludge rose from the deep. This was reminiscent of gravy-browning and three-year-old Easter eggs.

How can anyone sell this stuff? How can anyone buy this twice? And this was only a small one – a baby. The adult version must be like sucking the outlet of a nuclear power station.

I slumped into a seat. There was a pamphlet about fair trade, and how Starbucks paid some Nicaraguan Sancho a reasonable amount for his coffee so that he now had a mule to go with his 13 children, leaky roof and 15 coffee bushes. It made not screwing the little no-hope wetback into penury sound like the most astonishing act of charitable benevolence. And they just had to print a pamphlet about it, so we all know the sort of selfless, munificent, group-hug people we're dealing with.[16]

A second, and closely related, point involves striking the right balance between fake and real. The problem many consumers have with experiential environments is that they feel somewhat synthetic, decidedly sanitised, crassly commercial, and uncomfortably manipulative. It's not that they are unpleasant; it's just that they are unreal with an unpleasant undertow of exploitation. Little wonder that "authenticity" is the latest buzzword in experiential marketing circles.[17] If you can fake authenticity, presumably you're laughing all the way to the fast buck bank.

Nowhere is this better illustrated than in Disney's retrofit of 42nd Street, adjacent to Times Square in New York City. As I can personally attest, having experienced the place back in the 1980s, Times Square was once an unedifying urban environment – sleazy, run-down, threatening, riddled with drug dealers, panhandlers, and analogous low-lifes. It was Disneyfied in the late 1990s, and when I was there a couple of years back, 42nd Street was full of sightseers, theatre goers, family groups, and so on. And a good thing too, some might say. But it also felt unreal in that creepy, calculated, commercialised, Main Street USA way. It was a plastic card in stone and concrete. Or as the comic novelist Carl Hiaasen puts it in his tour de force on "Team Rodent":

Dateline: Times Square, November 1997...

Disney audaciously has set out to vanquish sleaze in its unholiest fountainhead, Times Square; the skanky oozepit to which every live sex show, jack-off arcade, and smut emporium in the free world owes its existence. For decades, city and state politicians had vowed to purge the place of its legendary seediness, in order to make the streets safe, clean, and attractive for out-of-town visitors. New Yorkers paid no attention to such fanciful promises, for Times Square was knowledgeably regarded as lost and unconquerable; a mephitic pit, so formidably infested that nothing short of a full-scale military occupation could tame it. As recently as 1994 Times Square swarmed unabashedly with hookers, hustlers, and crackheads and was the address of forty-seven porn shops.

Then Disney arrived, ultimate goodness versus ultimate evil, and the cynics gradually went silent. Times Square has boomed.

The dissolute, sticky-shoed ambiance of Forty-second Street has been subjugated by the gleamingly wholesome presence of the Disney Store. Truly it's a phenomenon, for the shelves offer nothing but the usual cross-merchandised crapola ... Yet somehow the building radiates like a shrine – because it's not just any old store, it's a Disney store, filled with Disney characters, Mickey and Minnie at play in the fields of Times Fucking Square. And evidently the mere emplacement of the iconic Disney logo above the sidewalks has been enough to demoralize and dislodge some of the area's most entrenched sin merchants ...

A few blocks away, Peep Land hangs on by its cum-crusted fingernails. Inside ... well, just try to get past the video racks. Sample: volumes one through five of Ready to Drop, an anthology featuring explicit (and occasionally team-style) sex with women in their third trimester of pregnancy. And that's not the worst of it, not even close. The shop's library of bodily-function videos is extensive, multilingual, and prominently displayed at eye level. Skin a-crawl, I am quickly out the door.

Revulsion is good. Revulsion is healthy. Each of us has limits, unarticulated boundaries of taste and tolerance, and sometimes we forget where they are. Peep Land is here to remind us; a fixed compass point by which we can govern our private behavior ... Team Rodent doesn't believe in sleaze, however, nor in old-fashioned revulsion. Square in the middle is where it wants us all to be, dependable consumers with predictable attitudes. The message, never stated but avuncularly implied, is that America's values ought to reflect those of the Walt Disney Company and not the other way around.

So there's a creepy comfort to be found amidst the donkey films and giant rubber dicks, a subversive triumph at unearthing such slag so near to Disney's golden portals. (Hey, Mickey, whistle on this!) Peep Land is important precisely because it's so irredeemable and because it cannot be transformed into anything but what it is ... Standing in Disney's path, Peep Land remains a gummy little cell of resistance.

And resistance is called for.[17]

The third and perhaps most profound question raised by the experiential paradigm is "why?" Why have experiences suddenly come to the fore? How come every consultant worth his or her salt recommends experience as the cure for contemporary marketing's ills? What is it with the experience economy anyway? Is it the latest twist in capitalism's convoluted evolution, as Pine and Gilmore claim?[18] Is it a neglected part of the marketing mix – the 4th P of place – that's finally getting its moment in the management sun? Is it yet another management buzzword that's taken off like the synergy, globalization, and six sigma of yore? Speaking personally, I suspect things go much deeper than that. My suspicion is that our enthusiasm for experiences, emotional branding, service-dominant logic, and suchlike are a collective defence mechanism-cum-rationalisation, a psychological reaction to the sheer intangibility of modern commercial life. The real economy of nuts and bolts and widgets – the manufacturing economy – has disappeared over the eastern horizon, but we westerners have somehow convinced ourselves that we don't really need it anyway. Because, hey, the creative economy, the hyperreal economy, the weightless economy, the wiki economy is where it's at.

This unease is encapsulated, I believe, in that quintessential exemplar of experiential marketing, the food court. The centrepiece of almost every shopping development nowadays, food courts are supposed to be practically perfect places where countless cuisines from around the world mix and match and meld in happy harmony and ecumenical accord. It's a mall world after all. Peace, love, and pass the condiments. The reality of food courts is anything but utopian, however. They're not so much gourmet as grisly, greasy, grotesque. If, as they say, the way to the world's heart is through its stomach, then a course of colonic irrigation is overdue, surely:

Food Courts: *Dishes from the four corners of the world! Left half-eaten, on paper plates, stacked up, on Formica tables.*

The food hall, or food court: the most monstrous part of the already desperate shopping centre "experience". It's like a horrible accident at an MSG factory.

And always, as well as the usual suspects, there are outlets that you never see anywhere outside of food halls. Singapore Sam Express. Quizno's Sub. What is that? Who is this Quizno? What is this for? Who are these people? WHAT DO THEY WANT FROM ME?[19]

Press 6 for Conclusion

So, where does all this leave us? My point is not that the experiential paradigm is hopelessly utopian or utterly futile. The empirical evidence – and indeed my own personal experience – clearly indicates otherwise. It's necessary to bear in mind, though, that there's a dark side to memorable customer experiences, that memorable customer experiences are easily derailed by factors outside imagineers' control, that memorable customer experiences are neither new nor the sure-fire secret of marketing success, that memorable customer experiences may even be a convenient excuse, a manifestation of our collective failure to face up to post-industrial reality. The west may be doomed, boys and girls, but at least we've got Disneyland.

Press 7 for Notes

1. Carù, A. and Cova B. (2007), *Consuming Experience*, Routledge, London; Gilmore, J.H. and Pine, B.J. (2007), *Authenticity: What Consumers Really Want*, Harvard Business School Press, Boston, MA; LaSalle, D. and Britton, T.A. (2002), *Priceless: Turning Ordinary Products into Extraordinary Experiences*, Harvard Business School Press, Boston, MA; Pine, B.J. and Gilmore, J.H. (1999), *The Experience Economy*, Harvard Business School Press, Boston, MA; Schmitt, B.H. (2003), *Customer Experience Management*, John Wiley, New York; Shaw, C. and Ivens, J. (2002), *Building Great Customer Experiences*, Palgrave Macmillan, Basingstoke; Sherry, J.F. (1998), *Servicescapes: The Concept of Place in Contemporary Markets*, NTC Business Books, New York.
2. Schmitt, B.H. (1999), *Experiential Marketing*, Free Press, New York.
3. Brown, S. (2003), *Free Gift Inside!!*, Capstone, Oxford.
4. Finkelstein, S. (2003), *Why Smart Executives Fail: And What You Can Learn From Their Mistakes*, Portfolio, New York; Ormerod, P. (2005), *Why Most Things Fail: Evolution, Extinction and Economics*, Faber and Faber, London; Sandage, S.A. (2005), *Born Losers: A History of Failure in America*, Harvard University Press, Cambridge, MA.
5. Brown, S. (2008), *Fail Better! Stumbling to Success in Sales and Marketing*, Cyan, London.
6. Brown, S. (2001), *Marketing–The Retro Revolution*, Sage, London.
7. Brown, *Fail Better!*
8. And let's not forget IKEA-rage. As Lowe and McArthur observe, "IKEA fucks with your head. All you want is some furniture: why do they want your sanity in return? The layout alone makes you feel like a lab rat. The stores are like psychoactive jigsaw puzzles with moving pieces, designed by a sick Swedish physicist with access to extra dimensions. They have what look like short cuts between adjoining sections, allowing you to pop through a little walkway from one part of the store to another. But where you end up won't be where you were trying to get to, even if the store map said it would be. Worse, if you decide you were better off where you were, and pop back through the hole, you won't end up where you started, but in a different section again. Sometimes on a different floor altogether. In a different branch of IKEA." Lowe, S. and McArthur, A. (2005), *Is It Just Me or is Everything Shit?*, Time Warner, London.
9. Moneypenny, M. (2008), "Down to earth", *Financial Times Magazine*, Saturday, 12 January, p. 8.
10. I'm not an anorackish obsessive, rest assured, let alone the doddery academic of legend. It's just that my professional peregrinations have taken me to many of the retail stores, restaurants, theme parks, shopping centres, et al. that are being hyped up by promoters of the experiential paradigm.
11. In the interest of brevity, I've kept my excerpts to a minimum. I have empirical evidence to support every point, but this chapter would be twice the length if I included it all. Also see Patterson, A., Hodgson, J., and Shi, J. (2008), "Chronicles of 'customer experience': The downfall of Lewis's foretold", *Journal of Marketing Management*, Vol. 24, Nos 1–2, pp. 29–45.
12. Describing things as nightmarish is particularly common. In addition to common or garden "nightmare", the stories are full of references to "recurring nightmare", "complete nightmare", "worst nightmare", "ultimate nightmare", "absolute nightmare", and "Nightmare on the High Street".

13. Other annoyances in the physical environment include garish colour schemes, inadequate toilet facilities, unpleasant lighting effects, dowdy merchandise displays, inhuman ticketing systems, and the unattractive overall gestalt (or personality) of the retail store.

14. Prominent among these is snotty sales assistants, who are either far too pushy and would say anything to earn their commission, or completely ignore the customer, preferring to chat among themselves and do anything other than the job they're paid for.

15. Craig, D. (2005), *Rip-off! The Scandalous Inside Story of the Management Consulting Money Machine*, Original Book Company, London.

16. Gill, A.A. (2003), "Table Talk: Firehouse", *Sunday Times Style Magazine*, 9 February, pp. 46–7.

17. Hiaasen, C. (1998), *Team Rodent: How Disney Devours the World*, Ballantine, New York, pp. 1, 2–3, 8–9.

18. Pine and Gilmore, *The Experience Economy*.

19. Lowe, S. and McArthur, A. (2006), *Is It Just Me or is Everything Shit? Volume Two*, Sphere, London.

CHAPTER 16

Manufacturing Memorable Consumption Experiences from Ivy and Ivory: The Business Model, Customer Orientation, and Distortion of Academic Values in the Post-Millennial University

MORRIS B. HOLBROOK*

Abstract

The recent blossoming of interest in "experiential marketing" has produced strong evidence, in the form of various promotional communications, that the experiential view has caught on with the business community. However, we must question whether this widely touted concept fits all situations in general or the special case of academia in particular. In this connection, recalling the wisdom of Dwight D. Eisenhower, several dangers result from running the university like a business. Anecdotal illustrations – bolstered by a more detailed example that involves the branding of the author's own business school – suggest painful analogies between the commercialization of education and the selling of toothpaste or the glorification of the shopping mall. One lesson to be learned is that the advisability of promoting a school as "Hot Hot Hot" comes across as "Not Not Not".

Introduction: Customer Value in the Consumption Experience

In line with the central theme of the present volume on *Memorable Customer Experiences*, no one would question the extraordinary degree to which an emphasis on the role of

* Morris B. Holbrook, W.T. Dillard Professor of Marketing, Graduate School of Business, Columbia University, New York, NY 10027. Please address correspondence to Morris B. Holbrook, Apartment 5H, 140 Riverside Drive, New York, NY 10024. E-mail: mbh3@columbia.edu. Telephone: 212-873-7324. The author gratefully acknowledges the financial support of the Columbia Business School's Faculty Research Fund.

consumption experiences in the co-creation of customer value has preoccupied marketing thinkers in recent years. When Holbrook and Hirschman first popularized this concept over 25 years ago,[1] they failed to give an adequate account in recognition of how the role played by consumption experiences in contributing to market success could be traced back through the work of Woods[2] to the seminal contributions of Alderson[3] and, from there, through the writings of Abbott[4] and Norris[5] back to the pronouncements of Keynes,[6] the insights of Marshall,[7] or even the original thinking of Adam Smith.[8] With rare exceptions,[9] recent advocates of the experiential view have ignored the work of Holbrook and Hirschman almost as naively as those authors ignored the foundations laid by their own intellectual progenitors. Nonetheless, despite or even because of this historical amnesia, a veritable flood of publications – mostly self-help books written by marketing management gurus – has inundated bookstores to offer insistent testimony on the wisdom of attending to the co-creation of customer value through the careful management of satisfying consumption experiences.[10] Most such books celebrate the virtues and successes of (say) Starbucks, JetBlue, Nike Stores, the Hard Rock Café, or Disney World – sometimes from a dangerously retrograde perspective, as in the cases of the oft-touted Krispy Kreme or Microsoft. Although, like a few others,[11] the present author has found such managerial self-help books surprisingly supportive of satire or even parody,[12] some commentators have pushed the role of consumption experiences in the co-creation of customer value in the direction of lionization, bordering on sainthood within the marketing community.[13] Indeed, writing in *The Wall Street Journal*, Frank suggests that – in a world dominated by "Market Volatility" – "Experiences Trump Things" and "Experience Is the New Luxury".[14] In short, any reasonable observer might conclude that the service-dominated logic of designing consumption experiences that build satisfaction by delivering maximum customer value has come to dominate our conventional wisdom on how to make money in the marketplace.

Evidence: Television Commercials and Print Ads

Not surprisingly, this trend in our thinking about the role of consumption experiences in marketing has manifested itself in the appeals and themes that appear ubiquitously in various television commercials and print advertisements. In this connection, the author has amused himself over the past few years by collecting samples of experience-oriented advertising in a persistent but haphazard way. In other words, when he has seen an exemplar of an experience-oriented ad on TV, in a newspaper, or in a magazine, he has written it down or torn it out and put it in a rapidly growing file. By now, this compilation includes a large number of case examples.

Overall, the multiplicity and variety of ways that advertisers and other promotional communicators have found to brag about the consumption experiences provided by their offerings appears quite astounding. Some use the word "experience" as a simple noun attached to the name of their brand or company – as in "The ABC Experience", where ABC = JetBlue, Land Rover, the Regent, Aruba, Acatama, RCS, Verizon, or the Wyland Galleries. Others regard "experience" as a verb that urges the reader or viewer to appreciate their brand or product – as in "Experience XYZ", where XYZ = Jablum's Coffee, Coca-Cola BlaK, Ambien, Saks Fifth Avenue, Downy, Bermuda, The Caribbean, Ely, Scottsdale, Colorado, Blu, The Nocturne Grand Piano, The Dark-Ride Cymbal, Lehman Brothers, Discovery

World, The Minneapolis Metrodome, The Esplanade Senior Residence, The Village, or New York City. Still others draw upon favorite cliché-laden modifiers such as "ultimate" to praise "The Ultimate RST Experience" – where RST = JetOne, Ocean Edge Resort, *The New York Times* Travel Show, Schweitzer Bed Linens, Broadway, Southport Jazz Festival, Ralph Lauren, DollGallery.Com, or Anchorage Center. However, the number of different ways to make the same basic experience-based claim must be seen to be believed. The following classification sorts these into various product categories.

CONSUMER NONDURABLES

Drinks

Jablum Coffee from Jamaica – "Experience Jablum's Blue Mountain Coffee" and "The Coffee Experience Beyond Compare"; "Critics' Choice" Wine Tastings – "Part of the New York Wine Experience"; Coca-Cola BlaK™ – "Experience BlaK™ ... Every sip is an experience"; Geerlings & Wade (wines) – "The Vineyard Experience"; Braun Tassimo Hot Beverage System – "Experience all the irresistible hot drinks you could ever wish for"; and Gevalia Coffee – "All You Need for the Perfect Coffee Experience".

Food

Fish Farm (French gourmet foods) – "Food as pleasure ... The Experience"; and Hillshire Farm Deli Select (premium lunch meat) – "Made with special touches for a delectably different taste experience!"

Miscellaneous

Ambien (sleeping pills) – "Experience Ambien CR for yourself"; Fancy Feast (cat food) – "Experience the very latest of the very best from Fancy Feast"; Clairol's Herbal Essence (shampoo) – "Experience the intensity"; Charmin Flushable Moist Wipes – "Experience the fresher feeling"; Downy and Tide (laundry products) – "Experience Downy and Tide Clean Breeze"; Tic Tacs (breath mints) – "Entertainment for your mouth"; Vicks VapoRub – "Experience the feeling of free breathing"; Freeman Facial Clay Masque – "Experience the revitalizing benefits of organic perfection"; Lauder's Beyond Paradise for Men – "Introducing the new experience in men's fragrance"; Jean Paul Gaultier "Le Male" Fragrance – "Lift here to experience"; and Saks Fifth Avenue – "Experience Saks Fifth Avenue For Her and For Him Fragrances".

TOURISM

Airlines

JetBlue Airlines – "The JetBlue Experience"; Alitalia Airlines – "Experience Italy with Alitalia!"; American Airlines – "Experience the allure of Europe"; British Airways – "Expectation: A better business class experience"; British Airways Sleeper Service[SM] – "Experience somnia"; JetOne – "Experience Ultimate Aviation"; Singapore Airlines – "Experience the comfort of the most spacious bed in the sky"; and Air Canada – "On your next international trip, experience our new Executive First® Suite complete with lie-flat beds, personal touch-screen TVs and ambient mood lighting."

Cruises

Alaska Cruisetours – "Unparalleled Experience, Unbeatable Value!"; American Express Mariner Club – "Extraordinary cruise experience"; Blue & Gold Fleet – "Experience Blue & Gold Fleet's New Breathtaking Bay Cruise Adventure"; Celebrity Cruises – "Come experience everything that makes a Celebrity cruise a true departure"; Cunard Ocean Liners – "Celebrate the Golden Age of Ocean Travel. Better Yet, Experience It" and "Experience the majesty of the sea"; Holland American Line – "The cruise experience you've been waiting for"; Holland America's new MS *Noordam* – "A classic cruise experience"; Magellan Residential Cruise Line – "The most extraordinary residential experience ever conceived"; Princess Cruises – "Experience Europe Like Never Before!" and "Experience the Small Ships of Princess"; Regent Cruises – "Experience the World Your Way" and "What defines the Regent Experience? … your wishes satisfied and your dreams fulfilled"; and Cruise West – "Experience America's Bounty" and "Each day of your Cruise West experience is carefully planned to showcase the true essence of California or the Pacific Northwest."

Other transportation

Land Rover (SUV) – "The Land Rover Experience" and "Experience the Freedom"; Mercedes-Benz of Huntington – "Experience Luxury at Affordable Prices"; Eurail – "Enjoy … experience … explore"; and New York City "A" Train – "This is the 'A' experience to Lefferts Boulevard. Stand clear of the closing doors and have an interesting morning."

Hotels

Regent Hotels & Resorts – "The Regent Experience"; Marina Hotel – "Experience African Hospitality"; Fairmont Hotels and Resorts – "There's Only One Way to Experience Summer"; Ginn Clubs & Resorts – "Reinventing the Resort Experience"; Hyatt Regency – "Make Plans Now to Experience Hyatt Resorts Puerto Rico"; Paradise Island's Atlantis Hotel – "An Experience Like No Other" and "Reward Yourself with a Unique Experience"; Intercontinental Hotels & Resorts – "Experience Adds. Vision Multiplies"; Mandalay Bay, Las Vegas – "The Glow … 10% off your entire Mandalay Bay experience"; MGM Grand Hotel, Las Vegas – "MGM Grand Offers Maximum Food & Beverage Experience"; SummerBay Resort – "Experience Las Vegas With a Free Two Night Stay!"; Trump International Hotel & Tower – "Experience a new level of sophistication in the heart of Las Vegas"; Caesars Palace – "The Caesars Palace Dining Experience"; Mohegan Sun – "A legendary getaway experience"; Ocean Edge Resort – "Only our 400 acre seaside Resort delivers the ultimate Cape Cod experience"; Rose Hall Resort, Jamaica – "A Contemporary Resort Experience Is Coming"; Temple Tower Hotel – "Experience the Power of the Temple Tower Club … experience the glory of Rome"; The Ritz-Carlton – "Reconnect®, a unique experience by The Ritz-Carlton"; Ultimate Resort Luxury Destination Clubs – "Experience The Ultimate Vacation™ Every Time"; Renaissance Vinoy (St Petersburg) – "Experience the Legend"; and Lido Beach Grill – "Sarasota's Newest Dining Experience Featuring Regional American Cuisine With a Mediterranean Flair".

Travel destinations

Aruba – "Aruba Experience"; Bermuda – "Experience Bermuda"; The Caribbean – "Experience the Caribbean"; Blue Rush Sports Camp – "Experience the Rush!"; New York – "Slow Down, Experience the True Great City"; Los Angeles – "Experience it"; Small town in Minnesota – "Experience Ely … The Ely experience could lead to an addiction … It's the memory of the total Ely experience that will make you come back for more"; Québec – "Providing Emotions Since 1534 … a land of emotions!… Experience … vacation memories you'll cherish and adore"; Orkney Islands – "A timeless experience"; Scottsdale, Arizona – "Experience Scottsdale … Bring your passion for life"; small town in north-eastern Pennsylvania – "Enjoy the Honesdale Experience!"; Hudson Valley, New York – "Follow the River… Experience the Hudson River Valley … Discover Albany"; and Greece – "Live Your Myth in Greece … Starring You … Amazing Sights, Diverse Experiences".

Travel tours

Country Walkers – "Step into the Experience … The experience of a lifetime … To enhance your Italian experience"; Dolphin Encounters – "The Experience of a Lifetime"; DreamCycle Tours – "Experience Colorado … Experience the grandeur of cycling along the shores of Colorado's Arkansas River"; Far & Wide Tours – "Adventure … Discovery … Experience … Experience the Best of New Zealand"; Lindblad Expeditions – "Explorations … New Expeditions, Fresh Experiences"; *The New York Times* Travel Show – "Be Part of the Ultimate Travel Experience"; and Travcoa Escorted Journey's – "Request your complimentary Travcoa catalog to experience the personal touch of an Escorted Journey".

Travel books

National Geographic – "It's All About the Experience … Experiential travel and the chance to bring home not just new pictures but a new perspective is the fastest-growing trend in the industry."

CONSUMER DURABLES

Electronics

Warner Brothers Entertainment – "Experience BLU … The Look and Sound of Perfect"; Acer Home Theater – "BlueExperience"; HP Computers – "Experience it now at Circuit City"; Harvey (electronics store) – "Grand. Experience"; JVC High-Definition Television – "The Perfect Experience … JVC's HD-ILA TV is designed to fit your lifestyle – and totally change the way you experience television"; Panasonic Television – "Experience the Undeniable Power of Panasonic Plasma"; Stressless Seating – "Comfort. Defining your home theater experience"; The Home Entertainment Show – "Experience the Lifestyle"; The Jitterbug Cell Phone – " Introducing the world's simplest, cell phone experience"; Outi Earphones – "Feel the Sound! Experience the Full-Body Sensations!"; E100 from iriver – "Experience … A New Method of Viewing Photos"; myvu Crystal – "a hands-free, full-screen private viewing experience"; shades 301 – "Eyewear to experience videos up close & personal"; and Intel Centrino Atom – "The best internet experiences start with Intel inside new mobile internet devices."

Other durables

Walk-in bathtubs – "The Safer Bathing Experience"; Mason & Hamlin Pianos – "Experience the new legendary Mason & Hamlin piano"; Yamaha Digital Pianos – "Experience the Nocturne Grand"; Schweitzer (sheets and pillow cases) – "For the Ultimate Linen Experience"; Tempur-Pedic Swedish Mattresses and Pillows – "Experience the kind of sleep you've always dreamed about"; and Volvo – "Experience Europe the Volvo Way ... Take a trip overseas where your custom-built souvenir is part of an unforgettable experience."

EVENTS

Broadway

Broadway Theater Musicians – "Live Music ... Experience It!"; Broadway.yahoo.com (DVD included) – "Here's Your Ticket to the Ultimate Broadway Experience"; and Cadillac with Broadway – "Cadillac Invites You to Win the Ultimate Broadway Experience".

Shows and films

Beauty and the Beast (musical) – "'Tis the Season to Experience the Magic!"; *Showboat* (musical) – "Carnegie Hall Proudly Invites You To An Exciting One Night Only Musical Experience"; *Memory* (play) – "A Rare Theatrical Experience to Treasure"; John Patrick Shanley's *Doubt* (play) – "An experience to last you a lifetime"; *Rescue Dawn* (film) – "Experience the Incredible True Story of One Man's Journey Home"; *Spirit* (film) – "Saddle Up and Experience the Spirit of the West!"; *The Magdalene Sisters* (film) – "Experience the Year's Most Triumphant Film"; *The Diving Bell and the Butterfly* (film) – "Amazing! You won't have a more emotional experience this year ... Astonishing. A remarkably rich experience"; Sundance Online Film Festival – "To experience the passion and excitement of independent film, just bring your Wi-Fi laptop"; and WalMart – "Experience the greatest movies ever".

Jazz and pop

Jean-Luc Ponty (jazz violinist) – "The Acatama Experience"; Sheffield Jazz Recordings – "Experience the Natural Sound of Sheffield Jazz"; New Orleans Jazz & Heritage Festival – "To everyone who experienced the healing power of music at Jazz Fest 2006 New Orleans says, 'Thank You!'"; Southport Jazz Festival 2003 – "We Give You the Ultimate 4 Day Jazz Experience!"; The Artists Collective – "Experience a Jammin' Jazz Getaway"; Cannonball Saxophones – "It creates one of the most free-blowing experiences you can imagine"; Neotech Saxophone Straps – "Experience the Innovation"; Zildjian Cymbals – "Experience the Dark-Ride"; www.ejazzlines.com – "Experience the web's largest and most user-friendly catalog of jazz"; www.jazzvoyeur.com – "jazz voyeur ... the visual experience"; Mike Longo Trio (jazz piano-bass-drums) – "Looking for a toe tappin', swinging New York jazz experience?"; Legends of Jazz with Ramsey Lewis – "Experience extraordinary performances @ www.legendsofjazz.net"; Gretchen Parlato (singer) – "Experience the magic"; The Town Hall World Cabaret Series – "Experience ... the drama of German Kabarett"; Volodos (classical pianist) – "Experience Tchaikovsky's Piano Concerto like never before!"; and Jimi Hendrix (rock icon) – "Are You Experienced?"

Other events

Nintendo Games – "Experience a New Way to Play"; Bodies, the Exhibition – "Real Human Bodies, Preserved Through an Innovative Process ... Experience The Human Body Like Never Before"; Discovery World at Pier Wisconsin – "Experience Discovery World during our Year of Discovery™"; Minneapolis Metrodome – "Experience Minneapolis Metrodome"; 3D Center of Art & Photography – "We invite you to explore the rich history of stereoscopic photography and revel in a truly visual experience!"; National Geographic Channel – "Don't Just Watch TV. Experience It"; Global Extremes, Mt. Everest – "Experience the Pinnacle of Live Television"; Related Urban Development – "New Yorkers dine out as an entertainment experience"; Rita's Petting Farm – "Hands on Experience with Petting Farm Animals at Rita's Stable"; The Dutchess County Fair – "Experience a Classic"; *Walking With Dinosaurs* (presented by Immersion Edutainment) – "The Live Experience"; The Power Within (motivational speeches by William Jefferson Clinton, Michael D. Eisner, and Lance Armstrong) – "Experience the Power Within"; American Marketing Association, 2007 Winter Marketing Educators' Conference – "Creating Value through Marketing Experiences"; and American Marketing Association (again) – "Experience unparalleled discovery ... An event you have to experience to believe ... M.planet".

EDUCATION

The Teaching Company – "Experience the Power and Beauty of English"; University School Milwaukee – "The Experience for a Lifetime ... Click here to experience the many faces of USM" and "The new USM website ... now offers hundreds of new ways to view the USM experience"; New York University – "Experience ... How Has NYU Changed Since You Were a Student?"; The Columbia Business School's On-Line Course-Listing Software – "Our ongoing commitment to improving the Angel experience"; *The Wilson Quarterly* (magazine) – "Discover the writing of the world's leading thinkers ... Experience *The Wilson Quarterly*"; Hands On! (group music lessons) – "A Musical Experience"; Despair Motivational Products – "Finally, you can experience all the pain ... without the indignity"; and *Firefly Lane* (novel by Kristin Hannah) – "Share the *Firefly Lane* Experience!"

HOUSING

Extell Condominium Residences – "Experience the Extell Choice"; The Watergate (apartment building) – "Experience the Rebirth of Washington's Premier Address"; VIP Realty Group – "Experience magnificent views overlooking Southwest Florida's Gulf Coast"; The St. Regis Residence Club – "Experience the exhilaration of the U.S. Open year after year with Membership in the St. Regis Residence Club, New York"; Bald Head Island – "Experience the Exceptional Nature of ... North Carolina's Premier Second-Home Community"; Oldfield (private club community) – "To Experience It All for Yourself, Only a Personal Visit Will Do"; Esplanade Senior Residences – "Experience ... The Esplanade

Senior Residences" and "You're Invited to Experience … Esplanade"; Hyatt in Briarcliff Manor (retirement community) – "Experience Luxury Senior Living"; On Prospect Park – "Experience the absolute in New York living"; and Greg D'Angelo Construction – "Builders of Unique Relationships, Experiences and Spaces".

SHOPPING

Bricks-and-mortar stores

RCS electronics store – "RCS experience"; Verizon Stores – "The Verizon Experience"; Wyland Galleries (Sarasota) – "Wyland Galleries Experience"; Ralph Lauren Store – "The Ultimate Experience"; Design Within Reach (DWR) – "Design Is a 3-Dimensional Experience"; Gracious Home (housewares) – "Experience"; Home Depot – "Your Opinion Counts! We would like to hear about your shopping experience"; Macy's – "Experience 5-star luxury"; and Trader Joe's – "Customer Experience: A Trader Joe's Love Story".

Online shopping

DollGallery.com – "The Ultimate Collector's Experience"; Go4AllSports.com – "The Premium Sports Shopping Experience"; and ShopHop.com – "The online shopping experience!"

Shopping areas

AOL Time Warner Center – "The most exciting and elegant shopping experience in New York City"; Anchorage Center – "Grand Cayman's Ultimate Duty Free Shopping Experience"; and Old Hyde Park Village (Tampa) – "Experience the Village".

Other

Fashion & Retail Day (New York City) – "Experience NYC".

FINANCIAL SERVICES

Lehman Brothers – "Experience Lehman Brothers"; Fidelity Investments – "Experience the value of fixed-income investing at Fidelity"; Commerce Bank – "Experience America's Most Convenient Bank"; First International Bank of Israel – "You experience the traditional Private Banking of the renowned World Wide Safra Banking Group"; Winslow – "Twenty Five Years of Green Investing Experience … It's a very exciting time to be a green investor"; and Jenkins & Gilchrist (lawyers) – "The experience you deserve … the Jenkins experience".

MISCELLANEOUS SERVICES

Utilitarian

Avis – "Please Tell Us about Your Avis Experience"; and Verizon – "You're invited to experience the Internet as it was meant to be" and "Come experience Verizon High Speed Internet for yourself".

Hedonic

Exhale Spa – "Explore exceed exist exclaim experience exhale"; Deborah Thompson Day Spa – "Experience the world of Marrakech ... It will be an unforgettable spa experience"; St. Tropez Tanning Essentials – "Experience the Luxury of St. Tropez Instant Sunless Tanning"; Gurney's Inn Sea Water Spa (Montauk, New York) – "A Gurney's Group Experience ... Groups of 5+ get a Champagne Toast"; and Kanine Kleaners (Milford, Pennsylvania) – "Located in the heart of prestigious Milford, we offer the ultimate grooming experience for dogs and cats."

Other

American Red Cross – "Experience the feeling of making a difference"; and Harvard Medical International – "Outdoor activities are often part of the travel experience, but what if you get hurt or get sun poisoning?"

Memorable Consumption Experiences in the Hallowed Halls of Ivy

Although he doubts that the ploy would have been legally feasible, the present author devoutly wishes that Holbrook and Hirschman had trademarked the term "experience" when it first dawned on them as a key concept 25 years ago. At a penny or two per usage, they would have collected millions or billions of dollars by now and could be sipping frozen margaritas on the beach in Aruba – enjoying the Aruba Experience – rather than toiling in the weed-filled vineyards of academia around various inhabitant-unfriendly parts of the north-eastern United States. However, their enthusiasm for the experiential perspective stops short of endorsing certain nearly sacrilegious uses to which the concept appears to have been put as it has attracted an increasing degree of support in all areas of marketing.

In celebration of the consumption experience, the business model – entailing an enthusiastic embrace of customer orientation in the service of commercialism – has appeared in any number of situations in which, arguably, it does not belong. Conspicuous examples include churches, hospitals, museums, and prisons.[15] But – most disturbingly, as brilliantly presaged almost 100 years ago by Veblen[16] – the business model has come to dominate the strategic thinking that governs the conduct of academic institutions.[17] As asked and answered by Delbanco,

What makes the modern university different from any other corporation? ... There is more and more reason to think: less and less. Driven by big science and global competition, our top universities compete for "market share" and "brand-name positioning," employ teams of consultants and lobbyists and furnish their campuses with luxuries in order to attract paying "customers" – a word increasingly used as a synonym for students.[18]

Symptomatically, in an e-mail circulated on November 19, 2007, that epitome of business sensibilities, The Donald himself, *trump*eted the opening of his very own school:

TRUMP UNIVERSITY is something I have thought about for a long time. I didn't want to put my name on anything having to do with education unless it was going to be the best ... That's why I assembled a team of some of the finest instructors in the world ... Some of them have not gone through the traditional education system. But they have gone through these tremendous hard knocks; gone out on their own, and succeeded.

Apparently, at Trump U, those educated mostly in the "school of hard knocks" will deliver inspirational vocational training to those seeking indoctrination into the Donaldian Ethos – for a price, of course.

At a less grandiose level, one would correctly expect the business model to govern the administration of almost any school of management.[19] For example, when the MBA program at Stanford University recently redesigned its course offerings, this effort was billed as a project in which "the business school will retool the M.B.A. curriculum to provide a highly customized experience".[20] So, not surprisingly, we find that – with a little help from the demonstrably inaccurate and biased ratings published by *BusinessWeek*[21] and *U.S. News and World Report*[22] – B-schools have come to view their students as consumers who must be pleased to the max via a dedicated pursuit of the customer orientation.[23] Typically, this pursuit translates into a single-minded focus on teaching practical applications of use on the job in ways designed to maximize the starting salaries of MBA graduates. One might argue that such a focus badly distorts the essence of academic values[24] and that B-school students should more properly be viewed as channels of distribution through which knowledge is disseminated to the broader community.[25] But amidst a commercial climate rooted in self-interest or even greed, such admonitions would fall on deaf ears in ways that can only prove disappointing and frustrating.[26]

How the Mighty have Fallen

When the present author arrived at Columbia University as a fledgling MBA student in 1965, the building that housed the Graduate School of Business bore an inscription on the wall immediately adjacent to its front door and clearly visible to all who entered. This inscription presented a quote from the Harvard philosopher Alfred North Whitehead: "A great society is a society in which its men of business think greatly of their functions."

From the current perspective, we would want to amend that statement to include women as well as men. As the author recalls, there were only two female students and one woman on the faculty back in his days as an MBA at Columbia (1965–1967). Obviously, times have changed the ratio of women to men that we find in the business world and in the B-schools. This change represents a step forward and upward.

But, more to the point, all will surely agree that Whitehead's words of wisdom set a lofty standard for the guidance of business thinking and practice – a noble ideal, to which businessmen and businesswomen alike should aspire, in the direction of working toward the creation of a great society and a better way of life for all its citizens.

Today, those inspiring words of A.N. Whitehead have disappeared from the wall of the author's *alma mater* – replaced by a new entrance to a renovated building that has grown in size to accommodate an increased number of corporate recruiters. But directly inside the new entrance, approximately 20 feet from the place where the inspiring words of Whitehead once stood, hangs a banner with the School's official honor code emblazoned on it. Like the old Whitehead quotation, this banner looms large as the first thing that greets the eyes of a visitor walking into the building that houses the Columbia Business School. It reads, in part, "As a lifelong member of the Columbia Business School Community ... I will not lie, cheat, steal, or tolerate those who do."

Few can fail to notice the remarkable decline in vision that has occurred over the past 40-plus years among those who plan the architectural environment of the Business School. Thinking greatly of our business function has been replaced by not tolerating prevarication, plagiarism, or pilfering. In other words, officially and even insistently, the aspirations of the Columbia Business School have fallen from those of building a great society to those of disowning petty crimes and misdemeanors.

A fuller version of the quotation from Alfred North Whitehead, written in 1932, expands on this theme:

> *The behavior of the community is largely dominated by the business mind. A great society is a society in which its men [and women] of business think greatly of their functions. Low thoughts mean low behavior, and after a brief orgy of exploitation, low behavior means a descending standard of life.*

If low thoughts do indeed "mean low behavior", and if that in turn "means a descending standard of life", the sacrifice of aspirations toward societal greatness in the service of preventing venal aspects of dishonesty and criminality might strike some as a very poor bargain – indeed, a form of ethical and spiritual bankruptcy.

But from where, we might wonder, does such a devolution of ideals arise, and from what untoward source of strength does it gain force? Ironically enough, the answer appears to stem from the widespread adoption of a business model for running the university and a concomitant subscription among academic administrators to the well-worn principle of customer orientation.

Trouble in the Ivory Tower

To repeat a point made earlier, one might expect such a state of affairs to prevail in a business school, where commercialism in the service of the bottom line rules the day. However, far worse than the distortion of academic integrity at a business school (not all that strong to begin with), because far more insidious in corrupting the principles that formerly guided liberal education (once a noble calling), this tendency toward bottom-feeding has now usurped the value system of the university as a whole. As universities driven by a concern for financial stability increasingly embrace the business model at all levels of academic life, the customer orientation takes over, with an emphasis on the student as the primary consumer of interest and with a consequent focus on pandering to the wishes and wants of the student population. In the words of Roger Bowen at the American Association of University Professors,

> *Presidents now are C.E.O.'s ... You no longer have treasurers, you have chief financial officers; you no longer have deans, you have chief academic officers. Faculty play the role of labor, students play the role of customer.*[27]

At the undergraduate level, this shift means that catering to the lowest common denominator of student tastes tends to displace disciplined scholarly inquiry. Teachers aim to please students by amusing them and hoping for favorable student evaluations. The focus shifts from an emphasis on education to a preoccupation with entertainment or edutainment[28] in a manner analogous to the ways in which network news programs have devolved in the direction of infotainment[29] or ... less politely ... bullshit.[30] Students now spend more time on their cell phones, pagers, PDAs, iPods, laptops, and text-messaging devices than they do with their books. Research for a term paper – in those rare cases in which research still happens – now consists largely of engaging with the Internet and googling the relevant key words. If this trend toward pandering to dumbed-down, lowest-common-denominator tastes continues, the day will soon arrive when colleges will offer little more than user-generated iEducation at the iSchool.[31]

At the graduate level, mere education gives way to a focus on preparation for a lucrative career. Classroom material leans toward an emphasis on practical training with on-the-job applicability. The old-fashioned community of scholars dissolves into a pool of knowledge providers infected with the banausic trade-school ethos. Aware that consulting-based war stories now carry more credibility than serious scholarship, professors who once undertook intrinsically motivated research in the spirit of pure curiosity now gear what few studies they still conduct toward billable hours and managerial relevance.[32] Thus, business interests now dictate research priorities in ways that distort or corrupt the integrity of academic values. When consulting replaces pure scholarship, those that pay the piper call the tune. And the tune modulates ineluctably from "The Hallowed Halls of Ivy" to "Brother, Can You Spare a Dime".

General Eisenhower and the New Industrial Complex

Once a military hero in the Second World War, then the President of Columbia University, and later the President of the United States, General Dwight D. Eisenhower gave a rather dramatic and deeply moving speech on the occasion of his retirement from public office in 1961 at the height of the Cold War. Specifically, Eisenhower warned of the dangers inherent in the simultaneous unbridled growth of the "armaments industry" and the "defense establishment" or what he called the *Military–Industrial Complex*, in which "This conjunction of an immense military establishment and a large arms industry is new in the American experience": "The total influence – economic, political, even spiritual – is felt in ... its grave implications."[33] He continued,

In the councils of government, we must guard against the acquisition of unwarranted influence ... by the military-industrial complex. The potential for the disastrous rise of misplaced power exists and will persist ... Only an alert and knowledgeable citizenry can compel the proper meshing of the huge industrial and military machinery of defense with our peaceful methods, so that security and liberty may prosper together ... Disarmament, with mutual honor and confidence, is a continuing imperative. Together we must learn how to compose differences, not with arms, but with intellect and decent purpose ... As one who has witnessed the horror and the lingering sadness of war – as one who knows that another war could utterly destroy this civilization which has been so slowly and painfully built over thousands of years – I wish I could say tonight that a lasting peace is in sight.[34]

In short, Eisenhower worried that, consistent with the interests of big business in general or with those of munitions merchants and weapons manufacturers in particular, the United States had armed itself with a massive arsenal begging for deployment and a huge military machine aching to deploy it. Put simply, warfare served the interests of those governed by the underlying economic and political realities. Subsequent actions of the United States abroad appear to have confirmed the reality of the crisis that Ike so prophetically anticipated.

Not surprisingly, however ironically, we find that the US military establishment itself has embraced the much-touted service-dominated logic of marketing. Recently, *Harper's Magazine* quoted a report by the RAND Corporation's National Defense Research Institute under the title "Enlisting Madison Avenue: The Marketing Approach to Earning Popular Support in Theaters of Operation". This report contained the following specimen of military-industrial advice:

While the term brand often refers to a product name (e.g., Lexus), it is more importantly construed as a collection of perceptions in the minds of consumers (e.g., expensive, luxury, Japanese, and so on). Virtually every organization or entity has a brand identity. The U.S. military is no different ... Brand identities rarely last forever, and a given product may require a brand update to fit new competitive environments ... Products that are thought to be superior from a business standpoint but fail to meet customer needs court failure. U.S. military should seek to tailor activities around projects that meet civilian priorities. The coalition can apply a similar approach to understanding indigenous perspectives regarding use of force and tolerance of civilian casualties.[35]

In other words, if you are going to bomb, kill, and maim local residents, try to do so in a way that meets "customer needs" and "civilian priorities".

With that dismal story as a background, it now appears wise to worry about the advent of a second crisis that we might refer to as the *Industrial–Educational Complex* – namely, the manner in which an adoption of the business model by universities, an embrace of customer orientation, a redefinition of students as consumers, a dedication to improving the consumption experiences of these student customers, a focus on the promotion of graduate careers, an embrace of the trade-school ethos, a rush toward the apotheosis of practical knowledge in the service of business interests, an acceptance of practitioner-targeted applied consultancy as a substitute for curiosity-inspired basic research, and a resulting distortion of academic values have led toward the corruption of scholarship and the devolution of education in the direction of commercialized edutainment and intellectual dereliction.[36] Thus, in a less famous but equally profound portion of his speech, perhaps drawing on insights gained in his former role as the President of Columbia University, Eisenhower added,

> *The free university, historically the fountainhead of free ideas and scientific discovery, has experienced a revolution in the conduct of research. Partly because of the huge costs involved, a government contract [or, we might add, a consulting opportunity] becomes virtually a substitute for intellectual curiosity ... The prospect of domination of the nation's scholars by ... the power of money is ever present ... and is gravely to be regarded.*[37]

Students as Shoppers

At some schools, the first few days of each term are referred to as the *shopping period* because at these times the administration invites students to wander aimlessly from class to class, trying to decide which course offerings they find most appealing and ultimately voting with their feet or, more accurately, with their rear ends. Any teacher who has endured the unpredictable ebb and flow of students roaming in herds in and out of early-term classes, with no sense of who is or is not a class member until deep into the syllabus, cannot have failed to notice the sad appropriateness of the *shopping analogy*.

Even so, a surprisingly vivid illustration of the dangers inherent in the Industrial–Educational Complex arrived in this author's e-mail in-box during the Fall semester of 2007. Specifically, by coincidence, two communications appeared in directly adjacent positions in the in-box, almost as if they had been sent by one guiding hand at precisely the same moment – which, in a way, they had.

The first of these two messages came from the *online shopping network* found on the World Wide Web at www.shop.com. This venture in e-commerce explained shop.com's desire to improve the quality of the *shopping experience* at its online website and invited the recipient of the e-mail to participate in a *survey* designed to develop guidelines for the improvement of *shopper satisfaction*.

The second message came from the Dean of Students at *a major graduate school of business* (which will remain anonymous). This dean explained his or her school's desire to improve the quality of the *student experience* at the relevant academic institution and invited the recipient of the e-mail to participate in a *survey* designed to develop guidelines for the improvement of *student satisfaction*.

Thus, the language of the two e-messages was almost indistinguishable. Message Number One began (with shaky grammar):

> *Dear Morris Holbrook ... As a customer on SHOP.COM, we value your feedback and would greatly appreciate your opinions on improving the shopping experience we provide to our customers.*

The message continued by describing the deployment of "an outside independent market research firm". It concluded with an appeal to participate in "a survey to better understand how we're doing in your eyes": "The survey questionnaire is online and may be accessed at any hour, day or night, using the link below and should take you about 20–25 minutes to complete."

Concomitantly to an amazing degree, Message Number Two began:

Dear [Addressees] ... I want to update you on the progress that we are making to improve [the school's] student experience – a topic that remains top of mind for the administration – and to request your help by providing feedback on ideas that we have generated over the past months. With your support, we can address student needs ... and contribute to how the School is perceived.

The message continued by describing "past student satisfaction surveys"; the deployment of a "strategy consulting firm ... to assist us"; and the school's dedication to "identifying customer needs and maximizing customer satisfaction" so as to develop "initiatives that could enhance the overall ... student experience". It concluded with an appeal to participate in "a short, 15- to 20-minute online survey" intended to "help us obtain a clear perspective on which of these initiatives ... will have the greatest positive impact on the student experience while at [the school] and beyond": "Once we have analyzed the results of the survey, we will begin implementing the initiatives that have the highest likelihood of improving student satisfaction." Shortly thereafter, this follow-up message arrived:

A few days ago I requested your help in providing feedback on ... an initiative to improve the student experience ... Our work included a review and analysis of the student satisfaction surveys ... We also enlisted the support of [a] strategy consulting firm ... Together, we developed a comprehensive list of potential initiatives that address ... the student experience ... Therefore, we request your participation in a short 20-minute survey by clicking on the link below.

Hot Hot Hot? Not Not Not!

The author's shock at discovering that the principles and procedures guiding the design of academic programs in at least one major business school follow a logic directly analogous to those that govern the appeal of an online shopping network recalls his far more bemused response to an apparently tongue-in-cheek promotional pitch that has attracted considerable attention on www.youtube.com – namely, the promo film for Appalachian State University entitled "Hot Hot Hot". This hilariously funny masterpiece of absurdity presents a high-tech theme song – complete with stirring appeals, panoramic visuals, a jazz orchestra, and a gospel choir – to advertise the benefits of attending ASU, where the essence of those benefits emerges with delicious satirical force as ... being cool and having fun. To quote the author's comments, posted on youtube.com,

Surely, in representing Appalachian State University, "Hot Hot Hot" instantiates the near-definitive postmodern masterpiece – an ironic, paradoxical, reflexive, self-parody – that brilliantly exposes the fallacies of regarding the university as a business and selling education like toothpaste or laundry detergent.

Every time the author watches this superb video, he collapses in helpless laughter. But he also recognizes a dark side to his mirth – namely, the deep sense that "Hot Hot Hot" at ASU profoundly reflects a widespread state of affairs in which the supremacy of the student's consumption experience over the university's intellectual mission will soon obliterate the community of scholars, the dedication to inquisitive learning, the integrity of academic values, the devotion to knowledge for its own sake, and other worthwhile goals that once shaped the educational mission but that have now succumbed to the quest for customer satisfaction in the form of favorable course evaluations, flattering magazine rankings, hefty consulting fees, lucrative career opportunities, and supportive student surveys. If this manifestation of the Industrial–Educational Complex continues to grow at its present rate, we shall soon find ourselves in a position where the view of education as a sort of glorified shopping experience in which the student as customer is king is all we've "Got Got Got."

For serious scholars who still care about the mission of the university and the integrity of its academic values, the time has come to be afraid. Very afraid. Ideally but improbably, the woeful if amusing example of ASU on youtube.com should evoke cries of "Not Not Not!"

Ivory Towers, Halls of Ivy, and the Branding of B-schools

One illustrative case of the dangers inherent in adopting the business model, pursuing a customer orientation, and treating students like consumers appears in the fretted efforts of the author's own school to forge its way in the highly competitive B-school marketplace by creating a new *brand identity*, *image*, and/or *reputation*.[38] We must admit that it makes some kind of tortured sense to regard a school's name as a sort of brand, comparable (say) to Crest toothpaste or Buick automobiles or Dell computers or Starbucks coffee.[39] And where we find brand names, we also find the tempting possibility of building *brand equity* – which, as appreciated by every devout disciple of Aaker[40] or Keller[41] – is another way of referring to financial benefits above and beyond those that an offering actually deserves by virtue of its quality or performance.[42] What self-respecting business school would not want to reap the lucrative payoffs from a high-profile, large-equity, crowd-pleasing, profit-maximizing *brand identity*?

So the brand-identity gurus with names like Gardner Nelson & Partners, Pentagram, and Fleishman Hillard moved into the author's school and worked with its staff to conduct focus groups, to think long and prayerfully about the school's meaning in the marketplace, and ultimately to decide on a new school logo. This new logo – featured at gsb.columbia.edu – retains the old mascot in the form of the Greek God Hermes, as represented by an insignia in the shape of the number four with a couple of horizontal lines through its lower stem. But the former name of the Graduate School of Business at Columbia University has now been officially transformed to "Columbia Business School" or, for short, "CBS".

As explained by the school's image-promoting alumni magazine:

This modern interpretation of the Hermes icon paired with a stronger and cleaner typeface for the Columbia Business School wordmark is designed to reflect the School's identity in the early 21st century ... The new logo is the visible symbol of Columbia Business School's commitment to strengthening its identity among students, faculty members and alumni, to showing the business world who we are and to fostering pride and ownership in the School's success.[43]

We might applaud the decision to retain Hermes as the CBS mascot and to keep the strange-looking four as the school's insignia. As recommended by Shimp[44] in borrowing from the work of Rescorla,[45] this unusual-looking symbol rarely if ever occurs in nature and should therefore be easy to associate with the school's name and its relevant connotations by virtue of the usual mechanisms of classical conditioning (frequent pairing together in advertising and other promotional materials). In this sense, the Hermes insignia resembles the Nike swoosh, which was also rarely encountered in nature until Michael Jordan and his celebrity friends got hold of it.

Furthermore, Hermes and his four-shaped insignia carry many favorable associations that could well bolster the image of the school and enhance the equity of its brand name. For example, as the Greek god of trade, commerce, and travel, Hermes suggests highly favorable connotations in the context of a business school with a focus on global enterprise.[46] Also, when turned on its side, the Hermes insignia resembles the skeleton of a fish – clearly an attractive emblem to students from Japan and other cultures where fish is a main staple in the diet or to others who happen to be hungry for a taste of seafood. Moreover, Hermes reminds us of the French retailer Hermès, noted for the high quality of its offerings, not to mention its expensive prices.[47] In addition, Hermes and his Roman equivalent Mercury lend their image to the FTD Flower Company, noted for rapid delivery of beautiful offerings. Beyond that, as messenger to the gods, Hermes gave his name to the field of hermeneutics, thereby evoking associations with communication and human understanding. Also, Hermes invented the lyre or harp and/or the panpipe or flute.[48] And, to top it all off, the Hermes insignia bears some resemblance to the caduceus symbol (search for "caduseus" on images.google.com) – the icon that stands for integrity in medicine, as represented by the Hippocratic Oath.[49]

True, we might notice that Hermes and his strange-looking four-shaped insignia also evoke certain potentially embarrassing negative associations. For example, besides representing trade, commerce, and travel in Greek mythology, Hermes also served as the patron of thieves and as the god of trickery and deception.[50] His associations with the number four remind many Asian students (Japanese, Chinese, Korean) of "death", a homophone of "four" in the languages of those countries. Several Asian students have complained to the author that they experience fear and trepidation whenever they see the four-shaped Hermes emblem. Such students often like the association of the rotated insignia with fish. But to Americans, the term "fishy" carries strong negative implications. Also, to southern Americans, who count "one", "two", "three", and then "foe", the number four recalls the concept of a dangerous enemy. Indeed, in Greek mythology, Hermes served as "the conductor of the dead to Hades"[51] – which means that when Hermes takes your hand, you know you are going straight to Hell.

On balance, we suppose, the positive associations of Hermes and his quadruplicitous insignia evoke an overall favorable pattern of associations with the Columbia Business School – especially among Greek-speaking, non-southern born-again Americans with a flair for French fashions. But what are we to make of transforming the school's name from "The Graduate School of Business at Columbia University" to simply "Columbia Business School" with its inevitable contraction to "CBS"? Is this new name in any way distinctive? Apparently not, because it corresponds exactly to the call letters of a famous and oft-mentioned American television network, as well as mirroring the well-known abbreviation of the Copenhagen Business School. Does the association of "CBS" with the Columbia Broadcasting System carry favorable connotations? Probably not, because the fortunes of the CBS network have fallen in recent years, especially among those not addicted to reality shows (*Survivor*, *Big Brother*, *The Amazing Race*) or to programs that celebrate the investigation of crime scenes in Las Vegas, Miami, and New York City (the *CSI* series). Does it make sense to downplay the erstwhile strong association with Columbia University as a whole? Perhaps not, given that the larger University – with all its celebrated history, famous graduates, Nobel Prize-winning faculty, and so forth – doubtless has a more favorable image than its Business School. Trading a name that identifies a school as "The Graduate School of Business at Columbia University" for an abbreviated but ungrammatical "Columbia Business School," with strong associations to the "CBS" television network (plus the leading B-school in Denmark) rather than to Columbia University, might strike some observers as trading down rather than trading up.

But far more important than any such minor quibbles with taste or style, the effort invested in transforming the brand identity and corporate logo of Columbia Business School impresses the author as a misplaced attempt to import the business model into an academic environment where, arguably, it does not belong. Tinkering with the brand identity of an institution once regarded as a fine graduate school at a major ivy league university and converting it into something that sounds like a branch of an unpopular but entertainment-oriented television network seems to pursue a customer orientation that panders to the student's memorable consumption experiences in ways that reduce education to something resembling toothpaste, soda pop, or laundry detergent. When Appalachian State University did this in a tongue-in-cheek video called "Hot Hot Hot", it seemed funny and even inspired in a postmodern, irony-laden, reflexively self-parodic sort of way. When the author's own school does it in a manner that evokes the ethos of commercialism misapplied to higher education, it seems dangerous, sad, and deeply threatening to the integrity of academic values.

Conclusions

Sometimes, it would seem, the quest for producing memorable consumption experiences can go too far. Despite the service-dominated logic of experience-based, co-created customer value that has swept the world of marketing in recent times, a university should not be viewed as a factory for the fabrication of useful facts and figures. However pleasing to its potential customers, a school should not be regarded as a career-oriented job-recruiting service. A professor should not be seen as a knowledge provider devoted to vocational training in the manner of a trade school. And a student should not be treated as an experience-collecting consumer but rather should be honored as one participant in a channel of distribution for the creation and dissemination of new knowledge to the community in general and to the world of business in particular.

In the last analysis, education differs from commerce in important ways. Anything that distorts the truly education-oriented perspective in the direction of a commercialized business model brings dishonor to the hallowed halls of ivy and diminishes the intellectual integrity of the scholars who reside in the ivory tower. Finding a snappier logo for the halls of ivy or tinkering with the brand identity of the ivory tower cannot disguise the fact that, in the process, we have sacrificed something sacred that deserved protection. Long after the student-consumers have forgotten their supposedly memorable consumption experiences in the hot-hot-hot world of edutainment at the service of career objectives, this incalculable loss will endure.

Notes

1. Holbrook, Morris B. and Hirschman, Elizabeth C. (1982), "The experiential aspects of consumption: consumer fantasies, feelings, and fun", *Journal of Consumer Research*, Vol. 9 (September), pp. 132–40. See also Hirschman, Elizabeth C. and Holbrook, Morris B. (1982), "Hedonic consumption: emerging concepts, methods, and propositions", *Journal of Marketing*, Vol. 46 (Summer), pp. 92–101; Holbrook, Morris B. (1987), "O, consumer, how you've changed: some radical reflections on the roots of consumption", in F. Firat, N. Dholakia, and R. Bagozzi (eds.), *Philosophical and Radical Thought in Marketing*, D.C. Heath, Lexington, MA, pp. 156–77; Holbrook, Morris B. (1995), *Consumer Research: Introspective Essays on the Study of Consumption*, Sage, Thousand Oaks, CA; Holbrook, Morris B. (2006), "Consumption experience, customer value, and subjective personal introspection: an illustrative photographic essay", *Journal of Business Research*, Vol. 59, No. 6, pp. 714–25; Holbrook, Morris B. (2008), "Consumers just wanna have fantasies, feelings, and fun!!", in B. Mittal (ed.), *Consumer Behavior: How Humans Think, Feel, and Act in the Marketplace*, Open Mentis, Cincinnati, OH, pp. 653–58.

2. Woods, Walter A. (1981), *Consumer Behavior*, North Holland, New York.

3. Alderson, Wroe (1957), *Marketing Behavior and Executive Action*, Irwin, Homewood, IL.

4. Abbott, Lawrence (1955), *Quality and Competition*, Columbia University Press, New York.

5. Norris, Ruby Turner (1941), *The Theory of Consumer's Demand*, Yale University Press, New Haven, CT.

6. Keynes, John Maynard ([1936] 1964), *The General Theory of Employment, Interest, and Money*, Harcourt, Brace & World, New York.

7. Marshall, Alfred [1920] 1961), *Principles of Economics*, 8th edition, Macmillan, New York.

8. Smith, Adam ([1776] 1937), *An Inquiry into the Nature and Causes of the Wealth of Nations*, The Modern Library, New York. See also Holbrook, Morris B. (1994a), "Pursuing happiness: American consumers in the twentieth century", *Journal of Macromarketing*, Vol. 14 (Spring), pp. 83–8; Lebergott, Stanley (1993), *Pursuing Happiness: American Consumers in the Twentieth Century*, Princeton University Press, Princeton, NJ.

9. LaSalle, Diana and Britton, Terry A. (2002), *Priceless: Turning Ordinary Products into Extraordinary Experiences*, Harvard Business School, Boston, MA.

10. Arussy, Lior (2002), *The Experience! How to Wow Your Customers and Create a Passionate Workplace*, CMP Books, San Francisco, CA; Carbone, Lewis P. (2004), *Clued In: How to Keep Customers Coming Back Again and Again*, Prentice Hall, Upper Saddle River, NJ; Honebein, Peter C. and Cammarano, Roy F. (2005), *Creating Do-It-Yourself Customers: How Great Customer Experiences Build Great Companies*, Thomson, Mason, OH; LaSalle and Britton, *Priceless*; Milligan, Andy and Smith, Shaun (2002), *Uncommon Practice: People Who Deliver a Great Brand Experience*, Pearson Education, London; Pine, B. Joseph, II and Gilmore, James H. (1998), "Welcome to the experience economy", *Harvard Business Review* (July/August), pp. 97–105; Pine, B. Joseph, II and Gilmore, James H. (1999), *The Experience Economy: Work Is Theatre and Every Business a Stage*, Harvard Business School Press, Boston, MA; Samuel, Larry (2003), *The Trend Commandments™: Turning Cultural Fluency into Marketing Opportunity*, Bang! Zoom! Books, New York; Schmitt, Bernd (2003), *Customer Experience Management: A Revolutionary Approach to Connecting with Your Customers*, John Wiley & Sons, Hoboken, NJ; Schmitt, Bernd

H. (1999), *Experiential Marketing: How to Get Customers to Sense, Feel, Think, Act, and Relate to Your Company and Brands*, Free Press, New York; Schmitt, Bernd H., Rogers, David L., and Vrotsos, Karen (2003), *There's No Business That's Not Show Business: Marketing in an Experience Culture*, Prentice Hall, Upper Saddle River, NJ; Shaw, Colin and Ivens, John (2002), *Building Great Customer Experiences*, Palgrave Macmillan, Basingstoke; Smith, Shaun and Wheeler, Joe (2002), *Managing the Customer Experience: Turning Customers into Advocates*, Prentice Hall, London; Tisch, Jonathan M. with Weber, Karl (2007), *Chocolates on the Pillow Aren't Enough: Reinventing the Customer Experience*, John Wiley & Sons, Hoboken, NJ.

11.   Brown, Stephen (2003), *Free Gift Inside!! Forget the Customer. Develop Marketease*, Capstone, Oxford.

12.   Holbrook, Morris B. (2000), "The millennial consumer in the texts of our times: experience and entertainment", *Journal of Macromarketing*, Vol. 20, No. 2, pp. 178–92; Holbrook, Morris B. (2006), "The consumption experience – something new, something old, something borrowed, something sold: part 1", *Journal of Macromarketing*, Vol. 26, No. 2, pp. 259–66; Holbrook, Morris B. (2007), "The consumption experience – something new, something old, something borrowed, something sold: part 2", *Journal of Macromarketing*, Vol. 27, No. 1, pp. 86–96; Holbrook, Morris B. (2007), "The consumption experience – something new, something old, something borrowed, something sold: part 3", *Journal of Macromarketing*, Vol. 27, No. 2, pp. 173–83; Holbrook, Morris B. (2007), "The consumption experience – something new, something old, something borrowed, something sold: part 4", *Journal of Macromarketing*, Vol. 27, No. 3, pp. 303–19.

13.   Holbrook, "Consumption experience, customer value, and subjective personal introspection"; Holbrook, Morris B. (1994), "Axiology, aesthetics, and apparel: some reflections on the old school tie", in M.R. DeLong and A.M. Fiore (eds.), *Aesthetics of Textiles and Clothing: Advancing Multi-Disciplinary Perspectives*, ITAA Special Publication #7, International Textile and Apparel Association, Monument, CO, pp. 131–41; Holbrook, Morris B. (1994), "The nature of customer value: an axiology of services in the consumption experience", in R.T. Rust and R.L. Oliver (eds.), *Service Quality: New Directions in Theory and Practice*, Sage, Thousand Oaks, CA, pp. 21–71; Holbrook, Morris B. (1999), "Introduction to consumer value", in M.B. Holbrook (ed.), *Consumer Value: A Framework for Analysis and Research*, Routledge, London, pp. 1–28; Holbrook, Morris B. (2005), "Customer value and autoethnography: subjective personal introspection and the meanings of a photograph collection", *Journal of Business Research*, Vol. 58, No. 1, pp. 45–61; Holbrook, Morris B. (2006), "ROSEPEKICECIVECI versus CCV – the resource-operant, skills-exchanging, performance-experiencing, knowledge-informed, competence-enacting, coproducer-involved, value-emerging, customer-interactive view of marketing versus the concept of customer value: 'I can get it for you wholesale'", in R.F. Lusch and S.L. Vargo (eds.), *The Service-Dominant Logic of Marketing: Dialog, Debate, and Directions*, M.E. Sharpe, Armonk, NY, pp. 208–23; Holbrook, Morris B. (1999), *Consumer Value – A Framework for Analysis and Research*, Routledge, London; Vargo, Stephen L. and Lusch, Robert F. (2004), "Evolving to a new dominant logic of marketing", *Journal of Marketing*, Vol. 68, No. 1, pp. 1–17; Lusch, Robert F. and Vargo, Stephen L. (2006), *The Service-Dominant Logic of Marketing: Dialog, Debate, and Directions*, M.E. Sharpe, Armonk, NY.

14.   Frank, Robert (2007), "When enough is enough", *The Wall Street Journal*, 21 December, p. W2.

15.   Brown, *Free Gift Inside!!*; Friedman, Richard A. (2006), "Well served as patients, dissatisfied as customers", *The New York Times*, January 3, p. F7; Holbrook, Morris B. (1995), "An American in praxis: the authority of the consumer", *Irish Marketing Review*, Vol. 8, pp. 143–6; Holbrook, Morris B. (1995), "The four faces of commodification in the development of

marketing knowledge", *Journal of Marketing Management*, Vol. 11, No. 7, pp. 641–54; Holbrook, Morris B. (1999), "Higher than the bottom line: reflections on some recent macromarketing literature", *Journal of Macromarketing*, Vol. 19 (June), pp. 48–74; Holbrook, Morris B. (2001), "The millennial consumer in the texts of our times: exhibitionism", *Journal of Macromarketing*, Vol. 21, No. 1, pp. 81–95; Holbrook, Morris B. (2001), "The millennial consumer in the texts of our times: evangelizing", *Journal of Macromarketing*, Vol. 21, No. 2, pp. 181–98; Holbrook, Morris B. (2001), "Times Square, Disneyphobia, HegeMickey, The Ricky Principle, and the downside of the entertainment economy: it's fun-dumb-mental", *Marketing Theory*, Vol. 1 (December), pp. 139–63; Holbrook, Morris B. (2005), "Living it up in Twitchell's branded nation: which way to the egress?", *Journal of Macromarketing*, Vol. 25, No. 2, pp. 233–41; Keat, Russell, Whiteley, Nigel, and Abercrombie, Nicholas (1994), *The Authority of the Consumer*, Routledge, London; Twitchell, James B. (2004), *Branded Nation: The Marketing of Megachurch, College, Inc., and Museumworld*, Simon & Schuster, New York; Twitchell, James B. (2007), *Shopping for God: How Christianity Went from In Your Heart to In Your Face*, Simon & Schuster, New York; Zepp, Ira G., Jr (1997), *The New Religious Image of Urban America: The Shopping Mall As Ceremonial Center*, 2nd edition, University Press of Colorado, Niwot.

16. Veblen, Thorstein (1918), *Higher Learning in America*, Transaction, New Brunswick, NJ.

17. Anders, George (2007), "Business schools forgetting missions?", *The Wall Street Journal*, September 26, p. A2; Aronowitz, Stanley (2000), *The Knowledge Factory: Dismantling the Corporate University and Creating True Higher Learning*, Beacon Press, Boston, MA; Bok, Derek (1982), *Beyond the Ivory Tower: Social Responsibilities of the Modern University*, Harvard University Press, Cambridge, MA; Bok, Derek (2003), *Universities in the Marketplace: The Commercialization of Higher Education*, Princeton University Press, Princeton, NJ; Crainer, Stuart and Dearlove, Des (1999), *Gravy Training: Inside the Business of Business Schools*, Jossey-Bass, San Francisco, CA; Delbanco, Andrew (2007), "Academic business: has the modern university become just another corporation?", *The New York Times Magazine*, September 30, pp. 25–30; Engell, James and Dangerfield, Anthony (2005), *Saving Higher Education in the Age of Money*, University of Virginia Press, Charlottesville; Fulton, Oliver (1994), "Consuming education," in R. Keat, N. Whiteley, and N. Abercrombie (eds.), *The Authority of the Consumer*, Routledge, London, pp. 223–39; Gabor, Andrea (2008), "Lessons for business schools", *strategy+business*, Vol. 50, pp. 111–17; Gould, Eric (2003), *The University in a Corporate Culture*, Yale University Press, New Haven, CT; Holbrook, Morris B. (1989), "Aftermath of the task force: dogmatism and catastrophe in the development of marketing thought", *President's Column, ACR Newsletter* (September), pp. 1–11; Holbrook, Morris B. (2004), "Book review – *Universities in the Marketplace: The Commercialization of Higher Education* by Derek Bok", *Journal of Macromarketing*, Vol. 24, No. 2, pp. 68–74; Holbrook, Morris B. (2004), "Gratitude in graduate MBA attitudes: re-examining the BusinessWeek poll", *Journal of Education for Business*, Vol. 80, No. 1, pp. 25–8; Holbrook, Morris B. (2005), "Marketing education as bad medicine for society: the gorilla dances", *Journal of Public Policy & Marketing*, Vol. 24, No. 1, pp. 143–5; Holbrook, Morris B. (2006), "Does marketing need reform school? On the misapplication of marketing to the education of marketers", in J.N. Sheth and R.S. Sisodia (eds.), *Does Marketing Need Reform? Fresh Perspectives on the Future*, M.E. Sharpe, Armonk, NY, pp. 265–9; Holbrook, Morris B. (2007), "Five phases in a personal journey through the troubled waters of academic values in a world of business: where's the beef?", *Journal of Public Policy & Marketing*, Vol. 26, No. 1, pp. 135–8; Holbrook, Morris B. (2008), "Compromise is so … compromised: Goldilocks, go home", *European Business Review*, Vol. 20, No. 6, pp. 570–78; Holbrook, Morris B. and Day, Ellen (1994), "Reflections on jazz and teaching: Benny and Gene, Woody and We", *European Journal of Marketing*,

Vol. 28, No. 8/9, pp. 133–44; Holbrook, Morris B. and Hulbert, James M. (2002), "What do we produce in the 'knowledge factory' and for whom? A review essay of *The Knowledge Factory* by Stanley Aronowitz", *Journal of Consumer Affairs*, Vol. 36, No. 1, pp. 99–114; Holmberg, David (2007), "Student evaluations", *The New York Times Magazine*, July 1, p. 18; Khurana, Rakesh (2007), *From Higher Aims to Hired Hands: The Social Transformation of American Business Schools and the Unfulfilled Promise of Management as a Profession*, Princeton University Press, Princeton, NJ; Kirp, David L. (2003), *Shakespeare, Einstein, and the Bottom Line: The Marketing of Higher Education*, Harvard University Press, Cambridge, MA; Lee, Felicia R. (2003), "Academic industrial complex", *The New York Times*, 6 September, www.wehaitians.com/the%20acade mic%20industrial%20complex.html (accessed November 2, 2007); Lewis, Harry R. (2006), *Excellence Without a Soul: How a Great University Forgot Education*, PublicAffairs, New York, NY; Newfield, Christopher (2003), *Ivy and Industry: Business and the Making of the American University, 1880–1980*, Duke University Press, Durham, NC; Readings, Bill (1996), *The University in Ruins*, Harvard University Press, Cambridge, MA; Sacks, Peter (1996), *Generation X Goes to College: An Eye-Opening Account of Teaching in Postmodern America*, Open Court, Chicago, IL; Rotfeld, Herbert Jack (2001), "Misplaced marketing: when marketing misplaces the benefits of education", *Journal of Consumer Marketing*, Vol. 16, No. 5, pp. 415–17; Shumar, Wesley (1997), *College for Sale: A Critique of the Commodification of Higher Education*, Falmer, London; Sykes, Charles J. (1988), *ProfScam: Professors and the Defense of Higher Education*, Regnery Gateway, Washington, DC; Twitchell, *Branded Nation*.

18. Delbanco, "Academic business", p. 26.

19. Anders, "Business schools forgetting missions?"; Crainer and Dearlove, *Gravy Training*; Gabor, "Lessons for business schools"; Holbrook, "Aftermath of the task force"; Holbrook, "Living it up in Twitchell's branded nation"; Holbrook, "Does marketing need reform school?"; Holbrook, "Five phases in a personal journey through the troubled waters of academic values"; Khurana, *From Higher Aims to Hired Hands*; Rotfeld, "Misplaced marketing"; Sykes, *ProfScam*.

20. Alsop, Ronald (2006), "Stanford offers custom classes for its students", *The Wall Street Journal*, October 10, p. B8.

21. Holbrook, Morris B. (1993), "Gratitudes and latitudes in M.B.A. attitudes: customer orientation and the BusinessWeek poll", *Marketing Letters*, Vol. 4, No. 3, pp. 267–78.

22. Finder, Alan (2007), "College ratings race roars on despite concerns", *The New York Times*, August 17, p. A16; Holbrook, Morris B. (2007), "Objective characteristics, subjective evaluations, and possible distorting biases in the business-school rankings: the case of U.S. News & World Report", *Marketing Education Review*, Vol. 17, No. 2, pp. 1–12.

23. Argenti, Paul (2000), "Branding B-schools: reputation management for MBA programs", *Corporate Reputation Review*, Vol. 3, No. 2, pp. 171–8.

24. AMA Task Force on the Development of Marketing Thought (1988), "Developing, disseminating, and utilizing marketing knowledge", *Journal of Marketing*, Vol. 52, No. 4, pp. 1–25; Holbrook, Morris B. (1985), "Why business is bad for consumer research: the three bears revisited", in E.C. Hirschman and M.B. Holbrook (eds.), *Advances in Consumer Research*, Vol. 12, Association for Consumer Research, Provo, UT, pp. 145–56; Holbrook, Morris B. (1990), "Holbrook's reply to Pechmann: prelude and poem", *ACR Newsletter* (September), p. 4; Holbrook, Morris B. (1993), "Comments on the report of the AMA Task Force on the development of marketing thought", in P.R. Varadarajan and A. Menon (eds.), *Enhancing Knowledge Development in Marketing: Perspectives and Viewpoints*, American Marketing Association, Chicago, IL, pp. 19–23; Holbrook, Morris B. (1998), "The dangers of educational and cultural populism: three vignettes on the problems of aesthetic insensitivity, the pitfalls of pandering, and the

virtues of artistic integrity", *Journal of Consumer Affairs*, Vol. 32, No. 2, pp. 394–423; Holbrook, "The four faces of commodification in the development of marketing knowledge"; Holbrook, "Book review – *Universities in the Marketplace*"; Holbrook, "Five phases in a personal journey through the troubled waters of academic values"; Holbrook and Day, "Reflections on jazz and teaching".

25. Holbrook, "Consumption experience, customer value, and subjective personal introspection"; Holbrook and Hulbert, "What do we produce in the 'knowledge factory' and for whom?"

26. Holbrook, "Marketing education as bad medicine for society"; Holbrook, "Compromise is so … compromised".

27. Quoted in Glater, Jonathan D. (2006), "Pay packages for presidents are rising at public colleges," *The New York Times*, November 20, p. A16.

28. Holbrook, "The dangers of educational and cultural populism"; Holbrook and Day, "Reflections on jazz and teaching".

29. Postman, Neil (1985), *Amusing Ourselves to Death: Public Discourse in the Age of Show Business*, Penguin, New York.

30. Frankfurt, Harry G. (2005), *On Bullshit*, Princeton University Press, Princeton, NJ: Holbrook, Morris B. (2005), "Marketing miseducation and the MBA mind: bullshit happens", *Marketing Education Review*, Vol. 15, No. 3, pp. 1–5.

31. Elliott, Stuart (2007), "For many campaigns, the little i's have it", *The New York Times*, August 10, p. C6.

32. Holbrook, "Why business is bad for consumer research"; Holbrook, "Aftermath of the task force"; Holbrook, "Holbrook's reply to Pechmann"; Holbrook, "Comments on the report of the AMA Task Force on the development of marketing thought"; Holbrook, "The four faces of commodification in the development of marketing knowledge"; Holbrook, "Marketing education as bad medicine for society"; Holbrook, "Five phases in a personal journey through the troubled waters of academic values; Holbrook, "Compromise is so … compromised"; Holbrook, Morris B. (1986), "The place of marketing research on the business–research continuum", in J. Guiltinan and D. Achabal (eds.), *Proceedings, Winter Educators' Conference*, American Marketing Association, Chicago, IL, pp. 11–15; Holbrook, Morris B. (1986), "Whither ACR? Some pastoral reflections on bears, Baltimore, baseball, and resurrecting consumer research," in R.L. Lutz (ed.), *Advances in Consumer Research*, Vol. 13, Association for Consumer Research, Provo, UT, pp. 436–41; Holbrook, Morris B. (1987), "What *is* consumer research?", *Journal of Consumer Research*, Vol. 14 (June), pp. 128–32; Holbrook, Morris B. (1987), "What *is* marketing research?", in R.W. Belk and G. Zaltman (eds.), *Proceedings, Winter Educators' Conference*, American Marketing Association, Chicago, IL, pp. 214–16.

33. Eisenhower, Dwight D. (1961), "Military-industrial speech", coursesa.matrix.msu.edu/~hst306/documents/indust.html (accessed November 2, 2007).

34. Ibid.

35. *Harper's Magazine* (2007), "Target audience", Vol. 315 (1890, November), pp. 21–2, at p. 22.

36. Lee, "Academic industrial complex".

37. Eisenhower, "Military-industrial speech".

38. *Hermes* (2007), "Columbia Business School: honoring the past, the school introduces a new visual identity for the 21st century", (Summer), pp. 12–15.

39. Argenti, "Branding B-schools".

40. Aaker, David A. (1991), *Managing Brand Equity: Capitalizing on the Value of a Brand Name*, Free Press, New York; Jevons, Colin (2006), "Universities: a prime example of branding going wrong", *Journal of Product & Brand Management*, Vol. 15, No. 7, pp. 466–7.

41. Keller, Kevin Lane (1998), *Strategic Brand Management: Building, Measuring and Managing Brand Equity*, Prentice Hall, Upper Saddle River, NJ.

42. Bello, David C. and Holbrook, Morris B. (1995), "Does an absence of brand equity generalize across product classes?", *Journal of Business Research*, Vol. 34 (October), pp. 125–31; Holbrook, Morris B. (1992), "Product quality, attributes, and brand name as determinants of price: the case of consumer electronics", *Marketing Letters*, Vol. 3, No. 1, pp. 71–83.

43. Herm*es*, "Columbia Business School", pp. 13, 15.

44. Shimp, Terence A. (1991), "Neo-Pavlovian conditioning and its implications for consumer theory and research", in T.S. Robertson and H.H. Kassarjian (eds.), *Handbook of Consumer Behavior*, Prentice Hall, Englewood Cliffs, NJ, pp. 162–87.

45. Rescorla, Robert A. (1988), "Pavlovian conditioning: it's not what you think it is", *American Psychologist*, Vol. 43 (March), pp. 151–60.

46. Herm*es*, "Columbia Business School", p. 13.

47. Ibid., p. 13.

48. Ibid., p. 12.

49. Ibid., p. 14.

50. Ibid.

51. Ibid.

Index

If you have found this resource useful you may be interested in other titles from Gower

Brand Risk: Adding Risk Literacy to Brand Management
David Abrahams
224 pages; Hardback: 978-0-566-08724-0

Commoditization and the Strategic Response
Andrew Holmes
248 pages; Hardback: 978-0-566-08743-1

**Gender, Design and Marketing:
How Gender Drives our Perception of Design and Marketing**
272 pages; Hardback: 978-0-566-08786-8

Making Ecopreneurs: Developing Sustainable Entrepreneurship:
Edited by Michael Schaper
248 pages; Hardback: 978-0-7546-4491-0

**Managing Market Relationships:
Methodological and Empirical Insights**
Adam Lindgreen
248 pages; Hardback: 978-0-566-08883-4

Visit **www.gowerpublishing.com** and

- search the entire catalogue of Gower books in print
- order titles online at 10% discount
- take advantage of special offers
- sign up for our monthly e-mail update service
- download free sample chapters from all recent titles
- download or order our catalogue